Artistic Choral Singing

Practical Problems in Organization, Technique and Interpretation

by

Harry Robert Wilson, 1901-

G. SCHIRMER, NEW YORK

44441c
X225

To

All of My Students

Past, Present and Future

PREFACE

The author has a faith, a faith in the power of music to bring something beautiful and spiritual into the lives of people. And so this is a book about catching the beauty in one kind of music, choral music.

Beautiful and spiritual things must be sought if they are to reveal themselves. In music that means participation. The person who joins a chorus is seeking, primarily, to satisfy through the medium of singing a longing for something beautiful and spiritual in his life. There may be social motives but the musical motive is invariably the stronger. The most natural and at the same time the most universal medium for experiencing music is that of singing. The total physical and emotional responses in the act of singing make it the most personal musical activity. Singing also affects the entire body more directly and more intimately than any other musical experience.

Therefore, choral conductors have a real human service to perform. We fear that all too often many of them fail to appreciate the golden opportunity and sacred privilege which is open to them. They fail to rise to the responsibility entrusted to them. The credo of our life is that people who sing in a chorus should become better people. If not, there is something wrong with the music or the conductor.

As a chorus grows from a nebulous beginning to maturity, what it becomes is largely due to the type of musical experiences the choristers have and the way which these experiences affect their inner selves and their relations with fellow members of the group. The choral conductor shares these experiences. Through his guidance he can bring joy and comfort to the singers by surrounding them with an environment of beautiful music, by introducing them to occasions where music is used in the expressions of their inner emotional and spiritual selves, and by seeing to it that music contributes to the awakening of social conciousness. This book was written to foster these human and musical values.

When choral conductors and students read a professional book like this one they sometimes are looking for some device or trick to try out at the next rehearsal. They are often more concerned with the *what* and *how* of conducting choral groups than with the *why*. If only they would realize it, a little search into the *why* of organizing and conducting choral groups will usually be their best guide in the selection of *what* and will often suggest the *how* that will best fit the situation.

With these thoughts in mind the author of this book has expressed as succinctly as possible the *why* of choral groups. This *why* is based on the general values of singing, the interest and needs of choristers in their search for beauty, and the unique purpose of choral singing as being the artistic performance of worthy music.

After this general picture of the *why* of choral groups which permeates the entire book, we are better able to point out to choral conductors what music should do for people and how choral singing fits into the picture. The *what* of the choral program consists of the types of groups, the organization and scheduling of choral activities, and suitable equipment and materials.

The *how* is not neglected but actually emphasized, for now we have a basis for choosing our methods and devices. When we realize what choral singing should do for people and when we are thrilled with the contribution it can make in their existence, our methods will not be heavy-laden and lifeless, but will evolve from sympathetic understanding and an enthusiasm for service. The *how* includes the gamut of methods for artistic choral singing: how to conduct, factors of interpretation, elements of expression, style and diction, developing tone, special vocal problems, rehearsal procedures, program building and the presenting of groups in performance.

And so for our readers, whether conductors, teachers, or students, the author hopes that this picture of the *why, what,* and *how* of choral singing will serve their own needs, increase their enthusiasm, and direct their efforts in the worthy purpose of developing artistic choral singing throughout the land.

HARRY ROBERT WILSON

CONTENTS

Chapter I

Values of Choral Singing

In this day of our highly developed a cappella choirs we sometimes lose sight of the fact that singing together has long been a joyful experience for people who wish to express themselves through music. The Greek drama had its singing chorus. The early Christians sang songs of faith at their meetings. Folk songs became a part of life in work and play by national groups. The ability to sing one's part in a madrigal was a social asset. Organized worship of God saw the flowering of church choirs throughout the western world.

The past fifty years are often referred to as the Renaissance in choral music. This renewed emphasis on choral singing is undoubtedly due in part to a normal reaction away from the dominance of instrumental music in the nineteenth century. A more decided influence is probably the amazing growth and expansion of music activities in our public schools. Most schools which in the past boasted one modest glee club may now have three or four singing organizations. As these singing groups flourished in our schools there was a corresponding increase in the numbers of such groups in the musical life of our colleges, communities and churches. People seek participation in these groups because of the values that such an activity has for them. These values may be recreational, social, cultural, spiritual or aesthetic. Perhaps we should clarify these values because they have a bearing upon our discussion.

CHORAL SINGING AS RECREATION

When a group of people come together to sing, the most immediate and obvious value for them is that of pure recreation. The pleasure is found in the activity itself. There is no necessity for a future goal of public performance. This type of informal singing encompasses all of the intrinsic values inherent in a recreational activity. It is fun, it is healthful, it is emotionally satisfying and it is a wholesome use of leisure time.

The question often arises whether this type of singing earns the distinction of being called choral singing. We are inclined to say that when a group of people sing together simultaneously, either formally or informally, it is choral singing. It is as true in music as in sports that a higher degree of recreational value is enjoyed with the improvement of the activity. However, it is a wise precaution never to lose or belittle this spontaneous pleasure of participation in the working for an attainment of a higher degree of technical and expressive performance.

Informal Group Singing

When several people come together to sing for their own immediate satisfaction and pleasure it is usually referred to as informal group singing. The accompanist is often the only leader. Or perhaps one of the better singers leads with his voice. The singing may be in unison or some attempt may be made to sing voice parts by ear or note. The song is the thing!

Singing of this type may represent many levels of artistry. It may be the hilarious singing at a lively party. It may be the sentimental singing around the campfire. It may be the voluntary singing of a group of students around the piano before or after a chorus rehearsal, an activity which we heartily condone. Or it may be the more refined and artistic singing of madrigals and folk songs around a table.

The old slogan that "a singing school is a happy school" can be applied to any social unit. A singing home will be a happy home; a singing church will be a happy church; and a singing community will be a happy community. In our development of choral singing let us encourage informal group singing. It should be a natural outgrowth of a program of choral activities and it will in turn nurture a greater interest in organized singing.

Classroom Singing

The classroom may be an organized group but the music should retain some of the qualities of informal group singing. That is, there should be immediate and spontaneous pleasure in classroom singing. The teacher is the appointed leader but the procedures used should not emulate the typical choral rehearsal.

However, concerted singing in the classroom should not be limited to having fun. When any group of people, whatever the age level, meets regularly to sing together, genuine musical values must be fostered to retain interest. Therefore, along with the immediate satisfaction which informal singing provides, let the students in the classrooms have the gratification which accompanies continuous and steady musical growth.

Assembly and Community Singing

When a large group of people come together to sing informally under a song leader, it is usually referred to as assembly or community singing. Congregational singing of hymns comes under this category. In this case the song leader may be the organist or the choir director. When these occasions are incidental, a spirit of informality should permeate throughout.* There should be no attempt on the part of the leader to turn the occasion into a choir rehearsal. This does not negate the possibility of obtaining musical effects through the singing of rounds, use of contrast in dynamics and style, and an attempt at singing easy parts.

When there is a series of music assemblies, as in schools, there should be a definite plan to gradually improve the singing of the entire school. This can be done by preliminary work in the classroom, by suggestion on the part of the leader, and by demonstration of selected choral groups to the entire assembly. Following this procedure we have heard standard choral numbers sung by an entire school assembly. The same procedures can be used to improve the congregational singing of church groups.† In the endeavor to improve the quality of singing in these situations the leader must take every precaution that the recreational values of informal group singing are not lost.

Barber-shop Singing

Many ardent followers of the unique art of barber-shop singing will object to the inclusion of it in the section on recreational singing. We are in complete sympathy with the aims of the active organization, SPEBSQSA, Society for the Preservation and Encouragement of Barber-Shop Quartet Singing in America. There is no question that barber-shop quartet singing is an art. The music sung cannot be taken too seriously but there is no doubt that the style of singing is unique. This style of singing will be treated in Chapter IV.

We have been guests at the national convention of the SPEBSQSA which includes much informal quartet singing, planned meetings for the improvement of barber-shop singing, and a contest of keen competition for national honors. We have been greatly impressed with the serious intent to obtain artistic perfection in this style of singing. With the advent of the participation of barber-shop glee clubs in the contest, many more men are enjoying the fine fellowship and emotional outlet which this music affords. Regardless of the work put into the task of raising singing standards, the meetings of this organization have the joyful quality of a recreational endeavor in music making.

* A complete discussion of community singing can be found in the author's book: "Lead A Song," Schmitt, Hall & McCreary Co., Minneapolis, 1942.

† Chapter 10 in the following book is devoted to the improvement of congregational singing: Wilson, H. R. and Lyall, J. L., "Building a Church Choir," Schmitt, Hall & McCreary Co., Minneapolis, 1957.

With the gradual vanishing of boys' glee clubs from our high schools and colleges, perhaps a remedy may be obtained from the experience of the SPEBSQSA. Since this type of choral music has such an appeal for young men, perhaps school glee clubs can be built around and expanded from the organization of several barber-shop quartets. As a glee club develops, the young men may be introduced to other types of music as well as barber-shop.

CHORAL SINGING AS A SOCIAL ACTIVITY

Music is by nature a social activity. Through the medium of tone and rhythm the composer wishes to share his emotional and musical experiences with other people. This is true regardless of the motivation, whether it be for fame or fortune or for personal satisfaction. To do this he needs to record his music in a permanent form. The performer, who may be the composer, wishes to share the music with listeners. The listeners, in turn, wish to share the music with each other.

A choral group is an ideal vehicle for people to share music with each other. The preponderance of choral singing in this country is done by amateurs. They sing for each other's amazement, as one singer deftly expressed it. These singers give of their time and energy to a choral organization for the immediate pleasure and fellowship which they receive from it. This spirit of friendliness should be nurtured because it is the life blood of every choral group. Sometimes professional singers lose this social attitude in their eagerness to attain prestige and make money. Their work may suffer as a result. In amateur groups the director must guard zealously the social values inherent in choral groups as he strives for and perhaps drives for a more perfect performance.

Community Choral Groups

With commercial entertainment sources such as radio and television, it has become increasingly more difficult to maintain community choral groups. The universal ownership of automobiles and the tempo of our daily living are additional competitors for people's time and interests. It seems true that the average amateur singer is reluctant to devote one night each week to a choral group.

This general character of our social culture may be accepted as inevitable or a sincere attempt may be made to counteract it with appealing choral activities. We have noticed that where there is a flourishing community choral group there is loyal devotion on the part of the members to a dynamic leader and to each other. This devotion is based upon sincere friendships. Therefore, it would seem that the organizers and directors of community choral groups should provide for sufficient social activity, as well as social environment at rehearsals, to enable these friendships to develop. The idea that such social environment is detrimental to musical attainment is erroneous. In fact, it is the very thing that gives music performance by these groups enthusiasm and delightful spontaneity.

Industrial Choral Groups

Industrial choral groups are the same as community choral groups except that they are more closely knit together with their identification with some industry or business. They are usually organized at the request of a group of employees or at the instigation of the employer. They usually represent one aspect of the recreational program of the industry or business. For this reason rehearsals should be social gatherings as well as musical events.

This recognition of the social values in an industrial choral group need not impair the desire on the part of the singers for artistic performance. In fact, the director may capitalize upon their sense of pride in representing their business or industry in a genuine cultural venture. We have seen industrial choral groups attain a level of performance worthy of the leading concert halls of the country. As pointed out before, fostering social values in a choral group need not weaken musical values; on the contrary, social values will tend to strengthen musical values.

School Glee Clubs

In the early period of their existence school glee clubs were as much social as they were musical organizations. This dual aim was implied in the term "glee." It was a very fortunate term for a school or college choral group. The term implied a preference for a certain type of choral composition somewhat in the same manner that a barber-shop quartet implies the type of music the group sings.

Many school glee clubs have been replaced by a cappella choirs. Perhaps this was a natural development in an effort to improve the quality of music sung by school choral groups. Something of worth may have been lost in this shift of emphasis on the type of music sung and in the change of names. It is true that we must be ever alert to improve the quality of music being performed by our school choral groups but not at the complete sacrifice of the social values inherent in the activity. There is no objection to the a cappella appellation if all of the "glee" is not taken out of the singing.

CHORAL SINGING AS A CULTURAL AND RELIGIOUS ACTIVITY

We have coupled the cultural and religious values of choral singing under one heading because in the field of music they are so often closely allied. The singing of a beautiful anthem has genuine cultural value and the singing of a beautiful choral composition, although secular, usually has true spiritual value.

There is a great heritage of choral music, largely in the field of religious music. Every choral group has the right to be introduced to this heritage of great choral literature. The adequate performance of such music has a real spiritual impact upon the participant. This effect upon the singers of a choral group is the paramount goal to which we should dedicate ourselves.

Oratorio Societies

These societies are really community choruses which confine their major efforts to the singing of the great oratorios. Since the type of literature which is sung attracts the better singers and musicians of a community a high level of performance can be attained. Moreover, since these singers are genuinely interested in a fine caliber of music they relish the opportunity to learn master choral works. As a result they are, as a rule, devoted to the organization and are faithful in attendance.

By the very nature of the music which is being learned the directors of these societies are usually outstanding musicians and command the respect of the singers. Also, there is generally the motivation of two performances of major choral works each year. The cultural and spiritual values for the singers in such a group is evident. The immediate recreational and social values are not as evident but are certainly present if to a lesser degree. In these groups the joy of singing together with other people is a genuine attraction but more often it is the thrill of learning and singing great music that welds the members together.

Motet Choirs

In communities which are not large enough to sponsor an oratorio society the motet choir can provide a cultural and spiritual experience for interested singers. It is similar to a church choir but it crosses denominational lines and does not limit its repertory to the sacred anthem. These choirs usually number from approximately sixteen to thirty-two voices.

As in the case of the oratorio societies the leader is generally one of the leading musicians of the community. Moreover, the repertory includes outstanding individual choral compositions, both sacred and secular, and many of the shorter choral works of the great composers. Therefore, each rehearsal is an exciting adventure which attracts singers who wish to perform fine music in a manner not often possible in the local church choirs. These choirs are motivated by being in constant demand for concerts and appearances in the community and environs. They can certainly be a cultural influence on the community and have, in turn, a genuine spiritual influence on the singers themselves.

School and College Choirs

Surely the choirs and choral organizations in our schools and colleges should exert a cultural influence on the institution as well as on the singers. Moreover, with the preponderance of religious music which is sung by these choirs they can have a decided spiritual influence if this music is treated and revealed in its true light rather than just limited to its technical and artistic aspects. So often these choirs give an adequate technical performance of a choral composition but completely miss the real import of the message of the music. This fact is reflected in the stoical faces and lackadaisical attitudes of the singers. When someone is genuinely inspired and uplifted it shows in the face and eyes.

The inspired leader will reveal the meaning of the music in such a manner as to enlist this response. He will use both words and music of the composition to do this. He will do this in a democratic way, which preserves the pleasure of singing beautiful music together. In fact, if he doesn't employ such procedures he will probably destroy the very responses from the singers which he is desirous of attaining.

Amateur Church Choirs*

The primary purpose of church choirs is to create a spiritual atmosphere that is conducive to worship. All other purposes are subordinate to this main one. The repertory of the choir is influenced by the musical tastes of the ministers and the congregation. The standards of performance are partly determined by the place music is given in the worship of an individual church.

In creating a spiritual atmosphere conducive to worship, the singers in a church share with the congregation the personal benefits inherent in such a situation. Such an atmosphere is largely dependent upon the quality of music and the quality of the performance. Cheap music sung poorly, regardless of how sincere, will not reach a very high level of spiritual meditation. For this reason church choirs are duty bound to work assiduously for an artistic level of performance.

* A complete presentation in developing amateur church choirs will be found in the following book: Wilson, H. R. and Lyall, J. L., "Building a Church Choir," Schmitt, Hall & McCreary Co., Minneapolis, 1957.

The wealth of beautiful music which has been written for the church gives the singer a genuine cultural experience as well as a religious one. Many of our greatest composers have devoted their most serious efforts to writing for the church. The success of an amateur church choir is also largely dependent upon the friendly *rapport* between the director and the singers and the feeling of comradeship among the members. The successful church choir will provide recreational and social as well as cultural and spiritual values.

CHORAL SINGING AS AN ARTISTIC EXPERIENCE

The perfection of musical performance seems to be the primary aim of most choral conductors. Too often however, this aim is motivated principally by the desire to impress an audience. This single aim is justifiable if the motivation is derived from a desire to realize the effect that artistic performance can have on the singers.

Aesthetic satisfaction is a subtle emotion. The recreational, social, cultural, and religious values found in choral singing are rather direct and obvious. Perhaps that is one reason why they are so quickly disparaged or dispensed with. Aesthetic values are elusive. They undoubtedly exist only where there is artistic performance in music, whether they are experienced through listening or participating.

Continuous and significant aesthetic experiences can have a profound effect on personality and character. They will develop an appreciation and sensitivity to cultural things, refinement in taste, and a more artistic and creative manner of living.

These ideas are clothed in rather embellished philosophic terminology. We are simply trying to say that singing beautiful music in an artistic manner will have a decidedly beneficial effect upon the singers. In addition, we are trying to say that artistic performance can be obtained without neglecting the other uses of choral activities. Artistic performance is unquestionably the ultimate goal. Moreover, with proper leadership, it can be attained by the average choral group. The idea expressed by some conductors that a choral group is only as good as its weakest member is without foundation. In a singing group the individual can rise to musical heights which are impossible for him through his own efforts alone. The test of the leader is to inspire the entire group to these artistic heights.

Professional Concert Choirs

The primary aim of a professional choir is to attain a standard of performance which will impress critics and audiences. The singers are paid money to achieve this aim. The director's reputation is dependent upon it. For this reason the recreational, social, and cultural values of choral singing are discarded as superfluous or inappropriate. Perhaps this may be why some of these choirs lose enthusiasm and spontaneity in their performance as they strive for perfection. The influence of these groups will be more pronounced if they can retain an amateur spirit as they attain professional standards.

Professional Church Choirs

Some church choirs, especially in metropolitan areas, employ a professional quartet of soloists and often pay a small stipend to all of the members of a choir. This policy does not change the purpose of the choir as stated in the section on "Amateur Church Choirs," namely, that of creating a spiritual atmosphere conducive to worship. It does not change the responsibility of the director to the ministers, the music committee, and the congregation in the selection of music. Nor does it change the practice of the choir to abide by the decisions of the administration of the church as to the place of music in the worship services.

However, it does usually give the assurance of the adequate performance of well chosen and appropriate music for worship. All of the personal benefits for the singers inherent in belonging to a church choir and the singing of beautiful music artistically must not be impaired by the fact that they receive some remuneration for their services.

Selected School and College Choirs

The primary purpose of all school and college choirs is to have a beneficial effect in terms of spiritual and aesthetic values upon the singers themselves. Sharing the music with an audience is a secondary purpose. Public performance can serve as a motivation to attain a high standard of performance but it should not be the dominating factor in the functioning and rehearsing of the group. In this way even selected school and college choirs differ in their emphasis from professional concert and church choirs.

However, it is a truism that in the singing of choral groups the quality of the experience is determined largely by the quality of the performance. If singers are to reap the full personal value from being a member of a choral group there must be an unrelenting effort on the part of the director and the singers to strive for perfection.

All choral groups should continue to strive for artistic performance but it is in the selected choral groups that this goal is feasible. Therefore they definitely have their place in the program of activities in any school or college. This does not mean however, that they should be the only representative choral groups in an educational institution. A choral program of activities should endeavor to strike a balance of values among the various organizations and within each individual organization.

Small Vocal Ensembles

More talented singers in a high school or college need a greater musical challenge than that represented by large choral groups. There should be opportunities for these singers to participate in small vocal ensembles, such as madrigal groups, octets, sextets, quartets, or trios. These groups should provide for the singers participating all of the personal values discussed in this chapter. Moreover, if the material is carefully selected it is within these groups that a quality of performance can be attained which will reward the singers with artistic experience of lasting value.

OUR PHILOSOPHY OF CHORAL SINGING

Throughout this chapter we have continually emphasized a definite point of view as to the function and value of choral singing in our culture. We insist that the chief concern is not what people can do to music but what music can do for and to people. So much of our choral singing is based on the first premise. Man was not made for music but music was made for man. Let us organize and direct our choral groups so that the music serves the singers. Let us not set music upon some pseudo-kingly throne which in some dictatorial fashion imposes a servile attitude on the part of the singers, precluding the attainment of the various personal values inherent in the activity.

A succinct review of the considerations which will enable us to accomplish these aims includes the following factors:

When any group of people comes together to sing it should be considered choral singing.

Recreational, social, cultural, spiritual and aesthetic values are inherent in all types of choral singing.

Regardless of the type of choral group all of these values should be fostered although with different emphasis.

Recreational and social values should not be deprecated in the effort to attain a high standard of performance.

Artistic choral performance should be the ultimate goal of every choral group because herein lies the unique personal values of choral singing.

Every choral conductor has the responsibility to reveal the music to the singers in a manner in which it will be an inspiration to them.

Chapter II
The Art of Choral Conducting

Conducting is a performing art. It is more than beating time. It is the art of interpreting music through rhythmical patterns, bodily attitudes and facial expressions. Besides being an art, conducting is also a craft. It involves a knowledge of and skill in rehearsal procedures which assures efficiency in learning and preparing the music for performance.

The good conductor has need of a basic, though flexible, technique in order to obtain quick musical results. Otherwise the rehearsal period becomes a listless experience for the ensemble and the spontaneity of the final performance is lost. This basic technique is the same for all kinds of musical groups, instrumental, choral, or combined, although various types of ensembles require some modification of the basic practice. The concern of this book is the conducting of choral groups and the principles prescribed will be primarily directed toward these groups.

THE CHORAL CONDUCTOR

It is a platitude to point out that the success of a musical performing group depends upon the conductor. It is also usual procedure to point out the personal and social traits which contribute to this success. These include appearance, sincerity, enthusiasm, patience, tact, sense of humor.

Personality

What is really important, however, is that the choral conductor have a magnetic personality. This means that people should feel drawn toward him. It means that they enjoy working with him. Some conductors obtain results working quietly while others rely on lively procedures and a fast rehearsal pace. Whatever method is used it will not compensate for a lack of understanding of people and a lack of "knowing his business." This "business" is to obtain musical results as quickly as possible.

The choral conductor should have enthusiasm! This does not mean that he goes through life at all times bubbling and scintillating. It does not mean that he resorts to wise-cracking his way through rehearsals. It does mean that he loves what he is doing and this love is reflected in the way he does things. This kind of enthusiasm is infectious. It grows out of genuine interests. Varied interests beget enthusiasm.

Therefore, the choral conductor should interest himself in life, people, literature and all aspects of music. To interest oneself in life is to strive to grow spiritually and intellectually through meditation, reading, study and association with others. To interest oneself in people is to devote one's talents to serving others. To interest oneself in literature means to expand one's viewpoint by reading the works of great writers, with emphasis on poets. He should be able to present a new choral composition to a group through meaningful and artistic reading of the text. Finally, he should not limit himself to a study of just choral music. It is a truism that "he who knows only one thing knows not that." His interest in and knowledge of choral music will mature through his interest in and study of all music.

Character

An individual's character is reflected in his personality. Character includes more than moral qualities although these are not to be disparaged. A choral conductor is committing suicide if he does not abide by the social mores of the community in which he is working. The whole idea of character can best be summarized by the following incident. A student, who was a fine musician with adequate control of conducting techniques, came to the author with the following inquiry: "How can I make a better conductor of myself?" The answer was: "Make a better person of yourself."

Physical Qualities

There are several factors to consider in discussing the physical qualities of a choral conductor. The most obvious one is *appearance*. A chorus reacts to the impression made by a conductor through his appearance. He does not need to be a Beau Brummel but he should be well-groomed. The best rule is to dress tastefully without endeavoring to startle the chorus with individual idiosyncracies of apparel. We hope the day is past when talent in music, and especially conducting, is identified with long, uncontrolled, flowing locks, and eccentric clothes and mannerisms.

Let us not overlook *energy*. Conducting is hard work and directing a chorus rehearsal requires plain physical endurance. The author has discovered that with the growth of musicianship and understanding of rehearsal procedures, equally high standards of performance can be secured with less expenditure of physical energy. There seems to be no substitute for this experience but we hope to point the direction in this book toward more efficient rehearsals.

Physical handicaps do not seem to be a barrier to success. We know successful one-armed conductors. Also, we know conductors who have overcome the handicap of extreme near-sightedness and in the case of one fine choral conductor, total blindness. One of the best conductors we know is quite crippled. Evidently the successful attributes of a choral conductor are independent of physical disabilities.

Man or Woman? We see no reason why there should be any discrimination in the matter of sex in discussing the desirable qualities of a choral conductor. Certain traits and abilities are recognized as the *sine qua non* of successful choral conductors. If a woman has these traits and abilities there is no reason why she cannot be eminently successful in this field.

Social Qualities

By "social qualities" we mean something more than just being socially acceptable, although this will do no harm. It means something different than being a good fellow. In fact, in certain situations, too much gregariousness with the organization may not be advisable; especially if it tends to form cliques. Probably the safest procedure is to maintain a reserved friendliness with all of the members of the group.

By "social qualities" we are referring to the approach in learning the music. Does the conductor actually feel that singers with whom he is working are more important than the music notes on the page? Is he willing to recognize and emphasize the social values inherent in the activities of the chorus as he endeavors to attain high performing standards? Does he employ patience and tact during the rehearsal period instead of being completely negative in his criticism? Does he see the advantage of appropriate encouragement and praise? A positive response to questions such as these indicates that the conductor has the social qualities necessary for this work with people.

Democratic Qualities

Democratic qualities are closely allied to social qualities. They recognize the fact that the chorus is organized to benefit the greatest number of singers possible, not just a selected few. Democratic behavior means the absence of snobbery. It enlists the opinions of the chorus on matters of organization, selection of music and even in the matter of the interpretation of music.

The autocratic conductor is often apprehensive of the opinions of the chorus and fearful of his exalted position. Therefore he drives the singers to cover up his limitations. The democratic conductor welcomes the opinions of the chorus and is humble in the service of his position. He strives therefore with the singers toward a common goal.

Dramatic Qualifications

By dramatic ability we mean the power to stir the imagination or emotions deeply. We do not mean the theatrical exposition, which suggests a more direct and blatant appeal to the emotions. We certainly do not mean melodramatic display, which suggests an inappropriately effusive demonstration. Nor do we mean a histrionic performance employing the gestures of seasoned actors. The choral conductor needs to be able to respond so completely to the various moods and emotions expressed in the music that he is able to convey these qualities to the singers to such a degree that they respond in a similar way. Only then will their singing be *expressive* as well as *impressive*.

Mechanical conducting patterns are only one facet of the art of conducting. Regardless of how florid or expressive these patterns may be, they will not replace the effective use of facial expression. We suspect that much of the spiritless singing that is heard today by choral groups is due to the stolid faces of the conductors. It is with the eyes and the face that the conductor can excite an emotional response to the contrasting moods of the music. There is a tendency for the singers to reflect in their faces and eyes the emotions expressed in the face and eyes of the conductor. As the music speaks through the conductor so shall the music speak through the singers. It is this ability to which we refer when we speak of the power of stirring the imagination and emotions of the singers deeply.

Musical Qualifications

Finally, let us consider the musical qualifications of the choral conductor. The Biblical quotation, "the first shall be last and the last shall be first" is certainly applicable to the discussion of these qualifications. No combination or accumulation of physical and social traits can offset the lack of musicianship on the part of the choral conductor.

It is true that choral conductors as a group have been the victims of disparaging remarks from professional musicians. They have been accused of "getting by" on personality with little musicianship to support it. In too many cases we are afraid that these accusations have some foundation. It is stated that this condition prevails because choral conductors are working primarily with amateurs, and it is necessary to know little more than these amateurs with their limited musicianship. But it is for this very reason that choral conductors should represent a high level of musicianship, so that these amateur singers can reap the benefits of inspiration that accrue from being associated with a fine musician.

General Background. To begin with, the choral conductor through self-study or college training should be well-grounded in an understanding of music in general. He should have a knowledge of the history of music, especially as it applies to the performance of the music of different periods and various composers. He should be sufficiently at home in the theory of music so as to be able to make an analysis of the form and structure of the music. The ability to do this will contribute to a more satisfactory performance. His knowledge in this area will also be useful in correcting editorial mistakes or making changes in arrangements in order to make them more adaptable to his own groups. His growing acquaintance with an ever larger repertory of usable choral compositions of various styles is a never ending study. His study must develop within him the power to discriminate between the fine and the cheap, the effective and the ineffective, the appropriate and the inappropriate.

Instrumental Study and Score Reading. A tendency of the choral conductor is to neglect any study of instrumental performance. Yet many of the master choral works which should be in the repertory of any fine chorus use orchestral accompaniment. Only through a study of the capabilities of all of the instruments is the conductor prepared to perform choral compositions which combine both choral and instrumental resources. It is accepted practice for the choral conductor to prepare the chorus and for an orchestral conductor to conduct the final performance. However, there is no question that if the choral conductor is capable of conducting the choral and instrumental combination, the chorus will be more responsive to his wishes rather than to those of an unfamiliar orchestral conductor. Therefore, it behooves the choral conductor not to limit his studies in score reading to choral music; he should be just as much at home reading a full orchestral score. Then he will be ready to take advantage of any opportunity or emergency to conduct combined instrumental and choral numbers.

Performance. As stated before, conducting is a performing art but the choral conductor needs to supplement this skill with subsidiary proficiency in piano and voice. Ability to play the piano will facilitate the learning of scores. Moreover, it will give him additional musical understanding of the relationship between a piano accompaniment and the voice parts. He can thereby better weld the voice parts and the accompaniment into a more artistic whole in performance. The choral conductor needs to sing well enough to demonstrate tone, dynamics, diction and phrasing. An abiding tendency of choral conductors is to talk too much. So much time can be saved and learning facilitated if the conductor can demonstrate adequately with his singing voice. The author has found in his own work that when his voice has been impaired through illness or overwork, his teaching effectiveness during choral rehearsals is considerably reduced. Archibald Davidson's sage advice to all choral conductors was: "Sing whenever you feel the inclination to talk!"*

* Davidson, Archiband T., *Choral Conducting.* Harvard University Press, Cambridge, p. 40.

Ear Training. The ability to know exactly what one wants in the interpretation of a piece of music depends upon imagination, discrimination, and experience. But the ability to obtain this interpretation depends primarily on keenness of hearing. The choral conductor must develop his musical instincts until he has a tonal and rhythmical imagery of the final product he desires. Otherwise the chorus will sing through material at rehearsals in a meaningless, haphazard fashion while a confused conductor searches for ways to improve the general effect of the singing.

With this musical imagery as a beginning the conductor must train his ear to realize the effectiveness of contrast in dynamics, that is, loudness and softness, crescendos and diminuendos. Then he must set about to make himself tone conscious so that he is able to eliminate the individuality of voices that do not blend, and is able to develop a sonorous, homogeneous quality in the ensemble. Then he must develop the skill to sing and hear each individual part so that the notes and rhythm can be corrected quickly and accurately. Finally, he must be able to hear the sound effect of accents, nuances and diction. All of this is a big order and grows out of experience. Without this keenness of ear, however, attention to detail is neglected, obviating artistic singing.

The Conductor as Teacher

In addition to these desirable personal and professional qualifications, an indispensible attribute for the choral conductor is teaching ability. Teaching is more than imparting knowledge; it is more than showing how; it is more than systematized training: teaching is a sharing of oneself with others. In this case the conductor shares his personality, his character, his philosophy of life, his musical knowledge, and his technical proficiency with a group of people who have willingly accepted his leadership. It is not a matter of a musical dictator and his musical subjects; it is not a matter of give all, take all: it is a matter of establishing a personal and professional *rapport* which will engender a feeling of unity and group pride in accomplishment. It is a matter of growing musically together in an artistic endeavor.

TECHNIQUES OF CHORAL CONDUCTING

A choral conductor should be a person first and a conductor second; he should be a musician first and a technician second. Too many conductors seem to feel that waving their hands in an accepted manner fulfills their complete function. We do not belittle the techniques of choral conducting but they must always be employed not as an end in themselves but as a means of creating a more musical and artistic performance.

Posture

Needless to say, a conductor should maintain a posture that is presentable and does not detract from the musical performance. It should be the aim of the conductor not to attract attention to himself but, rather, to the music. Crouching, dancing, and shadowboxing are neither suitable nor necessary to stir the chorus into an exciting performance. At all times the conductor should endeavor to conduct himself so that the music speaks through him.

The choral conductor should assume a posture in which the weight of the body is primarily on the balls of the feet. The right foot should be slightly forward if the conductor is right-handed. The arms should be in front of the body with the right hand slightly higher and forward. (Figure 1.) If the conductor is in position to beat time with one of his feet then he has not taken the correct position. Of course this position may vary somewhat with different types of music and some rhythmic music actually invites the tapping of the foot.

Figure 1

Posture for Conducting

Front View Side View

The Conductor's Back

Books on conducting usually discuss the conductor as he appears to the chorus. Yet his appearance to the audience is equally important. A graceful posterior view is also a part of the equipment of the conductor as a performer. Ludicrous movements by the conductor can completely distract the attention of the audience from the performance of the music. All of his movements, both front and back view, should reflect the mood and expressiveness of the music.

Extreme spreading of the feet makes an unattractive stance, especially for women conductors. Refrain from stomping your feet; it may drown out the music. The podium is not the place to indulge in bouncing up and down or jumping, frog-like movements. We recall a performance of "Over the Waves" waltz by a twelve-piece elementary school orchestra, conducted by a young lady who used movements that resembled an antiquated flying machine. Invite your wife or best friend to criticize your appearance from the audience. Memorize this slogan: "Important, too, is the back view."

The Use of the Baton

Should the choral conductor use a baton? Again may we emphasize that all movements employed by the conductor should be conducive to a more satisfying performance. If a baton is used, it should be thought of not as a mark of the conductor's authority, but as a device for making clear his intentions regarding the music .The baton serves to lengthen the arm. One wonders at the ever-increasing length of the baton. Are these conducting scepters really necessary to convey a clear beat and transport musical meaning, or are they just a form of theatrics?

Conductors who do not use a baton often receive the criticism that their beat is indefinite and lacks clarity. It is claimed that the use of a baton will help control the tendency to beat in a haphazard manner. This is undoubtedly true. On the other hand, the beat will be perfectly clear if the conductor will use his hands as if he were holding a baton. Moreover, there are often subtle nuances of words and phrasing in choral music which can be portrayed better without a baton. In fact, a baton can be a hindrance at times. Of course ultimately the decision belongs to the individual, and it should be based completely upon the manner in which he feels he can best interpret the music.

The author never uses a baton for a choral group, small or large, when the group is performing unaccompanied or with the accompaniment of a piano, organ, or small instrumental ensemble. However, when conducting large festival choruses, accompanied by orchestra or band, the extended beat effected by a baton seems necessary for clarity and precision.

Right-Handed or Left-Handed?

The question often arises whether a left-handed person should change to the conducting patterns of a right-handed person. This switch is advisable if he can do it without too much discomfort. Otherwise the singers in a choral group may become confused in following his conducting patterns, especially if the group is an unfamiliar one. If trying to make the change is too disconcerting to a person, then he should try at least to gain such freedom in the use of his arms that he is practically ambidextrous. All future instructions and diagrams are intended for right-handed conductors.

Choral and Instrumental Conducting

The basic techniques for conducting choral and instrumental groups are the same. That does not mean, however, that a person who has gained control of these basic techniques will be equally successful in conducting a chorus or an orchestra or band. There are individual problems for each group that are unique, and only continued association with each particular organization will enable a conductor to be equally successful in obtaining results with all types of performing groups. Also the musical equipment of different conductors tends to lend authority with corresponding performing groups. Some choral conductors have a tendency to disregard the conventional conducting beats and work out their own system. All we can do is to point out that they are limiting their influence and effectiveness. The discipline of orchestral conducting is a valuable asset for all choral conductors.

There are two basic rules to observe in conducting technique: (1) the design of the beat should be in front of the body, and (2) every beat should have a preparatory beat. There should be one focal point for the performers to watch, to aid them in sensing the rhythmical and interpretive qualities of the music. Therefore, the reason for the first rule is obvious, when one considers the amount of conducting that is done through facial expression. Moreover, flying arms are distracting to both performers and listeners and interfere with the poetic qualities of the music.

The value of the second rule lies in the fact that singers need some warning before starting to sing. Also, conducting movements immediately have more flow and cease to be merely a time-beating device. If followed, this basic rule will enable a conductor to indicate phrasing, nuance, dynamics, ritardandos, and accelerandos, all conducting "musts." An attempt will be made to demonstrate the meaning of this rule in the conducting diagrams.

In following the standard conducting movements the novice can keep these points in mind as a check: (1) the first beat of the measure is always down, (2) the last beat of the measure is always up; (3)

the beat just before the last beat is always out; (4) the other beats fill out the symmetry of the pattern.

It is very difficult to indicate the actual movements used by the best conductors. For this reason a book on conducting often indicates merely a stereotyped basic design which is mechanical in construction. In the following diagrams a facsimile of the basic design will be given, followed by a florid design approximating the desired conducting movements for interpreting music written in the basic rhythmic patterns. A dotted line will be used to designate the preparatory movement before each beat. Notice that the base of each beat is near one focal point in front of the body.

Diagram 1

Duple Meter
(2/4, 2/2, ¢)

Mechanical Pattern | Interpretative Patterns: Slow Tempo | Fast Tempo

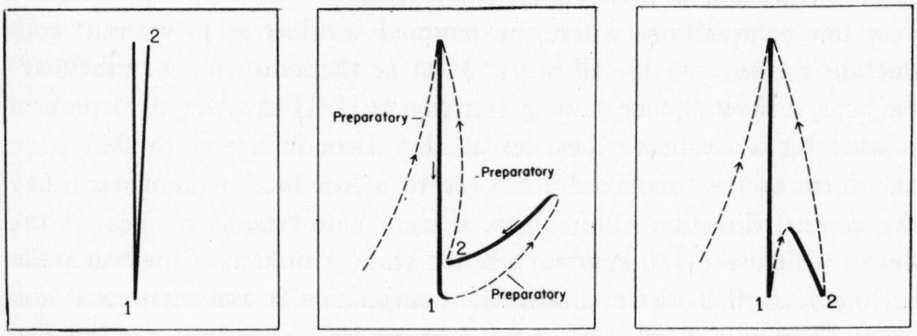

Diagram 2

Triple Meter
(3/4, 3/2, 3/8)

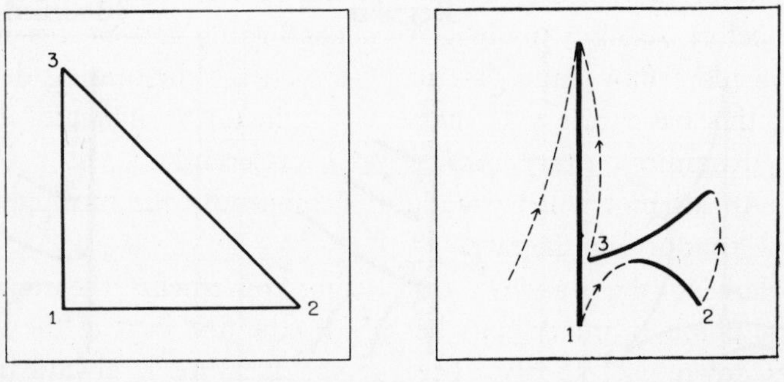

Diagram 3

Quadruple Meter
(C , 4/4, 4/2)

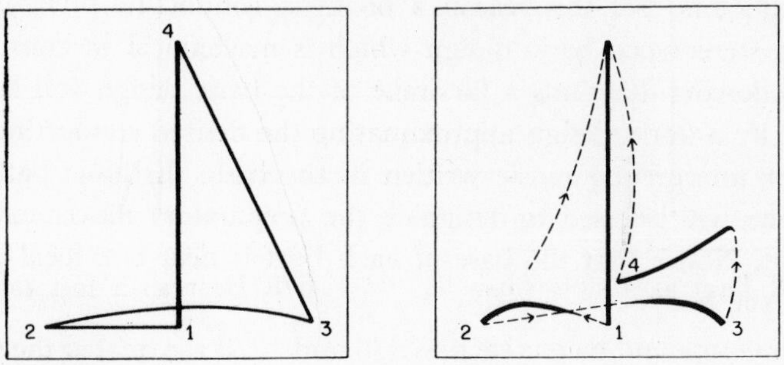

COMPOUND METER
(6/8, 6/4)

The following diagram, under "mechanical pattern," represents the traditional manner of conducting 6/8 or 6/4 meter. Today many conductors are changing to the pattern indicated as "regular", represented by the florid design. The reason for this change is quite evident: there are very few compositions where the tempo is so slow as to warrant conducting six beats to the measure. Most of them call for a "modified" *six* beat, a slow *two* beat, or a fast *two* beat. If the "regular" pattern is used for a *six* beat whenever needed, then it is easy to shift back and forth to the "modified" beat, or to a *two* beat, without changing the general direction of the basic design. The "modified" beat is the design which seems to indicate best the rocking motion of the barcarolle or lullaby in 6/8 meter. Unless the composition is extremely slow it is usually best to indicate 6/8 or 6/4 meter with a slow *two* or a fast *two* beat. Care should be taken to avoid conducting 6/8 meter as two groups in 3/4 time as this practice gives a false feeling of accent.

Diagram 4

Mechanical Pattern — Interpretative Patterns: Regular, Modified

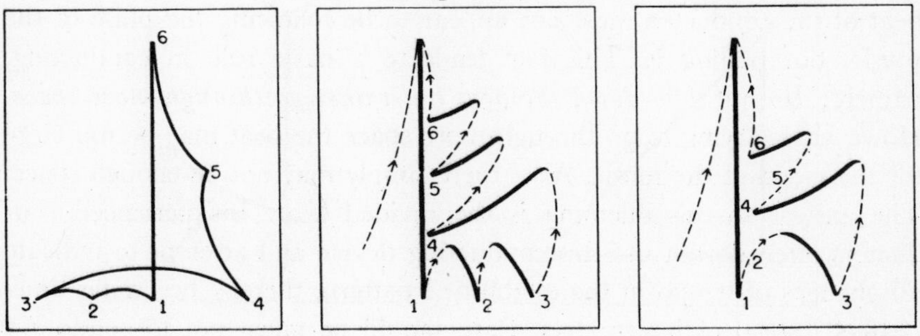

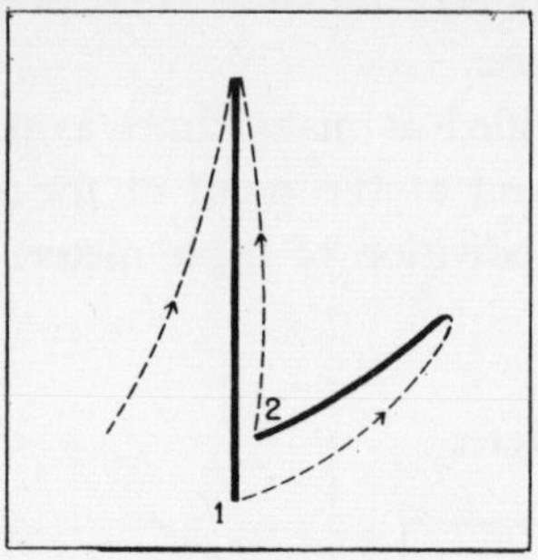

6/8 Beat as a slow *two*

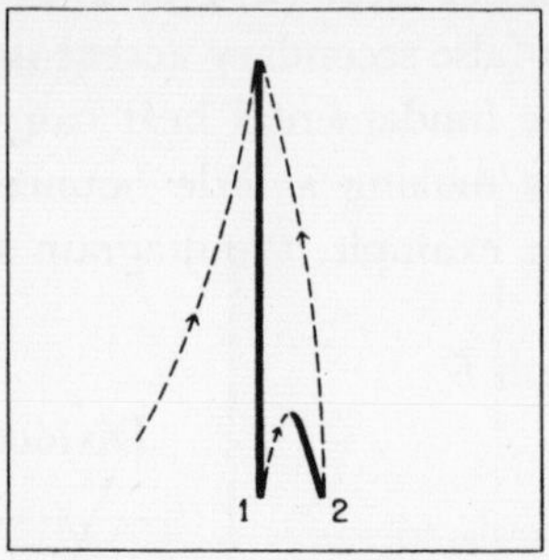

6/8 Beat as a fast *two*

Other compound meters such as 9/8 and 12/8 are treated the same as 6/8 meter. As pointed out in the previous diagrams 6/8 meter is fundamentally a duple measure with two subdivisions. Likewise 9/8 and 12/8 meters become triple and quadruple measures with the possibility of two secondary motions on each beat. In both of these meters each of the basic beats may be subdivided, as in the regular and modified interpretive patterns indicated for 6/8 meter. The manner in which subdivided beats are indicated is discussed in the next section.

Diagram 5

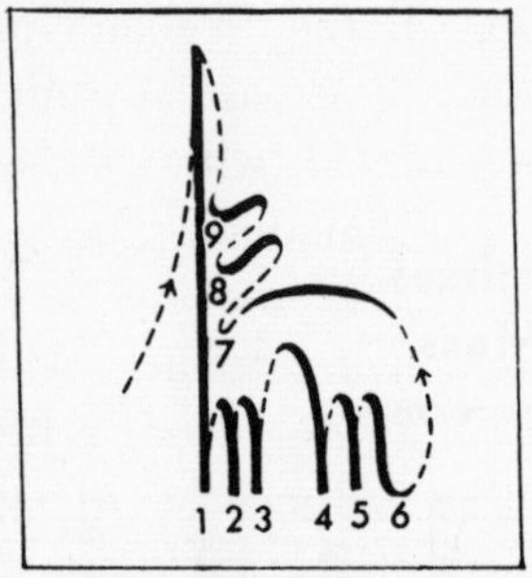

9/8 Beat

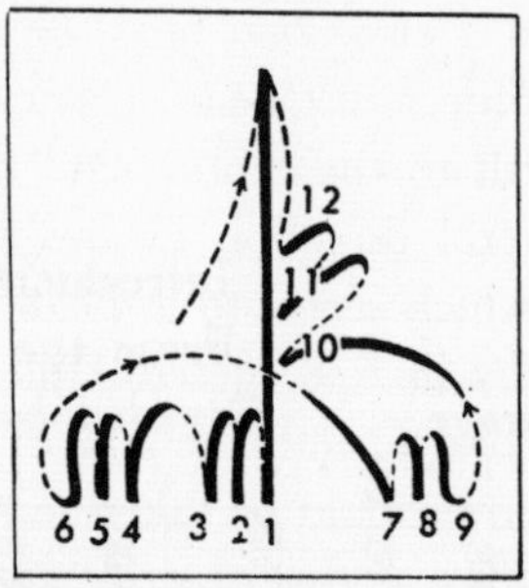

12/8 Beat

Divided Beats

Music is a moving art and so the beat must be kept moving. The beat of the conductor must not appear to be following the pulse of the music, but pulling it. This fact leads to a basic rule in conducting, namely: *Do not slow down the beat but rather go through more space.* However, in trying to go through more space the beat may be too large for the mood of the music. Also, there simply may not be enough space. The answer to this dilemma is the divided beat. Inexperienced conductors often do not use this conducting device and attempt to indicate all changes of tempo in the established pattern, thereby becoming timebeaters instead of interpreters. Care should be taken not to conduct a divided *two* beat (2/4 or 2/2) as a 4/4 or 4/2 measure. This practice gives a false secondary accent in the measure.

The fundamental beat can be subdivided as many times as necessary by making a little bounce of the hand at the point of the beat. See, for example, the diagram showing subdivision of triple meter.

Diagram 6

Divided Triple Meter

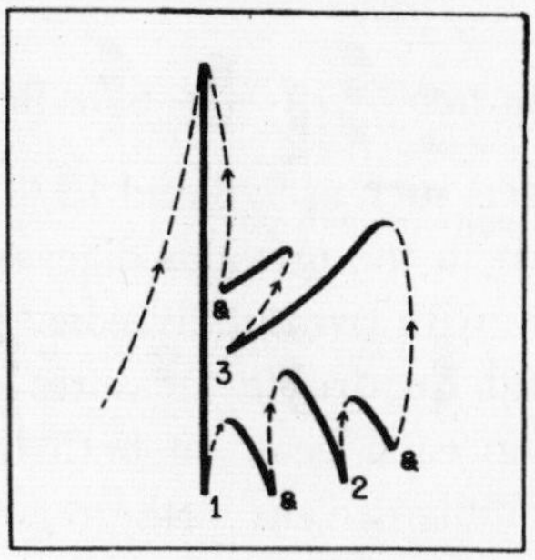

The other fundamental beats may be subdivided in the same manner. Subdivisions usually occur in very slow tempo, and in a *ritardando.*

Example 1

Introduction to Crucifixus
From the "B minor Mass" **Bach**

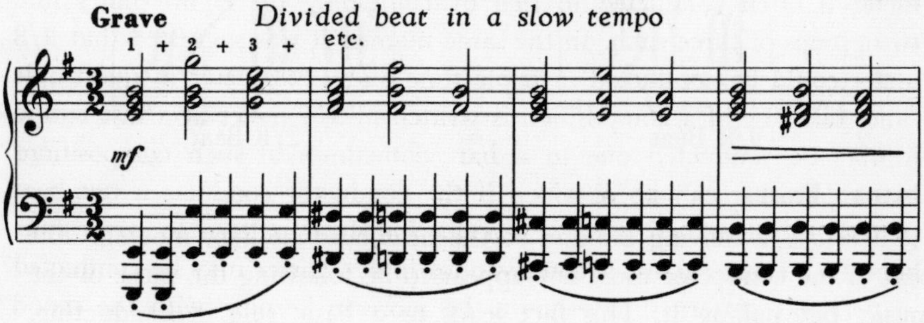

Example 2

Noël

Divided beat in a ritardando

Melville Smith

Grouping of Beats

The antithesis of the division of beats is the grouping of beats. If the reader will study the diagrams for 6/8 meter he will notice that this meter is often conducted in *two* by combining the eighth notes into two groups of three each. In the same manner it was suggested that 9/8 meter could be conducted in triple time and 12/8 meter in quadruple time. Likewise, if a composition is written in 3/4 meter at a fast tempo it may be conducted one to a bar. Sometimes in such compositions better phrasing can be obtained if the conductor conducts a two-beat pattern to cover two bars, or even a four-beat pattern to cover four bars. In a similar manner compositions in 4/4 meter may be conducted in two-beat pattern if it seems to be more in keeping with the mood of the number.

Irregular Meters

Irregular meters do not occur often in choral music and are usually considered as a combination of two common patterns, depending upon the phrase feeling. For instance, 5/4 meter is a combination of *three* and *two,* or *two* and *three*. Sometimes there is a dotted bar line to give the composer's intent as to stress. See example for *A Ballad of Trees and the Master*. Likewise, 7/4 meter may be thought of as a combination of *four* and *three,* or *three* and *four*.

Example 3

A Ballad of Trees and The Master

Wilson

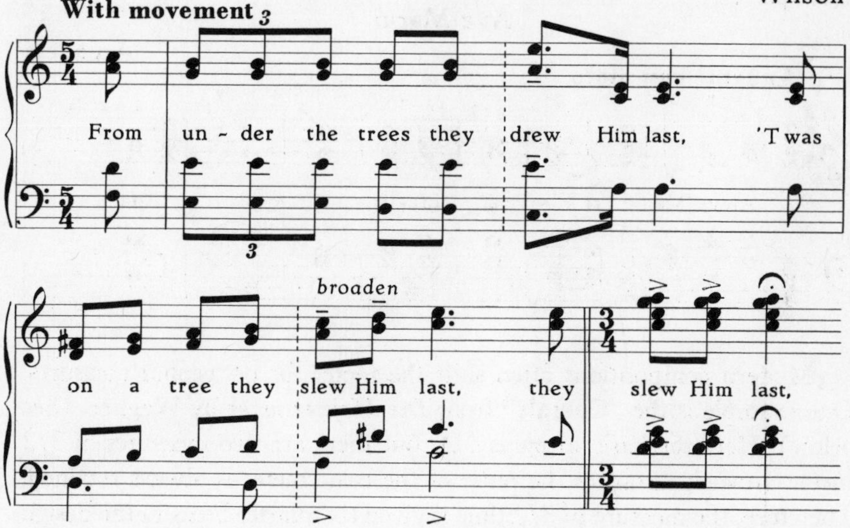

Because of the normal accent of the words in the text some conductors may feel that the measure does not divide itself naturally in one of the above combinations. They may feel that all the beats of the measure lead naturally to the first beat of the next measure. In such cases the design of the beat may move back and forth across the body the necessary number of times for the measure. It is well to remember when the top number of the meter sign is an odd number the movement for the second beat is always out. The following patterns approximate the design for such measures.

Diagram 7

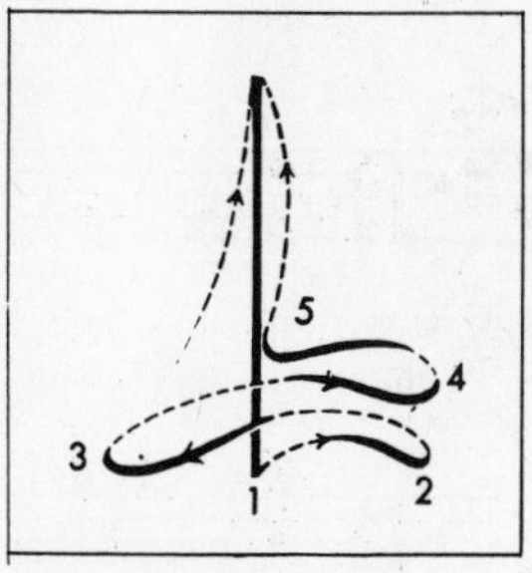

5/4 Meter

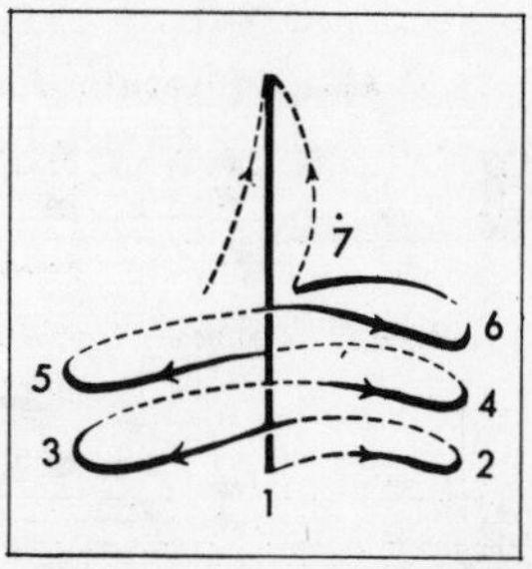

7/4 Meter

Some selections, such as *Ave Maria* by Arcadelt, have alternating duple and triple meters. These meters grew out of the normal accent of the words, which always offers the clue to the conductor in conveying the rhythmical feeling for compositions in irregular rhythms.

Example 4

Ave Maria

Arcadelt

Modern compositions often shift the meter for occasional measures. One example is the "Chorale" from *Die Meistersinger* by Wagner. (See below). Here the basic meter is 4/4, but there are two measures of 3/2 meter. In such instances the pulse of the basic meter is always retained. Therefore, the measure in 3/2 time is given six quarter beats in the design of a divided three beat.

Example 5 Chorale from "Die Meistersinger"

Wagner

More difficult are the instances, usually in contemporary music, where a basic quarter note meter such as 3/4 changes to 3/8 meter. As above, in these instances, the basic beat of the quarter note must be retained. The eighth note does not become the equivalent of the quarter note nor are the three eighth notes treated as a triplet. Such a measure is equivalent in time to a dotted-quarter note (♩.). It is usually beat as a grouping of three eighth notes in quarter note time (3/8 ♫♪ and). The example is taken from *In the Beginning* by Copland.

Example 6

In the Beginning

Copland

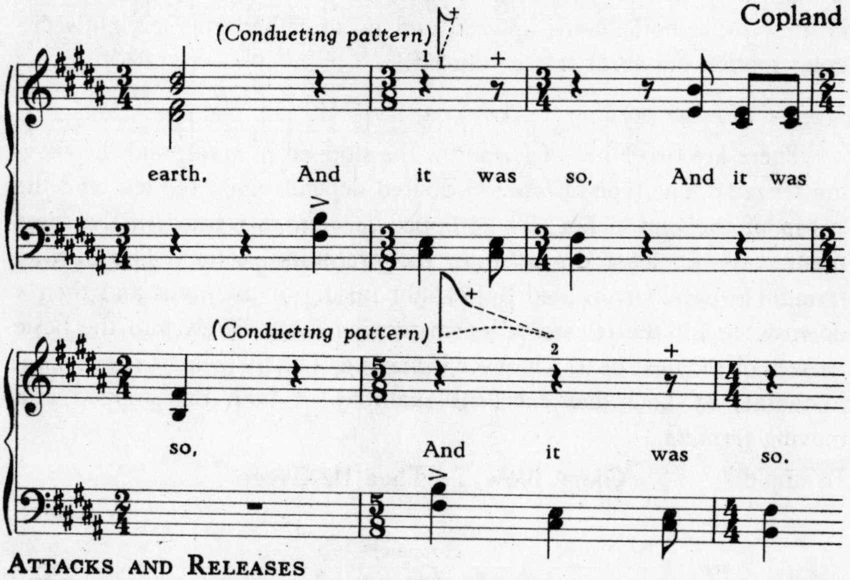

Attacks and Releases

Precision in attacks and releases are of utmost importance. They must be thoroughly prepared to be completely clear to performers. There are three kinds of attacks: (1) those beginning on the first beat; (2) those beginning on some other beat than the first; (3) those beginning on the last part of some beat of the measure.

Diagram 8

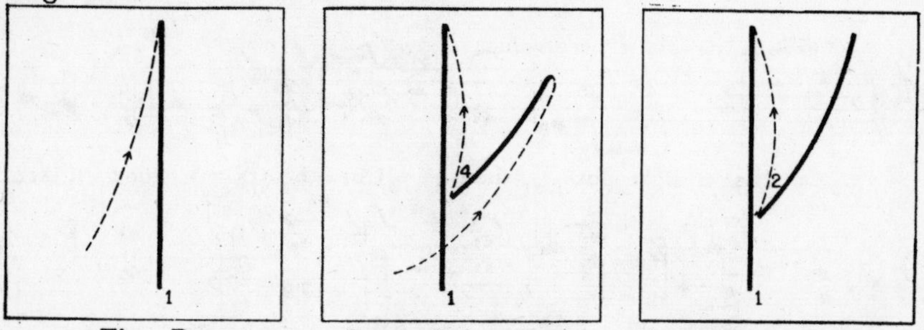

First Beat — Some Other Beat (Last Beat) — Last Part of a Beat (Part of Last Beat)

When the attack comes in an incomplete measure, it is well to avoid beating a full measure of preparation merely to set the tempo. This does not preclude the possibilty of the conductor's counting a measure silently to himself before giving the indication for attack.

As in the case of attacks, releases must be thoroughly prepared if any precision is to be expected from the ensemble. Conductors usually indicate releases in one of two ways, depending upon the mood of the composition, and the sharpness with which he desires the cut-off. For a sharp release he may draw his right hand upward and then bring it down quickly to the waist line for the cut-off. For a more gentle release he may bring both hands upward and in, and then give a slightly circular motion outwards for the cut-off.

Holds (Fermata)

There are two kinds of *fermatas,* the stopped *fermata,* and the moving *fermata.* The type of *fermata* desired depends upon the text and the sweep of the phrase line. The stopped *fermata* is treated in the same manner as a release described in the preceding section. The moving *fermata* is usually indicated by a slight raising of the hand and then a downsweep for the release, the arm moving immediately into the basic pattern of the next beat, whatever it may be. The following excerpt from a chorale by Bach has excellent examples of both the stopped and moving *fermata.*

Example 7 Glory Now To Thee Be Given

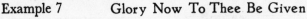

Bach

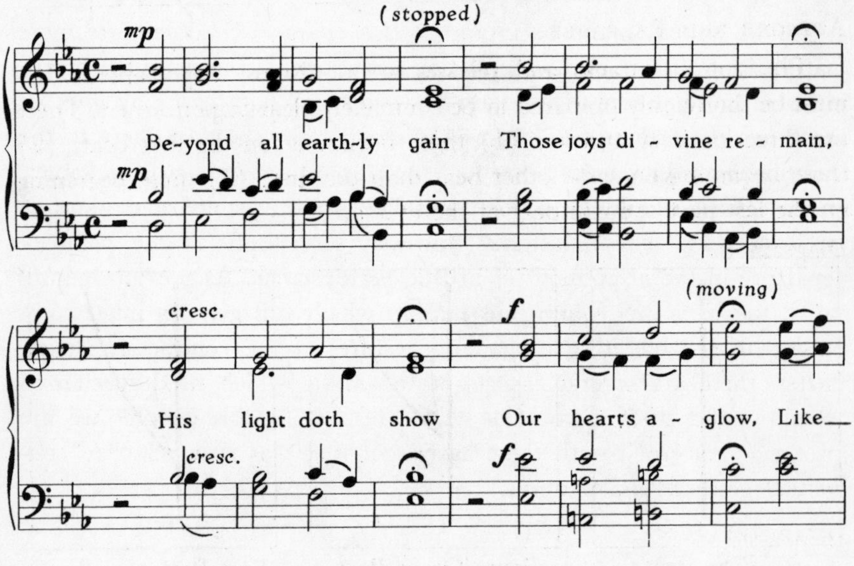

Use of the Left Hand

It is very amateurish for a choral conductor to use both hands continuously. The greater part of the conducting should be done with the right hand. The chief concern of the right hand and arm is to indicate the meter, and the rhythm. This responsibility does not obviate the use of the right hand and arm for dynamics and phrasing.

The left hand should not be used to beat time. Its movements should usually be independent of those of the right hand. The left hand should be used primarily to indicate cueing, accent, and dynamics. When a voice part needs to be cued, bring in the left hand with the right. When a certain beat or word needs to be accented, use the left hand with the right. Also, make use of the left hand for marked changes of dynamics. Reserving the left hand to be used judiciously for these purposes is the mark of a skilled conductor.

EXPRESSIVE CHORAL CONDUCTING

As we stated in the beginning of this chapter, conducting is more than beating time. Choral conducting is the art of conveying the meaning of a composition to a group of singers so that they may give an expressive performance of the music. Conductors should adhere to the traditional conducting patterns that have been presented in this chapter, and a chorus should be trained to follow these customary motions of the conductor. These patterns, however, serve only as the point of departure in the attainment of artistic performance. As previously indicated, the basis is a sound muscianship which will give an inner compulsion to the bodily attitudes and gestures of the conductor. Nevertheless, there are several aspects of the music which need specialized attention and study to obtain artistic results. In this chapter we are primarily concerned with these aspects of music as they relate to conducting gestures and patterns.

Interpretation

Generally speaking, there is one basic rule for the conductor with regard to interpreting music—look like the music! What does this mean?

First of all, the face and bodily attitude should reflect the mood and rhythm of the music. Secondly, all conducting techniques should be subservient to the will of the music itself. Let the music tell your arms where to go! Use flowing movements for smooth selections and crisp movements for rhythmical numbers. Use large movements for *forte* passages; small movements for *piano* passages. Vary the beat to indicate *crescendos, diminuendos,* and the tapering of phrases. Practice conducting in front of a full-length mirror. Do your conducting gestures and facial expressions reflect the mood and the style of the music?

Tempo

All writers on conducting have stressed the importance of the ability to set a correct tempo. The correct tempo is the one which enables the singers to perform the music with security and with expression. Composers ususally indicate their intent as to tempo with suitable terms in English or a foreign language, usually Italian. Careful composers give additional assistance by giving metronome markings. Do you know the meanings of these terms and these markings? Do you have a musical sense for setting the tempo for an *adagio* or an *allegro?* Can you come close to the tempo if the metronome marking for a quarter note is 72 (M.M. ♩ = 72)? Can you beat seconds (M.M. ♩ = 60)? A second is quite a long time. Then can you double this speed (M.M. ♩ = 120)? If you have these two basic tempi under control the others can be judged more accurately. Practice these basic tempi many times until you are sure of them. Check yourself with your watch. Here is a graded list of terms with the relative metronome markings. We say relative because of the wide variation of composers and conductors in their conception of tempo indications. Still they may be helpful to the novice conductor. Metronome markings may be given for any unit of time, such as the half, quarter, or eighth notes.

Italian	*German*	*French*	*English*	*Metronome Markings*
grave	same	same	very slow	mm 40- 50
largo adagio lento	langsam	lent lentement	slow	mm 50- 60
andante	same	same		
		moderement lent	medium slow	mm 60- 80
moderato	same	same	medium fast	mm 80-100
allegretto	same	same	rather fast	mm 90-110
allegro	lebhaft	vite		
vivace	schnell		fast	mm 110-140
presto	sehr schnell	preste		
		très vite	very fast	mm 140-160

Introductions and Codas

It seems superfluous to conduct an introduction when the accompaniment consists of just a piano or organ. The tempo can be quietly indicated for one or two measures and then the accompanist should be left to his own resources. Any variation of tempo or phrasing should be worked out in rehearsal. The same practice applies to codas when the accompaniment is a lone piano or organ. Naturally, if the accompaniment is some form of instrumental ensemble, introductions and codas must be conducted.

Rhythm

Time and rhythm are not the same thing, although they are related. Time is the pulse of the music and rhythm is the flow of the music. The beating of the pulse of the music must not interfere with the rhythmic flow of the music. The practice of conducting every note is often the habit of inexperienced choral conductors. This practice impedes and distorts the rhythm. Also, as a rule, conductors should avoid beating out rhythmic patterns. It is far better to continue the rhythmic flow of the meter. Singers will execute difficult rhythmic patterns with more assurance if the conductor gives them a strong metrical beat, than if he tries to indicate each note of the pattern. The following two examples will illustrate the practice which is the most advisable in maintaining rhythmic accuracy and continuity.

Example 8

Old Folks At Home

Foster

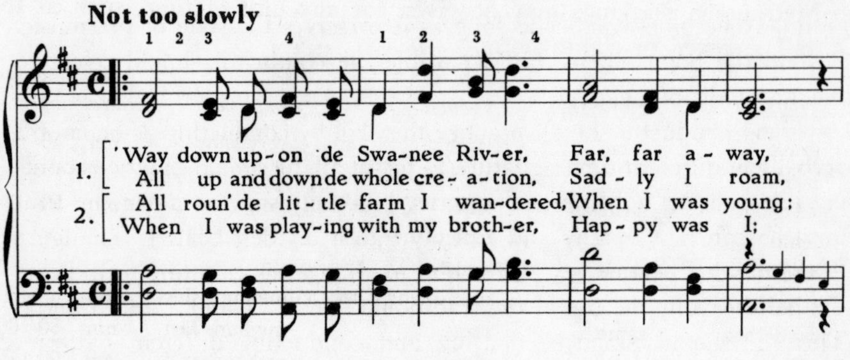

Example 9

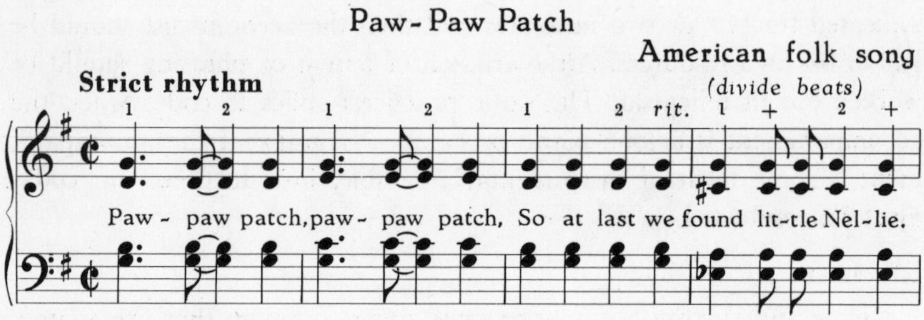
Paw-Paw Patch
American folk song
Strict rhythm
(divide beats)
1 2 1 2 1 2 rit. 1 + 2 +
Paw - paw patch, paw - paw patch, So at last we found lit-tle Nel-lie.

Ritardandos and Accelerandos

The ability to indicate steady ritardandos and accelerandos is a true test of a conductor. These changes of tempo within a piece must first of all be felt by the conductor and then the beat adjusted accordingly. We repeat that the beat does not follow the pulse of the music but there is a sense of leading it. Therefore, in slowing down the beat one must go through more space and in speeding up the beat one must go through less space.

Consequently, in making a ritardando the pattern of beat gradually becomes larger as long as it preserves the style of the music. Beyond the point where this is possible the conductor should resort to the divided beat. Conversely, in making an accelerando, the pattern of the beat gradually becomes smaller as long as it preserves the style of the music. Beyond the point where this is possible the conductor should resort to the grouping of beats.

Every conductor should practice this skill by conducting as he counts verbally in different time signatures. First of all, he should practice counting and conducting different patterns, gradually slowing down the beat until he can move easily and steadily into a divided beat. In changing to the divided beat, it is wise for him to change his counting to indicate the half-beats by the use of the traditional "and" (1 and 2 and 3 and). Then he should practice counting and conducting different patterns, gradually speeding up the beat until he can move easily and steadily into the natural grouping of beats. It is difficult to give musical examples to illustrate this skill, but the reader should be able to grasp the idea from the following excerpt.

Example 10

My Bonnie Lass She Smileth

Bottomley

In 4
meno mosso
Smile less,dear love,there-fore, And you shall love me more(yes,more),yes,
(there-fore),
In 2
accel. e cresc.
ff
In 4 again
rall.
a tempo
p
more and more,and more and more,And you shall love me more, Yes,more and more,Yes,
ff
p
accel. e cresc.
rall.
a tempo

Crescendos and Diminuendos

The problem of conducting *crescendos* and *diminuendos* is similar to the problem of conducting *ritardandos* and *accelerandos,* that is, in making *crescendos* the beat becomes larger and in making *diminuendos* the beat becomes smaller. However these changes of dynamics within a piece do not call for a change of tempo; therefore, in making *crescendos* and *diminuendos* there is no necessity of resorting to divided beats or the grouping of beats. There seems to be a natural tendency for conductors to speed up the beat when making a *crescendo* and to slow down the beat when making a *diminuendo.* This tendency must be guarded against unless the composer or editor indicates an *accelerando* with the *crescendo* and a *ritardando* with the *diminuendo.* These tempo and dynamic changes may be used in conjunction with each other or they may be divorced from each other. The conductor should endeavor at all times to follow the intent of the composer in treating these interpretive factors.

Phrasing

The art of musical performance is the art of phrasing. The key to artistic singing is a keen sense of rhythm, tone and phrasing. If through his beat the conductor can convey to his choral group a sense of musical phrasing, the singing will have more individuality and expressiveness.

This is especially true in singing music of a *legato* nature. Musical phrasing will counteract the prevalence of musical performance which is stilted and measured.

The ability to indicate a phrase line involves the rhythmical feel of pulling the beat and the continuous shifting and changing of the size of the beat. Then, at the end of the phrase there is a tapering of the size of the beat. There is usually no feeling of a pause at the end of the phrase but the conductor moves quickly to the next phrase by almost anticipating the beat. This conducting movement is similar in action to a singer recovering after a quick catch breath. A conductor can best gain the technique for indicating a phrase line by practicing the singing of melodic lines and adjusting his conducting movements to his own singing.

Conducting Legato Style

In the foregoing section a description of the technique of conducting individual phrase lines was given. In the early chants and much of the polyphonic music of the early Renaissance period there is a continuous *legato* quality. In this music there should be no feeling of a metrical measure nor should there be a feeling of definite pulse. Even in some of the homophonic music of later periods there are some pieces which need a similar smoothness to create an expressive mood.

In conducting this style of music one should take recourse to the technique of conducting chants, using a beat resembling the *arsēs* and *thesēs* which indicate the rising and falling inflection of the melody. This serves as a device for eliminating the stress on the beats, especially the first one in each measure. The basic figure is like a figure eight beat sidewise for duple meter. For triple and quadruple meter a small circle is indicated where it is appropriate, as illustrated in the diagrams.

Diagram 9

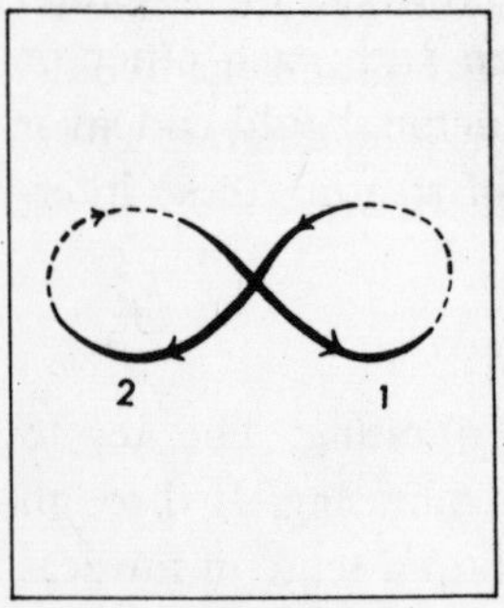

Duple Meter

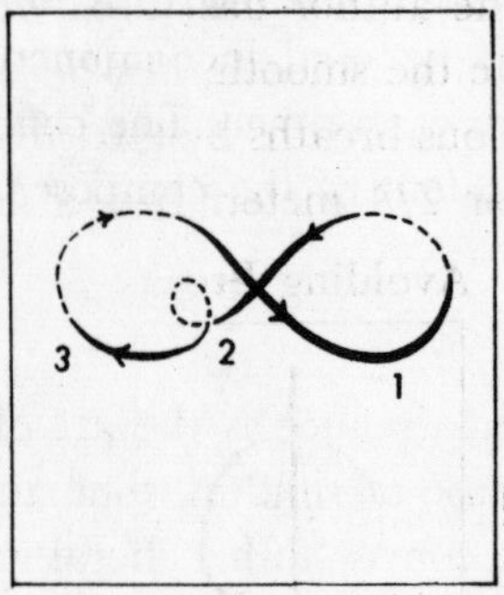

Triple Meter

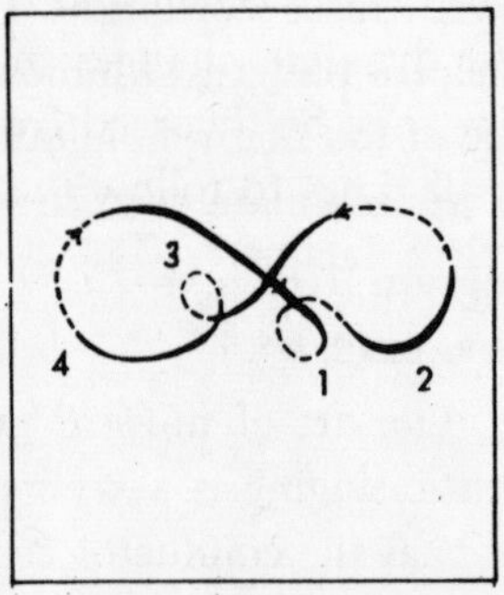

Quadruple Meter

Rests

Long rests need not be indicated by beats; their duration may be indicated by a sustained body alertness on the part of the conductor. In fact, over-emphasis in beating out rests can be positively distracting. The conductor can keep his place by counting quietly to himself. Short rests or single rests may be treated by negating the beat or by the use of a very slight movement.

These suggestions are not intended to imply that rests are not important in the performance of choral music. In fact, one criteria for determining a competent composer is his judicious use of rests. Rests do not denote a stopping of the rhythmical flow of the music. The movement of the music continues through the rest. The sense of this movement is usually more evident when the beats are not indicated by the conductor. Do not mistreat rests. They are often the loveliest part of the music.

Breath Indications

Editors today sprinkle choral music with breath marks (,) far too often, as a rule. A conductor should strive for long phrases, an earmark of artistic singing. Therefore, do not hesitate to eliminate breath marks when a more musical phrase line can be secured.

When a choir does take a breath, it should be like a musical punctuation, the sense of rhythm carrying on. The conductor conducts as if he were reading the text, with usually a slight tapering of the preceding phrase and with a slight anticipating of the following word, avoiding, however, giving it undue accent. Most singers have a tendency to accent any word following a breath, regardless of its normal verbal or metrical accent. If a conductor practices breathing with the singers, but without singing with them, he will soon sense the movements necessary in his conducting.

When a conductor desires to lengthen a phrase and eliminate what seems to be normal breathing places, he needs to adjust his conducting movements accordingly. The author has found that a forward circle is a helpful pattern to indicate the smooth, flowing rhythm and the avoidance of too many simultaneous breaths by the singers. The diagram gives the approximate pattern for 2/4 meter. It is a side view.

Diagram 10 Avoiding Breaks

Right Hand

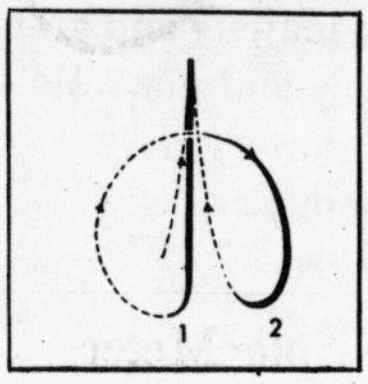

Side View

Soloists

As in the case of introductions it should not be necessary to conduct incidental solos when accompanied with a piano or organ. Likewise, duets and trios should be rehearsed sufficiently with an accompanist to eliminate the need for conducting. In the case of a quartet of soloists, the conductor should use his own judgment, but most conductors prefer to lead a quartet, especially if the music is difficult. When any combination of soloists are accompanied by a group of singers or instruments then they should be conducted.

Common Musical Terms

Every choral conductor should own a musical dictionary which he keeps at his side while he is studying and selecting music for his choral group. He should look up every term with which he is not familiar. In this way he will gradually gain an adequate knowledge of the terms necessary for his work as a conductor. Here are a few of the common terms for tempo and style and the type of beat which the conductor should use for their execution.

Term	English	Type of Beat
Largo	Very slow and dignified	Stately
Larghetto	Slow and measured	Firm
Grave	Slow and dragging	Heavy
Adagio	Slow and tranquil	Calm
Adagio non troppo	Slow but not too much so	Quiet
Andantino con expressivo	Slower than andante with expression	Smooth
Andante religioso	Rather slow and solemn	Sombre
Andante sostenuto	Rather slow and sustained	Even
Andante cantible	Rather slow and in a singing style	Flowing
Moderato	In moderate time	According to mood
Allegretto grazioso	Not as fast as allegro	Graceful
Allegro agitato	Fast and agitated	Excited
Allegro assai	Very quick	Lively
Vivace	Fast with spirit	Vivacious
Presto con brio	Fast with brilliance	Precise
Dolce	Soft and sweet	Delicate
Furioso	With great spirit	Emphatic
Maestoso	With majesty and grandeur	Dignified
Scherzando	Lightly and playfully	Bouncing
Vigoroso	With force	Vigorous
Legato	Smoothly	Undulating (see p. 34)
Marcato	Punched	Definite with rebound
Staccato	Detached	Crisp

Importance of Practice

No musician would dream of trying to become a fine singer, pianist, or instrumental soloist without devoting a long period of assiduous study to the development of the necessary technique and artistry. But many a music student seems to have the attitude that the technique and art of conducting can be attained from one or two semester courses in a college. As we have stated before, conducting is a performing art and requires the same diligent study and practice as any other medium. It is unquestionably true that the road to sound musicianship is the longer one. But with sound musicianship as a base, the musician still has to perfect the technique requisite for artistic choral conducting.

There are several ways in which this technique can be acquired. Study under fine teachers either individually or in classes, is one approach. It is wise to study with a teacher who can produce music with choral groups himself. This study must be supplemented, however, with individual practice. The ideal method of practice is to obtain the directorship of a small church choir or to organize a choral group of fellow students or interested singers who are willing to submit to your inexperience. No other study can match this practical experience in developing efficiency. In addition, however, other kinds of individual practice can be most profitable. It is helpful to impose on a friend who is a pianist and who is willing to play through a wide variety of choral literature while you conduct. Also, as previously suggested, it is extremely valuable to practice in front of a full-length mirror and sing through representative numbers while conducting. See if you can follow yourself.

THINGS TO REMEMBER

1. Study and develop the qualities necessary for your success.
2. Conduct—do not beat time.
3. Keep the beat in front of the body.
4. Be sure that every beat has a preparatory beat.
5. Beats must be adjusted for changes in tempo and dynamics.
6. Let the music tell your arms where to go.
7. Practice in front of a full-length mirror until you can follow yourself.
8. Let your body reflect the rhythm of the music.
9. Convey the mood of the music with your face and body—look like the music.

Chapter III

General Considerations for Interpretation

Interpretation of music is the revealing of its expressive qualities through performance. In choral music it includes the revealing of the poetical qualities of the text. It involves creating and re-creating. This is because composers do not leave works of art to posterity as do painters. They leave the medium and directions for producing a work of art. With the development of phonograph recordings we do have within the limitations of technical science a permanent record of someone's conception of a work of musical art. A page of the full orchestration of Stravinsky's *Sacre du Printemps* has the symmetry of a work of art in appearance. However, the music notes and rests on this page are not a work of art until they have been interpreted.

Therefore the choral conductor has two jobs on his hands in assuming the responsibility of interpreting works of musical art. He must, first of all, have the ability to *create the means* by which the music can be interpreted. In this case it is the organization and development of a choral group which can give an adequate performance of the music. Secondly, he must have the personality, temperament and musicianship to use the choral group to *re-create the work of art* according to the intent of the composer.

In the light of the foregoing remarks, the job of the choral conductor should be clear. He is not creating a work of art; he is re-creating one. On the other hand, he is not making a painted copy of a work of art. In fact, he is not trying to reproduce a piece of music; he is trying to breathe life into the dormant creation of the composer.

SINCERITY OF EXPRESSION

The position of the choral conductor or any musical interpreter can almost be described as a dilemma. Should he stick with rigidity to the notes or should he be free to consider them a relative facsimile of the intent of the composer? For that matter, to what degree is he confined to the design of the composer? Very few conductors take either of the extreme positions in resolving this so-called dilemma.

Music is both a science and an art. As a science one can be fairly objective about an approach to it, but as an art the approach to it will be primarily subjective. On the one hand, the choral conductor who tries to be completely objective in his interpretation will usually reveal the intellectual aspects of the music at the sacrifice of the expressive and poetical. On the other hand, the choral conductor who considers himself a creator and approaches the interpretation of the music from a completely subjective point of view often distorts the music beyond the original intent of the composer. It is in the latter interpretation where one finds the exaggerated tempos, the excessive rubatos, the drawn-out *fermatas,* and the bizarre tonal effects. It is safe to say that any choral conductor who assumes that he has the privilege to pervert the music beyond the limits of recognition of the original composition is on the wrong track.

There is such a thing as common musical feeling and understanding and such a thing as musical integrity. Authentic musicians seem to approach the interpretation of a piece of music with the same basic premise. They all speak a similar musical language with the corresponding variation found in the spoken or written word. Hence, we have the traditional interpretation of standard compositions. Every young or inexperienced choral conductor should acquaint himself with these traditions. Such a premise does not preclude a conductor's bringing a touch of the warmth of his own musical temperament to the performance of both new and old works. His own musical integrity dictates his sincere attempts to reveal the original artistic intent of the composer within the personal and musical limitations with which he understands and feels it. A guiding axiom for the choral conductor might be, *Do not try or strive for choral effects which are not inherent in the words and the music.*

UNITY OF EXPRESSION

A great composer's music is *unified.* At the same time one is always amazed at the variety in rhythmical, melodic and harmonic content. The music of an untalented composer seems to lack this richness of variety and at the same time it never seems to get anywhere. It is in such music that one often finds external rhythmic and tonal effects for the sake of the effects, rather than growing out of the internal musical expression of the total work. An element of this style of composition seems to have crept into the creative efforts of some contemporary composers. The first step in the expressive interpretation of a composition is the ability to recognize and understand with feeling the unified coherence intrinsic in it.

Therefore the choral conductor must strive for performances which hold together. He must be able to do this as he unfolds the rich variety within a composition. His specific rhythmic and tonal effects should evolve from the complete musical effect of the total work. He should avoid extremes when they are incoherent. The performance should go somewhere. Wagner stated that every composition should have at least one climax, although he himself was often accused of having too many. Look for the emotional climaxes whether they be soft or loud. Music should move people, physically and aesthetically. This approach endeavors to conceive the composition as a whole, without, at the same time, neglecting the infinite variety of detail which makes it a work of art. It is this approach which we will emphasize later in the discussion of both rehearsal procedure and public performance.

MOOD AND MODE

By *mood* we mean the atmosphere of emotional feeling which is inherent in a piece of music and portrayed by the performer. By *mode* we mean the manner in which the composer and performer project the atmosphere or mood. All art has mood and if a choral group fails to portray the mood of a composition the singing will be spiritless and inexpressive.

Very often choral groups perform with adequate technical facility, but leave little aesthetic impression upon the listeners. Moreover, the singers themselves seem to get very little emotional satisfaction from their own performance. This condition is reflected in the stoical faces of the singers, the lack of animation in their eyes, and the listlessness of their attitudes.

Why is this? Surely it must be found in the manner in which the music is introduced to the singers. Evidently, the emotional impact of the music is lost as they endeavor to gain control of the technical detail necessary for a public performance. Evidently they are never introduced to the poetical quality of the words or the artistic quality of the music. The mood and atmosphere surrounding the performance of a choral composition can be fostered in three ways: (1) encourage the singers to react physically to the emotional quality of the music; (2) engender a sensitivity toward the mood of the words; (3) build a musical understanding through the analysis of the music as it applies to expressive performance.

1. The emotional impact of the music can be partially realized by the reflection in the facial and bodily attitudes of the singers. A fine artist reflects the emotional qualities of the music, automatically. That

is the primary thing which makes him an artist. In amateurs it must be encouraged. Here is the key for the insistence of a positive bodily attitude, usually called correct posture, aside from the fact that it is conducive to better tone production.

When a hymn of praise to God is sung, the light of exultation should be in the eyes of the singers. When a jovial folk song is performed, smiling faces should accompany the singing. So often in the performance of such numbers, the smiles are delayed until the audience applauds exuberantly, as if the singers caught the mood from the listeners. Faces and bodily attitudes should reflect the mood of the music and directors should encourage the singers to "look like the music" while they are learning the numbers. Then the spirit of the song has a better chance of being retained and projected in performance for an audience. "Mood and physical response are so interdependent that paradoxical though it may sound—the response can sometimes actually appear to initiate the mood."*

2. In a choral composition the composer tries to enhance the mood of the words. Therefore if a sensitivity to the mood of the words can be engendered, a similar response to the mood of the music can be elicited more readily. Words with their literal meaning often make a more direct appeal to the emotions. Singers should know and feel what they are singing about. In Example 11 below an inspired reading of Psalm 150 will create the spirited atmosphere for the singing and study of the inspired music of Lewandowski. In Example 12 a quiet reading of the poem will instill in the singers the necessity for a smooth, flowing performance to paint the mood picture inherent in the words.

Example 11

Psalm 150

Lewandowski

* Greene, Harry P. *Interpretation in Song,* New York, Macmillan Co., p. 16.

Example 12

In Stilly Night

Brahms

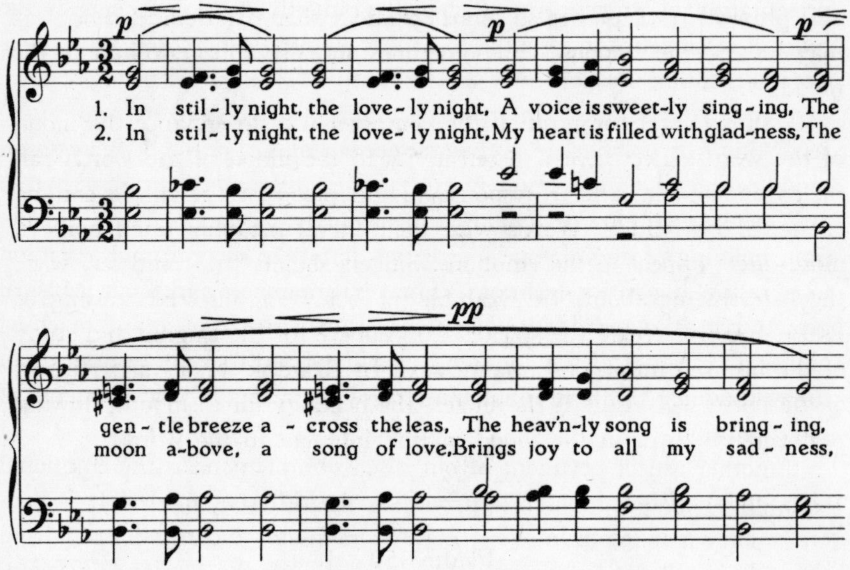

3. As important as physical reactions and emotional responses are to an impressive performance, they must be supported by musical understanding. We have found by experience that musical analysis, per se, is rather futile and a waste of time, but musical analysis as it applies to performance is invaluable. Although it is a mistake to believe that undivided attention to musical analysis will automatically result in an expressive interpretation, it is just as great a fallacy to believe that musical intelligence is not necessary for artistic performance.

For instance, in Example 11 above, it can be pointed out how the ascending arpeggio figure at the beginning produces an exultant mood. In the next section the percussive rhythmical figures on the word

"Hallelujah" give added meaning to the words in the duet being sung by the male voices. These rhythmic parts should be sung in a detached manner and should never cover the melody. Later in the composition, Lewandowski inverts the treble and the male parts. Recognition of this device adds musical understanding to the performance.

In Example 12 the composition can be played quietly and smoothly on the piano to illustrate how the flowing melody and lovely harmonies enhance the mood of the words. It is an excellent piece in which to study how musical phrasing adjusts to the verbal phrasing.[1] Also it can serve to illustrate the unmusical effect of singing a composition such as this one in regular, measured tempo in contrast to the judicious use of tempo rubato.[2]

Much of the remainder of this book is devoted to a discussion and presentation of procedures which will gradually develop in singers the musical intelligence so essential to artistic singing. Among the procedures we will mention are style and taste in composing and singing, importance of adequate technique in interpreting music, relation of words and music, recognition of polyphonic and homophonic music, effect of tempo and modification of tempo upon interpretation, difference between rhythm and meter, attributes of melody and harmony, import of form and design, building of choral tone, correcting habits of diction, and attention to phrasing, dynamics, fermatas, climaxes, ornaments and pitch. Musical growth is a slow and continuous process, but with patience and teaching ability on the part of the conductor it will evolve from an awareness, an understanding, and a gradual mastery of these factors and elements of interpretation.

Another aspect pertinent to our discussion of mood is the emotional character which composers attribute to the different modes. It is generally known that our modern major and minor modes emerged from the old church modes. Briefly, these modes were the Dorian, Phrygian, Lydian, Mixolydian, Aeolian, and Ionian, and their respective Plagel Modes. They are represented by the white notes on the piano beginning on D, E, F, G, A, and C in the order of a scale. It will be quickly seen that the Ionian mode is the same as our major scale.

If one plays these various modes or scales on the piano it will be observed that each one has quite a distinctive quality. The old musicians called the Dorian mode *Modus Gravis,* or the Grave Mode. It is interesting to note that they considered the Ionian mode or our present

1. Recorded by the University Concert Choir in album entitled *One God,* David Kapp Recordings.
2. Recorded by the Concert Choir of Teachers College, Columbia University, PAR Recordings.

major scale as secular and light-hearted in contrast to the more serious and sacred quality of the other modes. The purity of these modes gradually gave way to the alteration of cadences, introduction of accidentals, transposition, and the development of basic harmonic progressions.

It is a fascinating study to gain an understanding of the relationship of these old modes to the polyphonic music of the era. However, it is questionable to what degree it will influence a conductor in interpreting this beautiful music, sometimes referred to as the purest style of choral writing. The reason for this observation is the fact that the mood of each composition is so intrinsic through the close relationship of the words and music that it is evident to any musician without the exacting identification of the mode or the degree of alteration.

The same is not true of the more modern homophonic music. Take for instance the piano composition *Humoresque* by Dvorak. Indicated by the title he gave it, he evidently thought of it as having a humorous mood. However, as played sometimes as a violin solo it is made into a sentimental tear-jerker. Indulging in such theatrics is not permissable for the sincere choral conductor with musical integrity. To a comparative degree certain moods are commonly attached to our major and minor modes; that is, the major mode reveals a happy mood and the minor mode a sad mood. However, not all songs in a minor key are sad. Witness the Christmas carol, *God Rest You Merry, Gentlemen.* Nor should all songs in a major key be considered happy, for example, "God So Loved the World" from *The Crucifixion* by Stainer. With the expansion of harmony and instrumental color, other factors began to influence the mood of music besides the mode and the relation of words and music. In choral music, the words are still the point of departure for determining mood, and the conductor should exploit to the utmost their emotional quality in securing the atmosphere conducive to artistic performance.

STYLE AND TASTE

By style we mean not only the quality which gives distinctive character and excellence to a choral composition, but also the distinctive mode or manner of singing the composition which gives the performance of it character and excellence. By taste we include the meaning of style, namely the quality of distinctive character and excellence both in creating and performing a choral composition as well as the discriminative aesthetic judgment of knowing and feeling the worth of the composition and the performance of it. Style is more than stylishness and taste is more than personal preference.

For instance, there is a polyphonic style and a homophonic style of composition. An adequate performance of these styles is dependent upon an understanding of their contrasts. Through long association with certain types of words there have arisen sacred and secular styles of music. A composer who sets sacred words to secular music is showing poor taste. There are also consonant and dissonant styles in music. A composer who continually shifts from one to another is mixing styles. There are choral styles and instrumental styles. When a composer mixes these two types of styles in a choral composition the conductor is confronted with the problem of whether to give predominance to the verbal or musical phrase-line. In common usage to the layman are the terms *classic* and *popular* styles. The serious musician thinks of them as good and bad styles. Interesting and uninteresting, worthy and banal, enduring and transitory would probably describe their characteristics somewhat better. Then there are solemn and humorous styles, majestic and modest styles, intellectual and sentimental styles. The choral conductor must develop a sensitivity to these contrasting styles and be able to interpret them within the realm of artistic and musical taste.

The composer also has at his disposal more precise terminology to indicate the style of an entire composition, a section of it, a single phrase, or a melodic or rhythmical figuration. These terms are *legato, marcato, staccato* and *rubato.* These terms are also used to represent styles in singing and diction. They will be discussed thoroughly in later chapters. Briefly, *legato* means smooth music; *marcato* means punched music; *staccato* means detached music; and *rubato* means "robbing" time value from one unit of melody and giving it to another. Conductors and singers should think in terms of contrasting styles from the outset. In studying a choral composition a conductor should ask himself what part of the piece should be sung in *legato* style, what part *marcato,* what part *staccato,* and when *rubato* should be introduced. This will give a tangible approach to the interpretation of various styles in choral composition.

RELATION OF INTERPRETATION AND TECHNIQUE

These two bogies of performance, interpretation and technique, are another aspect of the subjective and objective approach to music. Interpretation represents the emphasis on the aesthetic and poetical qualities of the music, and technique the intellectual and scientific qualities.

The term *interpretation* was given priority in the heading of this section deliberately. It implies that technique is subservient to the interpretation. It does not decry the position of many performers in their insistence on surplus technique. It simply stresses the point of view that music is a work of art with the resultant natural emphasis on the emotional qualities intrinsic in this type of human experience. Since interpretation is primarily concerned with the bringing out of these emotional qualities, it is the function of the intellectual and scientific aspects of the music to contribute to the expressiveness of the music. We are not concerned here with a discussion of the different ways music can be appreciated; nor are we endeavoring to dissociate technique from feeling and emotion. We are trying to disclose the position of technique in welding all of the elements of musical expression into an artistic whole.

The choral conductor who over-stresses technical detail in his approach to a composition fails to see the proverbial woods for the trees. Such performances are usually over-academic and lack imagination. A chorus under this type of conductor often sings correctly but without verve. Such a chorus will look upon the *Song of Fate* by Brahms as merely another opportunity for an experience in singing a beautiful piece of music. The choral conductor who stresses the over-all expressive qualities of a composition may fail to recognize the different kinds of trees which make up the woods. His performance may have imagination but lack the attention to the technical detail which produces artistic results. His approach is correct but he may jeopardize the ends with inappropriate means.

A synthetic approach to the interpretation of a composition will harmonize these conflicting approaches. First of all, strive for a musical and expressive conception of the work as a unified whole. Then, analyze any difficulties and bring to bear any technical procedures which will alleviate performing difficulties. Then, put it together again; refine and give more attention to detail without nullifying the original conception of the music. This process goes on until an expressive performance is realized.

Remember, *expressiveness begets impressiveness!* A chorus that arrives at an artistic performance of the *Song of Fate* by Brahms with this approach will look upon it as more than an opportunity to sing another beautiful piece of music but as a privilege to share with others a presentation of the destiny of man.

RELATION OF WORDS AND MUSIC

Here we are on grounds which are a little less controversial than the ideas presented in the previous section. The relationship of words and music in a choral composition is usually described as a wedding of the two into a work of art. This would imply an equal emphasis on each one. On first consideration this observation would certainly seem to be true. Nevertheless, we usually refer to a choral composition as a musical setting of a selected text. We are aware that in certain cases words are adapted to an instrumental composition. We do not disparage this practice but it seldom comes off with satisfactory results. Translating is a different matter, but there are many difficulties in this craft which are almost insurmountable. However, these compositions were at least originally designed for vocal utterance.

Certainly music should enhance the poetical qualities of the text, or it would seem better to preserve the text in its literary form. The text has emotional and expressive qualities and the music should heighten these qualities. In this respect it is interesting to note that some texts lend themselves much more readily to a musical setting than others. Witness the number of times that some passages of the Bible and certain selections from classic poetry have been set to music.

In the light of these comments, the choral conductor is on solid ground if he approaches the interpretation of the music through the meaning and expressiveness of the words. This approach involves much more than attention to the pronunciation of the words so that they can be understood by an audience (even though this attempt is a worthy aim). It means approaching the expressive elements of the music such as tempo, phrasing, dynamics, climax, nuance, meter, rhythm, accent, and tone through the sense and poetry of the words.

Strange as it may seem, this is the very approach to use to make a piece of music sound like a choral composition and not a musical recitation, or a song without words. With this approach the words are never obscured, and the expressive qualities of the music are revealed. One is not more important than the other, but they are molded together to form an integrated whole. The same attention to the treatment of the words should be given to the setting of a familiar text, such as the *Lord's Prayer,* or to compositions based upon a single word, such as Randall Thompson's *Alleluia.* In a choral composition, lack of attention to the expressive qualities of the words will impede the interpretation of the contrasting moods and styles of the music. Without mood and style there is no music.

Perhaps we should make a few observations regarding music which employs humming and neutral vowel effects. Several composers have tried writing choral compositions based on various vowel sounds. They do not seem to be very lasting. Moreover, there is not a composition of Bach, Beethoven or Brahms which utilizes humming or neutral vowel effects. The implication is that serious or great composers do not consider such effects to be worthy of the choral art.

One might say that times have changed, and if these effects sound good, why not use them? The radio was instrumental in stressing the style of singing which devoted itself to extensive humming, "oohing," and "ahing." Perhaps these effects are appropriate for this style of singing, or more likely, they became popular as a result of the technical limitation of the radio. They do seem to be disappearing with the technical improvement of radio and television.

It is probably a question of adhering to the medium that best expresses an art. It is doubtful procedure to use voices to try to represent instruments. They are a feeble substitute and it would undoubtedly be better to use the instruments in the first place. Humming, if done correctly (See Chapter VIII), has a musical sound. Again, if it is not used as the imitation of something but as an individual musical effect, it surely has its place in lighter, secular compositions. It can be effective when used alone as an accompaniment for a soloist without the piano or organ. It can be quite striking in rhythmic effects in folk songs of the dance variety. The same is true of the various neutral vowel sounds. In other words, they have an artistic *raison d'être* if arranged or composed for a specific musical setting of a temporary (not necessarily contemporary) type.

Finally, the interpretation of a choral composition is not the interpretation of just music, but the interpretation of words and music. This may be the key reason why so many instrumental conductors are ineffective as choral conductors. A choral conductor whose books of poetry are not as worn or marked as his books of music is neglecting an extremely important phase of his development. We do have choral conductors who go into such transports over the poetry that they disregard the expressive elements of the music. These are the choral conductors who neglect their musical development, and are ineffectual as instrumental conductors. The solution is to meet the challenge of developing sensitivity to both poetry and music.

POLYPHONY AND HOMOPHONY

A composition is polyphonic when all of the vocal parts are melodious and equal in interest; a composition is homophonic when the melody is concentrated in one special part, usually the highest, while the other parts serve as an accompaniment to this single melody. There are many compositions which combine the features of polyphony and homophony to varying degrees.

These definitions give a lead for the interpretation of music which has the characteristics of either style. In polyphonic music there should be a blending of the various melodies. All of the parts are of equal importance. The final result should be a fusion of the voices into one beautiful, composite tone. In homophonic music, although there should be a blending of the voices, the melody should always be slightly prominent. Even though the melody shifts from one voice to another this rule remains in effect. It may be necessary for the conductor to shift voices to the part carrying the melody to attain this monodic effect. A conductor must be ever alert to bring out the short contrapuntal melodies which a composer often introduces in music of a homophonic style.

In polyphonic music the interpretation is truly inherent in the style. It seems almost self sufficient. Polyphonic music is universal music. A conductor should not attempt to bring to it too many individual interpretative ideas. He must accept the principle that polyphony is based upon words, and not words on polyphony. Then, if he will allow the music to flow according to the verbal accent and not be dominated by the conventional musical outlook based upon dance rhythms, he will soon realize the sheer beauty of this style of music.

Homophonic music based upon the romantic philosophy of individualism allows a conductor more freedom to experiment and introduce his own ideas of interpretation. This freedom is based upon all of the principles already in this chapter. The ability of the conductor to bring out the contrasting character of these two styles of composition is an important step toward artistic singing.

CONSONANCE AND DISSONANCE

Any consideration of consonance and dissonance will not be very fruitful if put on a basis of concord and discord, or what sounds harmonious to the ear and what sounds unharmonious. Combinations of tones that have been considered discords in one period of music have been accepted as concords in succeeding periods of music. It has always been recognized that much of the expressive power in music resides largely in the treatment of dissonance, and the emancipation of dissonance has been a dominating factor in the entire development of music.

For our needs we will consider a consonance as a combination of two or more tones which require no further progression to make it satisfactory, and dissonance a combination of two or more tones that require resolution. Dissonances are prepared and unprepared. If a conductor thinks of consonances and dissonances in these terms he will have something tangible on which to base his treatment of them.

In the polyphonic era dissonances were always prepared. Therefore, they were seldom harsh or disturbing. They evolved from the melodic line as determined by the rules of counterpoint. The dissonant harmony was the result of the combination of melodies, not an entity in itself. To give these dissonances a delicate, pungent flavor a slight stress, like a swell, is the usual treatment. The following example is a good illustration.

Example 13

Fire, Fire My Heart

Morley

In the polyphonic era dissonance and discord were terms which were often used synonomously. In modern music discords usually refer to a series of unresolved chords which become progressions that are entities in themselves. Dissonances are not necessarily discords, but are chords which require resolution according to the style of the music before they come to a satisfactory cadence or conclusion. These dissonances are prepared or unprepared. The prepared dissonance receives a slight stress and swell as described above, while the unprepared dissonance is usually given more emphasis. The following dissonances illustrate the difference.

Example 14

In Stilly Night

Brahms

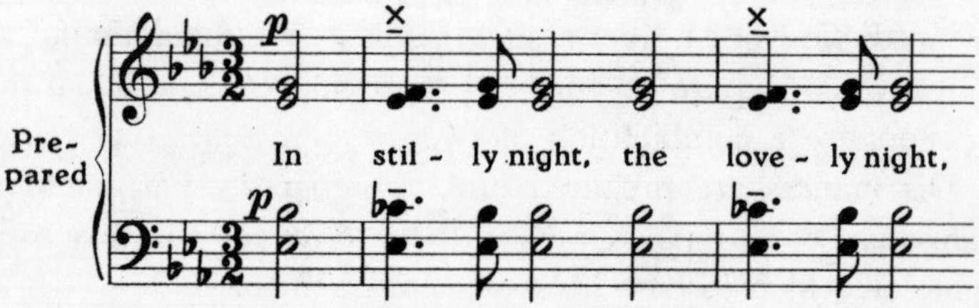

Example 15

Look To This Day

Wilson

One of the most satisfying musical effects is obtained by lingering on the dissonance of the chord just before the last chord of a composition. If this chord is held in soft selections and allowed to melt into the consonance of the last chord it produces a pleasant and soothing close. If the same treatment is given to these chords in a *forte* ending, a striking and brilliant musical effect is achieved.

Example 16

Long Ago In Bethlehem

Wilson

Example 17

Fanfare for Easter

Greyson

THINGS TO CONSIDER

1. Interpretation is a sensitive balance between creating and re-creating.

2. Sincerity of expression means having the musical integrity to abide by the poetical qualities inherent in the words and music.

3. Unity of expression means the ability to understand and interpret a choral composition as a coherent whole.

4. Mood is the emotional atmosphere intrinsic in a choral composition and mode is the manner of revealing it.

5. No style, no artistry. No taste, no appreciation.

6. Technique serves interpretation.

7. Words and music should be a happy, artistic marriage. The court of interpretation permits no marital difficulties or divorce in this union.

8. Music is melody and combinations of melody. You, as musical doctor, must treat melody, as your musical patient, and give it emotional health and artistic life.

9. Variety is the spice of life. Dissonance is the spice of music. Treat dissonance in a manner to give variety to your music.

Chapter IV
Basic Elements of Expression

The elements of music are the substances which the composer has to draw upon to write what he wishes to express in tonal-rhythmic patterns. After a choral conductor has an understanding and control of the considerations for expressive interpretation as presented in the previous chapter he must turn to the elements of expression as they affect the final interpretation of a composition. Attention to these elements is an open-sesame to a perfect performance. Hold the challenge of perfection ever before the chorus and through persuasion, tactfulness, and unwavering faith insist on the unremitting attention to the detail that will realize this goal.

TEMPO

Of all the elements of expression the one most basic to interpretation is *tempo,* or the speed at which the music moves. Wagner, in his monograph on conducting, stated that one could tell whether a conductor understood a piece of music or not by the tempo which he set. Still, it is a revelation to see the difference with which three outstanding conductors like Toscanini, Stokowski, and Mengelberg will take the first four notes of the *Symphony Number 5* of Beethoven. Obviously, the correct tempo is the one at which the music sounds the best.

Is there just one correct tempo? Do the acoustics of an auditorium have any effect on the proper tempo? Should there be any variation in the tempo when singing indoors or outdoors? Should a conductor vary his tempo of a number in light of the technical limitations of his chorus? How strictly should a conductor observe the tempo and metronome marks of a composer or editor? Unquestionably there is a correct tempo, but there is also some latitude from this tempo within which the effectiveness of the music is not impaired.

Tempo and Style

Many conductors hold to the premise that the tempo is inherent in the music itself. In other words, the style dictates the tempo. Even Brahms was supposed to have observed that tempo and expression marks were superfluous, because unless a conductor sensed these interpretative factors from the music itself, they would not have the musicianship to follow the directions of the composer. Though there is much truth in this position, it is not sufficient guide for inexperienced conductors who are not thoroughly acquainted with the various styles of choral music.

The inherent quality of the style of the music is undoubtedly the final criteria for the most effective tempos. Take for instance the majesty of the Handelian allegros as compared to the more rapid tempo associated with the term *allegro* in contemporary music. It is the lack of understanding of this change in the interpretation of the term *allegro* that causes some conductors to take the "Hallelujah Chorus" from *Messiah* at a tempo too fast to preserve the dignity and majesty of this stirring masterpiece. Also, prior to the music of Bach there was practically no indication of tempo by the composer. In modern editions of Renaissance choral music the tempo and expression marks have been supplied by editors. These marks are not infallible, and consequently they should be followed only as far as the editor has proved himself to be an authority in interpreting the style of music of this period. Again, the conductor, in the final analysis, must resort to the inherent quality of the music for the most effective tempo.

It can readily be seen that there is no substitute for musical understanding in the matter of deciding upon correct tempos. Even the so-called traditional tempos are not sacrosanct but may have been initiated by some daring individualist who was adding his own creative temperament to the conception of the music. The only safe guide for the young conductor is to: (1) make himself cognizant of the tempo marks as indicated by composer and editors; (2) familiarize himself with the traditional tempos of standard compositions as exemplified by performances of established conductors in concert and on recordings; (3) develop his own musicianship and understanding of styles until he can experiment with the tempos as dictated by the intrinsic qualities of the music.

External Factors Influencing Tempo

If the correct tempo of a composition is dictated primarily by the intrinsic qualities of the music, what room is there for any variation of this tempo? Are there any conditions external to the music which may warrant some latitude of tempo within narrow limits?

In judging choral festivals it is striking to notice the difference in tempo of the same composition taken by individual conductors under similar physical conditions. It is not unusual for several of these conductors to receive superior ratings. There are many factors in performance that determine a judge's decision aside from that of tempo, but it is significant that a variation in tempo does not necessarily nullify an acceptable performance.

Could it be that the variation in tempo is due to the individual temperament of the different conductors? The interpreter must make the music live again. The conductor must re-create the music. But there is an element of creation in re-creation. The conductor is not a rubber stamp or a submissive musical sheep. The conductor is dependent upon the composer but, in turn, the composer is dependent upon the conductor. Variation of tempo within limits may better suit the personality of some conductors. The music may sound better for one conductor at a slightly different tempo than for another conductor. No two roses are alike, but both may be beautiful. This factor does not give any conductor the privilege of disregarding, or even obliterating, the indications of the composer with exaggerated tempos. Within the confines of musical taste the conductor should establish a tempo which coincides with his individual artistic temperament.

Should the personality and ability of a chorus have any effect on the variation of tempo? Should a chorus of mature voices take certain compositions at a different tempo than a chorus of immature voices? Should the technical limitations of a chorus affect the tempo?

These questions are probably more a matter of selection of music than one of selection of tempo. Certain numbers which are suitable for well-trained choruses of mature voices should not be attempted by inexperienced choral groups with immature voices. It is quite feasible that a group of young people might take a lively dance number at a faster tempo than a chorus of octogenarians. One might raise the question whether the latter group should sing the number at all. Also it is quite possible that a conductor might favor a slower tempo for a very difficult number if a group could not cope with the technical problems at a more appropriately faster tempo. Again the question, should the group attempt to sing the number before it is ready? Also, if a young group is having pitch difficulties with a very slow number a slightly faster tempo may partially correct the problem. For programs or occasions where the singing of certain numbers is a necessity the slight adjustment of tempos would seem to have artistic validity.

How about tempos in high-vaulted, over-resounding auditoriums or churches, in contrast to low-ceiling, acoustically-treated auditoriums resembling radio studios? Again it is probably more a question of the choice of music. Rapid, brilliant numbers will usually not sound clear in the former, while the same number will be too penetrating in the latter.

It is a sign of musical discretion if a conductor checks a new auditorium where his choir is singing for the first time by listening to it from the back of the hall. He may find that in very resonant auditoriums certain numbers with rapid diction passages or intricate rhythmic patterns need to be taken at a slightly slower tempo for clarity. He may find that very slow numbers need to be moved a little to increase their effectiveness. He may discover that in halls which seem "dead" acoustically, a little livelier tempo throughout is better.

Another problem which confronts the conductor is the fact that most choral groups practice in small rooms with low ceilings. They get used to the sound of the music in these rehearsal rooms. In a large auditorium the music sounds quite different and a little slower tempo for fast numbers and a little faster tempo for very slow numbers may be necessary for a better musical performance. All of these tempo adjustments may be ever so slight, and can only be determined by the artistic sense of the conductor.

How about singing out-of-doors? The answer is "don't, if possible." Singing voices are so absorbed in the great outdoors that the results are invariably disappointing. We are not referring to informal singing on picnics or around a campfire. This condition can be partially corrected by the use of a properly built backdrop or shell. Usually only broad and majestic music of a sacred and patriotic nature will resemble to any degree the sound to which the chorus and conductor have become accustomed at rehearsal. Even the distortion of tone, balance, and dynamics which usually accompanies the use of a public address system is more acceptable to an audience than the complete lack of any enclosed platform. Without the assistance of microphone equipment, slightly faster tempos are usually necessary out-of-doors to guard against a listless performance. The reason for this adjustment out-of-doors is the lack of resonance found in an inside auditorium. Unless he is caught completely unawares, a conductor should insist upon a short rehearsal under the conditions where he is expected to perform out-of-doors.

None of the foregoing external factors (the individual temperament of the conductor, the personality or capability of the chorus, the variation in auditoriums, or the problem of singing out-of-doors) should be the initial criteria in determining the tempo of a composition. A conductor must always start with the music itself. Having done this, he should feel free to analyze any situation or problem with which he is faced, and make whatever adjustment to the tempo which he may believe preserves the effectiveness and integrity of the music.

MODIFICATION OF TEMPOS

We have been discussing the setting of tempos for an entire composition or for the large sections of a composition. Let us now consider the modification of tempos within a composition. A change of tempo within a piece implies the setting of a steady tempo from the outset. In other words, there must be the evidence of regularity in tempo before there can be some modification of it.

The establishment of a prevailing tempo can be fairly objective in accordance with the suggestions presented in the previous section. Any deviation from the established tempo within a composition is primarily a subjective urge on the part of the conductor to satisfy his musical feeling. Any choral composition, aside from rhythm numbers, which is sung throughout in a measured and inflexible tempo will usually sound academic and uninteresting. However, freedom on the part of conductors to modify tempos should not be interpreted as unrestricted license. Extreme and theatrical deviations of tempo can only be considered as musical heresy and have no place in artistic choral singing.

The more obvious modifications of tempo within a composition are usually indicated by the composers, arrangers or editors. *Rallentando, ritardando* or *slentando* are the terms most often used to indicate a gradually slowing down of tempo. *Calando* and *morendo* mean a gradually slowing down with a corresponding decrease in intensity. These changes of tempo usually appear after a climax or at the end of a section of a composition. *Accelerando, stringendo* or *poco a poco animato* are the terms prevalently used to indicate gradual increase in tempo. These terms are most often found leading up to a climax. They are usually accompanied by a *crescendo,* or an increase in intensity. *Allargando* is used to indicate a broadening of the tempo with a corresponding increase in the dynamic level. Many composers are now using English terminology. The key word in the proper manipulation of these tempo indications is *gradual.* Sudden changes are usually not in keeping with the intent of the composer.

It is in the subtle variation encompassed by these more obvious deviations from a set tempo that the individuality of the conductor as a musician and interpreter becomes apparent. Here is where his sensitivity to human emotions as represented in the words and the music transforms the stilted into a scintillating performance. It may be in the agogic accent of a single word, a subtle nuance of phrase line, the treatment of a *fermata,* or the introduction of *tempo rubato,* but it defines the difference between the ordinary and the impressive. These particular elements of expression are of such importance that they will be given added treatment in a later section of this chapter.

RHYTHM AND METER

Plato called rhythm "ordered movement," and John Dewey, in *Art as Experience,* defines it as "organized variation of changes". All definitions of rhythm stress the elements of movement or change. It is found in nature and all of life; the undulating of the waves, the variation of the seasons, the pangs of hunger, and the need for sleep. But the second aspect of rhythm is the quality of order or regularity. The point of departure is not regularity with movement or change imposed upon it but rather rhythm *is first of all* movement or change, and order or regularity *is brought to it.*

In music, rhythm is primarily the quality of flowing movement. The factor of order or regularity is represented by meter. It is sometimes referred to as *time,* which is an abbreviation for time-signature. We do not refer to 2/4 or 3/4 rhythm, but to 2/4 or 3/4 meter or time. The flowing movement is designated as the rhythmical pattern, and the regularity of beat is designated as meter or pulse.

In choral music, rhythm evolves from either (1) the natural cadence or inflection of the words, (2) the dance or bodily movement, or (3) a blending or fusing of these two. These factors give a conductor the approach to the treatment of rhythm in artistic singing.

When the melodic lines are based upon the inflection of the words, such as in the chants, early polyphonic music, and later homophonic music of a *legato* nature, the key to phrasing and conducting should be based upon the rhythm of the words. In music which emphasizes regularity of rhythm, such as madrigals of a lively quality, martial music of a patriotic nature, and folk or popular music of the dance variety, the regularity of pulse and meter should be stressed with a crisp, bouncing conducting beat. Music which blends these two basic types of rhythms, such as some of the baroque counterpoint of Bach and Handel, stirring anthems of a majestic quality, and much music of a folk type, compromises between following the natural rhythm of the words and following the regularity of the rhythm as represented in the meter. Contrast in style and mood in performance is dependent upon the ability of a conductor to exploit these basic rhythms.

Meter is the controlling factor of rhythm and the determining factor of conducting patterns (see Chapter II). The regular kinds are the simple and compound duple and ternary meters.

Simple duple — 2/8, 2/4, 2/2 or ₵
Compound duple — 4/8, 4/4 or C, 4/2
Simple ternary — 3/8, 3/4, 3/2
Compound ternary — 6/8, 6/4, 9/8, 12/8

The rhythmical pulse of these various meters is represented by stresses and slacks. These stresses and slacks are resolved by a slight prolongation and accent of the beats. They may be represented as follows:

Simple duple — |— ⌣|
Compound duple — |— ⌣ — ⌣|
Simple ternary — |— ⌣ ⌣|
Compound ternary — |— ⌣ ⌣ — ⌣ ⌣|

Although the type of measure gives order to variety and freedom in rhythm, if the alternation of stress and slacks is followed too regularly and too rigidly then a dull, stilted, even awkward performance results. It is similar to reading poetry in a sing-song, monotonous fashion. Music has a natural rhythm the same as poetry. In choral music the two should coincide.

The opposite extreme is to give the same stress to each note. Then a measure in 4/4 time would appear like this: — — — —. This practice is equally dull and stilted, except for special *marcato* effects as follows: >>>> . There must be a give and take between rhythm and meter. The procedure should be to develop the natural flow of the rhythm as represented in the words and music, retaining the stresses and slacks as represented in the measure to give the phrase unity.

There are times when the rhythmic patterns of the music should not match or be determined by the stress and slack of the meter or pulse. This is often determined by the desired emphasis of the words, but it may be dictated by the musical effect intrinsic in the phrase. In such cases it is expedient to warn the singers to stress or accent the unaccented beats. The normal metrical stress must give way to the stronger rhythmical urge intrinsic in the verbal and melodic line. Sometimes the stresses in the measure are deliberately altered, as in giving a slight accent to the second beat in a Viennese Waltz, or in the shifting of the accent in syncopated figures.

It is interesting to note the effect that time signatures have upon the rhythmical interpretation of the music. The time-signature which composers select for their music is also significant. Mozart wrote his beautiful *Ave Verum* in 4/4 time. Often it is sung in one beat to a bar or two beats to a bar. The three versions are as follows. The musical effect should be obvious.

Example 18

Ave Verum

Mozart

One to a bar

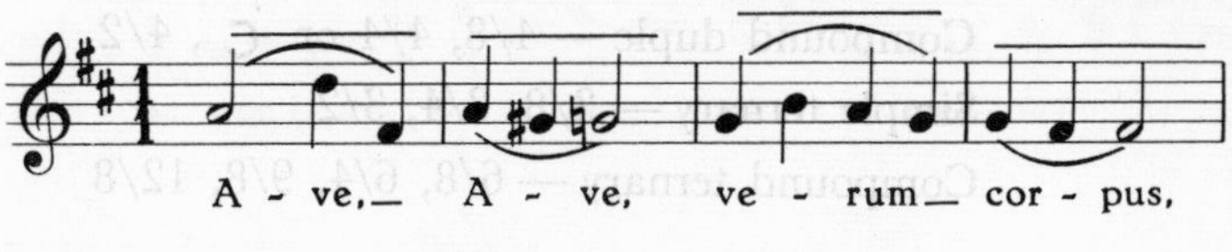

Two to a bar

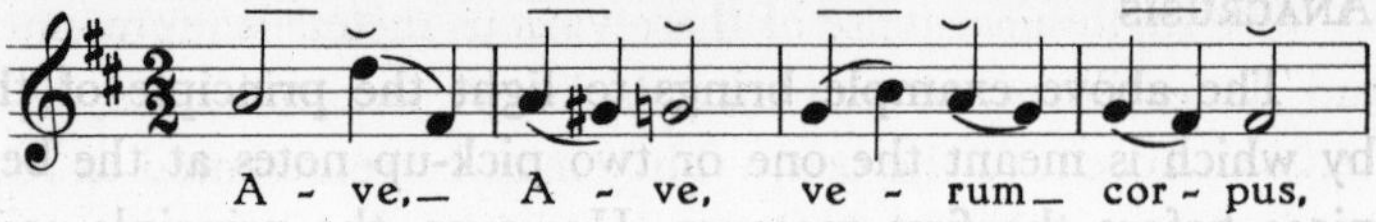
A - ve,— A - ve, ve - rum— cor - pus,

Four to a bar (as Mozart wrote it)

A - ve,— A - ve, ve - rum— cor - pus,

Another interesting observation is the effect of writing the cowboy song *Home on the Range* in ¾ time or ⁶⁄₈ time. It is published in both versions. Sing the two versions to absorb the contrast.

Example 19

Home on the Range

American folk song

Waltz style

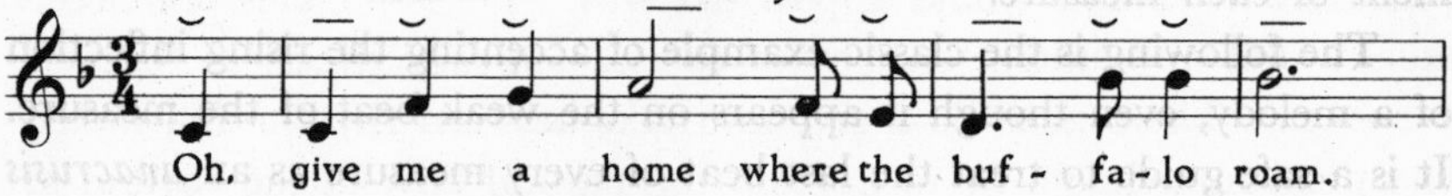
Oh, give me a home where the buf - fa - lo roam.

Smooth style

Oh, give me a home where the buf - fa - lo roam.

The time signature not only has an effect upon the style of rhythm, but also it is a factor in deciding the tempo. For instance, Schubert gave the time signature of ¢ or ²⁄₂ to his beautiful song *To Music*. The tempo indication is *moderato*. If it is taken at ¼ in that tempo it becomes a rather slow melody on the sentimental side. When taken in ²⁄₂ it flows along with artistic nuance.

Example 20

To Music

Schubert

Moderato

Thou love-ly art, my joy— and con-so - la - tion.

Moderato (as Schubert wrote it)

Thou love- ly art, my joy— and con so - la - tion.

Anacrusis

The above example brings to light the principle of the *anacrusis,* by which is meant the one or two pick-up notes at the beginning of a piece before the first measure. However, the principle can be applied to several notes, as in the example above, or in any last beat of a measure leading into the stressed first beat of the next measure.

In the above example the tendency is to stress the syllables on *love* and *my.* Always stressing the rising skip in a melody is the ear-mark of an amateur singer. Following the rule of not stressing the *anacrusis,* there will be no stress on the first three notes, regardless of the rising inflection. They will seem to lead to the stress on the word *art,* even though the melody skips down. There is a corresponding diminution to the note on the word *my* for the same reason. This illustration should give conductors an idea of the importance of studying the metrical treatment of each measure.

The following is the classic example of accenting the rising inflection of a melody, even though it appears on the weak beat of the measure. It is a safe guide to treat the last beat of every measure as an *anacrusis* leading to the first beat of the next measure. The effect on the phrasing in this example is apparent.

Example 21

And the Glory of the Lord
from "Messiah"

Handel

As often sung

Correct phrasing

Certain rhythmical figures seem to be confusing to inexperienced choral conductors, both as to accurate performance and interpretation. The following troublesome figures are the ones which seem to recur the most frequently.

1. 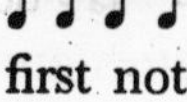 In this figure there is always a tendency to over accent the first note and rush the other three. Keep them even.

2.  This triplet figure is often sung as follows: . Do not over stress or prolong the first note. Keep them even.

3.  This figure in C or ₵ should receive the equivalent of two quarter notes . It is often performed as follows: .

The notes should fit this way: .

4.  These rhythms need to be practiced by the singers either by clapping them or singing with *la* on a single pitch. They need to be accurate to be effective. The conductor should beat the measure in a duple pattern, the common denominator of the two figures.

5. 
(performed)
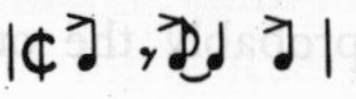

This figure in C or ₵ meter often occurs in modern arrangements of folk dances and popular songs. It is sometimes referred to as the Charleston rhythm because it is characteristic of that social dance. If the notes are given a slight direct accent and the dot is treated like a rest the dance effect is obtained.

MELODY AND HARMONY

Probably the most important criteria in expressive interpretation by a choral conductor is the musical wisdom and feeling which he brings to the manipulation of melodic lines. As previously pointed out, melody evolved from the plain-song based on the natural inflection of words. When melodies were combined under this principle, as in the early polyphonic music, the resultant harmonic progressions were a subsidiary consideration. With the emergence of harmony as an individual entity, polyphony, such as that of the baroque period of Bach and Handel, was based upon definite harmonic progressions.

With the evolution of homophony during the romantic period, melody became a single line with a suitable harmonic accompaniment to give it individuality and character; or, as in some cases, the construction and mood of the melody actually became dependent upon the mood of the harmonic progressions. Contemporary choral composers are endeavoring to reassert the dominance of melody by combining contrapuntal lines in a continuous shifting of meter.

In the early melodies based on the principle of the chant, or plainsong, there are a few problems of difficult rhythmic figures and unsingable intervals such as the augmented second or the tritone of the augmented fourth, (F to B) referred to in those days as "Si contra Fa Diabolus est In Musica"— the very devil in music. If you try to sing this interval without the assistance of instruments, you will readily understand the appellation. Later melodies based upon the dance and harmonic progressions incorporate complicated rhythmic patterns and difficult intervals which reflect the influence of instrumental music.

Aside from the further treatment of melody and harmony, which will be discussed in Chapter V under the various styles of choral singing, the broader aspects of interpretation are the same as presented in this chapter under the section on "Polyphony and Homophony"; namely, music that combines several melodies of equal importance should be blended into one tonal whole. Where a special emphasis is given to an individual melody it should be singled out for special treatment. This does not preclude that important harmonic passages should not have equal attention and even prominence. Nevertheless, the handling of the expressive elements in melodic lines is probably the one most important factor in artistic interpretation.

FORM AND DESIGN

Music expresses itself in tonal-rhythmic patterns. Form is the organization of these patterns into something unified and understandable. The symmetry by which this is accomplished is referred to as design. Therefore, it behooves the conductor to understand how the composer accomplishes this result. Lack of awareness of the form and design of a composition will give a vague and often distorted interpretation. It will lack unity of expression.

A composer has three resources at his command to give his musical ideas clarity and unity. These three resources are the same as those in verbal expression, namely, *repetition, variation* and *contrast*. In choral composition there is one additional resource which the Germans refer to as the *durchkomponierte* (through composed) style. In this style the mood and form of the words dictates the mood and form of the music. The composer permits his musical ideas to grow out of or evolve from the literal and poetical ideas expressed in the words. If there is repetition, variation, or contrast in the music, then it is inherent in the words.

In choral music, repetition is represented by the various stanzas of a hymn, carol, or song. Although the music is the same for each stanza, interest can be obtained in interpreting this type of composition by varying the manner in which the different verses are sung. Following the meaning and mood of the words, a modification of tempo can be taken for some verses; different combinations of voices can be used; transposed keys can be introduced; the accompaniment can be varied.

Theme and variation is employed more often in instrumental composition, but choral arrangers are beginnings to exploit the possibilities of this form. Many choral arrangements of folk songs, carols, hymns, and spirituals are being given this treatment. The use of humming and neutral vowel effects, shifting of melody to various voice parts, intricate rhythmical figuration as an accompaniment to the melody, introduction of solos with choral accompaniment, elaboration of harmonic progressions, and the utilization of introductions and codas are common practice among choral arrangers today.*

There are two dangers in these practices: the original song may be so distorted that the original mood and beauty will be lost in the maze of variation; or the tune, the distinctive quality of these songs, may be covered and buried under an avalanche of tonal and rhythmical complexity. It would seem that arrangers could curb their creative urges to the degree that the native, folk qualities are preserved, even in arrangements for concert purposes. It is difficult to condone the practice of "jazzing up" some of these charming folk songs and spirituals to appeal to popular tastes.

Contrast is the *sine qua non* of most creators of all of musical composition. From the simplest song-form to the most elaborate sonata-allegro form it has been the resource to which the great composers have turned to express their musical ideas. In choral composition, contrast is most often represented by the simple song form (A-B-A). An excellent example to study is the well-known *Kerry Dance* by Malloy, an expanded three-part song form (A-B-A, Trio, A-B-A). Here we have contrast in words, music, mode, and design. Moreover, the contrasts are so marked that the interpretation is obvious. When the contrasts are not so evident, the choral conductor must seek them out. Contrasts will be found between sections and within sections. They will be apparent in different styles of singing as previously pointed out. They will be lurking in the melodic line and the inner parts. Be ever alert to bring out contrasts for an impressive and thrilling performance.

PHRASING

An entire book could be written on the art of phrasing music. So many other factors of interpretation are reflected in the phrasing, and the approach to phrasing so often suggests the interpretation of these

* A complete presentation of these practices will be found in the following book: Wilson, Harry R., *Choral Arranging for Schools, Glee Clubs and Publication,* Robbins Music Corp., New York 19.

factors that we can hope to present here only a few fundamental guides to the many subtle nuances possible in singing phrase lines.

1. *Verbal phrasing should determine musical phrasing.* The development of melodic writing evolved from the natural phrase line of the words. The purest form of choral writing retains this aspect or it incorporates elements of an instrumental style. Therefore, the first step toward musical phrasing is for the singer to know what he is singing about. Consequently, it would seem that preliminary to the singing of a choral composition the poetry should be read as expressively as possible. This reading may be given by the conductor or a member of the group. It is rather a simple matter in a rhythmical chant like *Hospodi Pomilui* by Lvovsky. But even here the singers should know that they are singing "Lord, have mercy upon us" and not a phrase of nonsense syllables. The same approach is valid in Latin texts such as "Kyrie Eleison", also translated as "Lord, have mercy upon us."

When a choral group fails to grasp an understanding of phrasing a melodic line, the singers should read the words, not in a sing-song fashion, but in their natural inflection. Transfer this conception of the poetical line to the musical line. This approach is not giving a secondary role to the musical phrase line but it is the very device which will reveal its intrinsic qualities. We repeat that the key to phrasing choral music is found in the normal nuance and accent of the text.

2. *Fine choral groups invariably sing long musical phrases.* There is nothing more disconcerting than listening to a chorus sing four measures, then gasp, sing four more measures, gasp, *ad infinitum*. It might be referred to as "the four-square gospel of phrasing." Fine choral groups vary the phrase length, and are able to spin out what seem to be never-ending phrases. It is significant that the greatest composers seem to be the ones that can write the longest phrases and still retain musical interest. Witness the lengthy, enduring phrases in "Die Mainacht" (The May Night) of Brahms, which are the nemesis of many a concert soloist. Where a soloist may have vocal difficulty with such long phrases, a chorus, using the device of staggered catch breaths, can sing them with ease.

As suggested in the preceding paragraphs, music should be phrased according to the phrasing of the words. This would imply that the music should be punctuated according to the punctuation of the words. A strict adherence to this practice in some pieces would result in short, detached phrases of an inartistic nature. In some compositions, the sweep of the musical phrase line warrants unheeding the punctuation of the text which permits the music phrase to flow on to its complete fulfillment. Disregarding the punctuation of the words in such cases does not negate the axiom that the verbal phrase should determine the musical phrase. In fact, the verbal phrase is just being extended. It is interesting to note that there is a trend in both poetry and prose to eliminate punctuation marks, except where they are needed for clarity. The same procedure is applicable to music.

The following two excerpts are excellent examples of how musically satisfying it is to disregard the punctuation of the words to secure a long, beautiful musical phrase. If you try singing the two phrases observing the punctuation of the words, the unmusical, almost ludicrous effect is obvious.

Example 22

The Silver Swan

Gibbons

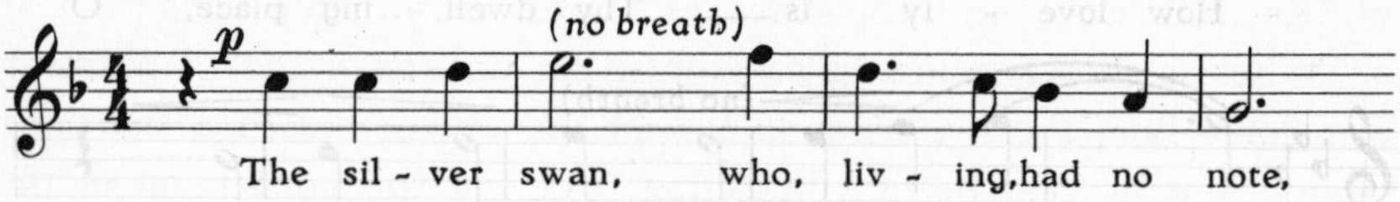
(no breath)
p
The sil - ver swan, who, liv - ing,had no note,

Example 23

Remember Now Thy Creator

Wilson

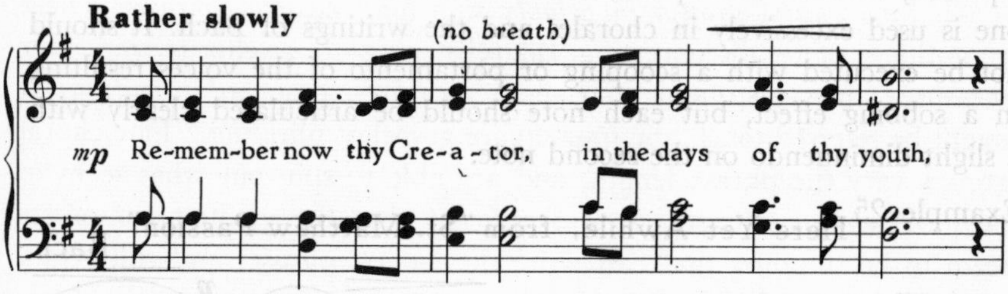
Rather slowly
(no breath)
mp
Re-mem-ber now thy Cre-a - tor, in the days of thy youth,

3. *To some degree a crescendo accompanies a phrase that rises and a diminuendo accompanies a phrase that falls.* This statement is an elementary guide to interpretation, employed without consideration of other factors. When followed rigidly there is a monotonous undulating of phrase line, sometimes compared to the in-and-out movements and resultant expression of an accordian. A graphic picture of this type of phrasing is as follows:

Diagram 11

In abiding by this precept, the unity of the phrase must always be kept in mind. Notes must be connected, and the variation in intensity must never give a suggestion of a group of short, disconnected phrases. This slight wavering of the phrase line follows the natural nuance and stress of the syllables of the words. It should not be pronounced as to distort the normal smoothness of the phrase line. Introducing choral effects which are not inherent in the words and music is an insincere form of expression. The following beautiful phrase illustrates this principle.

Example 24 How Lovely Is Thy Dwelling Place Brahms

Two common applications of this general principle of phrasing are found in a series of two-note slurs, and in three-or-four note slurs, especially in inner voice parts, that are chromatic in character. The first one is used excessively in chorales and the writings of Bach. It should not be executed with a scooping or portamento of the voices resulting in a sobbing effect, but each note should be articulated clearly with a slight diminuendo on the second note.

Example 25 Here Yet Awhile, from "St. Matthew Passion" Bach

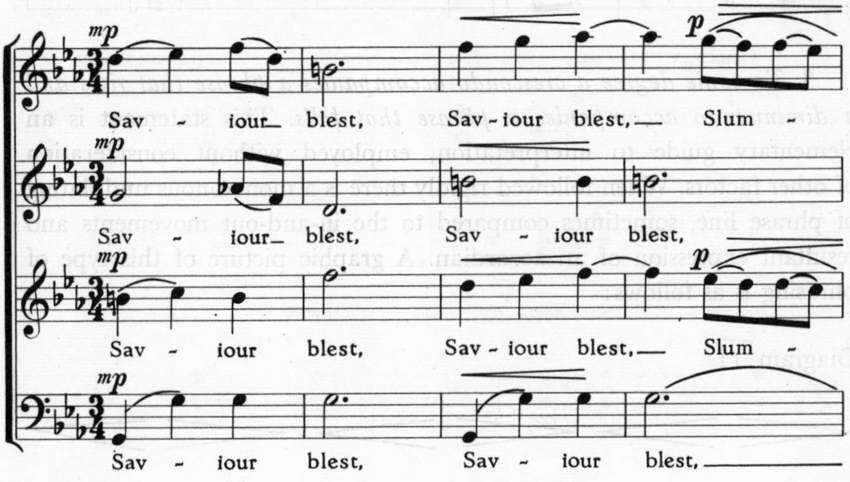

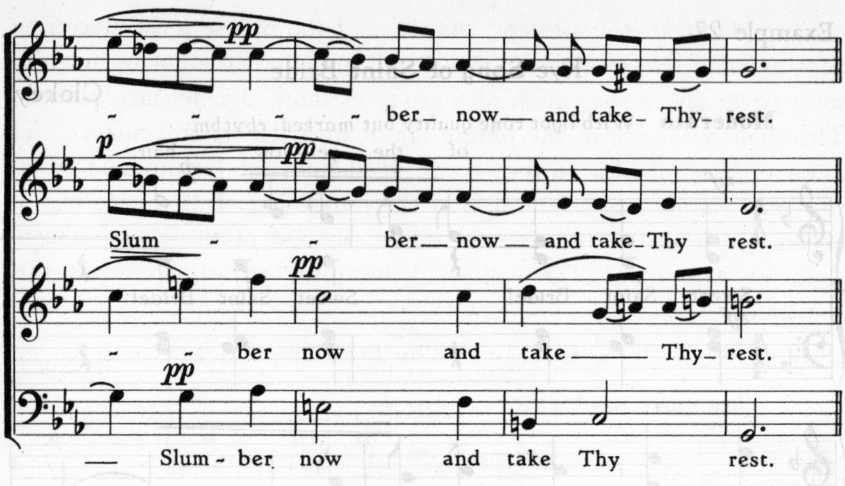

There are times when a delightful lilt can be obtained by diminishing to the peak of a phrase line. Kreisler, the violinist, was a master at this kind of phrasing. It is also inherent in the string quartet writing of the great composers. It has the same artistic effect as the tapering of the ends of phrases, even when the phrases end with a rising inflection. These instances should not be considered exceptions to our guiding premise, but should be considered expressive variation, the life blood of interpretation. The following two examples serve as illustrations.

Example 26

Come Where My Love Lies Dreaming

Foster

Example 27

Kye Song of Saint Bride

Clokey

4. *Melismatic melodies are phrased according to the intrinsic style of the music.* When a single word or syllable of a word is set to a series of notes it is called a *melisma.* A melody which is constructed of many of these ornaments is referred to as a *melismatic* melody. It was a technique used by the composers of the early chants to give emphasis or stress to a word or an important syllable of the word. The technique was retained in the early polyphonic writing. Composers used it not only to give emphasis to a word or important syllable, but also to give realistic expression to a word. In the choral music of the baroque period based upon measured, harmonic progressions with its emphasis on instrumental figuration, composers, such as Bach and Handel, set words to elaborate runs just as musical ornamentation, without, however, destroying the original function of the *melisma* or the rules of musical rhetoric. The following examples are illustrations of these three functions.

Example 28

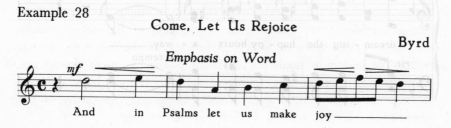

Come, Let Us Rejoice

Byrd

Emphasis on Word

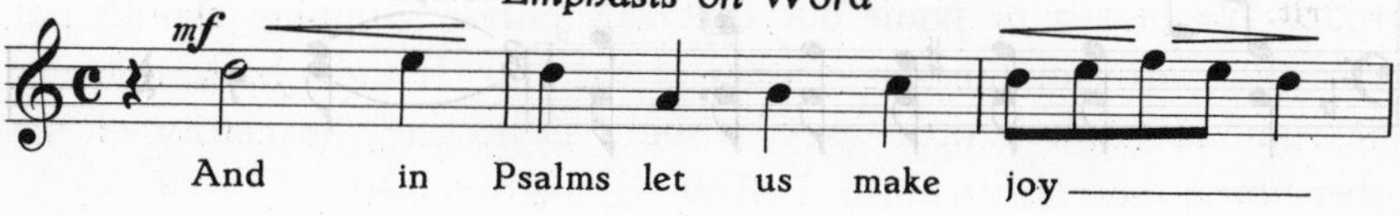

Example 29

Sweet Suffolk Owl

Vautor

Realistic Expression of Word

Example 30

For Unto Us a Child Is Born, from "Messiah"

Handel

Musical Ornamentation of Word

As stated in our heading of this section these types of *melisma* should be sung according to the intrinsic style of the music. In the first type the *melisma* is sung smoothly to coincide with the nuance of the word. In the second type the *melisma* is sung to bring out the realistic quality of the word. The notes should be distinct, but not detached, and the run is sung as a single phrase without secondary accents. In the third type the figuration is instrumentally conceived, and should have an instrumental interpretation. This requires a pronounced clarity of individual notes without disconnecting the notes. It must not sound like a series of notes with a similar accent on each note. Therefore, there needs to be a grouping of the notes, usually according to the sequences, with a slight stress on the first note of each group. We hasten to point out that this phrase grouping should not erase the clarity of the single notes of the run. If these basic notes of the run are given a little stress without neglecting the clarity of the other notes, the correct musical effect will be obtained.

Example 31

All Breathing Life from "Sing Ye to the Lord"

Bach

In polyphonic writing of this nature the contrapuntal lines must be distinct; otherwise the total effect is vague and diffused. The music may sound overpowering, but it will lack excitement. We feel that it is this want of clarity of contrapuntal lines that causes a lack of appreciation on the part of both singers and listeners to the brilliant eight-part writing of composers of the baroque and classic periods. The general rule for singing the runs in this music is that the detachment of the contrapuntal lines is in direct proportion to the number of parts. In other words, a single line should be treated as in the example above but as more contrapuntal lines are introduced devices need to be introduced to make each part distinct. In eight-part music of a brilliant type it is often necessary for the soprano and alto to sing runs semi-staccato, while the tenors and basses prefix each note with the aspirate *h* judiciously used.

With the advent of the romantic style of music the *melismatic* melody with its figuration and ornamentation gave way to melodies where each word and syllables of words were set to single notes. However, the characteristics of the earlier style were often retained in music of a polyphonic nature. Also the use of the *melismatic* melody is again being employed in the writings of modern composers and arrangers.

Example 32

Old Boat Zion

Shure

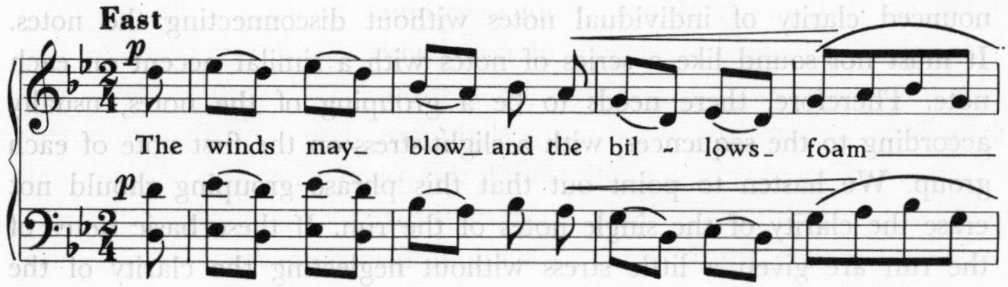

DYNAMICS

The loudness and softeness of music are referred to as dynamics. The term includes both volume and intensity. There is a general scale of dynamics which is familiar to, but not always observed by choral groups.

Term	*Abbreviation*	*English Equivalent*
Pianissimo	*pp*	Very soft
Piano	*p*	Soft
Mezzo-piano	*mp*	Moderately soft
Mezzo-forte	*mf*	Moderately loud
Forte	*f*	Loud
Fortissimo	*ff*	Very loud

It is a common observation that most choral groups sing with a dynamic range from moderately soft *(mp)* to moderately loud *(mf)*. Needless to say, this tendency usually results in uninteresting and unimpressive performances. School choral groups of young people are most often guilty of this style of singing. Undoubtedly this prevalence exists partially, at least, because of the limitations of these young voices. This condition does not have to be accepted by school choral conductors, because through proper vocal development, and the discerning use of tonal volume and balance, a contrast of dynamics can be secured. Impressive performances of many compositions are dependent upon a wide contrast of dynamics.

This scale of dynamics certainly had various meanings to various composers. Mozart seldom used dynamic indications of more than one *p* or one *f*. Most of his music sounds extremely well within these dynamic limits. In fact, much of his writing does not call for a wide range of dynamics. Tschaikowsky, on the other hand, did not hesitate to use such indications as *fff* and at the end of the first movement of the Sixth Symphony he uses the indication of *pppppp*. Undoubtedly composers have become more extreme with their markings, because they realize that neither instrumental nor choral conductors observe the traditional markings with enough precision to obtain a sufficient contrast of dynamics for effective performance of their music.

Dynamic Level

Intensity is a relative term. A moderately loud dynamic level for some choirs might be a moderately soft dynamic level for another choir. This difference in dynamic level may be due to vocal immaturity or limitations, or it may be the individual preference of the conductor. The normal dynamic level for a choir should be the point of departure from which extreme dynamic shadings should emanate. The individuality of a choir is often reflected in their level of tonal volume.

Soft-voiced choirs often sound aenemic in their interpretations. Many times these choirs are most effective for one or two numbers, but there is a sameness about their singing which makes an entire concert a rather listless affair. On the other hand, the choral groups of conductors who deride soft singing often lose artistry in their effort to be brilliant. If the dynamic level is too high then there is little opportunity for thrilling climaxes because all of the vocal resources have been used up.

Artistic interpretation is found in the compromise between these two levels of volume. Then the ears of the listeners are not dulled by the lack of variety in dynamics. A choral conductor through experimentation and experience will discover that he will obtain a better blend and balance of voices if he leans toward a softer dynamic level than if he favors a louder one, where voices may become forced and strident resulting in a loss of blend and balance.

Dynamic Balance

Intensity is just one factor in securing balance of voice parts. It has already been suggested that the melody should be prominent in homophonic music regardless of which part is singing it. The *tessitura* of the various voice parts also has a direct bearing on dynamic balance.

Tessitura refers to the general highness or lowness of a melody or voice part. Due to the vocal energy necessary to sing voice parts with a high *tessitura* they often sound louder than those parts with a low *tessitura*. It is often necessary to tone down high soprano parts and to build up low bass parts to achieve a balance of parts. Therefore one dynamic marking may not be equally suitable for all parts and must be adjusted to secure a musical performance.

One more particular in dynamic balance which seems to give concern to some conductors is that of the relative intensity of the various notes of a single chord especially those which are held at the end of a section or the final chord of a composition. The composer partially supplies the answer to this problem by the notes of the chord which he doubles. Unless an unusual effect is desired, the prominence of the notes of a chord is usually in this order: root, fifth, third. The intensity of the individual parts will depend upon the highness and lowness of the tones and the quality of the voices. At a moderate dynamic level in a medium pitch range the following chords would probably be sung thus:

Example 33

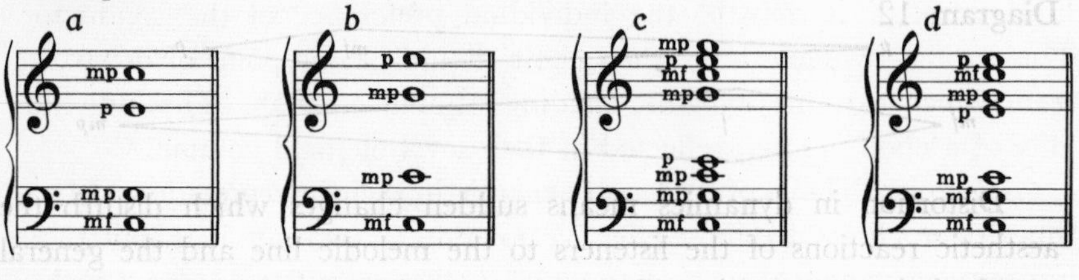

It is assumed in the above examples that the number of singers on each part is nearly equal. Naturally, in an unequal distribution of voices on various parts the different sections will have to sing more loudly or softly to produce a balanced chord.

Change in Dynamics

In all of the factors and elements of interpretation which we have discussed we have continually stressed the need for contrast. The same thing holds true in considering the function of dynamics.

The sudden changes indicated by the composer such as *piano subito* or *forte subito (sforzando, sfz)* are striking effects which should cause the conductor little trouble. It is a waste of time to practice continually the phrase preceding the sudden change and then expect the chorus to sing the *subito* properly. First of all practice the phrase indicated as *piano subito* or *forte subito*. Then the chorus will have a physical and tonal imagery of the effect desired. Now if the section leading into the *subito* is sung the chorus will automatically make the sudden change of dynamics desired.

A gradual change of dynamics is usually indicated by the terms *crescendo* and *diminuendo* (Abb. *cresc.* and *dim.)* Other terms which are a variation of these two indications are given in Chapter II. These terms are used so frequently that they are generally indicated by these graphic signs:

There are three considerations in the musical interpretation of these gradual changes in dynamics. The change of intensity should as a rule, be in proportion to the tonal volume level preceding and following the indication of change, the change should be so gradual that there is no distortion of dynamics in the execution of the *crescendo* and *diminuendo,* and the excitement of a *crescendo,* especially on repeated notes, is ample reason for a temporary disturbance of the regular flow of metrical accents.

From a soft *(p)* volume level, unless the *crescendo* is an exceedingly long one, the dynamic level will probably not rise higher than a *mezzo-forte (mf)*. Other levels of *crescendo* and *diminuendo* should be determined accordingly.

Diagram 12

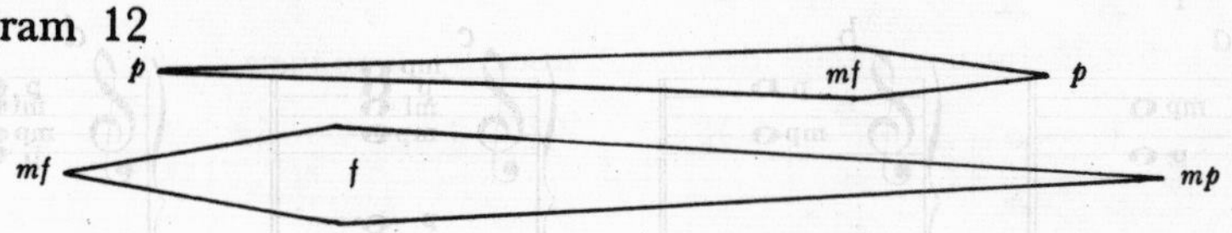

Distortion in dynamics means sudden changes which disturb the aesthetic reactions of the listeners to the melodic line and the general mood of the composition. Gradual changes in the dynamics of music should appear like the gradual changes of light and shade in classic painting. They should resemble the above diagrams, *not the following:*

Diagram 13

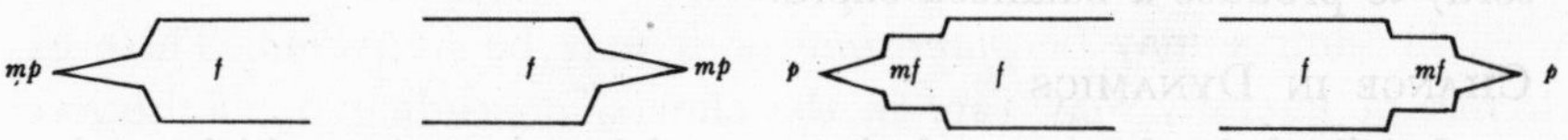

Such incongruous designs as those above give credence to the excellent statement of von Bülow, the famous German conductor, "*Crescendo* means *piano; diminuendo* means *forte.*" In other words, hold down the *crescendo;* hold up the *diminuendo.*

In ordinary *crescendo* and *diminuendo* the metrical pressures of the measure are retained, which give a slight undulating wave effect, without distortion, however. *Crescendos* on sustained tones or a series of repeated notes are most striking when the normal accents are temporarily discarded, as indicated in the two examples from *Messiah* below. In the second example, when sung by a large chorus, the conductor may achieve a better rendering of the phrase by having the first voices of each part sing the first three measures and having the second voices join in on the fourth bar. Then on the last measure for the *diminuendo,* the second voices of each part may drop out unobtrusively one at a time. This is just an expedient device and should not be necessary with a well-trained group or with smaller choirs.

Example 34

a. From "Messiah"

Handel

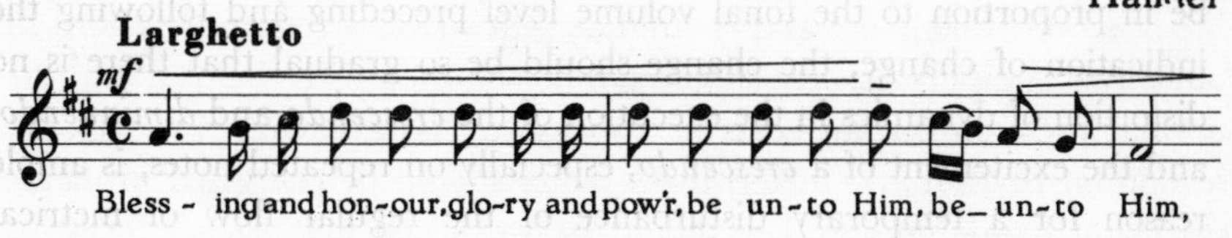

b.

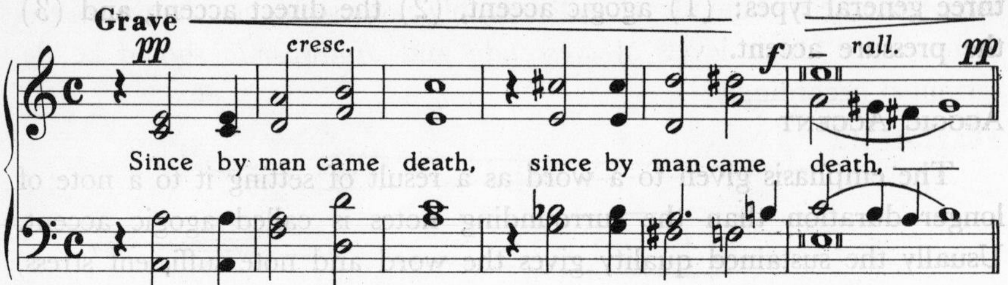

Climax

Every choral composition must have its musical climax, just as every play or story must have its dramatic climax. Any composer worth his salt realizes this and provides for it in the notes. Music that has no climax seems to lack unity. We say that it is "music that gets nowhere". The best advice we can give to you is not to sing it.

The climax may be *pianissimo* or it may be *fortissimo*. These extremes of intensity may vary in the climax, depending upon the level of tonal volume of the larger portion of the composition. The climax may be the last note, like the dramatic climax of a mystery novel, but if not, it will usually be near the end or the latter part of the composition. The reason for this position of the climax is that a piece of music unfolds like a story, and just as the author does not want to divulge his climax too soon, so the composer does not want to sap his musical ideas and resources too quickly.

The climaxes of choral compositions are so obvious that examples should not be necessary. They invariably coincide with the climax of the words. There may be intermittent smaller climaxes or apexes as in any good drama, but the conductor should use caution to reserve his vocal and dynamic resources for that final climax, whether it be a scintillating *pianissimo,* or a thrilling *fortissimo*. Sometimes, when learning a new composition, it is wise to practice the climax before singing the entire selection so that the singers will realize the musical and dramatic effect toward which they are moving and bending their interpretive efforts.

ACCENTS

The element in musical interpretation which shows that music has life is *accent*. Like pulse and rhythm, accent strikes a responsive chord to our physical nature. Accent should not be confused with the beat and the normal stress on certain beats in a measure. As was pointed out in the section on rhythm and meter, these pulses should be energized in measured and dance music; they should be weakened and even effaced in smooth, legato music.

There are countless nuances in dealing with accent but there are three general types: (1) agogic accent, (2) the direct accent, and (3) the pressure accent.

Agogic Accent

The emphasis given to a word as a result of setting it to a note of longer duration than the surrounding notes is called agogic accent. Usually the sustained quality gives the word and note sufficient stress, but it can be pointed up by giving it the treatment of a *tenuto* (—), which literally means to hold the note out to the full length of its value. In modern editions and arrangements it usually indicates a slight stress as well.

The importance of the agogic accent can be grasped when one understands that through its use, plus the inflection of the word and melody, the literal meaning of a word phrase can be drastically altered. This unique effect is illustrated in the following example. First of all, read the words following the accent and inflection suggested by the notation. Then sing the notes portraying the same literal meaning of the words. The result is striking and obvious.

Example 35

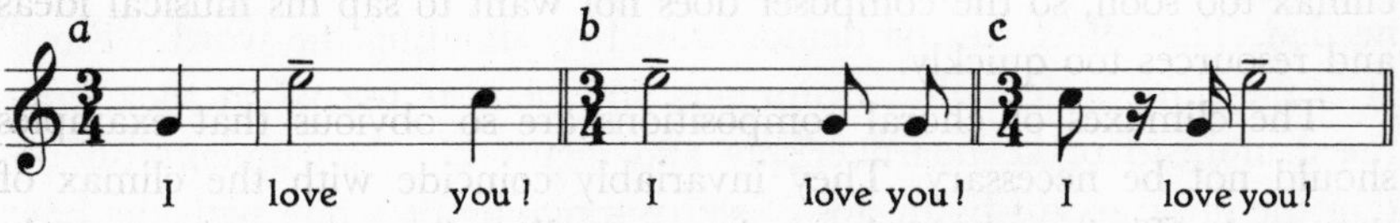

Further illustration can be shown by using the first phrase of the lovely old Christmas chorale, *Lo, How A Rose E'er Blooming* by Praetorious. It is composed of half-notes and quarter-notes, except for the alto part. The duration of the half-notes gives a slight agogic accent to the words set to these notes. When this is done a striking effect occurs, namely, the meter of the phrase seems to change naturally from a duple to a triple meter, and the words fall on natural accents. Then the phrase becomes the normal four-measure phrase, rather than the unusual five-measure phrase. Also in this meter there is no tendency for singers to breathe after the word "blooming" and destroy the beauty of the phrase. In instances of this kind agogic accent becomes almost synonomous with pulse and meter.

Example 36

Lo, How a Rose E'er Blooming

Praetorius

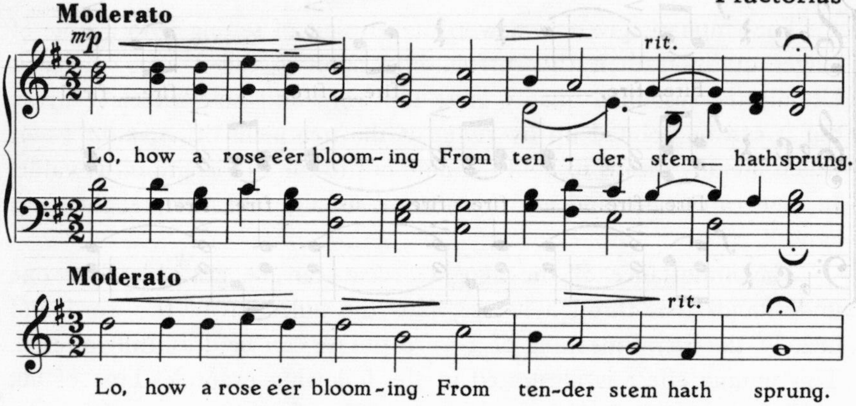

Direct Accent

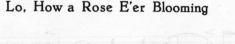

When words suggest great energy a percussive type of accent is needed. This effect can be demonstrated by shouting the word, "Fire!" It is the same accent that drummers and pianists use when they strike the drumhead or keyboard crisply and vigorously. Instrumentalists obtain the same accent by means of sharp tonguing or a bite with the bow. It is usually indicated by one of the following signs: ∧ , > , *sf* Too often it is conceived and executed by singers like a pressure accent, <>. It should be initiated with a glottis attack, that is, a stoppage of the vocal action with a sudden explosion of breath. In executing a direct accent, singers should not think of *crescendo* but of a sharp *diminuendo*.

The following exercise will give the correct technique. It may be spoken or sung on any convenient pitch: Ah, Ah, Ah, Ah, Ah. In choral compositions isolated direct accents should be practiced separately out of the musical context. When introduced into the musical context the amount of accent must always be in proportion to the tonal volume level, so that the effect will not sound distorted and inconsistent with the prevailing mood. A series of direct accents are performed as in *marcato* style, which will be discussed in Chapter V.

The following is a perfect example of the effect of direct accents:

Example 37

Fire, Fire My Heart

Morley

Pressure Accent

If slightly more stress on a word is desired than represented in the agogic accent, and less abrupt than the direct accent, the composer usually indicates the pressure accent. The usual marking for this effect is, <>. The pressure accent is vocal in character, while the direct accent, although possible with voices, is more instrumental in character. Direct accents are not found in early choral music. They were introduced in choral music as it was influenced by the development of instrumental music. Perhaps this is the reason why singers execute the pressure accent much more easily and naturally than the direct accent. As in all dynamic changes, the effect of the pressure accent should be in proportion to the tonal volume level of the prevailing mood and style. The following example should be sufficient illustration for the effect of the pressure accent as a common element in interpretation.

Example 38

With Drooping Wings

Purcell

FERMATAS OR HOLDS

When an interruption or pause in the flow of the music is desired it is indicated by a *fermata* or hold: · 𝄐 or 𝄑 . There are two kinds of *fermatas,* stopped and moving. In the stopped *fermata* there is a decided pause after the hold is made. In the moving *fermata* the next phrase is attacked immediately after the hold is made. The conductor must use his musical discretion in determining the type of *fermata*. The two basic criteria are in the verbal phrase, represented in the literal meaning of the words, and the natural sweep, or on-going-ness, of the musical phrase.

The following Bach Chorale contains examples of both types of *fermatas*. Except for the final one, the *fermatas* in the refrain *The Star-Spangled Banner* are moving *fermatas,* not stopped *fermatas* as they are usually sung. In the light of the two criteria above the reason is obvious.

Example 39

Break Forth, O Beauteous, Heavenly Light

Grande Pausa

Closely related to the *fermata* is the *grande pausa*. It is indicated as follows: 

. It holds a rest instead of a chord. It often follows a *fermata*. It is a device used by many composers to indicate an abrupt change of mood. A short break is sometimes indicated with a slanting double bar: // . Some conductors introduce *grande pausa* even when it is not indicated. Discretion is the better part of valor here, in order not to distort and even destroy sincerity and unity of expression.

Ornaments

In choral music the composer usually writes out the manner of performing all ornamentations. Still, a choral conductor in his study may contact the more common ornaments in old editions. The ornament of melodic runs and the *melisma* are discussed under "Phrasing."

Here is a list of those ornaments with which the choral conductor should be familiar. They are the stock-in-trade of all instrumentalists.

1. *Appoggiatura or grace-note*
   a. Accented *appoggiaturas* — two types

Long *appoggiatura*

Written  Performed 

Short *appoggiatura,* or *accaciatúra*

Written  Performed 

b. Unaccented *appoggiaturas*

Written  Performed 

2. *Turn* in Vocal Music

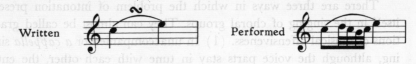

Written  Performed 

3. *Mordents*

a. Regular *mordent*

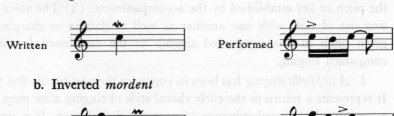

Written  Performed 

b. Inverted *mordent*

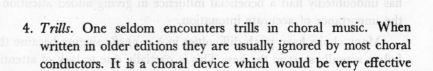

Written  Performed 

4. *Trills.* One seldom encounters trills in choral music. When written in older editions they are usually ignored by most choral conductors. It is a choral device which would be very effective but almost impossible to execute.

Written 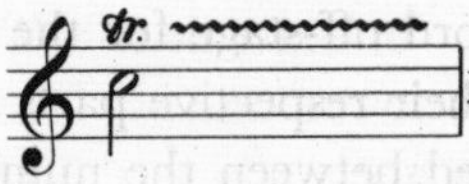

Performed 

5. *Glissando.* Occasionally used by modern choral arrangers for a novel or striking effect. Executed as a *portamento* by slurring the voices.

Written  Performed 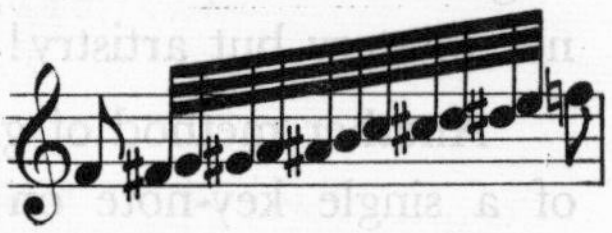

PITCH

Other factors of interpretation are futile if a choir sings consistently off pitch. It is probably the most exasperating element of choral performance with which the conductor has to deal. When Shakespeare wrote

> The man that hath no music in himself,
> Nor is not moved with concord of sweet sounds,
> Is fit for treasons, strategems and spoils,—

he certainly was not referring to the performance of the average choral group. The problem of intonation almost drives many a conductor to commit these iniquities, including murder.

There are three ways in which the problem of intonation presents itself in the singing of choral groups. They can almost be called gradations of musical offensiveness. (1) In unaccompanied or *a cappella* singing, although the voice parts stay in tune with each other, the entire ensemble flats or sharps uniformly from the starting pitch. (2) In accompanied singing the entire ensemble flats or sharps consistently from the pitch or key established by the accompaniment. (3) The voice parts sing out of tune with one another as well as flatting or sharping the given pitch in unaccompanied singing or the established key in accompanied singing.

1. *A cappella* singing has been in vogue for the past twenty-five years. It represents a return to the early choral style of singing after more than a century of the predominance of accompanied singing. It is unquestionably the purest style of choral singing, and the present renaissance has undoubtedly had a beneficial influence in giving added attention to the importance of accurate intonation.

Many choirs have pitch difficulties in *a cappella* singing because they fail to actually start in the key. This is partially due to lack of attention of the singers. But often it is due to the manner in which the pitch is given. Some conductors prefer a secretive method of giving the pitch. The choir is given the starting chord off-stage for the first number and is expected to retain the pitch of their respective parts as they march on the stage. Then a pitch-pipe is used between the numbers, which is inaudible, due to the applauding of the audience. It takes an experienced choir and considerable training to perform this stunt—training which might creditably be devoted to more important matters. The object is not mystery but artistry!

Another method of giving pitch for *a cappella* singing is the playing of a single key-note on some instrument. This method also involves considerable training in the ability of the singers to sing the pitch of their part from the key-note. It is difficult to understand this penurious attitude toward giving the pitch. One fails to see the artistic advantage. With such procedures too many choirs seldom start the piece in tune and in the proper key.

The third method is to play the beginning chord on the piano or organ with the melodic tone on top. The notes of the chord may be played simultaneously or they may be played singly from the bottom up to give confidence to the singers to obtain their respective pitches. They may hum their pitches inaudibly or better still they may think their pitches after hearing them played. Sometimes it is advisable, especially in dissonant numbers, to play the opening rhythmical figure. One caution should be emphasized and that is the desirability of giving the pitch in the mood of the composition to be sung. Nothing is more incongruous than to give a *forte* pitch when the piece begins *pianissimo* or to give a soft anemic chord when the piece begins *fortissimo*.

Although there can be no sanction for off-pitch singing, it is the writer's opinion that too great a fetish has been made of a chorus holding the given pitch in *a cappella* singing. Granted it is the goal for which to strive, still, a slight, uniform falling off of the pitch is seldom noticed either by the listeners or even the conductor. In rehearsal usually the final chord must be played before either the singers or the conductor can ascertain whether they are on pitch, sharp, or flat. Archibald Davidson concurs in this opinion.

> For my own part, I believe that the ideal of a correctly maintained pitch in *a cappella* singing is overemphasized. It is, perhaps, a by-product of our respect for instrumental accuracy. Naturally, one holds that ideal constantly before the chorus and expresses proper gratification when it is realized, but, provided the singing is in other respects satisfactory, a moderate departure from true pitch is not catastrophic when all four parts change practically simultaneously, not too suddenly, and in the same proportion, and when the basses are not crowded down to an inaudible pitch.*

2. Singing out of tune with an accompaniment is quite a different matter. A chorus that cannot sing in tune without an accompaniment is not likely to sing in tune when a piano or organ plays the voice parts. The sound of a chorus sagging below pitch and trying desperately to rise to the pitch of the piano is one of the most dismal experiences in music. It is better to stop the accompaniment and permit the voices to flat to their own content. In this situation, when the chorus is singing without accompaniment, there is a chance for some passages to be in tune, but if it is out of tune with the accompaniment nothing sounds good.

3. When voice parts are badly out of tune with themselves, accompanied or unaccompanied, the result is excruciating. Correct tempo, correct rhythms or correct execution of other elements of interpretation will not offset this musical monstrosity. Take heart, Choral Conductors, it is said that Brahms gave up directing a choral group of ladies in Hamburg, Germany because he could not get the ladies to sing on pitch. During this period, however, he wrote some of the most beautiful choral numbers which we have for three and four-part treble voices. Continued attention to the problem and experience in singing together are the only

* Davidson, Archibald T., Choral Conducting, Harvard University Press. Cambridge 1940, Pg. 37.

things which will conquer this bugaboo of singing out of tune.

The cure for this musical epidemic is an assortment of musical vitamins. First of all, the singers must learn to listen — listen to single pitches, chord blend, and to each other. Secondly, they must learn to sing with correct voice production, because lack of this technique is largely responsible for off-pitch singing ills. Chapters VI and VII will be devoted to this problem of voice production.

Here are a few quick remedies while the singers are undergoing a series of out-of-tune treatments.

1.) Insist that the singers energize themselves. Listless bodily attitudes beget "flatting." Encourage erect posture. Tell them to lift their faces. Look happy!

2.) If a choir consistently flats, raise the pitch of the piece one-half or even a whole step. The added energy required to produce their voices will keep them on pitch. Don't worry, the tenors will probably sing their part better.

3.) Sometimes a slight speeding up of the tempo on slow numbers will eliminate the tendency to flat.

4.) If the choir flats with an accompaniment, raise the pitch. Teach the accompanist to transpose from flat keys to sharp keys. Otherwise, teach the accompanist how to write out a transposed part.

5.) Use simple hymns to develop chord blend. Select single chords for tuning purposes.

6.) Check on those half-steps and those wide ascending skips. The singers must stretch for them. Sing on top of the tones, not on the underside.

7.) Singers usually sing sharp when they sing loudly in a high *tessitura,* and flat when they sing softly in either a high or low *tessitura.* Therefore if the ensemble or individual singers are sharping, tone them down a little. If they are flatting it may be necessary to raise the dynamic level, even at the sacrifice of the desired musical effect. We recall many times hearing the singing of a concert arrangement of *The Battle Hymn of the Republic*. Everything sounds satisfactory until the chorus comes to the soft stanza that begins, "In the beauty of the lilies", and the poor lilies droop a minor third. With this fiasco we will postpone the detailed discussion of this all-important element of interpretation until later chapters.

ATTACKS AND RELEASES

We have not placed this element of interpretation as the final one in this chapter because of its unimportance but because of its unique importance. We have discussed what should happen to the music between the start and the finish. Now comes the problem of how to begin and how to end. In Chapter II we presented the conducting technique necessary for the various types of attacks and the usual indication for releases.

First of all, the attack is not an assault, and the final release is not a sign of relief. They are a part of the entire interpretation. They must maintain the mood, the style and the dynamic level of the number. The attack is the beginning of the first phrase; the release is the ending of the final phrase. It is effective to establish the atmosphere of the piece before the attack and to hold it briefly after the final release. This is done by the facial and bodily attitudes of the chorus and conductor.

Precise attacks and releases are largely dependent upon a group of attentive singers. They must be trained to watch the conductor at all times, especially upon all attacks and releases. More detailed discussion of the handling of vowels and consonants which applies to attacks and releases will be presented in Chapter VI.

THINGS TO DISCUSS

1. Ultimate success depends upon placing standards of perfection in performance on both yourself and the chorus.
2. *Tempo* is the most basic element in interpretation.
3. The final criteria for effective *tempo* are the intrinsic qualities of the music.
4. Under certain conditions there is justification for a slight modification of *tempo*.
5. Rhythm means flow of movement while meter means regularity of movement.
6. The two bases for rhythm in music are the spoken word and bodily movement.
7. The choice of time-signature has a decided effect on the interpretation.
8. The principle of the *anacrusis* may be applied to the last beat of any measure regardless of the inflection of the melody.
9. In the last analysis, interpretation depends upon the treatment of melody.
10. Unity of expression is dependent upon a knowledge of the form of a composition.
11. The artistic reading of the verbal phrase line is conducive to the ar-

tistic singing of the musical phrase line.
12. Contrast in dynamics is a major factor in impressive performance.
13. Climaxes may be loud or soft but the dramatic appeal of music is dependent upon them.
14. Accents are as varied as human emotion itself. They give life to music.
15. Tonality, off-pitch, and out-of-tune are synonomous terms.
16. The attack is not an assault, and the final release is not a sign of relief.

Every choral conductor should have accessible at all times a pronouncing pocket-manual or dictionary of musical terms. It provides him with a capsule of knowledge of the detailed elements of music. It may even save him from embarrassment. The dictionary by Dr. Theodore Baker, published by G. Schirmer, is a good one.

Chapter V

Styles in Choral Singing

In Chapter III we pointed out briefly the relationship between style and taste. Style has to do with the distinctive character of a composition and the manner in which it is sung. Taste is a nearly synonomous term but it implies the element of discrimination. In this chapter we are concerned with the manner of singing choral compositions of different styles and types.

GENERAL STYLES OF SINGING

The mood or spirit of a song determines the style of singing. So much of the choral singing in our schools and churches is measured and spiritless with little contrast in either dynamics or style. The choirs sing as if they were reading poetry in sing-song fashion. Conductors and singers should think in terms of contrasting styles at the outset. These general styles of singing, as defined in Chapter III, may be described by the terms, *legato, marcato, staccato,* and *rubato.* Memorize these brief serviceable definitions. We repeat them for your immediate reference.

1. *Legato* means smooth music.
2. *Marcato* means punched music.
3. *Staccato* means detached music.
4. *Rubato* means "robbing" time-value from one unit of melody and giving it to another.

In *legato* singing the feeling of pulse and meter should be minimized and the stress should be on the natural inflection of the words. This style calls for considerable *rubato.* Regularity of pulse is the very thing that depletes the effectiveness of this style. There must be a freedom and flow of rhythm which should be indicated in the conducting motions of the director.

Instructing the singers to sing smoothly will not attain the desired results. They are too accustomed to singing beat by beat, measure by measure. The chorus must obtain a tonal imagery of the sound of *legato* singing. Such a conception can be acquired by having the singers *hum* softly the section to be sung *legato.* If preferred, the vowel *ooh* may be used instead of the hum. Then the chorus may gradually gain the ability to retain this same smoothness as it sings with words. *Legato* is secured by maintaining a consistent tone line while articulating the words. These techniques will be presented in the chapters on diction and tone.

In contrast, the *marcato* style of singing depends upon emphasizing the pulse, that is, each note is lightly punched. It is somewhat the same effect as singing a series of direct accents (see p. 78). Thus, each note seems to constitute a musical phrase. This style of phrasing can be portrayed graphically as follows: .

To attain the excitement and power of this style, loudness is not the primary consideration, although very often an increase in dynamics is indicated. The trick is to hit a note and diminish on it immediately, the same technique that is used to make a direct accent. It is necesary to stress diphthongs and final consonants to secure an effective *marcato* style.

There are varying degrees of emphasis in singing *marcato*. They are usually determined by the amount of stress a conductor desires to give certain words. When a composer or editor places accent marks above a series of notes, as in the following example, there is no question as to the interpretation. These notes and words should be well-marked as direct accents.

Example 40

Hospodi Pomilui

Lvovsky

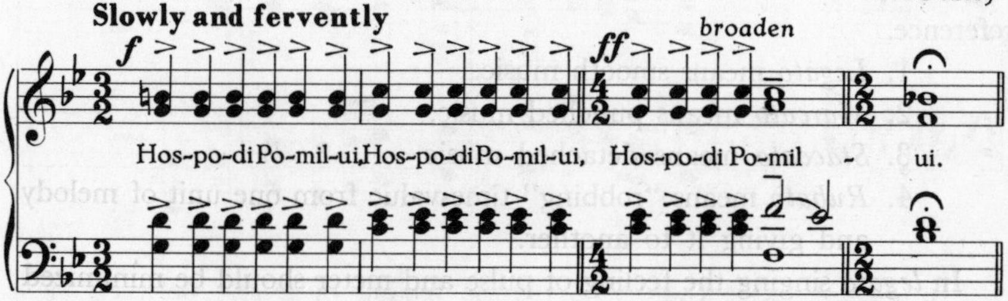

In contrapuntal numbers where there are slurs on the words, the degree of *marcato* is a moot point. We have mentioned previously that in the last analysis it is determined by the meaning of the words and the style of the music. If the words and music have an emphatic quality, the words must be stressed, and the contrapuntal lines must be clear and distinct. The more emphasis desired, the greater the degree of *marcato* needed. The more contrapuntal lines, the greater the degree of *marcato* necesary to give them individual character. The following example should resound with praise. The style is definitely *marcato,*

without being too detached. Therefore, there must be no portamento between slurred notes. This effect is secured by articulating a vowel on each note with a slight accent. The example below demonstrates this technique.

Example 41 Glory to God

Bach

In *staccato* style there is a precise feeling of a rest between each note, regardless of the tempo. It is necessary to read the words in a slower rhythm for the singers to gain this technique. It can then be transferred to the singing of the parts. *Staccato* style more closely resembles speech than *legato* style, and so the words are more easily understood even though the tempo is fast. The detached quality necessary for a *staccato* style is achieved by concentrating on the rests between the notes. In the following example (a) represents the original notation; (b) represents the tempo and notation the chorus should practice until the desired *staccato* effect is secured. Then the original tempo may be resumed. Further discussion of the techniques of *staccato* style will be presented in the chapter on diction.

Example 42

The Sledge Bells

Roberton

Leggiero e con spirito

The following example is interesting because the various styles of *legato, marcato,* and *staccato* are represented in four short measures.

Example 43

Cantate Domino

Pitoni*

Allegro con spirito

When a composer wishes a note or series of notes sung *staccato* he indicates it with a dot (.) above or below the note. If extreme sharpness is desired the composer uses a wedge-shaped stroke (′). *Mezzo-staccato* or *semi-staccato* is indicated by dotted notes under a slur. Some notes require *staccato* treatment when not indicated by the composer. These are usually determined by the meaning of the words, the position of the notes in the phrase line, or the musical effect desired. They are often

* Recorded by the Concert Choir of Teachers College, Columbia University, PAR Recordings, Box 209, Madison Square Station, NYC.

pick-up notes that need *staccato* treatment for clarity of attack. The following examples illustrate such cases:

Example 44

a. **Wassail Song** b. **Winter**

Vaughan Williams Wilson

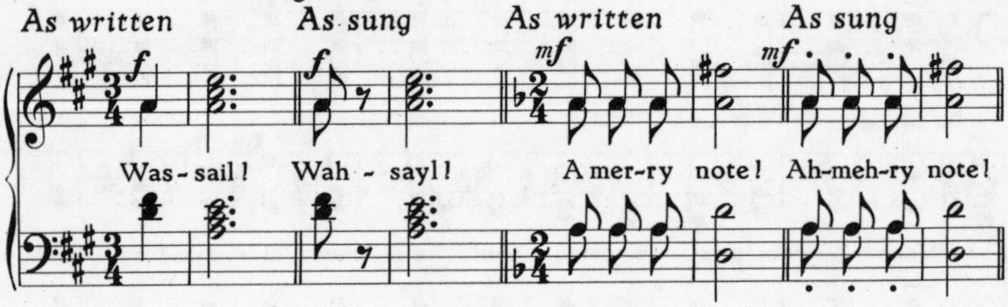

Rubato style, more often referred to as *tempo rubato,* is a subtle musical effect which few choral conductors seem to understand, let alone realize in performance. Most definitions are similar to the one given above, but its execution depends upon musical sensitivity, which is something more than intellectual knowledge. Baker's *Manual of Musical Terms* expands it as follows: "*Rubato* means dwell on, and (often almost insensibly) prolong prominent melody tones or chords. This requires an equivalent acceleration of less prominent tones, which are thus 'robbed' of a portion of their time value."

Little opportunity for *rubato* is found in the polyphonic style of the Renaissance and Baroque periods. It is in the homophonic style of the Romantic period of music that it is widely used. In choral music it evolves from the natural nuances of the words, but it is also intrinsic to instrumental music, as exemplified in much of the writing of Chopin. *Rubato* is more difficult to achieve with ensembles, either choral or instrumental, than with soloists. However, in *legato* music of a homophonic nature the discerning use of *rubato* not only eliminates the monotonous, measured style of singing so prevalent in choral groups, but it also gives a distinctive, artistic character to the performance.

It is most difficult to illustrate *rubato* in notation. It is of necessity left to the discretion of the performer. We will attempt to give an idea of the taking and giving of time in the following excerpt. The longer lines indicate the prolonging of the word or note, and the shorter lines indicate an equivalent speeding up of the time.

Example 45

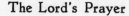

The Lord's Prayer

Wilson*

UNACCOMPANIED AND ACCOMPANIED SINGING

Between 1920 and 1950 unaccompained singing, especially by mixed choruses, was the vogue. The popularity of this style was undoubtedly due to the rediscovery of the beautiful *a cappella* music of the Renaissance period of polyphonic writing. *A cappella* choirs, beautifully robed, became the fashion. Not too many conductors knew what the term meant; some of them could not even spell it. Accompanied singing was frowned upon; it was actually considered inferior. At times, even such selections as "The Hallelujah Chorus" from *Messiah* were performed unaccompanied.

There are too many beautiful choral compositions with accompaniment for such a vogue to persist. The reaction set in, and rightly so. Every choral group should be able to sing, and should sing, both accompanied and unaccompanied numbers. The repertory in both styles of writing is so rich that every choral singer should have the opportunity and privilege of performing the great music of both styles. Every choral conductor has the duty to introduce his singers to the masterpieces of all styles of choral music.

* This composition is recorded by the Concert Choir of Teachers College, Columbia University, ABC-Paramount, New York City.

Unaccompanied or A Cappella Singing

A cappella singing has been called by so many authorities the purest form of choral art that it is superfluous to add our commendation. For that matter, we suppose that a string quartet or ensemble represents the purest form of string playing. It is just common sense that when there are no other interfering musical factors the individual character of singing voices will be more evident. This observation does not mean that all choral writing should be limited to just the musical resources of the voice alone.

Unaccompanied singing is the supreme musical test of a choral group. The performance must be superior for the music to sound beautiful. Without the rhythmical and tonal assistance from an accompaniment, both conductor and singers must be literally "on their toes" and devoted to their task. Nearly all editions of *a cappella* music today have a condensed accompaniment of the voice parts to be used for rehearsal. It may be necessary for inexperienced groups to rely upon this assistance in the first reading of a composition, but it should be dispensed with as soon as possible. With continual experience singers will listen more attentively, develop keener hearing, more assurance and self-reliance, and sing with better accuracy when they are not trying to follow their voice parts played on the piano. There is nothing like *a cappella* singing to give a choir a sense of blend and balance of voices, sensitivity of phrasing and voice-leading, accuracy of chording, and maximum growth in practical ear-training. Remember, physical stamina is often produced by throwing away the crutch; musical stamina can be generated by dispensing with the crutch of an accompaniment.

Aside from all of the other factors of interpretation which must be utilized in *a cappella* singing, there are three aspects which need special attention, namely: (1) the importance of tone, (2) the importance of intonation, (3) the importance of blend and balance.

1. *Importance of tone.* Since unaccompained singing is the purest form of the choral art, it is dependent upon the purest vocal tone possible. There is no accompaniment to help conceal individual, strident voices, assist in maintaining intonation, and lend support to blend and balance. The tone should be at once correctly produced, uniform in quality, and appropriate for the style of composition being sung.

Some conductors feel that voice-training is not a part of their responsibilities. They state that there is no time in choral rehearsals for such training. This attitude may be a defense against a lack of knowledge. Still, in his work with choral teachers throughout the country, the author has found that it is in the area of tone production that conductors need and request the most help. We feel that the principles of voice production can be made sufficiently direct that choral singing will improve when some attention is given to it. A discussion of the development of choral tone will be treated in Chapter VII.

Other conductors devote their attention only to securing a homogeneous tone quality from the group. There are expedient procedures for accomplishing this. Use a round, neutral vowel which does not have too much variation in individual color, such as *ooh, oh,* or *aw*. Have the chorus vocalize hymns, or the pieces being learned, on one of these vowels. Then endeavor to make all of the tone on this color when the words are being sung. Continual use of *ooh* will develop a rather dark, hollow quality; *aw* will develop a rounder, more virile sound; *oh* is a compromise between these two colors. The main objection to limiting tone production to these procedures is that so often the resultant uniformity of tone causes the choir to sound the same on everything that it sings, regardless of the style of composition. One or two numbers in this *timbre* may be most impressive, but there is a lack of variety for an entire evening's concert.

The above statement intimates that all styles of composition should not be sung with the same tone color. A light-hearted madrigal such as Morley's *Now is the Month of Maying* is usually portrayed with a brighter tone than a sacred composition of the polyphonic era such as Ingeneri's *Tenebrae Factae Sunt*. The same tone color is not used for an American folk-song as for a Brahms love song. A barber-shop quartet number has a brand of tone all its own. Although a uniform tone quality is always desired, the type of tone color should vary with the style of composition.

2. *Importance of intonation*. This essential element of expression in artistic singing was briefly presented in the previous chapter. Since it is so dependent upon correct tone-production it will be given further treatment in Chapter VII. At this point let us review the more common remedies for poor intonation.

a. Don't make a fetish if a choir drops slightly in pitch when singing unaccompained, if it is uniform and does not impair the musical effect.

b. Flatting in pitch can often be offset by raising the key of the composition (a simple thing to do in *a cappella* singing) or by increasing the tempo slightly in slow numbers.

c. Sharping is usually due to the forcing of voices. Tone them down!

d. Out-of-tune singing requires more careful attention to chord blending, wide interval skips and chromatic passages.

3. *Importance of blend and balance*. In singing which does not

have the support of an accompaniment, blend and balance are paramount. This statement implies a nearly equal distribution of voices on each part. In situations where this is not possible, voice sections may be arranged and intermingled in such a manner as to offset this lack of equal distribution. The purity of the *a cappella* style is so dependent upon these two factors that an entire chapter is devoted to them. (See Chapter IX)

Accompanied Singing

The statements in the foregoing section do not imply that all of the factors of interpretation, including tone, intonation, and blend and balance are not important to the singing of accompanied choral compositions. Nevertheless, it is true that accompaniments have been used as a cover-up of musical limitations, a support for voices and, on occasion, the dominating interpretive factor in the performance.

An instrumental accompaniment which is worthy of the name should be an additional musical element. It should add another *timbre,* amplify the scope of dynamics, increase the pitch range, and extend the gamut of expression. The singing of accompanied choral compositions involves both the style and the media of accompaniment.

Style of accompaniment. There are four general styles of accompaniment: (1) duplication of the voice parts; (2) expansion of the voice parts; (3) repeated chords, rhythmical figures or use of arpeggios; (4) a completely independent musical entity which contributes an important element to the composition.

1. The duplication of voice parts cannot by any sense of the musical imagination be considered an accompaniment. Such an accompaniment does not represent an additional expressive element; in fact, it can actually detract from the purity and uniformity of the voices. The percussive quality of the piano does not blend with voices and it actually influences the style of singing. We are convinced that much of the measured, inartistic singing in the schools today is partially the result of the continual use of the piano for accompaniments. The organ at least has the sustained quality represented in fine choral singing.

2. When a choir needs the assistance of an accompaniment and none is provided except the duplication of the voice parts, then the accompaniment may be expanded to give added support. This may be accomplished in the same way that an organist expands the hymn-type of accompaniment to support and encourage congregational singing. The simplest way of expanding such an accompaniment is to play the three upper voices, soprano, alto and tenor, in the right hand, and to play the bass part in octaves with the left hand. The chord of three

top notes may need to be adjusted so that it can be played within an octave to accommodate the normal stretch of the hand. Some choral arrangers are providing this type of accompaniment for compositions of a hymn-like character. Although it does not provide much musical contrast or variety it often supplies the support and encouragement that a young, inexperienced choir needs. The following example is an illustration:

Example 46

To American Youth

Wilson

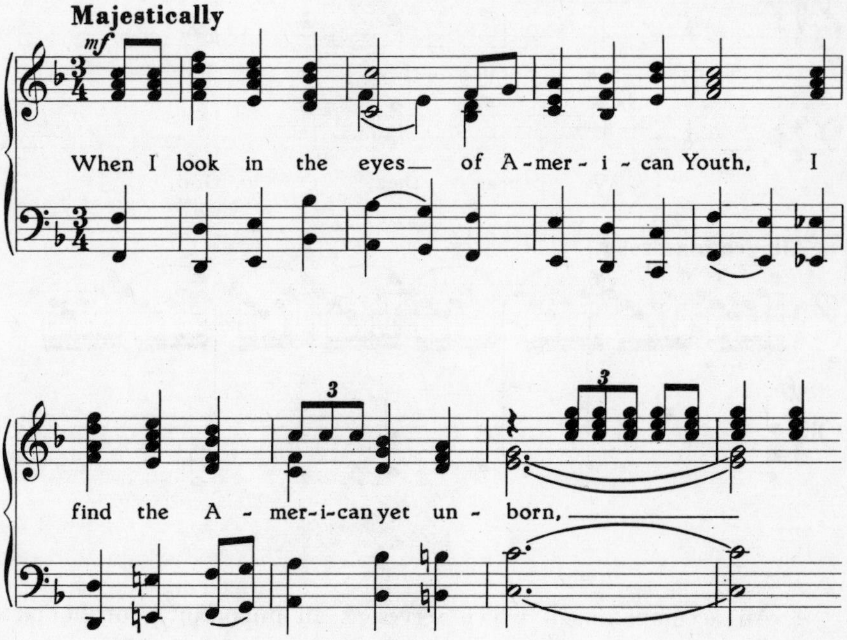
Majestically
mf
When I look in the eyes— of A-mer-i-can Youth, I
3
3
find the A - mer-i-can yet un - born, ——

3. The simplest way of giving individuality to an accompaniment is through repeated chords and rhythmical figures or the use of arpeggios. It is an unobtrusive type of accompaniment which gives support without detracting from the choral effect of the voice parts. Many of the great composers used this style of accompaniment in writing songs in order that the melodic line or the important role of the solo voice would not be covered up or diminished. These accompaniments serve the same musical function in choral compositions, as illustrated in this example:

Example 47

Te Deum

Holst

4. An accompaniment which serves as an important contribution to a choral performance is one that is a musical entity in itself. In other words, it sounds like a musical composition when played by itself. The interpretations of such choral compositions become an interplay between the singers and the accompanist. The choruses from the great oratories are representative of the style of this accompaniment. Although these accompaniments are invariably written for orchestra, many modern composers writing for church choirs and school choral groups are making use of the added color of piano and organ accompaniments with an individual quality.

The choral conductor must take care that accompaniments of this style do not become the "tail that wags the dog" and sound like piano solos. After all, they are accompaniments regardless of their musical texture; they must continue to play that role in an artistic performance of choral music. Here is an example:

Example 48

Devotion

Strauss

MEDIA OF ACCOMPANIMENT

There are several types of instrumental accompaniment being currently used for choral singing. Those employed most often are (1) the piano, (2) the organ, (3) rhythmic instruments, (4) small instrumental ensemble, (5) full orchestra, (6) concert band. A brief consideration of each one may be fruitful.

1. *Piano*. The piano is a percussive instrument, and some conductors may question its musical virtues as an accompanying instrument. Notwithstanding its limitations, it is undoubtedly the most efficient instrument for music study. That makes it by far the best instrument to use for choral rehearsals. Even though at the performance a different media is employed for accompanying, it is still advisable to use the piano to learn the music. It is still the indispensable instrument in school and church.

The limitations of the piano as an accompanying instrument are the result of the tonal divergence from sustained singing voices. But this percussive tone quality is the very thing which makes it the most appropriate accompanying instrument for dance numbers and choral compositions with a marked rhythmical character. When a marked contrast is desired between the voices and the accompaniment the piano is the instrument to use. When a similarity and blend of *timbre* is desired between the voices and accompaniment, sing the number *a cappella* or use another media of accompaniment.

2. *Organ.* In contrast to the piano a sustained quality of tone can be produced on the organ. Therefore, the organ serves as an ideal instrument when a similar *timbre* between the voices and accompaniment is desired. For this very reason, however, it is not as well suited to accompany dance and rhythm numbers as is the piano. Also, humming and neutral vowel effects in choral arrangements are invariably covered up with an organ accompaniment. Nevertheless, in the hands of an artist the organ can serve as an excellent substitute for an orchestral accompaniment. This attribute makes available the great choral masterpieces for the church service. Here it is the "King of Instruments."

3. *Rhythmic Instruments.* Composers and arrangers are experimenting with introducing instruments of the percussion section in accompaniments for choral numbers. Spanish dance numbers employ castanets, triangles, small cymbals, and other typical instruments. We know an effective setting of *The Lord's Prayer* by Edward Wald for treble voices and tympani. Novelties use such instruments as xylophone, wood-blocks, tom-tom, and large cymbals. Such accompaniments definitely come under the heading of innovation and experimentation. They are often played by members of the chorus. They are only suitable when a marked contrast is desired between the voices and the accompaniment, or when a little spice and variety is desired for a specific program.

4. *Small Instrumental Ensemble.* More and more choral conductors are endeavoring to enrich their programs by using a few orchestral instruments with the piano or organ as an accompaniment for appropriate numbers. This idea is especially suitable in numbers written with orchestral accompaniment, but which use a solo instrument. The author recalls the beautiful effect of using a violin solo with organ in a performance of the "Benedictus" from the *Missa Solemnis* by Beethoven. We have heard an excellent performance of the motet, *Jesu, Meine Freude* by Bach where an accompaniment of a string quintet was used. This motet, written for five voices, is usually sung unaccompanied or with an organ accompaniment. Brass instruments with organ can often be introduced in the compositions of Gabrieli, and in those of other composers of brilliant church music. The possibilities in this type of accompaniment are unlimited, and the choral conductor who explores them will reap rich

rewards in being able to present more interesting programs.

5. *Full orchestra.* Some of the greatest music ever composed was written for chorus and orchestra such as the *Mass in B minor* by Bach. Beethoven turned to the combination of chorus and orchestra in his *Ninth Symphony* when he had seemingly exhausted the resources of the orchestra alone.

It is a thrill for a chorus that has practiced a choral work with piano to join forces with an excellent orchestra for a final performance. It is a tragedy, however, for a chorus to work for weeks to perfect a choral work, only to have the performance jeopardized by an inadequately trained orchestra. When chorus is used with orchestra there must be complete understanding between the conductors in regard to the preparation of the groups, and who will conduct the final performance. There is little doubt that the singers will sing better for the conductor with whom they have rehearsed. However some choral conductors are reluctant to conduct combined groups. If the orchestra conductor is to conduct the final performance he should arrange to rehearse with the chorus alone at least once. This will expedite the final combined rehearsal.

In using an orchestra for an accompaniment, a large orchestra is not necessary. After all, the orchestra is supposed to sound like an accompaniment. It is wise to use only the better players, even to the extent of shifting first violins to second violin parts. Some teachers hesitate to do this for fear of hurting the feelings of some of the young people in the orchestra. The author has never run into one situation in his conducting career where the players would not prefer to sit out, rather than impair the artistry of the performance.

6. *Concert band.* With the mushrooming of concert bands in practically every school in the land, attempts to combine choruses and bands have flourished. Serious contemporary composers have been experimenting with their possibilities. Most festival programs which include choral and instrumental groups endeavor to program at least one combined number.

Unlike the orchestra, the tone quality of the band is similar to the tone quality of a chorus. It is sometimes referred to as the instrumental *a cappella* choir, because of the unformity of *timbre* of the instruments. For this reason a band has a tendency to cover up voices.

Only a small band of not more than thirty is necessary to accompany a chorus, regardless of its size. It is difficult to play brass instruments softly. This is especially true of inexperienced players. Therefore a full band is likely to over-power the singers.

Too often a band conductor is not familiar with choral procedures and a choral conductor is not familiar with band procedures. The question as to who should conduct the final performance is a debatable point. In such cases it would be judicious to divide the conducting responsibilities.

THE ACCOMPANIST

This is not a book on the art of accompanying, but we can recommend one: *The Unashamed Accompanist,* by Gerald Moore. Why should the accompanist be ashamed; he is one of the most important cogs in the musical wheel. Very often the singers follow the accompanist more than they follow the conductor. In fact, in some choral performances it has appeared that the conductor was following the accompanist!

This should not go to the accompanist's head, however. We have heard anthems sung in large metropolitan churches which sounded like an organ solo with choir accompaniment. The accompanist should not lead the choir, nor should he follow the singers. The accompanist and the conductor combine to make a musical team. He should be sensitive to the conducting gestures of the director and support the choir in a manner conducive to an artistic performance.

In schools choral teachers must devote time to the training of accompanists. Too often an otherwise adequate choral performance is ruined by an inexperienced accompanist. A good accompanist can expedite the learning of the music beyond measure. He needs to be able to play voice parts in open score. He needs to have sight-reading facility. He needs to be able to make simple transpositions, especially changing flat keys into sharps, and vice-versa. These skills need attention and practice. Students seldom receive this type of instruction from piano teachers, who endeavor to make soloists, not accompanists.

Several accompanists should be trained, in case of an emergency. The author recalls training seven high school accompanists during a two-day festival engagement; it was more difficult than training the chorus. However, do not use student accompanists who are completely inadequate. It is not good education to give training to one student at the expense of the musical growth of fifty or sixty other students. When a natural accompanist is discovered, the muse of music is watching over you. Don't embarrass him for his technical limitations and don't make him the butt of your jokes. Treat him kindly.

STYLES OF MUSIC PERIODS

A volume could be written on the characteristics of choral compositions from different music periods and by various composers. We can only hope to mention the significant aspects of these styles, both as to period and type, that relate directly to our discussion.

Pre-Renaissance Period

Until the ninth century practically all music was monodic in character and consisted of a single, flowing melody with sacred words, variously called *plain-song, plain-chant,* or just *chant.* The melodic line followed closely the natural inflection and accent of the words and syllables. It is still used in the service of the Catholic church today, and in a modified form in the Church of England.

The Chant. The chant is seldom used by choral groups on concert programs unless possibly on a very special one, illustrating the historical development of music. However, chants are wonderful songs for singers to sing in order to gain a sensitivity to a flowing phrase line, to relate the verbal and musical accent and nuance, and to acquire a homogeneous, pure tone. Conductors can likewise profit from the study and singing of chants. The beating of the *arsis* and *thesis* (rising and falling inflection) has a tendency to free his conducting gestures on all styles of *legato* music. The diagram for this type of beat can be found in Chapter II, on page 34.

Some composers make use of the Anglican style of chant for narrative texts and free rhythmical effects. There are usually two ways in treating these passages. In the traditional style of the following passage it is best to give each syllable equal time value except key words which should be sustained as long as necessary to give them emphasis.

Example 49

Now about that time, from "Upon This Rock"

Wilson

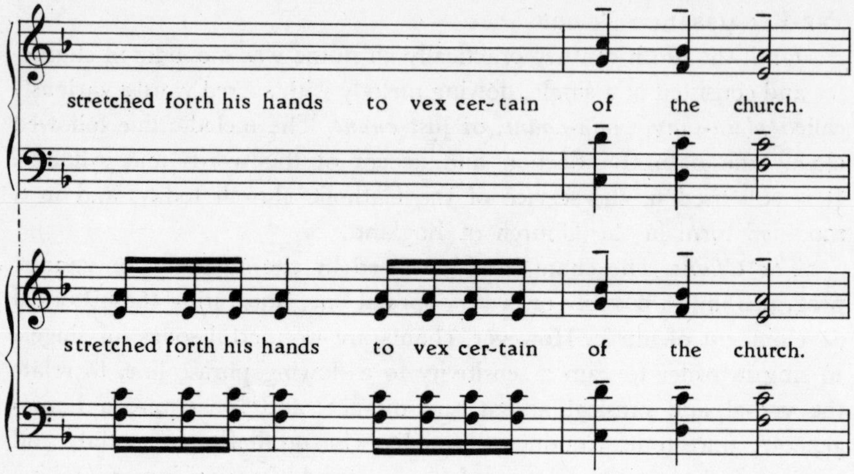

When a composer uses the chant style for exciting rhythmical effects as in the following example, the author maintains a strong rhythm and retains a metrical quality in keeping with the normal accent of the words.

Example 50

Woe Unto Them, from "The Peaceable Kingdom"

Thompson

Mosso con veemenza (with vehemence)

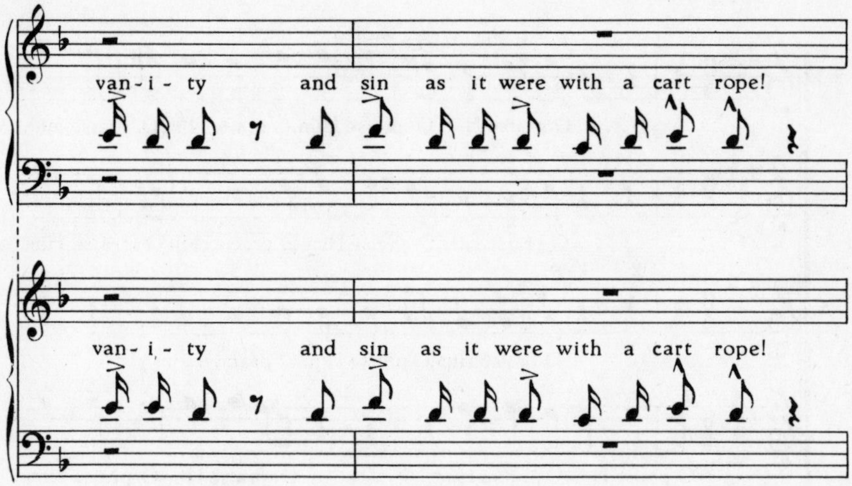

Organum. The use of the *organum* probably had its beginnings in the ninth century and continued until approximately the middle of the twelfth century. As this style of writing developed, there were several species of *organum*. We are interested only in *strict organum*, which was simply the singing of the melody at the interval of the fourth or fifth. The American Indian chant is an example of this style of writing. Naturally, singing the same melody at the interval of the fifth produced the nemesis of all theory students, a series of parallel fifths. This modern harmonic rule arose from the fact that later music was based on contrary motion, not parallel motion.

We are not interested in *organum* as a style of writing for concert choral performances. Conductors should realize, however, the extent to which contemporary composers are returning to this medieval device in searching for fresh, musical effects. In fact, it is again being used so much that it is already losing its freshness. The modern composer usually inserts a middle note between the fifths which gives the impression of a succession of triads, an effect familiar to the early writers by the way. Since each note supposedly represents a melody, each line should be sung with equal dynamic level. In the first section of the *Brazilian Psalm* Jean Berger uses the device in antiphonal manner most effectively.

Example 51

The Brazilian Psalm

Berger

Descant. As opposed to *organum,* in which parallel motion was the rule, in the twelfth century we find the first attempts at polyphony with contrary motion in the parts. These early beginnings were called *descant* (originally *discant),* which meant singing against a *cantus firmus* (fixed melody). Since the descant was freer in style, and did not follow rigidly the syllables of the words, some kind of metric device was necessary. Consequently, rhythmic modes were developed to correspond to the melodic modes mentioned in Chapter III.

Since the descant did not always fit the words, it was usually sung on a neutral vowel, so we see that the *oohing* and *ahing* of today is nothing new. Later more melodies were added to the *cantus firmus,* usually in the tenor part, and by the end of the thirteenth century there were several styles of composition. Thus we had the beginnings of the ***motet.***

Modern choral arrangers have adopted and adapted the descant to their own uses to attain new musical effects. When employed, it is invariably found in the soprano voice to give a lift to the choral parts. Community songbooks are filled with descants to familiar hymns and Christmas carols. It literally dresses up these old songs in a new hat. Arrangers seem to use the descant in the following manner: a florid melody against part-writing of a homophonic nature, or high sustained tones against part-writing of a more polyphonic nature.*

The descant is generally sung on a neutral vowel, either *ooh* or *ah*. Sometimes it is played by an instrument, such as the flute or violin, as an *obbligato*. It should never be too pronounced and cover the other voice parts. One or two singers on the descant for every twenty-five voices on the parts will usually give a correct balance. Needless to say, descant singers should have high voices of a pure quality.

Renaissance Period

From the fourteenth century until the end of the sixteenth century we find the Golden Age of Choral Composition. Instruments had not been perfected sufficiently to stir the imagination of the creators of music, and so they turned to voices. The fixed scientific rules for composition of an earlier period were being supplanted by a more imaginative approach. The one piece of choral music which was a precursor of things to come was *Sumer Is Icumen In* (Summer is A-coming In) by John of Fornsete, written around 1240. It is actually a two-part *rondel* (or ground bass) on which a four-part canon has been superimposed. It represents not only a historical turning point, but also a fine concert number. Every choir should have the delightful musical experience of singing it. In addition, choral conductors should familiarize themselves with the works of Jannequin, Arcadelt, Morales, Vittoria, Hassler, Gabrieli, Marenzo, Morley, Gibbons, Weelkes, Byrd, Orlando di Lasso, and Palestrina.

Polyphonic music flourished, with the development of the canon, the motet, and the madrigal, which will be treated separately in the next section. Based upon the early rhythmic and melodic modes this music was metered but not measured. It still followed the verbal phrasing of the words. It was a combination of equal melodies, not a group of melodies based upon harmonic progressions. Modern ears find the resultant harmonic effect dull and monotonous. It is horizontal, not vertical music. The interest lies in the blending of the individual melodic lines.

* Rules for writing descants will be found in the author's book: "Choral Arranging for Schools, Glee Clubs, and Publication" Robbins Music Co., New York, 1949, p. 49.

Interpretive Considerations. In the polyphonic music of this period there are no subordinate parts. A singer sings his part as an individual melody. When there seem to be melodic figures in his part which need emphasis, a singer should sing it accordingly. When there are phrases that need to be subdued, such as a series of repeated notes, a singer should sing it in that manner. When a singer seems to yield in this respect to another part it is only because his part at that place gives him no opportunity for making it prominent.

This interpretation of melodic lines in early polyphonic music holds true regardless of whether the parts move in *coincident,* that is the same, or *independent* rhythm. It also holds true whether the parts are based on canonic imitation or whether they are completely dissimilar in character. For this reason it is sound procedure to practice each part separately, not just to learn the notes, but to get a musical conception of the melodic line. Then when these melodies are blended together a beautiful and expressive performance will be realized. For additional suggestions for interpretation, see the section on "Polyphony and Homophony" in Chapter III.

Antiphonal singing. The practice of antiphony was introduced very early in the history of the Christian church. It first consisted of two sections of a congregation answering each other in chant style. It later became a musical response from the audience to the chanting of the clergy. As polyphony developed it gradually changed into musical responses between the choir and soloists. In this form it became quite a vogue in choral composition. Two of the most famous works in this style are the *Gloria Patri* by Palestrina and the *Echo Song* by Orlando di Lasso.

This style of singing is very effective in concert. It may be performed in two ways. The choir assumes its position on the stage while off-stage, usually in the rear of the auditorium, are stationed soloists or a small ensemble. The choir sings a phrase as indicated in the music and the small ensemble answers. The answering group should sing with similar tone, diction, tempo, rhythm, dynamics, and phrasing. When sung correctly, a beautiful effect is the result. The other method is to place the soloists in the middle of the choir on the stage. Then the answer is sung very softly in contrast to the louder singing of the choir. The same echo effect is achieved, although it is not quite as impressive to an audience as placing the soloists off-stage. The placing of singers in the rear of the auditorium complicates staging, so most conductors prefer the latter method of retaining all singers on the stage.

Baroque Period

The kernel of ideas that are associated with one period of art invariably evolve from those of a preceding period. The Renaissance period was concerned with a rather severe style of antique, classic art. From this style there arose a new one which emphasized curved lines and ornate decoration. It is usually referred to as the Baroque period of art.

In music, this period is roughly represented between the dates of 1600 and 1750. It saw the expansion of several choral forms: the anthem, the motet, fugue for voices, the cantata, the oratorio, and the mass. Until 1600, instruments were subservient to singing voices and were often used to replace one of the vocal parts. After this date composers became interested in the individual expressive and technical qualities of instruments as a musical media. Harmony developed into a musical entity not completely dependent upon melody. The period saw the experimentation and development in writing music for several combined choirs with elaborate instrumental accompaniment.

Choral conductors should not overlook the works of the representative composers of this period: Monteverdi in Italy; Heinrich Schütz in Germany; Henry Purcell in England. They should saturate themselves with the works of Bach and Handel, who brought the Baroque epoch to a towering climax and definitive close.

Interpretive Considerations. The music of this period was still based upon polyphony, but with more flexible contrapuntal rules of writing. The interest in instruments affected the choral style. Instead of the instrumental writing being vocal in style, the vocal writing became somewhat instrumental in style. The music was not only metered, but measured. Instead of harmony being the result of the combination of melodies, melodic writing became influenced by and dependent upon harmonic progressions.

Since much of the vocal writing of this period reflects an instrumental approach, the interpretation must have the precision and clarity of an instrumental performance. Each contrapuntal line must be distinct and clear, or instead of fusion of the melodies one will have confusion of the melodies. The normal accent of the syllables must conform to the metric accent of the measure. Harmonic progressions as such must be given their share of attention in giving the full expressive import to unusual effects. There is a striking example of this harmonic treatment at the end of the "Crucifixus" from the *Mass in B minor* by Bach. A slight stress and *tenuto* on the chord marked gives a spiritual, as well as a musical effect of surpassing beauty.

Example 52

Crucifixus from "Mass in B minor"

Bach

For suggestions regarding the singing of the elaborate runs often found in the music of this period, see the section entitled "Accent" in Chapter IV, and the remarks and example under *Marcato* in this chapter.

Classic Period

After 1750 we find a rapid development and expansion of the symphony orchestra. Also, by this time the opera had become an established media in the musical life of the people. Consequently the composers devoted their major efforts to writing for instruments and the solo voice.

The text ceased to be the dominating factor in musical form. The controlling element in form became the music material and melodic line. Definite musical forms evolved which largely determined the musical content. The music retained polyphonic characteristics, but it was measured, instrumentally conceived for the most part, and the expressive qualities were regulated by the accepted forms.

The Classic Period is the age of Haydn, Mozart and Beethoven. Most of their choral compositions are found in major works. Many of these have been published separately. The *Mass in G* and the *Seven Last Words* by Haydn and the *Requiem* by Mozart are within the capabilities of many mixed choirs. The *Missa Solemnis* by Beethoven is a prodigious work which should only be attempted by experienced choral societies. Pergolesi and Gluck also made important contributions to the choral literature.

Interpretative Considerations. Since the principal melody was made the main factor in Classical composition it must receive the major share of attention in interpretation. Counterpoint and harmony are subservient factors. All the dynamic contrast and nuance inherent in the melodic line must be brought out. Many of the choral works reflect the influence of Bach and Handel. In these cases similar interpretive considerations are in force, although the music of this period, except for the overpowering Beethoven, has a delicacy, grace and lyric expressiveness that is the stamp of the classic style. Little *a cappella* music is available, so the accompaniment must be treated as an independent musical factor with individual characteristics of its own in achieving an impressive performance.

Romantic Period

After the French Revolution and with the individual freedom exemplified with the later Beethoven, music turned to Romanticism. This style appeals primarily and very stongly to the imagination and the emotions, and stresses these imaginative and emotional qualities with all the means that are available. For this personal expression composers employed an infinite variety of new devices — rhythmic figures, melodic shapes, harmonic combinations, and color effects.

To express this romantic aspect of their musical feelings, composers employed more open, fluid forms. This practice is in marked contrast to the classic composers' use of more closed, fixed forms in which to express their musical ideas.

The influence of the Romantic spirit in music permeates the entire nineteenth century, although in the latter part it branched out into different paths. The creative output is still predominantly in the fields of the orchestra and the opera. However, many of the great composers of this century contributed immortal works for choral literature. These include Schubert, Mendelssohn, Schumann, Berlioz, Liszt, Wagner, Verdi, Brahms, and Franck.

Interpretive Considerations. The rich texture of the music of this period calls for a rich interpretation. The personal, emotional style suggests a personal, emotional approach to performance. Melody is supreme. Other interpretive factors are subservient to the free expression of the melody. Dynamic contrasts are intrinsic to the style. *Tempo rubato,* through the genius of Chopin, becomes an indispensable ingredient in performance. In the austere style of Brahms we find the successful fusion of the Romantic and the Classic. Consequently, the interpretation of his music requires more reserve of feeling and extreme effects.

Russian Church Music. An offshoot of the Romantic Era was the development in Russia of liturgical music for the church. It is very significant for the choral conductor, because it provides him with many superb *a cappella* numbers to include in the concert repertory of his choir. Several composers of worth became interested in adapting the old chants to the musical needs of the church of the nineteenth century. Among these composers were Glinka, Bortniansky, Lvoff, Schvedoff, Tchesnekoff, Tchaikovsky and later Rachmaninoff and Gretchaninoff.

This music although sacred, has many of the characteristics found in the secular music of the period. We find the enriched harmonies, the expansion of pitch and dynamic range, the emphasis on a dominating melody, rhythmical variety, and contrasting emotional moods. However, the composers achieved these effects with music that is chorally conceived, as well as extremely favorable for the singing voice.

Interpretative Considerations. Although romantic in tendency, this choral music of the Russian church must retain its sacred character in performance. Therefore the romantic qualities should be treated with reserve. It is purely vocal in character so the parts should be given equal importance and consideration. Contrapuntal lines are reminiscent of the early polyphony. In sections based upon chord repetition there should be a perfect blend and balance of the notes of each chord. However, this music represents a personal expression of religion, and should be interpreted in a much more subjective manner than the more objective expression in the sacred music of the Renaissance period.

Modern Period

Romanticism reached its high point in the works of Brahms and Wagner. The latter part of the nineteenth century saw a diffusion of its ideals and principles. Realism in literature evoked a similar quality in music. Racial and national characteristics influenced different styles.

Composers became obsessed with the idea of creating something new, that is, to invent a new style. They turned to primitive rhythms, modal techniques, "back to Bach", the impressionism of the painters for color, new harmonic systems, counterpoint uninhibited by rule, cacaphony, inexhaustible dynamic effects, and the gamut from unrestricted emotionalism to staid intellectualism. The period since 1900 has been one of experimentation.

Interpretive Considerations. In modern music the choral conductor must adjust his interpretation to the dominant style of the composition. Worthy composers do not mix styles. This gives the conductor a tangible key to the merit of a composition. Often the music is technically difficult in rhythmic patterns, melodic figures, and harmonic texture. The conductor must ask himself if the music is worth the amount of rehearsal time necessary for its preparation for performance.

Some modern compositions sound well when a mass effect is attained while others require infinite attention to detail. Don't fall into the error of judging this music on one reading and hearing. It is often a strange sound to both singers and listeners. Some fine modern music in contemporary style has been written which merits the same care in preparation as the music of earlier periods.

Choral Arrangements. The schools and colleges of our country have experienced a renaissance in singing during the past forty years. Not only do we find *a cappella* choirs in most high schools and colleges, but also the schools boast of general mixed choruses, girls' glee clubs, male glee clubs, various small ensembles, and children's choirs. Aside from the mixed voice groups there is not enough suitable, original material for the various voice combinations. Moreover, much of the original writing of outstanding composers is too difficult for the technical and musical ability of many of these groups. To meet this need there has arisen a completely new type of music creator: the choral arranger.

Choral arranging is an old art. The composers of the Renaissance often took an old chant or popular song as a *cantus firmus* around which they would weave beautiful counterpoint. Bach used the chorales of Crüger and Luther for many of his masterpieces. Many of the great composers have often turned to their native folk songs for inspiration. In nearly all of these earlier practices the composers turned to familiar melodies only as a source for their creative imagination. The final result was far more extended and original than what we usually refer to as a choral arrangement.

Today, choral arranging is not limited to composers; there are many musicians who devote their writing solely to the making of choral arrangements. There are six types of these especially designed choral arrangements.

1. *New editions of standard choral compositions where an optional part or optional notes are included to avert vocal range problems.* Some of these editions simply indicate tempo and interpretive markings. Others limit the original contribution to a translation or new set of words.

2. *"Watered-down" versions of original compositions to make them available for inexperienced choirs.* Many of these versions reduce and mutilate the original beyond recognition. As a rule, it is far better to limit the choice of music to original compositions written in good taste.

3. *The transcription of choral compositions, usually for mixed voices.* These can be performed by different combinations of voices, such as SAB, SA, SSA, SSAA, TB, TBB, or TTBB. It is undeniably true that there is not enough worthy material for these combinations. If the arrangements are written with integrity and maintain as far as possible the musical intent of the composer, they have their place.

4. *The transcription of an instrumental number for choral groups.* When a composer conceives his music for an instrumental media it is extremely precarious to attempt to arrange it for another media. First of all, it is usually unvocal. Secondly, there are generally so many changes necessary that the mood and style of the original composition are completely distorted. Unless such an arrangement preserves the quality of the original it should be avoided.

5. *Arrangements of art and popular songs for different combinations of voices.* Many composers have turned serious efforts to the writing of beautiful songs. Many of these songs seldom reach the ears of students and the joyful experience of performing them is overlooked. Young singers can become acquainted with this large body of vocal literature through choral arrangements. Unquestionably these songs sound better when sung artistically by a soloist, but again, if the arrangements are written in good taste, they provide the choral conductor a welcome repertory for limited voice combinations.

6. *Creative arrangements of folk songs, spirituals, hymns, and carols.* If he is talented, the arranger who emulates the practices of earlier composers in taking a familiar melody as the inspiration for his creative imagination can make a permanent and worthy contribution to the choral repertory. A search for this type of choral arrangement will be fruitful to the choral conductor.

Most choral arrangements for school groups are meticulously edited. They leave nothing to the imagination of the interpreter. Breath marks are scattered all over the page; far too many of them as a rule! Choral conductors should not hesitate to adjust and adapt these expedient and temporary arrangements and transcriptions to the musical ability of their own groups. Never toy with the music of master composers, but any choral conductor has the same musical prerogative as anyone else to make choral transcriptions and arrangements to serve his needs.*

STYLES OF COMPOSITIONS

There is an overlapping in a discussion of the styles of music periods and styles of compositions. Furthermore, a detailed treatise could be written on the styles of individual composers. Remarks and examples concerning the interpretation of the music of individual composers are scattered throughout this book. At this point we can hope only to point out helpful hints in the intepretation of different types of choral compositions.

Sacred Choral Compositions

All of the great composers have been inspired by the belief in a Creator. The greater percentage of fine choral music has been written for the church. These compositions have taken many forms. (Carols and spirituals, although sacred, are considered folk songs and are included in the next section.)

Chorale. The chorale is a hymn written in syllabic counterpoint. It was used by Martin Luther as a congregational song during the Reformation and was undoubtedly derived from the early chant and the German folk song. It exerted a profound influence upon the development of choral writing, especially in Germany. Chorales are excellent pieces for choral groups to study and sing. However, with a few exceptions, they do not serve as interesting program numbers.

There are several features of a chorale which should be considered when performed as a concert number.

a. It is sacred in character and should be so treated. It should not be looked upon as a musical exercise in harmony and couterpoint.

b. Usually every beat is divided in at least one voice part except at the cadences. Therefore, when the chorale is written in quarter-note time the feeling of the pulse is the eighth-note although the conductor should beat in four, not in eight. This rhythmical treatment will highlight the counterpoint.

c. The phrases should be distinct and clear. The degree of *marcato* will vary according to the dynamic level. The softer the singing the more *legato* it should sound. *Tempo rubato* is out of place.

* See the following book for helpful hints in arranging: Wilson, H. R., *Choral Arranging for Schools, Glee Clubs and Publication,* Robbins Music Corp., N. Y. 1949.

d. In congregational singing the length of the *fermatas* is fixed, being usually one beat longer than the duration of the note. In concert singing it varies, and should be determined by the flow of the verbal and musical phrase. The meaning of the words is the key for the treatment of *fermatas* in chorales. The occasional practice of disregarding the *fermatas* completely by singing the chorale as one continuous phrase (through the use of staggered breathing), is out of character.

Anthem. The anthem as an individual composition was derived from the older term *antiphon* meaning a musical response. Today it has no particular architectural form, and the term is used loosely to represent any religious song. Typical anthems are written for the church service. In performance, the sacred character should be unimpaired with theatrical or secular treatment. Few anthems are suitable for a choral program of various styles; they are usually reserved for concerts of sacred music.

Motet. The motet was a creation of the Renaissance period. Although musical evolution became concentrated in the secular aspect of the art after this period, the form of the motet continued to develop through the writings of master composers such as Bach. The motet is a sacred composition in polyphonic style. It is interpreted according to the style of the counterpoint in which it is written. Because of its extended musical treatment and its universal, rather than personal quality, the motet is usually very suitable for the sacred group in a choral program.

Fugue. Vocal fugues are nearly always sacred compositions. Therefore, they are usually designated as motets. A motet is contrapuntal, although not necessarily fugal in character. The identifying element of a fugue is the exposition, or the announcement of the subject consecutively in different voices. Aside from the treatment of these fugal entries it is interpreted similarly to a motet of the same style.

The fugal subject, which is usually announced in a single part, should be sung firmly and convincingly at the dynamic level indicated by the composer. There should be a sufficient diminuendo at the end of the subject in order that the second voice can be heard easily. As succeeding voices are added, the other parts should remain subservient to the one singing the fugal subject. This interpretive procedure is seldom indicated by the composer on the score. This balance of parts must be achieved within the dynamic level of the composition. Consequently, if the indication for singing the subject is *mp* the other parts must adjust their singing to this level regardless of the markings. When this procedure is employed throughout the fugue, following the continual shifting of the subject among parts provides an exciting musical experience. In the *stretto,* or the overlapping of themes (which usually occurs at the major climax), it may seem inadvisable to reduce the volume of any part. In such places the fugal entries may be brought out by marked accents or brilliant tone quality.

Cantata. Originally a vocal chamber piece in the style of an operatic aria, the cantata was gradually transformed into a larger, semi-dramatic form, quite similar to the oratorio, but much smaller in extent. It usually includes one to four soloists with chorus. Bach wrote more than two hundred sacred cantatas, and most of them are excellent for program purposes. Aside from its religious nature, the form of the cantata has been used by many composers for a secular work. A short cantata may often represent the highlight of a choral concert.

Oratorio. The oratorio and opera developed simultaneously around the year 1600. While choruses became a diminishing part of the opera, in the oratorio they became increasingly important. For this reason the oratorio serves as a major work for qualified mixed choral groups. However, is should not be attempted unless there are adequate soloists available and unless provision can be made for an accompaniment played by a superior organist or a well-balanced orchestra. Otherwise a more modest vehicle should be presented for concerts. The general style for choruses in most oratorios is polyphonic. They are often a descriptive part of the dramatic action, and they should be so treated in performance. This gives a continuity and unity to the entire interpretation.

Mass. From the beginning of its development the Mass has always been a musico-liturgical form. Practically all composers have used the Latin text of the Mass as the inspiration of their most devout music. The *a cappella* style of Palestrina gradually evolved into a more dramatic setting of the text with full orchestra accompaniment, such as the *Mass in B minor* of Bach. The individual choruses of the Mass are not quite as closely related as those of oratorio, and serve as excellent concert pieces. They should be performed not as a display of technical achievement, but with the religious spirit in which they were composed.

Secular Choral Compositions

Because secular music makes use of a text that is not Biblical or definitely sacred, it should not be considered flippant. Much secular music has both serious and spiritual quality.

Madrigal. The madrigal is the term loosely applied to the several forms of secular choral music which flourished during the Renaissance. It reached its peak in the Elizabethan period and the literature of the secular part-song contains no finer music than these English madrigals. They are polyphonic in character, but in a much lighter vein than the sacred music of the period. As a result, a more lyric tone and style are used in the performance of these numbers. Otherwise all of the consideration in interpreting the polyphonic music of this period also pertains to the madrigal.*

Folk Song. Folk songs have served as the stimulus for composers from the early beginnings of music. They have had a decided influence, especially in the secular development of both choral and instrumental forms. As a musical source for creative musical ideas they have been invaluable. However, folks songs should not be considered as sacrosanct, but each one should stand on its own merits as suitable for choral programs. Choral arrangements of folk songs have become a fixture on the concert programs of most choral groups. There are all kinds: dance songs, play-party songs, ballads, religious songs (including spirituals), humorous songs, and carols. They have been arranged for practically all combinations of voices.

Worthy arrangements will preserve the spirit and character of the original folk song. In the performance of a folk song the "melody is the thing". It should never be lost in a maze of rhythmic, contrapuntal or harmonic indulgences.

Love Songs. Someone has remarked that about fifty per cent of all vocal music is love music. The accuracy of this comment bears little import, except to point out that conductors are confronted with the predicament of how to treat this bulk of choral music. May we interject one caution? Do not sentimentalize sentimental music! Love songs have a tendency to be over-sentimental. They are filled with saccharine words, lush melodies, and juicy harmonies. It is wise to stick to settings of classic poetry. Study the *Liebeslieder* (Love Songs) of Brahms to absorb how this delicate subject can be dealt with in good taste.

Patriotic Songs. There seem to be two common tendencies in the performance of patriotic songs. One is to sing in an indifferent, desultory manner, and the other is to vocally "wave the flag on high." Sincerity is what is needed here, both as to the composition and the method of performing it. The best way to express patriotic fervor is not necessarily by means of vociferous vocalization. *The secret of artistry is restraint.* Uncontrolled patriotic enthusiasm is often insincere. Sing to your country as you would sing to your God.

Nature Songs. Songs of nature are descriptive. They do not need to paint a picture, but they should give an impression of the realistic

* An excellent and exhaustive treatise on the singing of madrigals can be studied in the following book by an outstanding authority: Scott, C. H., *Madrigal Singing*, Oxford University Press, London and New York, 1931.

quality described in the words. The gamut of impression, and consequently of expression, may range from that of a field of flowers to a thunder storm. Beethoven gave the clue for the interpretation of this type of music when he made this remark about his *Sixth Symphony,* "More of an impression than a painting." The *Songs of Nature* by Dvorak are the epitome of taste in capturing the moods of nature in choral song.

Humorous Songs and Novelties. Tread carefully in selecting songs of this type for your choral program. Many conductors question the notion that music should be funny. There is humor in a scherzo by Beethoven, but it certainly is not funny. The significance of music is definitely not focused in its power to make people laugh. Music that invites guffaws is likely to be unworthy of serious rehearsal by a choral group.

The effectiveness of humorous numbers is usually centered in the words and rhythmic effects. The words must be articulated almost in the manner of speech. Rhythmic figures must be accentuated. If there is a joke, it must be highlighted. An excellent example from instrumental music is the beginning of the second movement from the *Surprise Symphony* by Haydn. In selecting and performing humorous songs and novelties, we repeat: "Tread carefully"!

Barber-shop Song. The compact harmony in the low register of male voices gives barber-shop singing an individual, pungent quality. There is a unique skill and art in performing it. The male quartet is the best vehicle for making it attractive, but even male choruses are turning to it for at least part of their musical diet. (Some girls' groups are trying to capture its musical essence, but the effect is not the same in the higher register of the female voices.)

The parts in barber-shop singing are tenor, lead, baritone and bass. These names give a clue for its performance. The lead sings the melody and it must always be pronounced. Perfect blend of voices is essential. The quality of the voices is not a primary consideration but they must be of the same timbre. In fact, this style of music does not seem to reveal its concealed beauties when rendered by so-called trained, or operatic voices. In this music, harmony is king. Linger on those "swipes", an endearing term of the cult for the extreme, spicy harmonies.

Remember, barber-shop singing is as American as apple pie. It represents one phase of the lost art of improvising in choral singing. Now through the efforts of the SPEBSQSA (see page 3), bona fide barber-shop arrangements can be secured that retain some of the unique qualities of choral improvisation.

Popular song. What shall we say? If we are going to sing popular songs, let us sing them well. That means careful selection of the ones worthy of serious study. *You'll Never Walk Alone* by Rogers-Hammerstein is that type of popular song. Many of the better Broadway musicals contain choral music that is finding a rightful place on concert programs.

Many arrangers of these songs do not understand the problems and limitations of the amateur school chorus. Therfore, do not hesitate to adapt a commercial arrangement so that your group can learn it quickly, such as singing a section in unison where the harmonies are especially difficult. If humming and neutral vowel effects are not worthy of the effort and time to master them, they should be eliminated. Temporary music may be treated in a temporary manner.

In performing these arrangements it is not necessary to emulate the choral groups in the entertainment world. If one of these groups is used as a model, select one that sings with legitimate tone production. Continued use of the so-called straight, jazz tone will be detrimental to the singing of standard repertory.

SUMMARY

Sometimes a test will drive home salient points. After studying the chapter you should answer at least twenty items correctly. Page references are given for the correct answers.

1. *Legato* means _______ music. p. 88.
2. *Marcato* means _______ music. p. 88.
3. *Staccato* means _______ music. p. 88.
4. In _______ singing the feeling of pulse and meter should be minimized. p. 88.
5. In _______ style singing each note seems to constitute a phrase. p. 89.
6. In _______ style of singing there is a feeling of a rest between each note. p. 90.
7. The musical robbing of time is referred to as _______. p. 88.
8. The supreme musical test of a choral group is _______ p. 94.
9. The important factors in *a cappella* singing are (1) _______ (2) _______ (3) _______ p. 94.
10. An accompaniment should be more than the duplication of the _______. p. 96.
11. _______ choral compositions should not be considered inferior to _______ numbers. p. 93.

12. The is the best instrument to use for rehearsals. p. 99.
13. The should combine with the to be a musical team. p. 102.
14. Modern composers make use of the techniques of both and from the Pre-Renaissance period. p. 105.
15. The interest in music lies in the blending of the individual melodic lines. p. 107.
16. and brought the Baroque period to a towering and definitive close. p. 109.
17. The should receive the major consideration in the interpretation of Classic and Romantic music. p. 111.
18. In selecting modern music for performance the conductor should ask himself if it is worthy of the necessary for its preparation. p. 113.
19. Many of the great composers have often turned to their for inspiration. p. 113.
20. The greater percentage of fine choral music has been written for the p. 115.
21. The is a sacred composition in polyphonic style. p. 116.
22. The term is loosely applied to several forms of secular music which flourished during the period. p. 117.
23. Worthy arrangements will preserve the and of a full song. p. 118.
24. The secret of is restraint. p. 118.

Chapter VI

Diction in Choral Singing

Diction is the use, choice, and arrangement of words and the manner of expressing these words in speech or song. The secret of artistic choral singing depends upon beautiful diction. The diction of the words in a choral composition is the responsibility of the poet, but the manner of expressing the words in performance is the responsibility of the conductor and the chorus.

Expressive diction is contingent on correct pronunciation. Correct pronunciation gives meaning and provides intelligibility to diction. Articulation involves the manipulation of the vocal organs in producing intelligible pronunciation. Enunciation refers to the degree of articulation used for clear pronunciation. Articulation and enunciation make the words understandable and distinct. The term diction is loosely used to include pronunciation, articulation, and enunciation.

RELATION OF DICTION TO INTERPRETATION

In chapter III we discussed the relationship of words and music as a factor to be considered in interpretation. Choral music has a dual character. Since it combines two arts, poetry and music, it follows that conductors and singers should have an understanding of both of them. In this wedding of poetry and music, as in any marriage, happiness is dependent upon complete and lasting union "until death do us part." Divorce is disaster. The conductor is the musical judge who must appease all differences between them.

Clearness of Pronunciation

Words lend specific meaning to a choral composition and the music emphasizes their meaning by reflecting and enhancing the emotional quality. Obviously, the words should be clearly and correctly pronounced in order that their meaning can be easily understood.

Most choral conductors strive honestly to produce clear pronunciation, but in the end they compromise with the lethargic speech habits of the singers. These habits include both careless and colloquial pronunciation. Neither is to be condoned in choral singing. Slovenly articulation, as a rule, produces slovenly singing. Conductors must be relentless in their insistence upon adequate enunciation of words for clear articulation. The composer's music was suggested by the words, so it is only by intelligible pronunciation of the words that the listeners have a clue to the animating source of the music.

Printing words on the program. Some conductors endeavor to escape the dilemma imposed upon singers and listeners alike by having the words printed on the program. This procedure may give the singers a feeling of relief in the demands of clearness of pronunciation placed upon them. It may enable the listeners to relax more as they follow the words while the music is being sung. The composer, however, would undoubtedly prefer that the listeners give their undivided attention to his music in order that its beauty may be fully appreciated.

In reality, the printing of words on the program does not relieve the singers from any of their responsibility of making the words clear. Intelligible pronunciation is just a first, self-apparent step toward artistic interpretation. The mood of the music is dependent upon the style of diction. The diction is determined by the manner of pronunciation. Consequently, the emotional and poetical qualities of the music are rooted in the articulation and enunciation of words. Therefore, the same care must be given to the words when singing a familiar text, such as *The Lord's Prayer* or a composition composed on one word, such as *Alleluia*. There is more validity in printing words on a program when the music is extremely contrapuntal and the various voice parts are continually singing different phrases of the text.

*Approaches to pronunciation.** The author has observed two extreme approaches to the problem of pronunciation. A satisfactory compromise between these two methods seems to be the acceptable solution.

1. *Under-definition.* Diction that is unintelligible is due to carelessness and indifference. There is no coloring of the vowels and the consonants are flabby and slipshod. As a result the music has an anaemic quality and drivels on to a bloodless end. This calibre of singing produces such shining examples as *Swee Tin Lo,* which, upon examination, is not the name of a Chinese philosopher but a delightful metamorphosis of Tennyson's *Sweet and Low.*

This approach commits the sins of omission rather than those of commission, and in music, as in life, they often are the most damning. Singing in this manner shows that no thought has been given to the

* Roberton, Hugh S., *Festival Booklet Number Two,* Paterson Sons and Co., London, p. 18.

poetical qualities of the words and their significance in the performance. Any choral conductor who takes this attitude toward expressive diction, regardless of his concentration on the music, has failed in his sacred trust to convey to the singers the beauty of the composition.

2. *Over-definition*. Some conductors are meticulous to a fault in their approach to diction. Their only goal seems to be to obtain clearness of utterance at all cost. It is made an end in itself instead of a means to an end. When clearness of utterance becomes a fetish it is a detriment to the whole musical effect.

Such a practice is usually accompanied by abnormal differentiation of vowels, exaggerated consonants, and unattractive facial and lip movements. The continuity of the music is usually affected, and consequently, musical interest evaporates. The problem of the singer is to be able to enunciate the words and still retain the flow of the rhythm and the design of the phrase-line. In all fairness, we should add that the practice of over-definition is rare compared to the prevalence of under-definition.

3. *Naturalness*. Lying in between these two extreme approaches is a natural way of pronouncing words. It goes without saying that the natural way must also be the correct way. What is natural in one part of the country may not be natural in another. Naturalness and habit (or custom) are not synonomus terms.

Naturalness of diction depends upon correct production of vowels, definite formation of diphthongs, and clear articulation of consonants. These three factors need continual attention and will be discussed individually in later sections of this chapter. Natural diction results in the establishment of correct habits of pronunciation. Natural diction that is intelligible and does not distort the movement of the music is true expressive diction.

Diction and Style

A composer will usually write his best music when he has fine words as the impetus of his creation. It takes a master composer to rise above the dictates of a banal text. Handel seemed to be one of these composers. It is sometimes said that Handel could set the laundry list to great music. It must be added that he undoubtedly composed his most profound music to inspired religious texts.

Given fine words and fine music, our next concern is the style or excellence of performance of the composition. The preceding chapter was devoted to the styles of singing. Reread it and apply every suggestion to the matter of diction. *Legato, marcato,* and *staccato* styles in singing employ similar techniques in the pronunciation of words.

These contrasting styles, *legato, marcato,* and *staccato* are actually developed through the technique of appropriate diction. In *legato* singing much use is made of all diphthongs and the singing consonants — *l, m, n, ng,* and *r*. Final consonants, especially those just referred to, are carried over to the next word. In articulating these consonants in a *legato* style they are doubled, as in the following example. This technique minimizes the stress on pulse and measure which is the musical characteristic of this style.

Legato Style

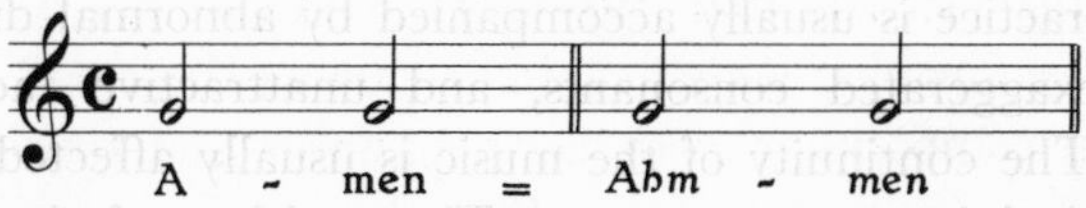

To attain *marcato* style there is a "bounce" to the diction. Diphthongs and ending consonants are sounded immediately. The effect may be pictured as follows:

Marcato Style

Staccato diction employs the abrupt beginning and ending of words with a definite feeling of a rest between each syllable.

Staccato Style

The same care must be given to the diction of words in accompanied music as in unaccompanied music. An accompaniment is not a substitute for the contribution of words to a choral composition. Furthermore, an accompaniment should not obscure the text so that it is unintelligible in spite of the efforts of the singers to articulate clearly.

Styles of choral music of various periods are also sustained by the diction, that is, the choice and arrangements of words and the manner of pronouncing these words. This is equally true of different styles of compositions. Style is inextricably interwoven with words. Expressive diction engenders expressive music.

Diction and Tempo

In what way can an expressive musical element such as *tempo* be affected by diction? Remember, different poems have their own tempo. This is especially true when the poetry is read aloud, which, by the way, gives a valid reason for this practice. The tempo of the music is suggested to the composer by the tempo of the words.

1. Tempos which are so fast that the words are completely unintelligible are inexcusable. The rapid tempos of instrumental music have probably been influential in this tendency on the part of some conductors. In fast, light numbers set a tempo that will enable singers to control articulation of the words and permit listeners to grasp them.

2. In slow numbers the tempo must not drag to the degree that the diction is lifeless, as well as being difficult to understand. These numbers actually require more concentration on diction by both the singers and the listeners than the faster numbers. Set a tempo where the words have meaning without misinterpreting the mood of the music.

3. Choral compositions with florid passages and runs are a special problem. Except for the dramatic effect that a run may give to certain words, florid passages usually reflect the dominance of instrumental music. It is very difficult for listeners to concentrate on words in this type of music. In fact, by the time a word is finished they have forgotten how it began. Luckily, most of this type of music is written to familiar Biblical texts. All the principles of the styles of singing and styles of diction apply to the pronunciation of words set to florid passages and runs.

Diction and Phrasing

As we have stated before, the verbal phrase should coincide with the musical phrase. The composer should set the words to musical phrases which permit singers to render the sense of the text accordingly. The problem here is often closely related to that of corresponding accents. However, sometimes it is a matter of the inflection and meaning of the words, controlled by the nuances of the music.

The following short example shows how misplaced accents upon the syllables of a word can affect the artistic quality of a phrase. Attention to such minor nuances is the very thing that gives finesse to phrasing.

Example 53

"Hallelujah Chorus" from Messiah

Handel

The following example is a longer phrase whose beauty depends upon the synchronization of words and music. The words should be read aloud in a flowing line. Notice how all of the words lead to the emphasis on the word "joy." Although the music is metrical, all of the notes should be considered as an *anacrusis* to the climax on this word. It represents the climax to the verbal, and the musical phrase. Both the rising inflection of the melody and the fan-shaped progression of the harmonies contribute to the musical effect of the phrase line.

Example 54 **A Thing of Beauty**

Wilson

Sometimes the contour of the music phrase dictates the treatment of the diction. This problem was touched upon in Chapter IV in regard to the relation of the musical phrase line with punctuation.

In the following example the beauty and refinement of the two-and three-measure phrases, in contrast to the stereotyped four-measure phrase, are the chief charm of the piece. Slight stress is given to the important words and syllables at the peak of each phrase. The phrase then tapers to a close regardless of the metric accent of the words. This translation is from the German, but the same problem exists in the original language. It serves as an ideal number to give singers a sense of artistic phrasing.

Example 55 **Love Song**

Brahms

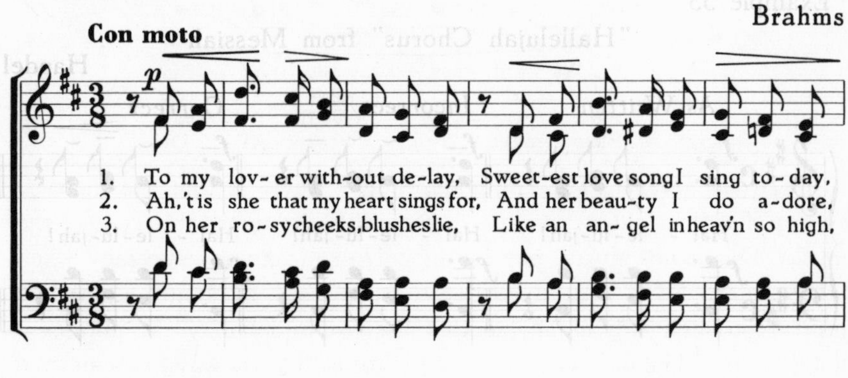

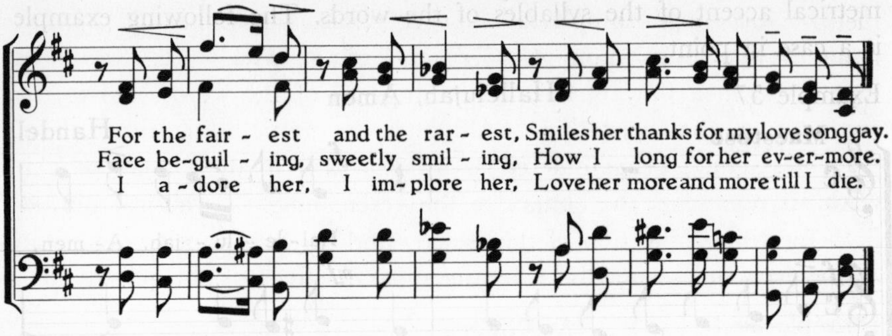
For the fair - est and the rar - est, Smiles her thanks for my love song gay.
Face be-guil - ing, sweetly smil - ing, How I long for her ev-er-more.
I a - dore her, I im - plore her, Love her more and more till I die.

Diction and Accent

Accents in music are of many kinds. The techniques for singing the more common ones were presented in Chapter IV. Accents in choral music should adhere to the normal accent of the words. Accents of the words vary according to their inflection, their meaning, and their importance. As a result some emotional accents are caressed and fondled, dramatic accents may be stressed and struck, and playful accents are sometimes light and tripping. Marks of accent are relative, not absolute. The nature of the accent is reflected in the style of diction.

Misplaced accents. In Chapter IV it was pointed out how a change in the accent and nuance of the phrase "I love you" not only changed the inflection, but also actually changed the meaning. A similar experiment can be performed with the shifting of stress on the capitalized words in the following smooth, flowing phrase as it is sung to the old familiar air. Undue accent on certain words, besides impeding the flow of the melodic line, also draws undue attention to words that convey their proper meaning without the added stress. The final one will coincide most closely to the musical phrase if a slight *decrescendo* is made on the second syllable of "Afton."

Example 56

Flow Gently, Sweet Afton

Spilman

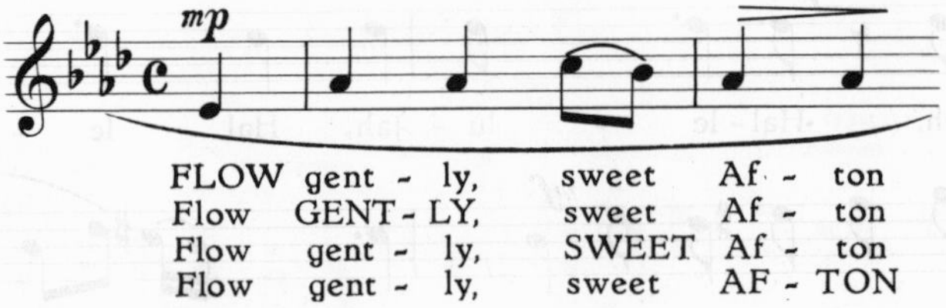
mp
FLOW gent - ly, sweet Af - ton
Flow GENT - LY, sweet Af - ton
Flow gent - ly, SWEET Af - ton
Flow gent - ly, sweet AF - TON

Metrical accents. The composer should see to it that the metrical accent of words follows as closely as possible the metrical accent of the music. This is not always possible in polyphonic music, especially when the counterpoint is measured. For that reason each contrapuntal line must be treated individually so that the rise and fall of the phrases is not distorted. The metrical accent of the measure gives way to the normal metrical accent of the syllables of the words. The following example is a case in point.

Example 57 **Hallelujah, Amen** Handel

Ordinarily a composer gives added duration or a rising inflection of the melody to the stronger syllable of a word or the important word of a phrase. However, in Example 53, a rising inflection in the melody was given to the relatively unimportant word "sweet." The tendency is to accent this word because of the rising inflection even though it comes on a weak part of the measure. The instruction in such cases is to tell the singers to diminish to the peak of the phrase.

In bi-syllabic or multi-syllabic words the normal accent should be followed as long as it agrees with the contour of the phrase line. This is especially true in tapering the ends of phrases. The conductor must be doubly careful to follow this style of diction when the composer gives equal value to each syllable, as on the word "Afton" in the preceding example quoted. This rule is apparent in the following example but invariably the singers will hold the last note too long, giving the final syllable undue attention besides impairing the artistic phrase as the composer wrote it.

Example 58 **Panis Angelicus**

Franck

*Rhetorical accent.** Expressive diction is made possible through rhetorical accent, a skillful and artistic use of speech. It is closely allied with metrical accent but, at the same time, it is not confined to or controlled by music meter. It is the safest shield against misplaced accents. Also, it is the antithesis of the common fault of singing every

* Coward, Henry, *Choral Technique and Interpretation,* Novello and Company, London.

syllable with equal force. In singing, although the inflection of the word is governed by the notes, the proper balance of the word-accent need not be interfered with. This fact is not grasped, as evidenced by the prevalence of the misplaced accent, in the following classic phrase. (See also Example 53.)

Example 59

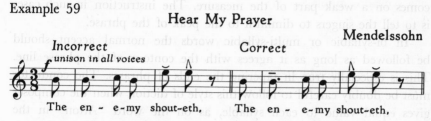

Hear My Prayer

Mendelssohn

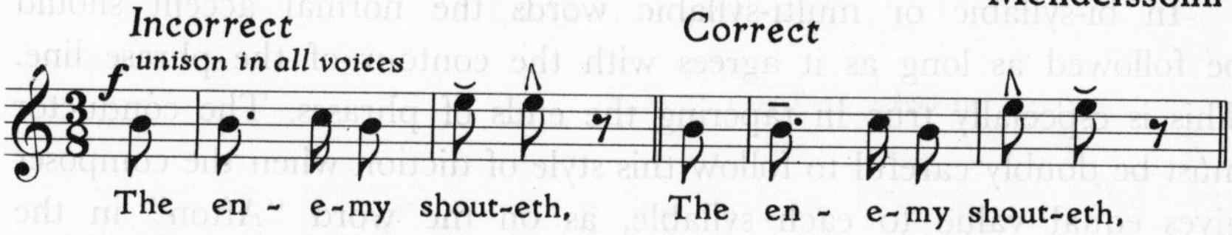

The rules of rhetorical accent should be followed even when an unaccented final syllable is carried over to a new measure as in the following examples.

Example 60

The Nightingale

Tschaikowsky

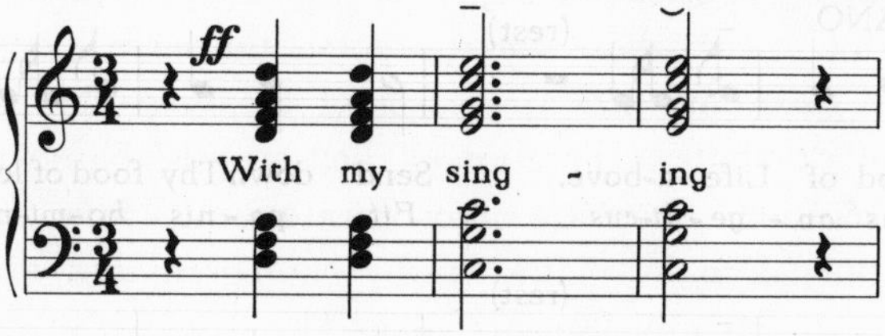

Example 61

O Give Thanks

Old round

Example 62

Gloria Patri

Palestrina

Accent of key words. Nearly every phrase has a key word of dramatic or descriptive import. This word should be given the kind of attention which will epitomize the expressiveness of the phrase or sentence. It may need emphasis, sometimes vividly, sometimes subtly, according to the mood. Search for these words in every phrase. Here is a typical example.

Example 63

The Twenty-Third Psalm

Wilson

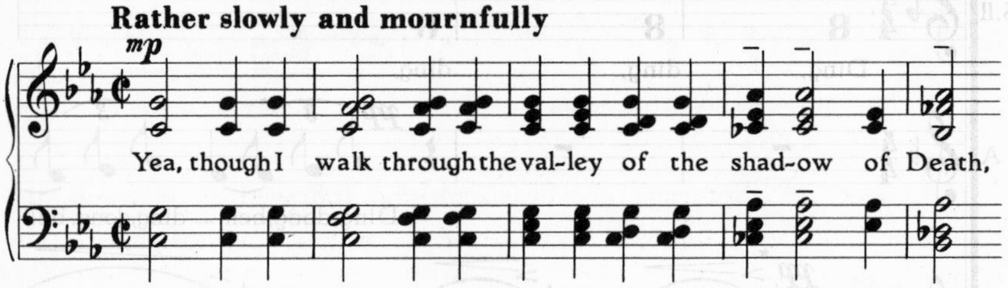

Onomatopoetic effects. Formation of words in imitation of natural sounds or use of words whose sound suggests the sense is referred to as onomatopoeia. *Buzz* and *hiss* are words of the first type, and *hush* is an example of the latter. Imitation of bell sounds, banjo accompaniment, and percussion effects are other illustrations. These choral effects have been indulged in by many worthy composers and are especially appreciated by singers and listeners alike. The first two examples below are striking effects of bell sounds while the third example, from the sixteenth century French repertory, is a delightful portrayal of a cackling hen. The trick in executing all of these onomatopoetic effects is to close the vowel immediately and sing on the consonants.

Example 64

The Bells of St. Michael's Tower

Knevett-Stewart

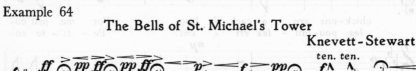

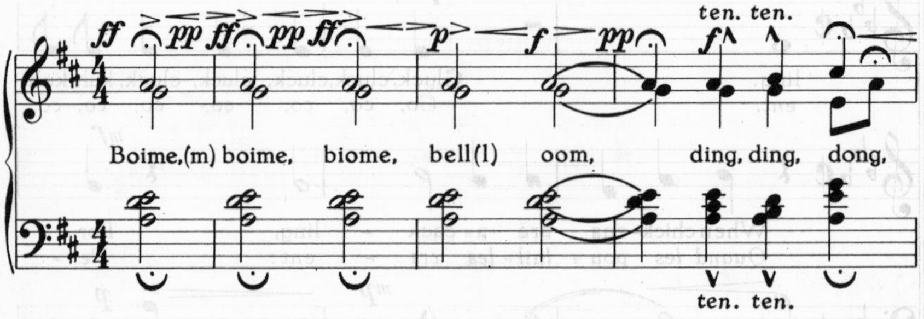

Example 65

Full Fathoms Five from "Three Shakespeare Songs"

Andante misterioso Vaughan Williams

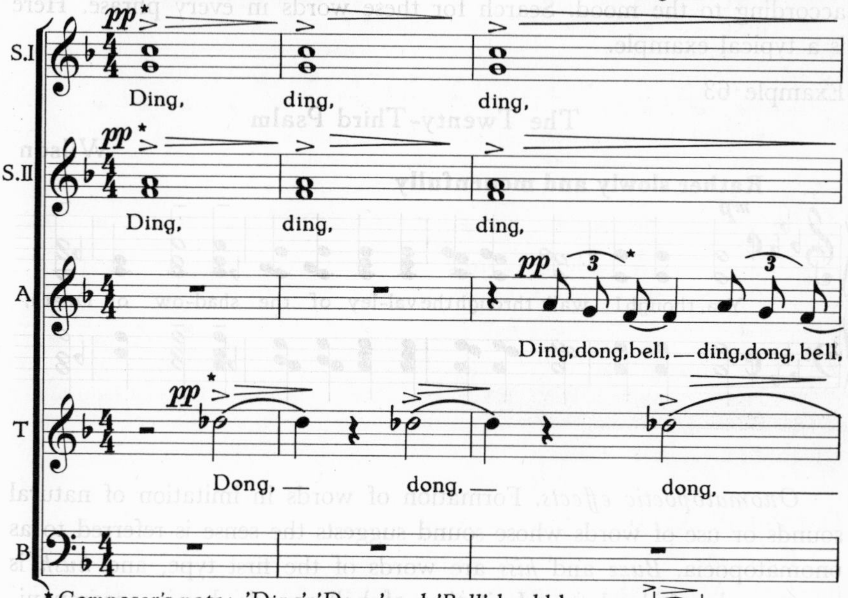
pp*
S.I
Ding, ding, ding,
S.II
Ding, ding, ding,
A
pp 3 *
Ding, dong, bell, — ding, dong, bell,
T
pp*
Dong, — dong, — dong, —
B

*Composer's note: 'Ding', 'Dong' and 'Bell' should be sung Di-ng Do-ng Be-ll

Example 66

He Is Good And Handsome (*Il est bel et bon*)

Passereau

Fast with animation

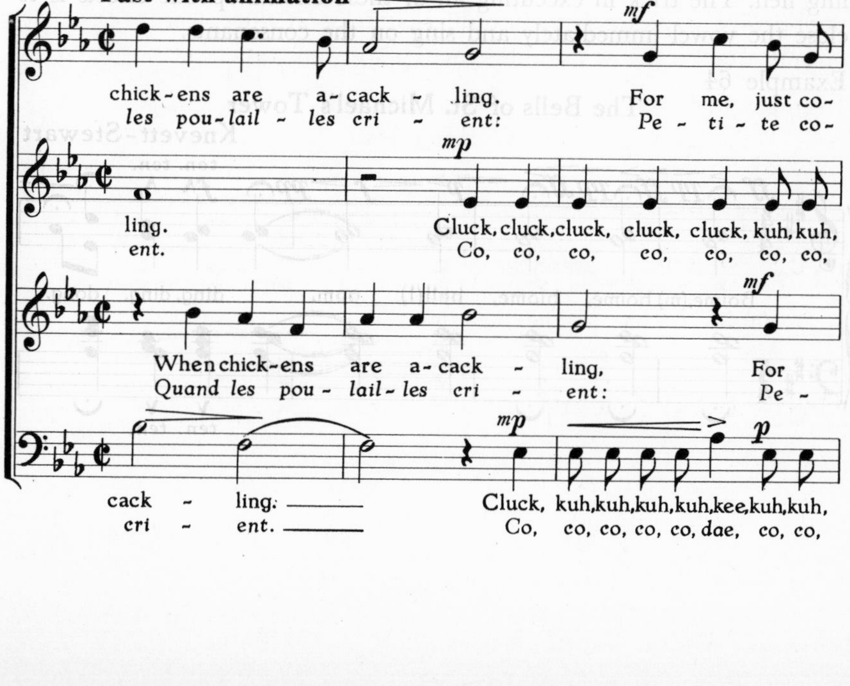
mf
chick-ens are a-cack - ling. For me, just co-
les pou-lail - les cri - ent: Pe - ti - te co-
mp
ling. Cluck, cluck, cluck, cluck, cluck, kuh, kuh,
ent. Co, co, co, co, co, co, co,
mf
When chick-ens are a-cack - ling, For
Quand les pou - lail - les cri - ent: Pe -
mp p
cack - ling: — Cluck, kuh, kuh, kuh, kuh, kee, kuh, kuh,
cri - ent. — Co, co, co, co, co, dae, co, co,

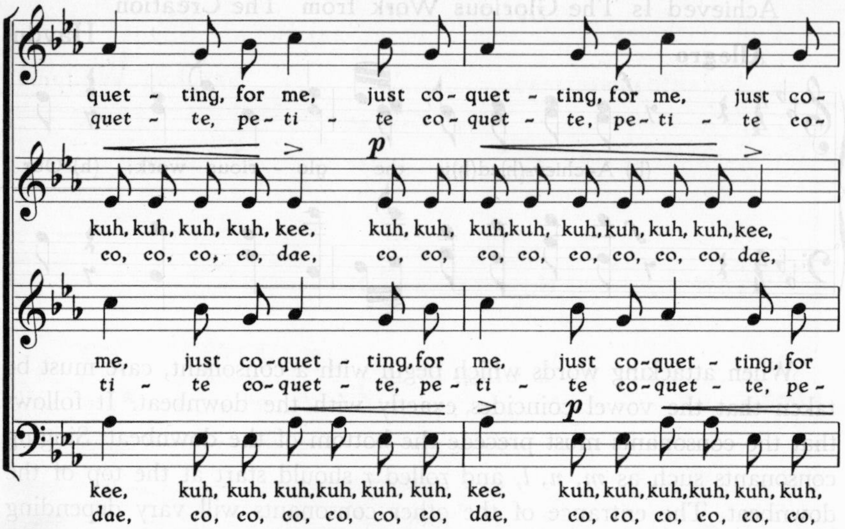

Diction in Attacks and Releases.

Everyone knows that a chorus should start together and stop together. A good beginning and a good ending partially erases minor pitfalls in the middle. Some of the basic principles for attacks and releases were introduced in the preceding chapter.

Even with a well-trained chorus it is difficult to obtain a uniform attack on a word beginning with a vowel. Such words require a glottis attack of the vocal action, and this is almost impossible for several singers to do simultaneously. Therefore it is a wise procedure to use an unobtrusive, aspirate *h* to introduce attacks on these words, especially on soft attacks. Below are different types of illustrations.

Example 67

O Bone Jesu

Palestrina

Example 68

Achieved Is The Glorious Work from "The Creation"

Haydn

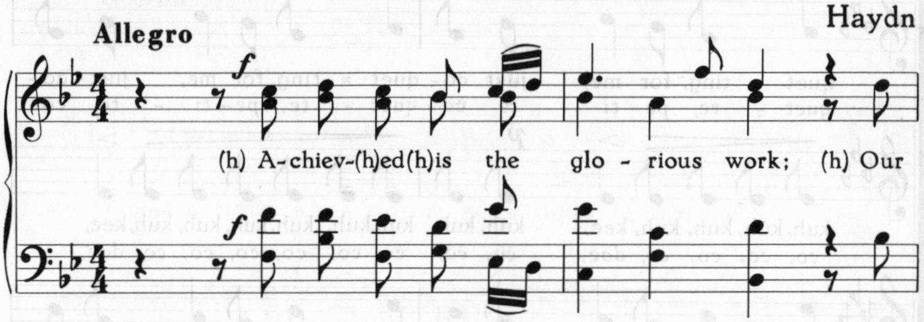
Allegro
f
(h) A-chiev-(h)ed(h)is the glo - rious work; (h) Our
f

When attacking words which begin with a consonant, care must be taken that the vowel coincides exactly with the downbeat. It follows that the consonants must precede the bottom of the downbeat. Singing consonants such as *m, n, l,* and rolled *r* should start at the top of the downbeat. The entrance of the other consonants will vary depending upon the effect desired. Explosive consonants such as *c, k, s, p,* and *t* may be pronounced simultaneously with the vowel sound at the ictus, or point, of the beat. This treatment of consonants is necessary so that the listeners can understand the words as well as grasp their musical significance.

Example 69

Now Thank We All Our God

Crüger

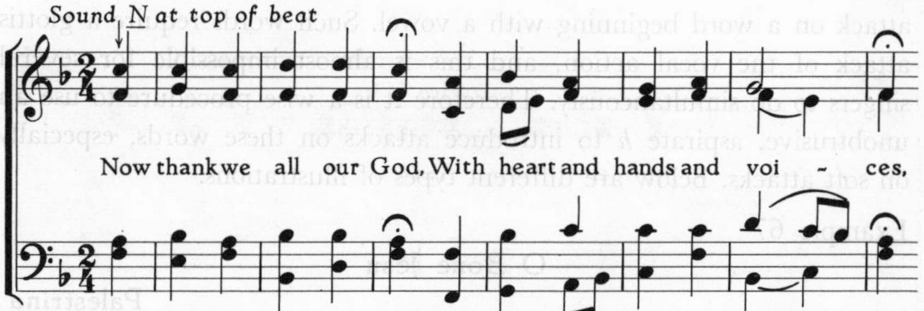
Sound N at top of beat
Now thank we all our God, With heart and hands and voi - ces,

On the final release, the explosive consonants like *k, p,* and *t* should be sounded on the dynamic level of the preceding vowel. If the vowel is soft the consonant should be soft; if the vowel is loud the consonant should be loud, even to the degree of sounding a neutral vowel after the articulation of the consonant. This dramatic device may become an affectation if indulged in during the body of the text, such as the lusty baritone singing "Olduh, Manuh Rivah" for "Old Man River." The following example should clarify this principle.

Example 70

Cindy

American folk song
Arr. by Wilson

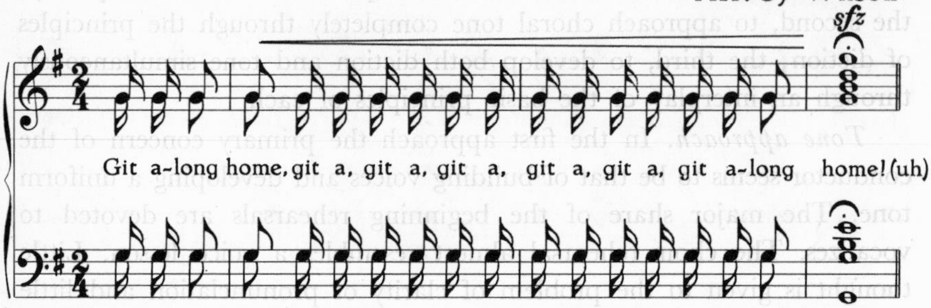

When the release is on a word ending with one of the singing consonants *m, n,* and *l,* the consonant should be sounded when the conductor starts up with the cut-off beat. In a *forte* release this change can be quite sudden, but in a *piano* release it should be gradual and smooth.

Example 71

Over Hill, Over Dale, from "Three Shakespeare Songs"

Vaughan Williams

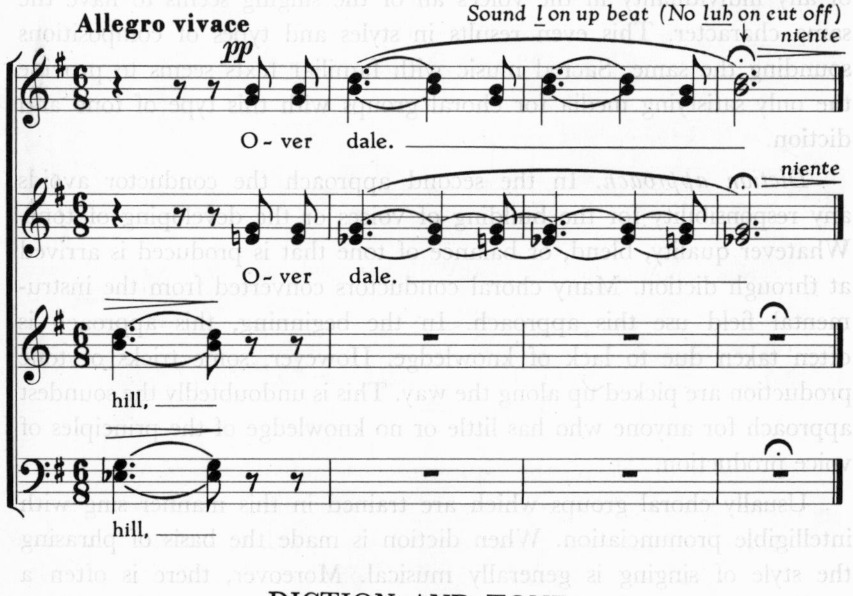

DICTION AND TONE

At this point we are not concerned with the problems of tone production. Chapter VII will be devoted to these problems. Let us turn our attention here to the relationship between diction and tone and how they affect each other. There seem to be three approaches in rationalizing the principles of diction with those of tone. The first is to develop a choral tone and then to adapt the diction to this quality; the second, to approach choral tone completely through the principles of diction; the third, to develop both diction and tone simultaneously through an interplay of the basic principles of each.

Tone approach. In the first approach the primary concern of the conductor seems to be that of building voices and developing a uniform tone. The major share of the beginning rehearsals are devoted to vocalizes. The choir rehearsal almost resembles a voice lesson. Little thought is given to the problem of clarity of pronunciation and little regard is shown for the interpretive factor of expressive diction.

These choruses do often develop a beautiful tone. Many times, however, they sound like a pipe organ with only one stop or registration. The voices have only one timbre and all diction is encompassed within this single tone color. Usually, to secure tonal blend, this timbre is on the dark side and the vocal alignment is on an *aw* or *oh* color. This continuous quality makes clarity of enunciation extremely difficult.

The sound may be musically satisfying but it is almost impossible to understand what the choir is singing. Moreover, with the elimination of any individuality in the voices all of the singing seems to have the same character. This even results in styles and types of compositions sounding the same. Sacred music with familiar texts seems to provide the only satisfying media for choral groups with this type of tone and diction.

Diction approach. In the second approach the conductor avoids any responsibility for the building of voices or the developing of tone. Whatever quality, blend, or balance of tone that is produced is arrived at through diction. Many choral conductors converted from the instrumental field use this approach. In the beginning, this approach is often taken due to lack of knowledge. However, some tricks of tone production are picked up along the way. This is undoubtedly the soundest approach for anyone who has little or no knowledge of the principles of voice production.

Usually choral groups which are trained in this manner sing with intelligible pronunciation. When diction is made the basis of phrasing the style of singing is generally musical. Moreover, there is often a quality of naturalness in the performances of these groups that reflects sincerity of expression. Also, there is attractive contrast of style in the singing of different types of compositions.

However, when this approach is used choral groups sometimes

lack blend and balance. The individuality of the voices has a tendency to cut through, especially in *forte* singing. Lack of understanding of voice production may cause pitch difficulties (usually flatting) in very soft singing. Then the all-important factor of an over-all musical tone may be missing. If the general sound is not moving, attention to other interpretive factors is rather futile.

We must face the fact that tone is the dominating emotional and artistic requisite in artistic performance. Therefore, this approach, with all of its favorable attributes, has serious limitations. In professional and experienced amateur groups the diction approach would seem to be the one most expeditious to artistic singing, but in inexperienced and young groups, direct attention must be given to building voices.

Combined diction and tone approach. Why divorce two things that are as dependent upon and as interwoven with each other as diction and tone? The effectiveness of choral music is governed by the close relationship of diction and tone. The acme of artistic singing is reliant upon beautiful tone *and* expressive diction. How shall we approach the problem? We must work in a manner so that diction will aid tone and tone will aid diction.

As the old Italian voice teachers used to say, "Chi parle bene, canta bene": He who speaks well, sings well. But this isn't as easy as it sounds. There is always the question of a person's musicality. The adage does point up the fact that the singing voice should improve with the development of the speaking voice, and vice-versa.

It is very difficult to produce the tone correctly and sing with expressive diction while giving attention to rhythm, notes, phrasing, and other factors of interpretation at the same time. Nevertheless, if diction is going to be used in the development of tone it must be related to singing, rather than a speaking situation. One procedure is to chant the words of the song on a single pitch in the rhythm of the music. Singers should be encouraged to use free jaw and lip movement in order to form round vowels and diphthongs, and to articulate carefully all consonants. This procedure is illustrated by the chanting of *The Lord's Prayer* in rhythm.

The opposite procedure is to approach diction through tone. Sing the melody of an easy number on a neutral vowel which is the basic color desired for the group. The same melody should then be sung with the words while the group endeavors to retain the same vocal production. The individual quality of vowels, diphthongs, and consonants should be articulated, but encompassed by this basic color.

The author always instructs a chorus to line the *forte* singing on an *aw* form. This vowel eliminates the tendency for strident voices to be prominent without causing the other voices to become too dark and colorless. Therefore, the melody of a loud composition may be vocalized on a round *aw* vowel, followed by singing the words in this same tonal alignment or color. This can be done without sacrificing the individuality of vowels and diphthongs. With experienced groups, or in familiar music, the same procedure can be used, with the group singing the voice parts.

Example 72

And the Glory of the Lord from "Messiah"

Handel

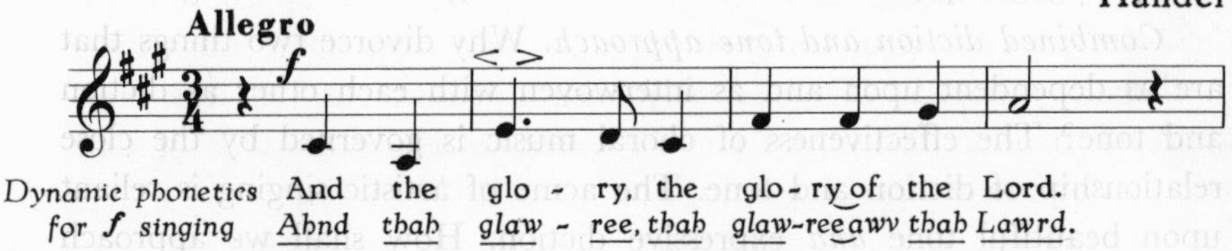

The method of vocal production described above is too weighty for soft singing. When it is used, flatting of pitch often results. Line *piano* or *pianissimo* singing on an *ooh* or *ah* (not *uh*) vowel, depending upon the basic color desired, to enhance the mood of the piece. Then the same procedure as above should be followed. Sing the melody or parts on an *ooh* or *ah* vowel and then sing them with words, keeping the basic color of the vowel used. *Ah* gives a brighter color and *ooh* a darker one.

Example 73

For Unto Us a Child Is Born from "Messiah"

Handel

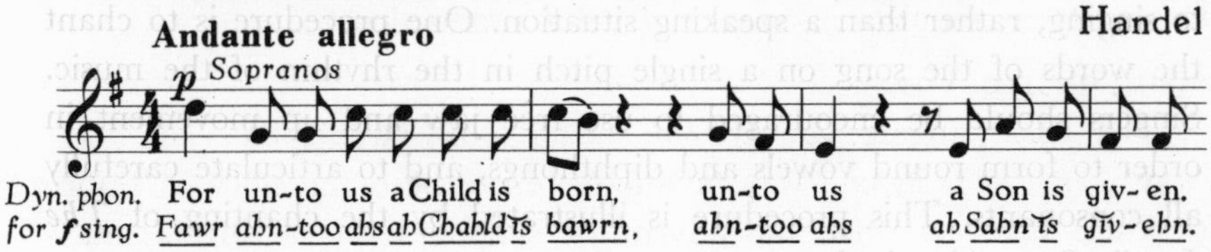

In general styles of diction and singing, as *legato, marcato,* and *staccato,* the same procedure may be used. Simply vocalize on the melody or parts in the style of singing called for by the music. Use *aw* for *forte* singing, *ooh* or *ah* for *pianissimo* singing. Then pronounce the words in the same style within this tone color, as presented earlier in this chapter. The above examples may serve as illustrations for *legato* style and diction.

In *marcato* singing, introduce an aspirate *h* with each vowel when vocalizing on the melody. Since *marcato* singing is usually *mf* or *f,* care must be taken that the same *aw* vowel is used as when singing *legato.* In *staccato* singing, vocalize on the melody or parts with a detached *ah* vowel. This vowel is used because most *staccato* passages are light and bright. While retaining this basic color, sing the music with detached words and with a feeling of a rest between each word. (See section on "Diction and Style")

Not only must the tone be pleasing and musical, but it must be appropriate. The tone of a madrigal differs from that of a motet, a popular song from that of a classical number, a barber-shop arrangement from that of an opera chorus. The types of tone appropriate for these different forms of composition will be discussed more thoroughly in the next chapter. Here we only wish to point out that the same approach as described above may be taken to secure the type of tone suitable for the composition being sung.

THE FUNCTION OF VOWELS

The quality of the voice is determined by the formation of the vowels. We often remark to singers, "Your voice is what your vowel is." In choral groups the aim is to secure the homogeneity of voices while retaining the individual character of the different vowels. The conception of vowel determines whether a voice is dark, hollow, strident, pinched or nasal. The first step is to establish a feeling, or physical imagery, of the singing resonance, and then to hold in memory this singing resonance while forming the different vowels. (Chapter VII is devoted to a complete discussion of voice production.)

Basic Singing Vowels

The basic singing vowels, *ooh* (who), *oh* (woe), *ah* (lah), *ay* (way), *ee* (we), in one way or another have been the stock in trade for voice teachers since the advent of singing lessons. Singers must learn the sight, sound, and feel of these vowels. Correct habits of vowel formation beget fine singing.

OOH — (*who*). This vowel must not be pronounced in the front of the mouth, which results in a thin tone; nor should the lips be puckered too much, which results in a hooty tone. To secure the correct resonance for this vowel, sing an *oh* vowel and gradually change it to *ooh.* The resulting tone will have roundness and depth. Using the prefix of *h,* as in the word "who", encourages correct formation.

OH— (*woe*). This vowel is really a diphthong, *oh-oo*. It is formed by sustaining the open *oh* sound, altering to the *ooh* sound just at the end. This vowel should not have a closed sound by mixing the *oh* and *oo*. The open quality is obtained by forming the vowel with a sense of largeness and roundness in the back of the throat. Also, using the prefix suggested in the word "woe" will secure added roundness. To prevent too dark a quality on this vowel, sing *ah* and gradually change it to *oh* by keeping the mouth open and rounding the lips slightly.

AH — *(lah)*. This is the "work-horse" vowel. In forming it, the jaw should be dropped, tongue flat (not curled back), with a sense of the back of the mouth being arched, as in a half-yawn. Sometimes repeating the word "are" several times on a single pitch will establish this sensation. Care must be taken not to sing the vowel *uh* for *ah*.

AY — (way). This vowel, as in the case of *oh,* is really a diphthong. Prefixing the vowel with the consonant *w* as in "way" will bring the lips into play. When this is coupled with a dropped jaw, the vowel will have roundness and depth. Avoid the "spreading" of this vowel, with the resulting blatant quality. Sustain the correct vowel form and sing a soft *ee* just at the end.

EE — (*we*). This vowel is naturally brilliant to the point of being piercing. Secure roundness by singing *ooh,* gradually changing it to *ee*. Also, practice using the prefix *w* as in "we" which will encourage a slight pursing of the lips in singing this vowel. Avoid spreading the lips, or grimacing when singing this vowel.

Other Vowels

As mentioned before, the basic singing vowels are *ooh*, *oh*, *ah*, *ay*, *ee*. Because we call the above vowels "basic" does not mean that they are more important than the other vowels. As previously indicated, these are the vowels that are used to establish the tonal and physical imagery of singing resonance. With this imagery as a basis the other vowels are formed with a similar resonance. There are many variations of vowels but the more common ones are *oo* (took), *aw* (laud), *oh* before *r* (between *oh* and *aw* as in Lord), *oh* (between *aw* and *ah* as in God), *uh* (love), *uh* before *r* (turn), *à* (between *ă* and *ah* as in dance), *â* (between *ā* and *eh* as in care), *eh* (let), *ĭ* (sit). Although a "Guide to Pronunciation" in any standard dictionary may give slight deviations from these vowels, if the choral conductor has an aural and mental understanding of the ones listed, he will find his needs served.

The next step is to realize how these vowels draw their resonance from the five basic singing vowels. The best initial practice is to connect these vowels with their basic vowel on a sustained speaking tone as follows: *ooh-oo, oh-aw, ah-aw, ah-uh, ah-à, ay-eh, ee-ĭ*. Many other combinations are possible but these are sufficient. Remember to retain the same basic resonance while varying the vowel. The next procedure is to sing these combinations on the single pitches of the descending scale. Then words containing these vowels should be sung on these pitches, taking care that the vowels are not changed as the consonants are pronounced.

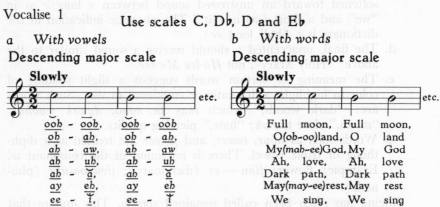

Vocalise 1

Use scales C, D♭, D and E♭

a *With vowels*

Descending major scale

Slowly

etc.

ooh - ooh, ooh - ooh
oh - ah, oh - ah,
ah - aw, ah - aw
ah - uh, ah - uh
ah - à, ah - à
ay eh, ay eh
ee - ĭ, ee - ĭ

b *With words*

Descending major scale

Slowly

etc.

Full moon, Full moon,
O(*oh-oo*)land, O land
My(*mah-ee*)God, My God
Ah, love, Ah, love
Dark path, Dark path
May(*may-ee*)rest, May rest
We sing, We sing

Further application of this procedure may consist in singing phrases of music with the vowel sounds alone. Follow this practice by repeating the phrase with the words, retaining the same vowel sounds as the consonants are pronounced. The following example illustrates this procedure.

Example 74

Alleluia

Thompson

Lento

pp
Phonetics Ah - ay - ooh - ah, ah - ay - ooh - ah, ah - ay - ooh - ah
Words Al - le - lu - ia, al - le - lu ia, al le - lu ia
pp

Special Cases

Several aspects of vowel formation seem to be perennial problems in the difficulty they cause conductors as evidenced by performance at concerts and festivals.

a. The article "the" is pronounced as *thee* before words beginning with a vowel or a silent *h*: "*thee* evening," and "*thee* hour;" it is pronounced as *thuh* before words that begin with a consonant: "*thuh* Lord," also, "*thuh* heavens."

b. "La" should be pronounced as *lah* not *luh* regardless of how fast the tempo. Madrigals lose their sparkle when the refrain is sung on *luh* instead of *lah*. The same holds true for carols such as "Deck the Halls." This is an example of permitting a consonant to interfere with the proper vowel formation. It usually signifies that the voice was not produced correctly in the first place.

c. Sustained prefixes as *di* in "divine" and *be* in "beloved" should not sound as *dee-vine* and *bee-loved*. This vowel should be softened toward an unstressed sound between a long *e* as in "we" and a short *i* as in "sit." The phonetic indication in the dictionary is *e*. (half long *ee*).

d. The final, unaccented *y* should receive a sound similar to the above: "Holy Mary", not *Ho-lee Ma-ree*.

e. The meaning of certain words suggests a slight shading of color to highlight a dramatic or emotional quality. Such words are: "dark woods," which may be sund, *dawrk woohds;* "moan," close the *oh;* "hate," piercing quality.

f. Words such as *hour, tower,* and *flower* are treated as a diphthong or triple vowel. There is no sound of the consonant *w*. Example: flower; *flou — er* (dictionary); *flow-oo-uhr* (phonetic).

Singing has often been called sustained speech. This implies that speech is the point of departure for singing. Tone gives the sustained quality to both speech and singing. The function of vowels is to give blend, color and variation to the sustained quality of artistic singing.

USES OF DIPHTHONGS

Many choral conductors not only make no use of diphthongs as they affect diction in music, but also as in the use of *a cappella* they have not even taken the trouble to learn how to spell the word. This negligence probably arises from the fact that most singers, even in this country, are trained on the Italian language. In this language there are no diphthongs. In words with a double vowel, such as "tuo" both vowels are written out. As a result the purity of each vowel is easier to retain. In English, singers have difficulty in thinking of two vowels when they only see one. It is certainly true that many of our soloists and choruses might as well be singing in Italian as far as intelligibility is concerned.

Diphthongs are simply compound vowels and should be sounded distinctly, especially in *legato* singing. The following are examples of diphthongs: day (*day-ee*), my (*mah-ee*), high (*hah-ee*), thou (*thaw-oo*), new (*nee-oo*), know (*no-oo*), joy (*jaw-ee*). The emphasis and length given to the different components depend upon the word and the style of the music. In all diphthongs except the diphthong *ee-oo* (as in the word "new") the first component is given greatest stress and length, although the final one must be sounded briefly. In "new" the reverse is true.

In an effort to sustain a uniform vowel some choruses and concert singers simply neglect the diphthong to the degree that it is inaudible. A graphic picture of their singing of the words "I know", would appear like this: *Ah-ah-ah noh-oh-oh.* On the other hand, popular singers in their efforts to "put across" the words are prone to sound the shorter component of the diphthong much too long. Their singing appears as follows for the same words: *Ah-ee-ee-ee noh-oo-oo-oo.* Normal pronunciation is the best rule to follow in this matter, but care must be taken by a chorus to make all components of diphthongs sound alike and together, if diction is to be clear and expressive. Example: *Ah-ee noh-oo.*

To obtain this uniformity in the singing of diphthongs, it is often advisable to give them metrical treatment. In fast *marcato* style the length of the unstressed component of diphthong will be quite short, while in slow *legato* music it will be slightly longer. Even in detached *staccato* music the diphthong must be rapidly sounded. If this principle is pointed out to the chorus in several different styles and tempos of music its execution will become automatic. Some publishers are endeavoring to publish music with the phonetic spelling of words, including the diphthongs, underneath the text. These are helpful to gain an understanding of the principle, but a chorus should soon be independent of such aids.

The principle of the metrical treatment of diphthongs is best demonstrated by a few examples. This treatment of diphthongs must not sound stilted and unnatural, but must fit in with all of the principles of diction that have been previously described.

Example 75

O Mary, Where Is Your Baby ?

Louisiana folk song

Arr. by Frackenpohl

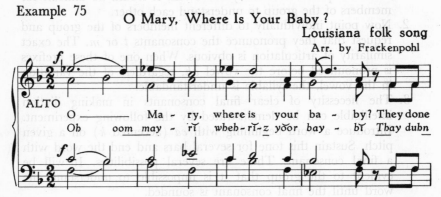

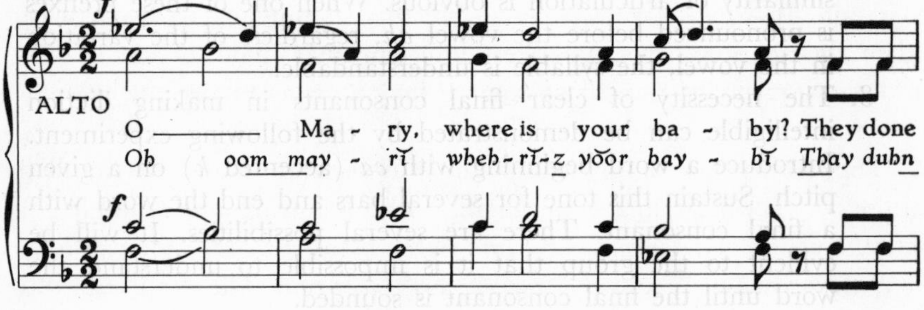

Example 76

How Far Is It To Bethlehem?

English carol
Arr. by Pfautsch

With simplicity

TREATMENT OF CONSONANTS

Whereas the character of tone is determined by vowel formation, intelligible diction is dependent upon the clear articulation of consonants. Try these experiments with the chorus:

1. Point individually to different members of the group (ten or twelve will be sufficient) and ask them to pronounce the vowel *ah*. The variation will be evident to the members of the chorus. It may need to be repeated. In fact, there is usually enough variation to cause the group to realize that if intelligible diction required uniformity of vowels, it would be difficult for members of the group to understand each other.
2. Now point individually to different members of the group and request that they pronounce the consonants *t* or *m*. The exact similarity of articulation is obvious. When one of these prefixes is pronounced before the vowel *ah,* regardless of the variation in the vowel, the syllable is understandable.
3. The necessity of clear final consonants in making diction intelligible can be demonstrated by the following experiment. Introduce a word beginning with *ca* (accented *k*) on a given pitch. Sustain this tone for several bars and end the word with a final consonant. There are several possibilities. It will be evident to the group that it is impossible to understand the word until the final consonant is sounded.

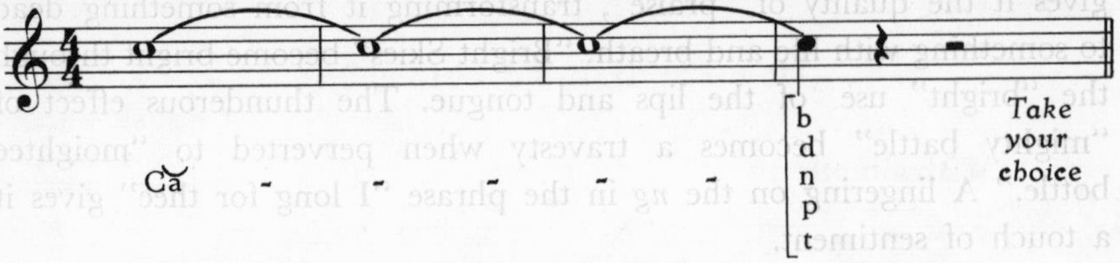

The above experiments are simple devices for demonstrating to a chorus the importance of consonants. In the average voice studio, singers hear so much about the importance of vowels as they relate to voice production that they lose sight of the extraordinary importance of consonants in artistic singing. Sometimes an ounce of demonstration, like the above experiments, is worth a pound of talk and explanation.

Neglect of consonants is oftentimes due to slovenly or careless speech habits. It is practically useless to instruct a chorus to "sing as you speak." This is especially true when one observes that a simple and direct question, such as "What did you eat?", degenerates into the colloquial, "Whajuheet?"

Overcoming Inertia

Inertia is present in many aspects of choral work, such as listless posture, or the lackadaisical manner of walking on and off the stage, but nowhere is it so evident as in the physical habits necessary for perfect diction. The first step is to inspire the singers to an awareness of the powerful impact of words and the desire to utilize their effectiveness in their singing. The second step is to stimulate their intellects to a realization and understanding of the factors involved in clear pronunciation. The final step, and possibly the most important, is to overcome the physical inertia of singers to establish habits of precise and flexible articulation.

1. The first step is achieved when the singers know what they are singing about and respond to the poetical quality of the words. This demands using music with words that have a beauty of imagery or feeling. Can they drink in the musical and poetical loveliness of these words?

> How sweet the moonlight sleeps upon this bank!
> Here we will sit and let the sounds of music
> Creep in our ears: soft stillness and the night
> Become the touches of sweet harmony.
> The Merchant of Venice — Shakespeare

This response to poetry must be accompanied by a feeling for the imagery and beauty of individual words. The singers must sense that in the word "alleluia", it is the liquid sound of the consonant *l* which gives it the quality of "praise", transforming it from something dead to something with life and breath. "Bright Skies" become bright through the "bright" use of the lips and tongue. The thunderous effect of "mighty battle" becomes a travesty when perverted to "moightee bottle." A lingering on the *ng* in the phrase "I long for thee" gives it a touch of sentiment.

2. Too many choral conductors take for granted that singers understand the problems involved in clear diction, while as a matter of fact most of them have little conception of the different kinds and types of consonants and the use of the appropriate articulators needed for their enunciation. A detailed description of the various consonants will be treated in the next section.

To stimulate singers with a realization of the most common weakness in pronunciation, the author, by appearing hard of hearing, has them chant the following slogan at varying degrees of intensity.

Leader: What is the weakest thing about the performance of choirs?

Choir: They do not finish their words! (mp)

Leader: What was that?

Choir: They do not finish their words! (*mf*)

Leader (Holding his hand to his ear) Louder!

Choir: THEY DO NOT FINISH THEIR WORDS! (*f*)

In this manner, results are achieved.

3. Physical inertia of singers is overcome by suggestion, persuasion, and coercion, although this final method must be used with tact. It is accomplished by insistence on clarity of diction and an everlasting vigilance that correct habits of articulation are being practiced. It depends upon flexible movement of facial muscles, lips, tongue and jaw. To eradicate immobility, it may be necessary at first to exaggerate these movements. Some conductors use "tongue-twisters" in an effort to develop this flexibility. An example for the consonant *ch* could be, "church chaps chirp chants cheerfully." Seldom is there time in rehearsals for such practice. Also, it is far more psychologically and musically sound to utilize the texts of the music being studied for development of correct physical habits.

The following device has proved efficacious for the author in establishing flexible movement of the articulators:

Ask the singers to imagine that they are speaking to a deaf person, so that it is necessary to make themselves understood completely through lip movement. The words are formed together simultaneously with the leader demonstrating. If the composition is a metrical one the words can be pronounced, or should we say formed, in the same way to the rhythm of the music. Some singers may find it easier to imagine speaking to someone across a room in which another person is sleeping. The trick is to make yourself understood by the other person without awakening the sleeper. The words are formed inaudibly with the lips. Such a poem as *Sledge Bells* by Edgar Allen Poe is a good one for this practice. The same physical movements should be retained in singing the music.

Example 77

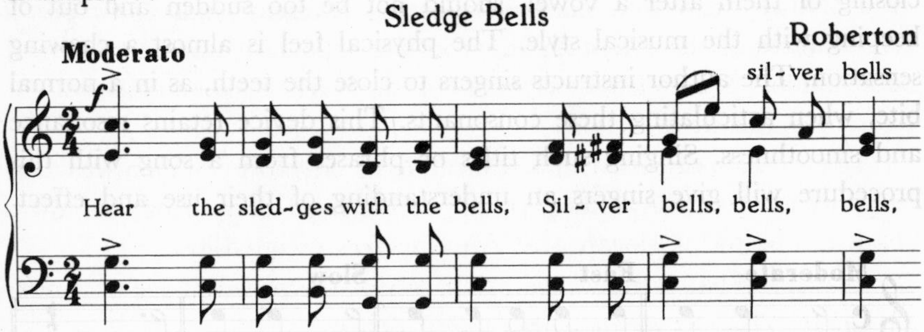

Classification of Consonants

For general consideration there are two kinds of consonants, resonant, and non-resonant, sometimes referred to as voiced, and unvoiced. Both kinds are equally important, because each has a unique function in giving meaning and emotion to the flow of sound based on the vowels. The resonant consonants are *b, d, g, j, l, m, n, r, v, w, z, ng* and *th* (as in *thine*). Time must be given for the pronunciation of these resonant consonants or they may be confused with non-resonant consonants. For instance, if the resonant quality of *G* is not sounded in the word *God,* it will sound like *cod.*

The length of time given to the pronunciation of these resonant consonants varies with the mood of the music and the resonant nature of the consonant itself. It has already been pointed out in the section on "Diction in Attacks and Releases" that the sounding of these consonants precedes the ictus, or point of the beat on attacks, and anticipates the cut-off beat at the end. The same principle applies to the body of the composition: they are sounded before the beat and are sung on the same pitch as the vowel which is sung on the beat. Failure to sing them before the beat causes lack of clarity in diction; failure to sing them on the same pitch as the vowel causes scooping, and musical inaccuracies.

These consonants vary in their degree of resonant quality. The ones which are most resonant and take the longest time for articulation are: *l, m, n, ng,* and *r.* These consonants are so expressive, especially in *legato* singing, that the author refers to them as the "singing consonants". As previously pointed out, in attacks they must be sung at the top of the beginning beat and in release they usually anticipate the final cut-off by one, or even several beats. They are invaluable in retaining the flowing smoothness of the music and the connection of words. Their importance in this function can be demonstrated in such titles as "To Music," "Dancing and Springing" or "Long, Long Ago."

The anticipation of these consonants before the vowel, or the closing of them after a vowel, should not be too sudden and out of keeping with the musical style. The physical feel is almost a chewing sensation. The author instructs singers to close the teeth, as in a normal bite, when articulating these consonants. This device retains resonance and smoothness. Singing such titles or phrases from a song with this procedure will give singers an understanding of their use and effect.

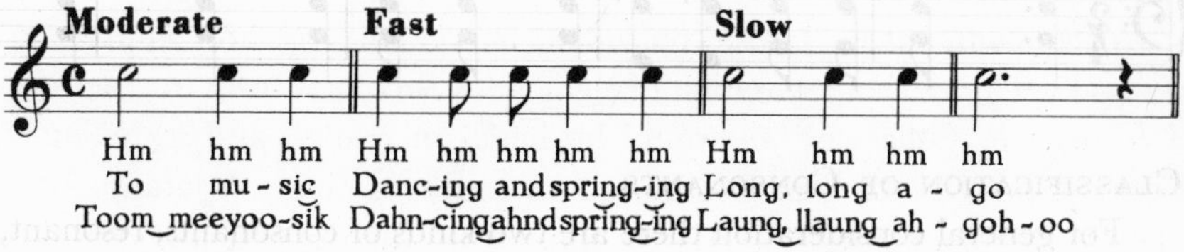

Consonants represent the abrupt stoppage of all sound, or the brief replacement of vowel sounds. They are further classified according to the articulators used in the stoppage or replacement of sound.

Labial or lip consonants. The consonants using the lips primarily for articulation are *b, f, p, w,* and *v.* Very active lips are necessary for their pronunciation. *B, w,* and *v* have resonance, while *f* and *p* are void of resonance. If the necessary resonance is not given to the consonant *b* in a word such as "big", it will sound like "pig." A complete stoppage of sound is needed for *p,* as in the word "pop." A short prefix of the vowel *oo* is needed to articulate the consonant *w* (woe=oo-woh). Unless *v* is voiced, it will sound like *f.* (*Very* becomes *fairy*).

Dental consonants. These consonants are *d, l, t,* and *th.* The point of articulation is the upper teeth. A flexible tip of the tongue is necessary for their pronunciation. *D, l,* and *th* (thine) are resonant; *t* and *th* (thank) are not. Unless time is given to voice *d* at the beginning and end of words, it will sound like *t.* (Thus the Biblical king, David, degenerates into Tavit.) The same is true of voiced *th* and unvoiced *th.* (See section on Connecting Words.) *L* is a singing consonant (see above), and should be so treated. Its singing quality is beautifully demonstrated in the word "alleluia." A safe slogan is, "Linger on the l's."

Palatal consonants. When the stoppage of tone is behind the front teeth, as in *g* (gem), *j, r, y* (ye), *ch* (chin), *sh* (she), and *zh* (vision), they are referred to as palatal consonants. *G* (soft), *j, y,* and *zh* are slightly resonant. *R* has considerable resonance while *ch* and *sh* have none. As pointed out in the above sections, the voiced consonants must be sounded carefully or they will sound like the unvoiced consonants, (gem becomes chem). The consonant *r* is a trouble maker. For clarity it should always be rolled at the beginning of words. The amount of time depends upon the dramatic effect desired: (Praise = pr-r-r-ay-eez). In the middle of a verbal phrase roll the *r* with just one flip of the tongue: (O praise ye = Oh-oo pr-r-ay-eez ye). It is a singing consonant but it is unmusical as well as unvocal when sustained too long on the end of words such as *her, earth, world,* and *father*. In such words sustain the vowel and pronounce the *r* with a flip of the tongue at the end: (Her = huh-uh-uh-r, not huh-er-er-er.)

Nasal consonants. These consonants *m, n,* and *ng* are referred to as nasal because of the sensation of their resonance, not from the method of formation. Otherwise, *m* would be labial, *n* dental, and *ng* palatal. They are priceless tools in sustaining tone and retaining a *legato* quality. They were treated fully at the beginning of this section and will be treated again in the next chapter, the discussion of choral tone.

Gutteral consonants. The term itself implies the position for the formation of these consonants, *g, k,* and *qu*. *G* has resonance, the others do not. The chief problem is to give (not kive) sufficient time for the resonant *g,* so that it won't sound like *k*.

*Aspirate consonant.** One of the most useful consonants in the alphabet is the aspirate *h*. It has no resonance, but regardless of this lack, it has musical as well as dramatic function. Some of these functions have been described previously but will be reviewed briefly at this point.

1. Be sure to utilize the slightly percussive quality of the *h* at the beginning of words in order to bring out their significance, as well as to contribute to the rhythmical quality and flow of the music. (From the *Elijah:* "*H*elp, Lord", not *elp Lord.*) (From the hymn: "*H*oly, *H*oly, *H*oly", not *oly, oly, oly.*)

2. The salutary use of introducing an *h* in initial attacks was discussed in the section, "Diction in Attacks and Releases", and demonstrated in Example 64 and 65. This device gives more precise, uniform attacks in such cases by avoiding the glottis stroke of the vocal action. An explosive *h* is not used in these instances, as it is too obvious. It is

* Davidson, Archibald T., "Choral Conducting". Harvard University Press, Cambridge, 1940.

most useful in very soft attacks, but it can also strengthen the impact in *forte* attacks.

3. Related to the foregoing device is the insertion of the consonant *h* before any word beginning with a vowel to avoid a glottis attack on the word. This use adds clarity to the diction and accent to the rhythm in *marcato* style of singing. Again, the *h* must not be so percussive or explosive in these cases as to be disturbing. It certainly gives these words life and vitality. (See Example 65.)

4. In slurs between two notes, especially in wide skips, the repetition of the vowel plus the insertion of an *h* eliminates the enervating quality of a misplaced and mishandled portamento.

Example 78

Grosse Messe in C moll

Mozart

A - - - - - - - - - men.
May be sung
A - (h) a (h)a - (h) a (h)a - (h)a (h)a - - (h)a - - - men.

5. As suggested in Chapter IV, under "Melismatic Melodies", the insertion of an *h* before each note in runs where there are several contrapuntal lines will add clarity to these runs. The degree of detachment of the notes with this device depends upon the number of contrapuntal lines, the dynamic level and the style of the music. In soft, smooth music it should not be used. It seems to be especially helpful to tenors and basses in singing *marcato* runs. Sopranos and altos have less difficulty in singing runs without the need of this mechanical device. The ideal technique is to separate the notes sufficiently for clear runs by the proper articulation of the vowel on each note. When there is neither sufficient time nor singing experience to gain this technique, then the expedient *h* is the answer.

6. Probably the most frequent use of the ever-serviceable *h* is its introduction between two adjacent vowels in such concoctions as *"gowon"* for "go on," *"toowold"* for "too old", and *"myyown"* for "my own." If these words are sung by inserting an unobtrusive *h* between them, the meaning becomes clear and the rhythm is preserved. Example: "go (h) on", "too (h) old", "my (h) own". Admittedly,

this is a mechanical method, but it is the kind of device to which a choral conductor must resort to obtain clarity of diction. If at first it appears overdone, by habitual use it becomes a tool as natural as any other technique in artistic singing.

Sibilant consonants. S, z, sh, ch, and soft *c* are sibilants, and they can be troublesome. *Z* has some resonance, but the others are non--resonant. These consonants can be especially disagreeable when singing over the radio or in making a recording. In the first instance they give the impression of static, and in the latter they may cause one to wonder if the needle isn't worn out. Sustained hissing on these consonants gives a most unmusical, even ludicrous effect. On the end of words, articulate these consonants precisely, but briefly. Attach these consonants, and most consonants for that matter, to the second syllable of a word: not *mas-ter,* but *ma-ster.* This avoids the danger of *mas-s-ter.* When two *s's* occur together, one *s* may be omitted. "This song" may be sung, *thi-song.*

Connection of words. Occasional comment has been made concerning the connection of words. However, since it seems to cause some conductors much confusion and torment, perhaps it will be profitable to outline some basic rules for connecting syllables or words in singing. The problem is more acute in *legato* singing than in *marcato* or *staccato* singing. These rules are applicable primarily to the *legato* style.

1. Carry the consonant of the first word over to the second unless it changes the meaning.

2. When the same consonants occur together between words, usually omit one of them.

3. When two non-resonant consonants occur between words, pass over the first one quickly.

4. When a singing consonant occurs after a vowel, anticipate the consonant, with the resultant feeling of doubling the consonant. If the pitch changes, the first consonant is sung on the preceding pitch.

5. As suggested above, insert an unobtrusive *h* between words where two vowels occur. Do this also between words where the meaning is distorted by carrying over the first consonant.

6. Between words that are connected by *th,* use the resonant form.

7. In words that end with a diphthong, be sure to articulate the second syllable of the diphthong while moving to the next word.

8. Use any device at your command to obtain clarity of diction and to retain the mood and style of the music.

In *marcato* diction, since words are somewhat detached, smoothness is not the primary problem. The same rules apply as in *legato* singing, but the consonants receive definite accents. Consequently, clarity of diction is more easily obtained.

In *staccato* diction the words are detached. Therefore, double consonants can be pronounced, if the tempo permits, and less stress is placed on the resonant consonants.

SINGING IN FOREIGN LANGUAGES

Most of the conductors who read this book will use music with an English text. Many college choirs and even an occasional high school choir enjoy performing in French, German, or Italian. We assume that no conductor will try this experiment unless he is adequately familiar with the pronunciation of these languages. With this background the same rules of diction apply to these languages as those for English, presented in this chapter.

The practice of singing in Latin is a different matter. Numerous standard oratorios, masses, and many early sacred numbers were composed to be sung with Latin text and they sound better that way. It is difficult to make translations for this music while retaining the normal accent of words and the nuance of the phrase lines. Also, the English equivalent of many Latin texts is familiar to music audiences and congregations so, consequently, they have an understanding of what is being sung. Therefore, unless there is some liturgical objection, choirs should be able to sing in Latin, and choral conductors should be cognizant of the pronunciation and translation of the texts. When there is no translation in the score, the conductor should write out the literal translation of each word on his copy, so that he can make the choir conversant with the text they are singing.

We feel that it is important to give the accepted rules of Latin pronunciation in the body of this chapter, rather than bury the presentation of these rules in an appendix. There is an unwritten agreement among choral conductors to use the accepted pronunciation of the Roman Catholic church, sometimes referred to as the Italianized pronunciation. It is different from the classic Latin taught in schools, and this often causes confusion. The best chart we have seen is the one by Dr. Becket Gibbs and we present it here with his permission.

ITALIAN PRONUNCIATION OF LATIN

By Becket Gibbs, Mus. D.

It is generally acknowledged that every country boasts of a variety of pronunciations of the national language, especially in England, with its 52 counties, each with its own peculiarities of speech. Germany and France are similar, with the nothern and southern, or high and low forms of speech. Although the Latins as a race have ceased to exist, their language has passed into the safe-keeping of the Roman Catholic Church. The so-called Italian pronunciation might more appropriately and more truthfully be called the Roman pronunciation, inasmuch as the Florentine differs from the Roman, both cities boasting of their more correct form of speech. But the seat of Ecclesiastical Government being in Rome, the following rules have been most carefully collected from the best authorities in that city. Euphony has dictated the final directions, all of which have been approved by those who ought to know.

In the following phonetic spelling *aa* indicates long English a as in late; *ee* long e, as in seat, etc. Each vowel has one uniform sound whose quality is not substantially changed by its quantity. It is the neglect of this elementary principle which produces the half-Italian, half-English pronunciation which we so often hear.

a This vowel has a full, open sound, as in father, not only in open vowels like *amo* (ahmo), but also in closed ones like *nam* (nahm).

e An exact equivalent for this vowel cannot be found in our language. The nearest we have is the *a* in fare, or the *e* in met. Careful practice soon acquires it. The flat *a* as in fat is to be avoided.

ae and *oe* equal *aa*.

i This vowel is always pronounced as *ee*.

o is sounded *oh,* as in for (fohr).

u is sounded *oo*. For example, *cum* is pronounced koom and *salutaris* is sah-loo-táh-reez.

au is pronounced like *ou* in the English word thou.

th is always pronounced as the *t* in Thomas. For example, *thronum* is pronounced tróh-noom.

z is pronounced as *dz*.

c before *i, e, ae,* and *oe* is always *ch* as in *caeli* (cháa-lee). At all other times it is pronounced as *k* . It is never pronounced as *s*. When the Latin *c* is followed by *ae, oe, i,* or *e* and preceded by another *c,* the first *c* is pronounced as *t* and the second *c* as *ch,* as in *ecce* (aat-chaa). Another instance is *buccellas* (boot-cháal-lahz).

ch is always pronounced as *k.*

g is always soft before *e, i, ae,* and *oe* as in the Latin word *genitóri* and in the English word general.

gn is *ny;* for instance, *magnam* is pronounced máh-nyam and *dignum* as dée-nyoom.

h is alwalys silent, except in *mihi* and *nihil.*

sc before *e, i, ae,* and *oe* is like *sh* in English. Thus, *suscepi* is pronounced soo-sháa-pee or even sooz-sháa-pee.

j is always treated as y. Thus *jam* is pronounced yahm.

ti when preceded and followed by a vowel is equivalent to tsee. Thus, *laetitia* is pronounced laa-tśee-tsee-ah and *patientia* (pah-tsee-áan-tsee-ah). When preceded by a consonant and followed by *a, o,* or *u,* it has the ordinary sound of *t,* as in *Christiani,* which is pronounced kree-stee-áh-nee.

An excellent exercise for testing one's accuracy in pronouncing the vowel sounds is to be found in reading the vowel sounds of a Latin text, passing smoothly from one to another with what might be termed a kaleidoscopic effect. Thus the utmost color may be secured from the vowels, without which vocal music would more represent an engraving than an oil or water-color painting, which is what vocal music should exhibit. For instance *et cum spiritu tuo* (*aa oo ee ee oo oo oh*) should be practiced (all voices in unison and in monotone, with perfect equality of each vowel). Again, the well-known hymn *O salutaris hostia* (*oh ah oo ah ee oh ee ah*) should be practiced. Another is *Tantum ergo sacramentum* in this form, *ah oo aa oh ah ah aa oo.* This method, though tedious at first, becomes interesting, while the results attained add much beauty to choral performances.

Certain words may give some trouble. The following list is far from complete, but it contains many words that are often mispronounced. The list might be added to indefinitely but it is hoped that it will be helpful to the choral conductor who desires a correct and colorful pronunciation of the Latin.

Alleluia. The first *l* may be treated as a musical consonant, the tip of the tongue being raised to the back of the upper teeth, keeping it there while the *l* is sounded. For the second *l,* the tongue drops to its natural position in the lower jaw. All words with double *l* may be treated in the same way.

Excelsis. This should be pronounced aag-sháal-seez. The *x* is sounded as *gs* and the *c* like *ch*. When these come together, the *x* loses its *s* sound and is softened down to *gg* and the *ch* is softened to *sh*. It is better to pronounce final *s* as *z,* as in the English words bees, seas. *Deus* as dáy-ooz. The *z* sound gives a better finish and has been approved by Roman authorities as a more agreeable ending to such words.

Fa-ctus, san-ctus, etc. Note that the *ct* in such cases belongs to the second syllable and is not divided, as is usually heard fahk-tooz, sahnk-tooz, etc. Such words should be fáh-ktooz, sáhn-ktooz, etc. There are many words with this double consonant effect and all are similarly treated. *Sanctam* (sáhn-ktahm); *catholicam* (kah-tóh-lee-kahm); never forgetting that the *th* is sounded as in the English word Thomas.

Aegypto (aa-gée-ptoh)
apparebit (ap-pah-ráa-beet)
ascendit (ah-shaán-deet)
buccellas (boot-cáal-lahz)
descendit (daa-sháan-deet)
dixit (dée-gseet). The *x* belongs to the second syllable.
ecce (aát-chaa)
et filio (ate fée-lee-oh)
et spiritu (ate spée-ree-too)
excita (aag-shée-tah)
exquisita (aags-qúee-see-tah)
gloria (glóh-re-ah)
inimici (ee-née-mee-chee)
patri (páh-tree)
propterea (proh-ptáa-raa-ah)
radix (ráh-deegs)
sancto (sáhn-cto)
tui (toó-ee)

SIGNIFICANCE OF WORDS*

Bright is the ring of words when the right man rings them,
Fair the fall of songs when the singer sings them.

There may be clarity of pronunciation, correct formation of vowels, and proper treatment of consonants, and yet still the words may lack significance of meaning. The beauty and spirit of the music should enhance the beauty and spirit of the words. It is in the beauty and spirit of the words that one finds the true poetic significance. It is trite

* Roberton, Hugh S., Festival Booklet #2, Paterson Sons and Co., London

to say that words are important; it is commonplace to say that they are over-powering. They are the life-blood of a choral composition, the source of musical inspiration.

> Blow, bugle, blow, set the wild echoes flying,
> Blow, bugle, answer, echoes, dying, dying, dying.

A fine reader of the above couplet can make one actually hear the rise and fall of the echoes.

> A thing of beauty is a joy forever:
> Its loveliness increases; it will never
> Pass into nothingness; but still will keep
> A bower quiet for us; and a sleep
> Full of sweet dreams, and health, and quiet breathing.

See Example 51 for a setting to this lovely poem. Notice the quiet lilt of it, the melodious nuances, the divine music in the mood of it. Study of such a poem is not enough; it must be absorbed. Not until the singers are saturated with the quiet nature of the poem can the setting be sung artistically. Technical finish may make words "a thing of beauty"; it is feeling and understanding that make them "a joy forever".

CHAPTER REVIEW

Here is a true and false quiz to test yourself on this important chapter. Reference pages are given for the correct answers. If you miss more than five questions you had better re-study the entire chapter. In fact, only a perfect score should satisfy a serious student of choral conducting. Mark true (T) or false (F) in the blank.

1. _____The secret of artistic choral singing depends upon beautiful diction. pg. 122.
2. _____Colloquial pronunciation is acceptable in choral singing. pg. 122, 123.
3. _____Slovenly articulation produces slovenly singing. pg. 123.
4. _____The printing of words on the program relieves the singers of the responsibility of making words clear. pg. 123.
5. _____Naturalness in diction, and habit or custom in diction are synonymous terms. pg. 124.
6. _____A conductor should give equal consideration to the words and music in selecting numbers for the chorus. pg. 124.
7. _____More care should be given to the diction of words in unaccompanied music than in accompanied music. pg. 125.

8. _____The tempo of the music is primarily determined by the tempo of the words. pg. 125.
9. _____Sometimes the contour of the musical phrase dominates the treatment of the verbal phrase. pg. 127.
10. _____The normal metrical accent of the syllables of the words is subsidiary to the metrical accent of the measure. pg. 128.
11. _____In attacks the vowel coincides with the downbeat; the consonants precede the ictus, or point, of the beat. pg. 135.
12. _____Tone should be developed first and then diction adapted accordingly. pg. 137.
13. _____Line loud singing on an *aw* color and soft singing on an *oo* or *ah* color. pg. 139.
14. _____The same tone should be used for all types of compositions. pg. 140.
15. _____The quality of voice is determined by the formation of the vowel. pg. 140.
16. _____Most choral conductors overstress diphthongs. pg. 143.
17. _____Singers should sing as they speak. pg. 146.
18. _____The first step in overcoming inertia is for singers to know what they are singing about. pg. 146.
19. _____The weakest factor in the singing of most choirs is that they do not finish their words. pg. 147.
20. _____Only vowels have singing resonance. pg. 148.
21. _____Resonant consonants precede the beat and are sung on the same pitch as the vowel. pg. 148.
22. _____The same rules for diction of English do not apply to foreign languages. pg. 153.
23. _____The beauty and spirit of the music should enhance the beauty and spirit of the words. pg. 156.
24. _____It is not a responsibility of a choral conductor to read the text to the chorus. pg. 157.

Chapter VII

Developing Choral Tone

Music is based upon giving form to tonal-rhythmic patterns. All art has rhythm and form. The unique element of music is tone. Even with all of the aspects of performance being adequate, if the tone is inappropriate for the music sung, the performance will suffer. Range of melodic parts, contrast in dynamics, establishment of mood, proper diction—all depend upon the ability to develop voices.

As we suggest in the previous chapter, the choral conductor should not side-step his responsibility in developing the voices of his chorus. He is jeopardizing the quality of the performance of the group unless he does assume this responsibility. Naturally, there is little time in a chorus rehearsal to give voice lessons, at least of the traditional studio variety. However, there are basic principles in singing applicable to all voices. These can be utilized in a rehearsal and will build singing voices.

Fortunate are conductors who inherit mature voices of pleasing quality. The primary problem then is simply one of establishing a homogenous voice quality within the group. Most choral conductors are presented with a heterogeneous group of voices, undeveloped and unspoiled. They may be labelled as strident, pinched, nasal, hollow, breathy, or anemic. Sometimes they seem to encompass all of these epithets. Here lies a musical and educational challenge! The personal, social and aesthetic values of choral singing as described in Chapter I are fundamentally dependent upon the free use of the singing voice. How can anyone enjoy singing if his voice cannot respond to the demands placed upon it?

The ability to develop young people's voices requires a thorough knowledge of the basic principles of singing. There is so much controversy in the field of voice teaching that the average choral conductor is completely bewildered. Some choral conductors follow fads by copying some eccentric type of tone used by a particular choir. This is questionable procedure. The safest thing to do is to use the great vocalists of the present and past as models. Luckily, recordings of the great artists are available to study.

Unless a choral conductor makes himself cognizant of the principles of voice production, his choral groups will be limited in what they can sing well. Some choral numbers require vocal power to be effective. The choral conductor must understand how to increase the dynamic potential of the singers without injuring the voices. Also, the perpetual lament is that the range of most choral music is too high for young voices, especially tenors and basses. This belief limits the repertory to compositions of modest dimensions and watered-down arrangements. Young people can and are being taught to use their voices to meet the expressive demands of all but the most taxing choral works. In this chapter we hope to throw some light on these problems.

TONE FOR CHORAL AND SOLO SINGING

Voice production is the same for solo and choral singing. True, the tone of the choral singer must be colored so that it will blend, but it is not darkened to the degree that it sounds hollow. Nor is all vibrato eliminated — tremolo, yes, but the aliveness in the tone is retained.

It is a strange and entirely fallacious idea that a person uses his voice differently when singing a solo than when singing in a chorus. Choruses which practice this principle sing ensemble sections with one type of tone, while solo passages are sung with a different tone. The effect of this approach is unmusical.

A usual reason for the variance in tone is due to the singer's having studied the solos with an individual voice teacher and then having been forced to adjust his technique for ensemble choir singing. The practice has caused friction between individual voice teachers and choral conductors in many of our colleges. In some cases voice teachers have forbidden their students to sing in the choir. Undoubtedly, there will always be disagreement among voice teachers, but if a choral conductor will devote himself to understanding the basic principles of singing as demonstrated by artist-singers, such instances will be reduced to a minimum. This suggestion does not necessarily imply slavish imitation, but practices based upon knowledge and sound procedures.

APPROACH TO TONE

Sound procedures are based upon an intelligent goal, a realization for what one is striving. It is impossible to take a step-by-step approach to vocal development, but it is sensible to have some organization in the presentation of the various techniques in singing. This will eliminate the all-too-prevailing "try this and that," "hit or miss" system of vocal training.

Tonal Imagery

A singer should have an aural conception of the tone he desires to produce. He needs a tonal image to guide his efforts. A choral group should also have such tonal imagery. Listening to the singing of fine artists and choral groups, either in concert or on recordings, is one way to develop a tonal image. Demonstrations by the conductor, if he is able, or by other students, is another. If the group can hold the image of this tone as they practice, striking results may be achieved. Different sections of a choir should practice singing melodies, or their parts, separately at an *mp* dynamic level. As they listen to each other, the tonal delinquents will realize their errors and adjust their singing to the basic tone of the group. This procedure is quite different from having sectional rehearsals to learn notes. It is designed to obtain a correct and uniform tone.

Some choral conductors and many voice teachers fear that this approach will produce imitation and unnaturalness, to the detriment of young voices. They point out that many young tenors have been ruined by trying to imitate Caruso. If taken literally, this caution might be valid. Little is accomplished in any endeavor without a goal, however, and little progress will be made by a singer unless he has as a goal some tonal image.

Some conductors approach vocal production completely through tonal imagery. It certainly would be a musical paradise if young people learned to use their voices well just by listening to fine singers. But sadly enough, it isn't that easy. Besides having a goal, one must work and practice. In addition to an image of a beautiful singing tone, a choral group must practice in some detail before it can produce the kind of tone necessary for artistic singing.

Physical Imagery

This approach to the tone involves the physical sensations felt by a singer. Some private voice teachers have made a fetish of the approach. Singers are confronted with such minute instructions as to "lower the larynx", "raise the larynx", "raise the uvula", "groove the tongue", "spread the pillar of fauces", "expand the inter-costal muscles", "pull in the stomach," ad infinitum.

Evidently the belief behind this type of teaching is that if one has the proper sensation of all of the separate muscles involved in the singing act, the voice will be correctly produced and sound beautiful. This leads to complete disillusionment. A singer should have a physical feel for producing the voice, but it is a total conception. Specific instructions may be given to members concerning the vocal act of which he has conscious control, such as the jaw, the lips, the tip of the tongue, and the head. Beyond this it is better to develop physical imagery through tonal techniques.

Combined Tonal and Physical Imagery

Instead of resorting to one type of image, it is far more expedient to aid the singer in gaining gradually both a tonal and physical image of correct voice production. In this approach the conductor will alternate between the two, utilizing the one which seems to improve the tone for singing a complete composition, a phrase, or a single word. This approach may be presented by the following diagram:

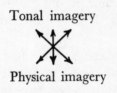

Tonal imagery

Physical imagery

} fosters correct voice production.

Natural Singing

Probably a few observations should be made regarding the belief that singers, especially choral singers, should just sing naturally. This belief is invariably held by someone who has had no experience in developing choral groups. A person doesn't sing naturally anymore than he walks naturally or plays the violin naturally. With training, a person sings or walks correctly, or at least he should.

It is very obvious, if one takes the trouble to observe his fellow man, that what many people call walking naturally is incorrect. They have never been taught to either sit, stand, or walk correctly. So many people have developed faulty speech habits over the years that their natural singing voices, if they had any, have been affected. Much of the poor choral singing in the schools today can be attributed to permitting the young people just to "sing naturally".

If natural habits were synonomous with perfect habits, there would be no need for education. Unfortunately this is not so, even in singing. It is a false assumption to consider daily habits as natural. If so, what is natural for one person is unnatural for another. In fact, unless voices are developed they cannot even meet the technical demands of the major portion of the beautiful choral music which is available. Our goal should be to develop the young voices in our care so that they sound natural and can be utilized to their maximum power and beauty.

TESTS OF A CORRECT TONE

What we need in vocal study are some standards or tests from which we can be assured that our methods are valid. The author has set up a list of achievements against which he tests the effectiveness and efficiency of his vocal procedures. They are: freedom, range of pitch, range of dynamics, flexibility, intonation, and durability. All of the suggested vocal procedures in this chapter are presented as a means of attaining the standards implied in these tests.

Free Tone

The first premise which a choral conductor must accept is that a singing tone is free. On this principle of voice production all teachers agree. But from this point on, complete subjectivity becomes evident. One teacher will label one type of tone as being free, another will prefer a different type, and a third will defend vigorously still another type as being the only free tone. Here is where the checks, or tests become useful. If a tone meets the standards of the tests, it is free.

The tone should be of the quality and quantity adequate for the music to be sung. Consequently, the tone must be freely produced, without undue physical tension, full and vigorous for *forte* singing, rich and vital for *pianissimo*. A wide range of dynamics is necessary for contrasting moods, and a correctly produced tone with ringing resonance is necessary to maintain pitch.

How can we fill this big order? The secret is to be found in singing with a free, open throat. Remember, the voice functions like an organ pipe! Strident tones, nasal tones, hooty tones and excessively dark tones are produced by a pinched, closed throat. Therefore, the basic necessity for the free singing tone is to get the throat open so that interference is avoided. Then the work of singing will be done predominantly by the large body muscles. The author has found the following exercise to be the most successful in securing this correct physical condition for singing, namely, the open throat. He uses it at nearly every rehearsal in order to release voices and eliminate rigidity, the prime cause of faulty tone production.

Vocalise 2

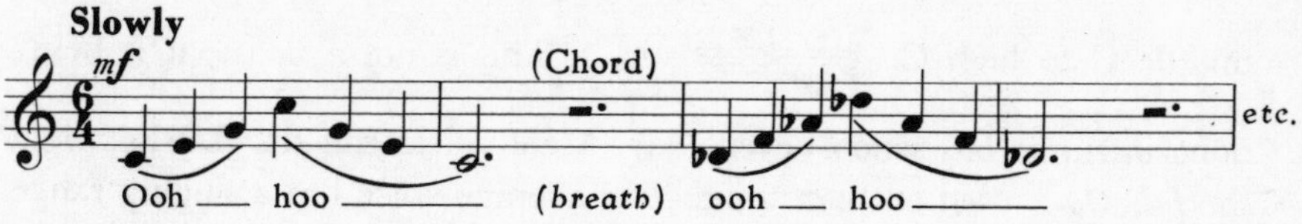

Procedure:

1. Sing on an *oo* vowel. To sing the correct *oo,* first sing an *oh* vowel; then change to *oo* by closing the lips slightly, retaining the space of an *oh* in the back of the mouth.
2. Place the first two fingers of the left hand between the teeth with the second (or middle) finger on top. More free emission of the tone is assured in this manner; also, stridency and thinness of tone will disappear if the proper *oo* vowel is used. See figures below.
3. Start on middle C and vocalize an octave or more. (Naturally, in the notation and execution of all vocalises, it should be understood that changed male voices are singing one octave lower than treble voices.)
4. Male voices will shift easily to *falsetto* or semi-*falsetto* at G or A♭, depending upon their development, when the exercise is sung softly. Above F, the *oo* vowel will gradually change to *aw* or *ah* in treble voices.
5. On the top tone, push the right hand down with palm open, and then forward in a gliding motion. This motion prevents the head from rising and assures contact of the tone with the breath.

Figure 2

a. b. c.

Range of Pitch

An extended range of the voice is the first test of free tone production. If a choral conductor cannot develop the high notes of his singers, especially tenors, to meet the requirements of the normal choral repertory, then he can be assured that his vocal procedures are wrong. The average group of treble voices (female voices and boys' unchanged voices) from the sixth grade to maturity can sing the above exercise from middle C to high C.  This is not a boast; it is being done in numerous schools every day. Male voices can do likewise when the *falsetto* is used on high tones. The average voice has a singing range of at least two octaves when it is properly produced. Below is the normal range for different types of choral voices and the range to which they can usually be extended with training. These ranges are for high school, college, and adult voices. Pitch ranges for younger voices will be presented with the discussion of these choral groups. Voice ranges for specific choirs will be given in Chapter X.

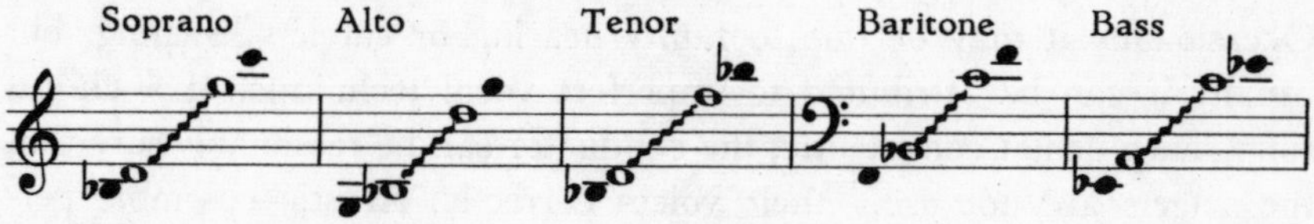

Range of Dynamics

The second test of free vocal production is the ability to sing both loud and soft. Contrast of dynamics is one of the criteria of artistic singing. Radio crooners usually have vocal difficulty when trying to sing *forte;* opera singers often are not effective in soft passages. These dynamic limitations reduce the repertory which each type of singer can perform impressively.

As mentioned previously, too many school choirs limit their range of dynamics from *mp* to *mf*. Most groups can sing softly if just a little attention is given to this skill, but it takes training and development to sing *forte* with a musical tone. Voices should not be pushed past the point at which they sound forced. This caution is especially applicable to young voices.

Some conductors contend that soft singing is the true test of tone. Experience in listening to hundreds of choirs of all age levels points, rather, to the unmistakable fact that loud singing which is beautiful is a more reliable test. Soft singing may become anemic, but loud singing so often has a tendency to become strident and downright disagreeable. Regardless of such controversial opinions, it is the responsibility of a choral conductor to extend the dynamic range of his chorus within the limits of the maturity of the voices. Procedures suggested in this chapter should be helpful.

Flexibility

A free voice is a flexible voice. Tight voices and dark, heavy voices seldom have flexibility. There is a high correlation between flexibility and beautiful tone. Flexibility is also required to sing runs, melismatic melodies, and ornaments. Flexibility in a voice indicates that there is little wrong with the production. It is also a sign of good musicianship. If a choral conductor has only little knowledge of the principles of voice building, he can rest assured that developing flexibility in the voices of his group is a safe procedure.

Intonation

The problem of intonation continues to arise in our discussion. We have suggested ways to eliminate this choral nemesis. We will pursue the culprit further in presenting vocal techniques later in the chapter.

The ability to sing on pitch is an immediate test of vocal production. Occasionally it may be due to faulty hearing or careless listening, but usually it can be attributed to imperfect vocal technique. If a chorus sings sharp or flat consistently, the conductor can be reasonably sure that the singers are not using their voices correctly. Artistic ensemble performance becomes impossible without the ability to sing on pitch. It is one of the responsibilities of the choral conductor to understand the principles of singing sufficiently to overcome this persistent bogey to choral performance.

Durability

There are two aspects to this test of vocal technique; one is the immediate staying power of the voices, the other is the preservation of the voice over a period of years. The first one serves as a continuous check, while the second can only be determined after a long period of the use of the singing voice.

If the voices of the choristers become tired and hoarse after an hour of vigorous rehearsing, they are using their voices improperly. The conductor should understand the psychology of rehearsal sufficiently to avoid having the singers sing at the "top of their lungs" on a very demanding piece for the entire hour. Voices must be used vigorously to develop, but they must be used correctly.

There is no question that undue demands are placed on young voices in one-day festivals in the high schools. Often these young people rehearse intensively for five or six hours in one day, giving a full evening's concert that night. At the end of such a strenuous day both voices and bodies are certain to be tired. Hoarseness may be evident in some of the more enthusiastic singers. However, young voices recover quickly from these choral marathons and no harm is done unless repeated too frequently.

A more serious problem is the endurance of the choral conductor's voice. A long teaching and rehearsing schedule each day is bound to impair the voice eventually, unless it is extremely hardy and perfectly produced. Few voices will survive the demands of continuous talking and singing imposed upon high school choral teachers. Therefore, it behooves them to learn to use the voice properly both for speaking and singing in order that it may be preserved for purposes of demonstration. Otherwise, their efficiency as teachers and conductors is reduced.

The voices of professional singers, when not abused, retain their beauty to an advanced age. Invariably such long enduring voices have a lyric, youthful quality. Perhaps here is the key for the development of durable voices.

TECHNIQUES OF TONE PRODUCTION

As suggested above the techniques of tone production should be approached through a combined and reciprocal tonal and physical image of the desired tone. Then assurance of vocal freedom should be checked by the foregoing tests of range of pitch, range of dynamics, flexibility, intonation, and durability. The author approaches all of his vocal techniques with these standards as a test of perfection.

Some teachers claim to use only a scientific method in teaching singing. Much as scientific data has contributed to the teaching of voice, there are still many controversial facts. The teaching of tone production can be made fairly scientific, but the teaching of singing is an art and consequently enjoys a high degree of subjectivity. Since the science and art of singing cannot, or at least should not be separated, complete objectivity is impossible. Nevertheless, the choral conductor should be cognizant of the acoustical and physiological factors in tone production and take them into consideration in his vocal methods.

Posture in Singing

Correct body posture begets correct tone production. This is not a panacea for all vocal ills, but without it, free tone production becomes increasingly difficult. Telling a group to "stand up straight" is not enough, although it is a beginning. Admonishing a group of lackadaisical youngsters to "sit with two feet flat on the floor" is another step in the right direction. Correct posture gives a choir personality and stage presence.

The posture for singing should reflect what is known of voice production in relation to the opening of the throat and the position of the head. Correct vocal tone results from the mental and physical coordination of the entire body. Therefore, the body should be held in an erect and alert position which is conducive to this free, coordinated mental and physical activity, whether the singer is standing or sitting. Relaxation is not a negative factor in voice production, but it results from positive mental attitudes arising out of muscular freedom. When a fine singer delivers that thrilling climax, he is not relaxed; he just looks and acts relaxed. To create the impression of performing a physical endeavor without effort, the body must be coordinated.

Again, the throat functions like an organ pipe. Therefore, in order to keep the throat clear and open, the head must be perpendicular to the shoulders and body, not tilted forward, back, or sidewise. The position of the head is very important. Any deviation distorts the tone. Raising the head or protruding the chin causes whiteness and stridency of tone, while dipping the head tends to cause darkness and thickness. If the body moves, the head moves accordingly. It should remain on center. The body should have a compact feeling of being all in one piece.

Standing posture. In performance singers in a choral group usually stand in an acceptable posture as far as stage presence is concerned. However, they are often lacking in the fundamentals of correct singing posture. Inadvertently, the singers are jeopardizing the excellence of the performance. Correct posture is not something that happens by chance; it must be practiced. These six major points should be observed:*

1. *A straight spine* — provides a main supporting structure upon which the movements of the entire body are coordinated and activated.
   Caution: Do not stand humped over or sway-back.
2. *An erect head* — allows the muscles of the throat to act without interference.
   Caution: Chin should not be raised, protruded or lowered. Head should remain perpendicular with the shoulders and body — should not be tipped sidewise.
3. *A comfortable high chest* — permits free breath action.
   Caution: Position should not be strained and the shoulders should not be strained or pulled back.
4. *A slight expansion of the lower ribs* — combines with the chest position to serve as a framework for deep, controlled breathing.
   Caution: Only expand the ribs to the point that the stomach muscles are pulled in straight. Too much expansion will cause tension.
5. *A position with the feet slightly apart and the right foot a few inches in advance of the left* — provides the singer with a sense of well-being, poise, and alertness for action.
   Caution: Do not rest on the heels; the weight of the body should be supported primarily by the balls of the feet.

* Peterson, Paul W. "Natural Singing and Expressive Conducting," John F. Blair, publisher, Winston- Salem, 1955, p. 10.

6. *A balance of the body weight slightly forward* — coupled with the position of the feet assures proper action of the back muscles and general coordination of the entire body.
   Caution: Do not lean forward too far or bend at the hips.

Sitting posture. Most choruses sit more than ninety percent of the time. Rehearsals are usually conducted with the singers in a sitting position, although there should be moments of change when they stand to sing through a number which they have been practicing. Therefore, correct sitting posture is an important, if not an indispensible ingredient for successful rehearsals.

The conductor must be adamant in his insistence on correct sitting posture at rehearsals. There will be sighs and groans, but if singers catch the spirit of accomplishment, the weak flesh will be strengthened. Even if a choral teacher in the schools has little success in teaching the youngsters to sing well, if he teaches them to stand and sit in a position conducive to good health and well-being, he will have fulfilled a major share of his educational mission. A rigid sitting position should not be retained throughout a rehearsal. There should be moments of relaxation, but the correct posture should be resumed while singing.

The important features of the standing position should be incorporated in the sitting position. If a chorus sits correctly, it will sing as well sitting down as standing up. There are two additional instructions for correct sitting posture:

1. *Place both feet flat on the floor* — emulates a standing position.
   Caution: Do not cross legs at the ankles or knees.
2. *Maintain a straight spine with the body tilted slightly forward from the back of the chair* — provides for free bodily and vocal action.
   Caution: Do not slouch in seat and put arms around the backs of chairs. Rehearsal chairs should be of the type to encourage correct posture. Otherwise, the conductor doubles his work.

The author uses this device to obtain correct posture from choral singers: Place the ends of the middle fingers together with the elbows pointing out. Place the hands against the stomach with the palms up, elbows still pointing out. Pull the elbows forward a couple of inches without permitting the chest to lower or cave in. Retain the feeling of this position when the hands drop to the side or when sitting down. The head must be perpendicular to the shoulders, as indicated in the following figures:

Figure 3

a. Correct Standing Posture

b. Incorrect Standing Posture

Figure 4

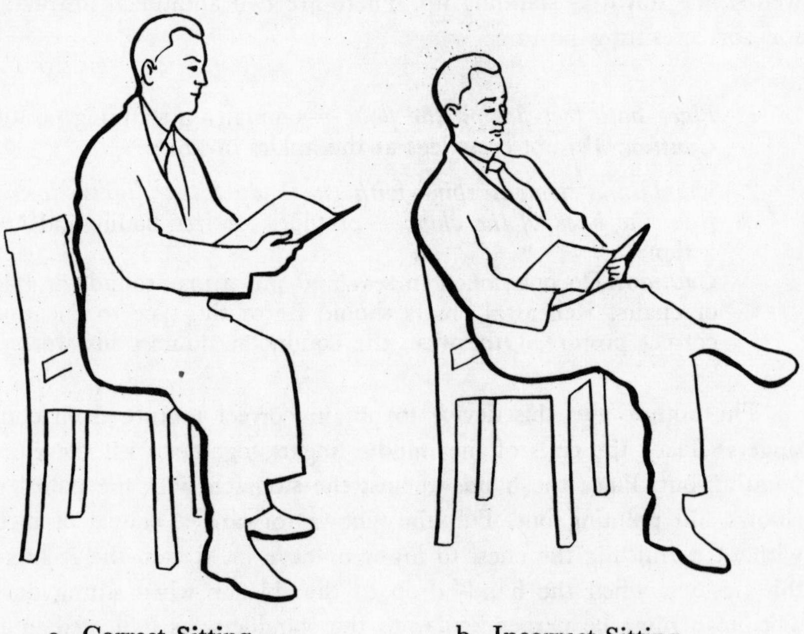

a. Correct Sitting Position

b. Incorrect Sitting Position

Figure 5

a. Incorrect
Chin Tilted Up

b. Incorrect
Chin Tilted Down

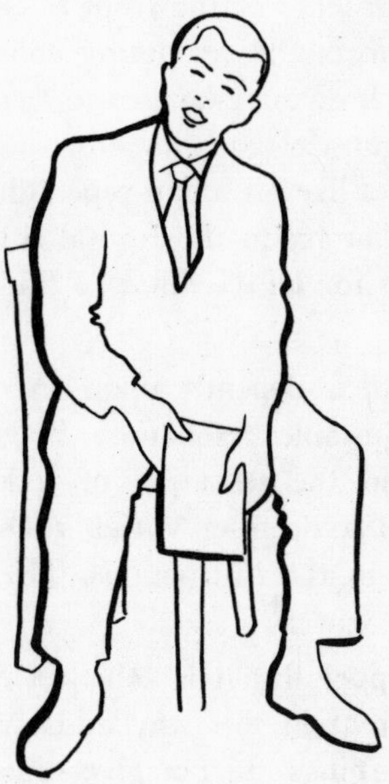

c. Incorrect
Chin Tilted Sidewise

RESONANCE

Begin with the development of vocal resonance; it is the forerunner of correct habits of breathing and diction. Resonance is really the determining factor of the quality of the voice. Breathing aids the development of resonance, and diction must not interfere with resonance while singing a song. The sound of a chorus depends upon the resonance with which it sings.

A beautiful singing tone must have roundness and fullness, coupled with carrying quality. This latter quality is sometimes referred to as "ping," "focus" or "forward placement." These terms are permissable when used to describe quality, but when used to indicate physical sensation they often defeat their own purpose. Any attempt to develop resonance by direct control invariably brings restriction and tension of the throat muscles, with the resultant faulty production. Do not direct the voice on the teeth, in the nose, or in the "masque." Make no attempt to project the voice. The voice must be allowed to sing!

Singing resonance is dependent upon a free, open throat. It is futile to tell singers to open their throat; they must produce their voices in a manner which will open the throat. The resonating column must be firmly opened throughout. The laryngeal pharynx, the oral pharynx, and the nasal pharynx are adjustable resonators; the post-nasal cavities and sinus cavities are non-adjustable resonators. (There should be no sense of resonance *in* the nose or the front of the mouth.) All of these resonators combine to form the resonating column. It is the vibrating air in this column which gives resonance to the voice, not the sense of vibration in the teeth, muscle tissue, or bone tissue. We point out once more, the voice resonates like an organ pipe. There seems to be a circle of resonance from the larynx to the frontal sinuses. The figure on the next page may be used for all reference to the physiological factors of vocal production.

Full singing resonance depends upon expanding the lower and upper throats, the adjustable resonators. Practice Vocalise 2, under "Free Tone", to obtain the sensation of a low, open throat. It is achieved by singing on a deep-set vowel, such as *ooh,* following the various steps indicated in the instructions. The same sensation should be transferred to other vowels.

Expansion of the upper throat is achieved by "arching" the upper throat. Shaping the throat in this way adds "ring" to the resonance. May we repeat the warning: do not give direct instructions to shape the throat in any manner. Its shape should result from the way in which vowels are formed.

Figure 6

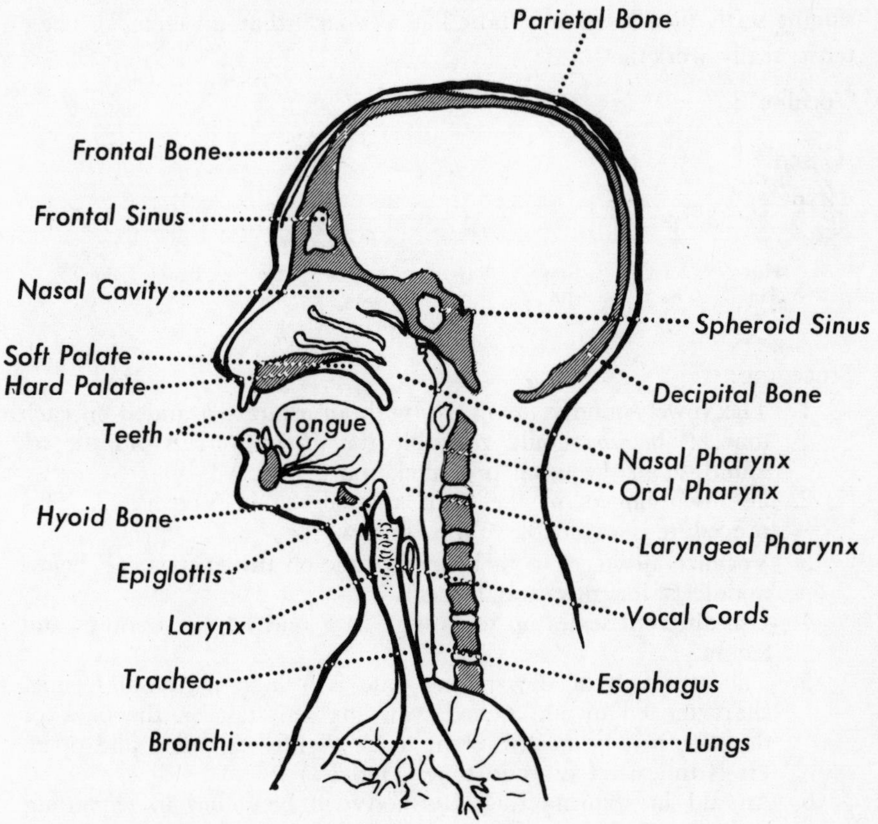
Parietal Bone
Frontal Bone
Frontal Sinus
Nasal Cavity
Soft Palate
Hard Palate
Teeth
Tongue
Hyoid Bone
Epiglottis
Larynx
Trachea
Bronchi
Spheroid Sinus
Decipital Bone
Nasal Pharynx
Oral Pharynx
Laryngeal Pharynx
Vocal Cords
Esophagus
Lungs

The "arched" tone can be secured quickly by requesting students to sing the descending scale using *haw* or *hah,* as in the act of "snoring." The author instructs young students as follows: "Snore more and sing less and you will sound better." Keep the dynamic level from *mf* to *mp.* Use the *aw* vowel for *mf* singing and the *ah* vowel for *mp* singing. In singing softly the sensation is more like a "snarl" than a "snore." (These terms really work).

Vocalise 3

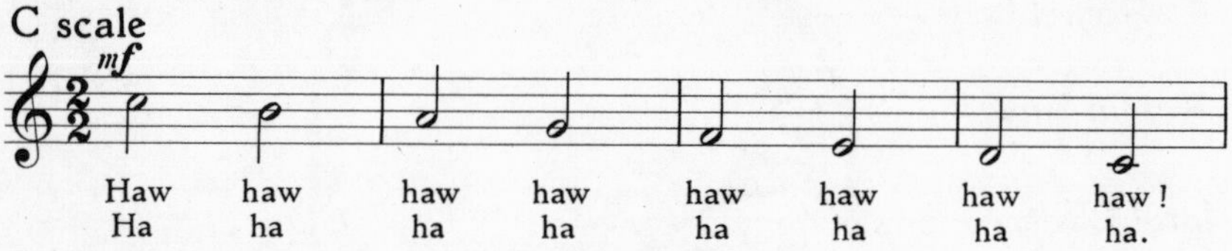
C scale
mf
Haw haw haw haw haw haw haw haw!
Ha ha ha ha ha ha ha ha.

Procedure:

1. The vowel sound is *aw* or *ah,* with an aspirate *h* added on each tone. (The *ah* should resemble the *ah* in *star.* Avoid the *uh* sound, as in the usual pronunciation of *love.*)
2. Use two fingers in the same manner as in Vocalise 2. This procedure is invaluable to free the jaw.
3. Vocalize all voices to their lowest tone on this exercise (F below middle C for altos and basses).
4. Use different scales up to as high as F and F♯ for sopranos and tenors.
5. The sensation of the singing tone is a high postnasal feeling, characterized by an arched, yawning sensation in the back of the mouth. The nostrils seem to be slightly extended and open. (It is the secret of good tone. Find it!)
6. An aid in securing this sensation will be found in extending both lips slightly and raising the upper lip until part of the front teeth show. (This lip position is not to be confused with the so-called smiling position which has a tendency to overwiden the tone.)

When this "circle of resonance" seems to be established it should be transferred to each vowel. However, within this sensation each vowel has its own resonating characteristic. The "circle of resonance" can be impressed upon students with the following exercise: place two fingers of the left hand between the teeth as instructed on p. 164. Then, starting on an indefinite high pitch and sliding down, make a sound like a siren and simultaneously make an outward circle with the right hand. This exercise never fails to bring hilarity, but the singers get the idea.

In review, the singing resonance employs all of the air spaces of the head and throat except the nose and the front of the mouth. The sensation is an expanded low throat and an arched upper throat. The resulting tone is deep and full, combined with "arch" and ring ("focus," if you will, although it is a misleading term). The following statement explains it succinctly.

Singing resonance results from {
- low, open throat; deep-set vowel; use *ooh*.
- high, arched throat; open-arched vowel; use *aw* and *ah*.

PRINCIPLES OF BREATHING

Some old Italian voice teacher started all the argument by remarking, "He who knows how to breathe, knows how to sing." And so many voice teachers today begin the teaching of singing with a presentation of the principles of breathing. Let us state emphatically that the procedures of breathing in singing should not precede or be separated from the act of phonation and diction. Singers who become overly breath conscious to the detriment of establishing resonance and habits of diction, seldom sing artistically and expressively. This is especially true in a choral group. A conductor should keep his instructions on the principles of breathing to a minimum. As we have stated throughout this book the approach and emphasis is on the musical message.

The above observations do not imply that correct breath habits do not contribute to voice production. On the contrary, they are very important in the act of phonation. An entire book could be written on the principles of breathing. However, only those factors which contribute directly to the singing resonance need concern the choral conductor.

There are two aspects of breathing that have gained status in the nomenclature of all voice teachers, namely, breath support, and breath control. The popular impression of these terms seems to be that breath support "holds up the tone" in some mysterious fashion, and breath control indicates conservation of the air so that singers can sustain a long phrase on one breath. Another popular misconception is the idea that one needs a large quantity of breath to sing. The idea leads to exercises in chest expansion which usually result in tension detrimental to singing.

Breath support is dependent upon the direct contact of the resonance with the breath. If the low throat is expanded and open just above the vocal action this contact is provided. Any restriction in this area makes breath support impossible. No singer can support a tone by pushing down or lifting up. It is a matter of the tone resting down on the breath. *Breath balance* is a better term. Abdominal muscles should remain firm;

they should not collapse (that is, the abdomen should not protrude), nor should they suddenly be drawn in and lifted. The abdomen should retain its position as in good posture.

Breath control is dependent upon the efficiency of the vocal action. Breath, in singing, cannot be emitted evenly either by mental or muscular control. If the throat is firmly open from singing with correct resonance so that there is no interference in the act of phonation, the vocal chords will gradually adjust in a manner which will control (or conserve) the breath. This condition is the only answer to the voice that is "breathy" or "fuzzy." The interpretive factors in singing long phrases are not a problem in a choral group because the singers can "stagger their breaths" without the break in rhythm being noticeable. Therefore, they should be instructed to breathe frequently and quietly so that the tone retains its vitality.

Inhalation. A person has two openings through which he can inhale; the nose and the mouth. He should breathe through the nose to remove dust particles from the air and for sustained physical exercise (running a mile for instance). For intermittent physical exercise where quick breaths are needed he should breathe through the mouth. Since continual quick breaths are needed for singing, all singers, both soloists and choristers, should breathe through the mouth.

The idea that people breathe more correctly through the nose than the mouth is absurd. If they breathe incorrectly through the mouth it is very likely that they will breathe incorrectly through the nose. In fact, with the prevalence of some form of nasal obstruction, such as head colds, catarrh, or deviated septums, in taking quick breaths more people are likely to breathe incorrectly through the nose.

It is very important that correct posture be retained during the act of inhalation, that is, shoulders should not be raised, the chest should not cave in, and the abdominal muscles should not collapse and protrude. There is a resultant slight expansion of the lower ribs and the back muscles. Hold those abdominal muscles firm!

This condition of inhalation is not possible unless the throat is open for singing. Therefore, the shape of the resonating column must be formed before the breath is taken. This preparation is possible by breathing on the form of the vowel to be sung.

The author has found this procedure very helpful in giving choristers the correct conception of inhalation and its relation to singing. First of all, assume correct posture, either standing or sitting. Then form the lips, the mouth and the throat in the form of singing *aw* (remember that "snoring" feeling). Take several breaths, with the right hand making a corresponding outward circle. The breath stream seems to be drawn against the roof of the back of the mouth. If continued for several breaths the roof of the mouth becomes slightly dry. Inhalation of the breath in this manner should produce an audible *aw* like a whisper. When this occurs the singer can be assured that the breath action and the shape of the resonators are correct. The same procedure should be followed for other vowels.

Exhalation. The term exhalation is really an unfortunate one. It implies that the singing tone is the result of a stream of breath being directed out of the mouth. Nothing could be further from the truth. As soon as the breath passes over the vocal chords it has no further effect on the tone. The air not the breath stream, vibrates in the resonating column to produce the tone.

Proper exhalation results from correct inhalation and the shaping of the resonators for the act of phonation. The singer must never direct the breath stream. Directing the breath stream into the mouth, the nose, or the "masque" simply causes tensions and a throaty quality of tone.

The condition for exhalation should be the same as the condition for inhalation. Both the shape of the resonators and the form of the vowel are retained. Returning to the exercise of breathing in on the vowel *aw,* attempt to sing this tone on a comfortable pitch; second space *a* is good. Sing as if in the act of inhaling, that is having a sense of drawing the tone in and over. The feel of singing is "in" not "out." As the author often admonishes his choristers, "Sing to yourself, no one else wants to hear you." This "drawing in" sensation as one sings assures the retention of the correct form of the vowel and the corresponding shape of the resonators as well as the proper exhalation. The author practices this procedure consistently with all types of choral groups.

Catch breaths. In singing, quick breaths are required to avoid interfering with the flow of the rhythm and phrase line. All of the procedures described above are applicable to taking catch breaths. Posture must be correct, breathing muscles firm, resonators shaped and vowels formed for the act of phonation. The following exercise is helpful and should be immediately applied to troublesome places in works the chorus is singing.

Vocalise 4

Procedures:

1. Place the hands in front of the body, palms up, elbows out.
2. Form the lips, the mouth and the resonators to sing *ah*.
3. Take a catch breath on this form, drawing the hands out at the same time. This movement of the hands represents the breath action.
4. Sing immediately on the completion of the breath. The two actions seem almost simultaneous. All breathing and singing muscles are held firm.
5. Repeat several times as indicated in the vocalise.

Sustained breaths. Most choral groups lack resonant power and vitality of tone. In the development of these vocal attributes attention to breath action can make a definite and valuable contribution. Lack of these qualities results from singers being unable to retain the conditions of singing, that is, vowel forms, shaped resonators, and firm breathing muscles while sustaining tones. The sensation is that of keeping the breath against the tone by seemingly drawing it in as one sings.

This exercise is priceless in developing resonant power and vitality of tone with choral groups of all types and age levels. The chorus stands and turns sidewise so that there will be room for bodily action. Correct singing posture is assumed. Arms are crossed in front of the body with the palms up. This causes singers to lean slightly forward. Sing the vowel *aw* on each note of a descending scale while drawing the hands outward keeping the arms waist high with the elbows pointing out. There must be a feeling of resistance to the hands, as if stretching a strong rubber band. This drawing of the arms and hands corresponds to breath action. The author remarks to the choristers, "Your hands are your breath." Sustain the tone until the arms are extended sidewise, then cut off the tone with a flip of the hands.

To develop vitality in soft tones, practice the same vocalise using the vowel *ah*. Smile a little, but do not grimace. This mouth position will tend to lighten the vowel and take some of the weight out of the resonance, an important factor in soft singing if pitch is to be maintained.

Vocalise 5

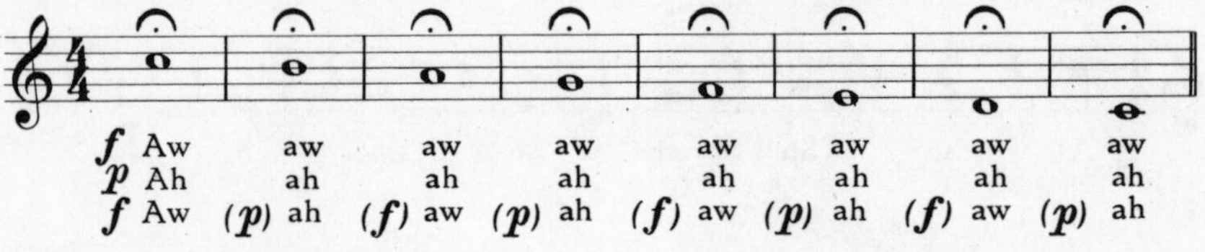

Procedures:

1. Cross the arms in front of the body, palms up, elbows out.
2. Form the lips, the mouth and the resonators to sing *aw* in loud singing, *ah* in soft singing.
3. Take a deep breath on the *aw* or *ah* form depending upon the dynamic level. When done correctly it is an inhaled whisper on these vowels.
4. Sing immediately upon completion of the breath. Draw the arms and hands straight outward, keeping them waist high. Retain consistent lip and mouth formation, shape of resonators and firm breathing muscles. Draw the tone in as if continuing the act of inhalation.
5. Practice one loud scale, then practice a very soft scale.
6. Alternate between loud and soft tones on a descending scale.
7. Apply the same vocalise to other vowels.
8. Use different scales from C to E♭.

Vowel Formation

As an introduction to this discussion, reread the section in Chapter VI on the "Function of Vowels". In that chapter vowels are treated as a factor in diction. In the present chapter we are more concerned with vowels as a means for vocal development, although these two functions of vowels can scarcely be separated.

As we have pointed out under "Resonance" in this chapter, beautiful vocal production is dependent upon the formation of a deep-set vowel and a high-arched resonance. All fine tone has these two basic characteristics. The physical imagery is a yawn-like feeling in the throat while the nasal passages seem open, as if in the act of snoring. This last sensation is the mysterious one for most singers to feel. It comes from the result of a high, palate position as if one were smiling behind the teeth.

These basic conditions of singing must be retained as the various vowels are formed. Otherwise, they will hinder correct vocal production rather than aid it. The resonators must not change as adjustments of the jaw, tongue and lips are made to form the vowels. Some conductors attempt to avoid this difficulty by having choristers use a minimum of mouth and lip movement in forming vowels. The singing which results is colorless and lacks variety. The chorus sounds as if it were vocalizing, instead of singing a piece of music.

The circle or column of resonance from the low throat to the front sinuses must not be continually altered as vowels are changed. Therefore, vowels must be formed so as not to interfere with the established resonance. If pronounced in the mouth over the tongue, in the mouth under the tongue, or in the oral pharynx or back of the mouth, resonance will change as vowels are changed. If pronounced in the nose there will be a consistency of resonance but it will be pinched and throaty with a most unpleasant sound.

To describe any particular locality for the pronunciation of vowels is very difficult. There is a sense of resonant vibration throughout the circle of resonance. The concentration of resonance seems to be above the roof of the mouth in the area behind the eyes and nose. However, there should be no attempt to direct the resonance to these cavities; the sensation of resonance here is the result of correct vowel formation. Again form the mouth and lips for an *aw* vowel. Inhale through the mouth on this *aw* form. Where the stream of breath is sensed — this is the area where all vowels should be formed. The area is on the roof of the back of the mouth in the soft palate area. When all vowels are formed in this area with the described "drawing in" feeling while singing, the circle of resonance is completed, vocal action is free, and the tone is supported and controlled by the breath. Study Figure 6.

Although all vowels should be formed in the area described above, they vary in their physical imagery or sensation of resonance. There must be movement of jaw, lips and tongue to give the various vowels their distinctive color. For simplification, all vowels can be classified into two kinds: closed and open. In singing closed vowels the mouth remains somewhat closed except on high notes. In singing open vowels the mouth opens in an elongated position at least the width of the index and middle finger. On all vowels the mouth is open more on high notes than on low notes.

Closed vowels. The closed vowels are *ooh* (who), *ee* (we), and *i* (win). The basic form for all of these vowels is the *ooh* vowel as presented in Vocalise 2. The closed vowels *ee* and *i* should be formed in the same way. Sing an *ooh* vowel and then sing an *ee* or *i* vowel with the same sensation, except for more concentration of the vowel. There should be the same feeling of depth, the same amount of space in the back of the mouth, and practically the same position of the lips except that a few teeth show on the latter vowels. See Figure 6. Only when sung in this manner will these vowels be round and deep.

The practice of singing these vowels a little too openly, especially in the male voices, causes thinness, reediness, and stridency. When tenors sing these vowels too openly, throatiness is caused, which results in flatting on high notes. A physical device to offset this tendency is to sing the *ee* and *i* vowels with slightly pursed lips as in the diagram and with the middle of the tongue touching the upper teeth, that is, arched in the back with the tip pulled away from the front teeth. The same tongue position should be used by treble voices in singing these vowels in the lower and middle part of the range of the voice. For acoustical reasons all closed vowels are more open when singing high notes, consequently the position of the tongue flattens somewhat as the mouth is opened to sing these higher tones.

Open vowels. All vowels except *ooh, ee,* and *i* are open vowels, regardless of the language being sung. The basic form for all of these vowels is the *aw* vowel for loud singing and the *ah* vowel for soft singing as presented in Vocalise 3. These vowels must also be deep-set so that they will be round and full. There is a corresponding sensation of resonance in the post-nasal and frontal sinus cavities, that is, the cavities behind the nose and eyes. The resonance gives ring and clarity to the tone. This formation gives a complete circle of resonance described in preceding sections. Without this balance of resonance, tones become throaty, and either pinched and strident, or dark and hooty, depending upon which resonance is predominant.

A list of open vowels can be found in Chapter VI under "Function of Vowels". The jaw must be completely free for all of these vowels and the mouth opened at least the width of the index and middle finger together. The tongue is relatively flat in singing these vowels, the tip not being curled under or up. The contour of the lips is away from the teeth, not pressed against them. Some of the teeth show. See Figure 7. With the dropped jaw there is a sensation that the upper part of the face is slightly lifted as in an expression of surprise. This latter sensation is particularly helpful in forming an arched throat with the resultant ringing tone. In opening the mouth care must be taken that the lower jaw does not protrude, the jaw and lips are not pulled back, or the upper lip pulled down while the lower lip bares the teeth.

Figure 7

Correct Mouth Position for Open Vowels

Lower jaw protrudes

Lips pursed

Grimace-tight jaw

Lower teeth bared

Incorrect Mouth Positions for Open Vowels

Connection of Vowels

Practice the connection of both closed and open vowels, as presented in Vocalise 6. In *mf* and *f* singing work from an *aw* vowel; in *mp* and *p* singing work from an *ah* vowel. If the *ay* and *eh* vowels are too brilliant, work from an *oh* vowel using the same formation. This device gives them color. Be especially careful of the *uh* vowel. It appears in so many short words that are on unaccented parts of a measure. Some teachers use this vowel as a basic color for a chorus. Blend can be secured in this manner, but top (or arched) resonance is eliminated. Consequently, the voice has a closed color throughout and flatting in pitch invariably results. The *uh* vowel should approximate the *ah* form to about the same degree that the *ee* vowel approximates the *ooh* vowel. This can be done and still retain the characteristic color of each vowel.

The following vocalise is excellent for obtaining a smooth connecting tonal line. Corresponding lip, tongue and jaw movements are given.

Vocalise 6

C scale, descending

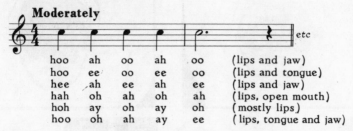

hoo	ah	oo	ah	oo	(lips and jaw)
hoo	ee	oo	ee	oo	(lips and tongue)
hee	ah	ee	ah	ee	(lips and jaw)
hah	oh	ah	oh	ah	(lips, open mouth)
hoh	ay	oh	ay	oh	(mostly lips)
hoo	oh	ah	ay	ee	(lips, tongue and jaw)

Procedures:

1. Sing entire vocalise on scales in the middle part of the voice, C, D♭, D and E♭.
2. In singing each set of vowel sounds use a mirror to see if indications of movement are being followed.
3. Note that the final vocalise moves from a closed position to open and back to closed.
4. In the same manner practice any vowel connections which may be causing trouble.

Diphthongs. A complete treatment of diphthongs as they relate to diction was presented in Chapter VI. They are simply compound vowels with the components being of different length. Therefore, in vocal development the individual vowels are used. Naturally, all of the principles and procedures presented in this chapter on resonance, breathing and vowel formation apply equally to the singing of diphthongs.

Figure 8

Relative Positions for Singing the Different Vowels

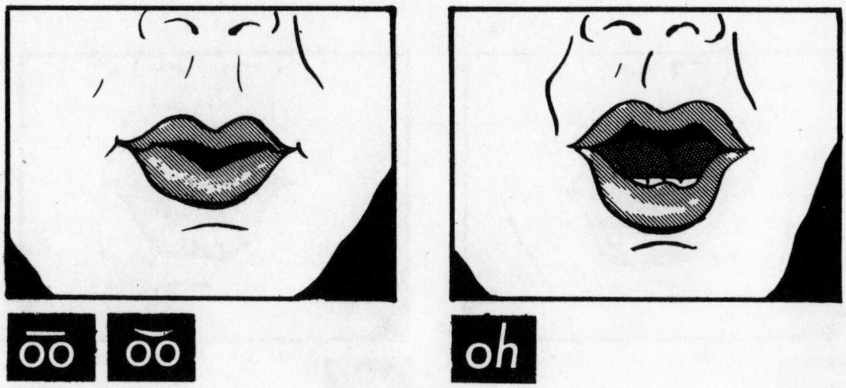

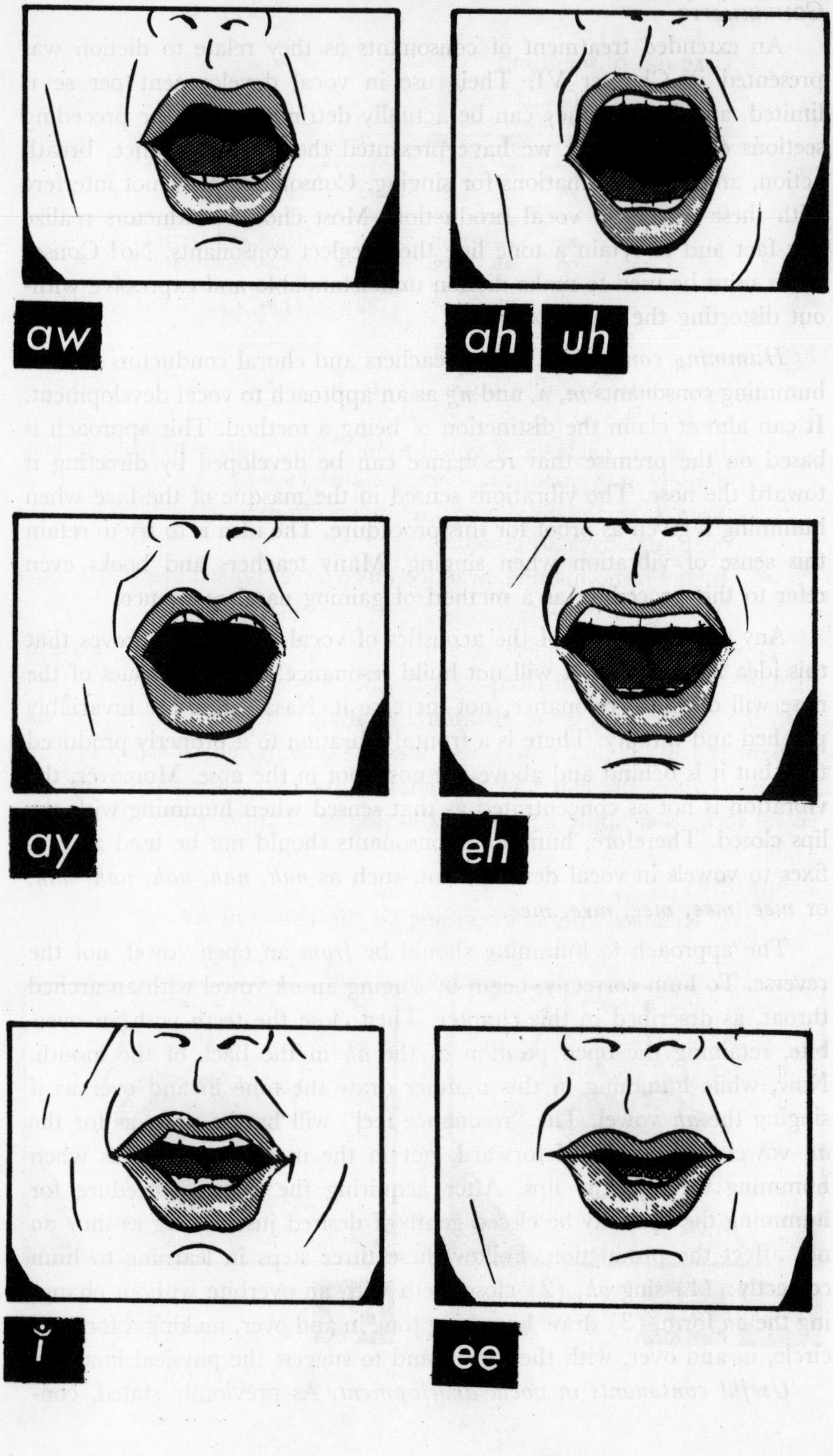
aw
ah
uh
ay
eh
i̇̆
ee

Consonants

An extended treatment of consonants as they relate to diction was presented in Chapter VI. Their use in vocal development per se is limited, and in fact, they can be actually detrimental. In the preceding sections of this chapter we have presented the basic resonance, breath action, and vowel formations for singing. Consonants must not interfere with these factors of vocal production. Most choral conductors realize this fact and to retain a tone line they neglect consonants. No! Consonants must be used to make diction understandable and expressive without distorting the singing tone.

Humming consonants. Many teachers and choral conductors use the humming consonants *m, n,* and *ng* as an approach to vocal development. It can almost claim the distinction of being a method. This approach is based on the premise that resonance can be developed by directing it toward the nose. The vibrations sensed in the masque of the face when humming is given as proof for this procedure. The idea is to try to retain this sense of vibration when singing. Many teachers and books even refer to this procedure as a method of gaining nasal resonance.

Any scientific study of the acoustics of vocal production proves that this idea is fallacious. It will not build resonance. The soft tissues of the nose will diminish resonance, not increase it. Nasal tones are invariably pinched and throaty. There is a frontal vibration to a properly produced tone but it is behind and above the nose, not in the nose. Moreover, the vibration is not as concentrated as that sensed when humming with the lips closed. Therefore, humming consonants should not be used as prefixes to vowels in vocal development, such as *nah, nah, nah, nah, nah,* or *mee, mee, mee, mee, mee.*

The approach to humming should be *from* an open vowel, not the reverse. To hum correctly, begin by singing an *ah* vowel with an arched throat, as described in this chapter. Then close the teeth with an overbite, retaining the open position of the *ah* in the back of the mouth. Now, while humming in this manner draw the tone in and over as if singing the *ah* vowel. The "resonance feel" will be the same as for the *ah* vowel very high and forward, not in the masque or nose as when humming through the lips. After acquiring the above procedure for humming the lips may be closed gently if desired just as long as they do not affect the production. Follow these three steps in learning to hum correctly: (1) sing *ah,* (2) close teeth with an overbite without changing the *ah* form, (3) draw humming tone in and over, making a forward circle, in and over, with the right hand to suggest the physical imagery.

Useful consonants in vocal development. As previously stated, consonants have a tendency to impede resonance not develop it. However, there are three consonants which may contribute to correct vowel formation, the real key to vocal production.

The aspirate *h* is helpful at the beginning of a vocalise to avoid a glottis attack or undue rigidity in the vocal action. We describe in the preceding chapter its many uses in the matter of diction. In this way it can serve to advantage in developing high notes, as in the following vocalise where it contributes to the task of keeping the low throat open. Its use will also assure the initial contact of the tone with the breath.

Vocalise 7

Progress up by half steps

The *rolled r* after a vowel is very helpful to develop the sense of an arched throat with the resulting feeling of resonance that is high and over. There is no advantage in rolling the *r* before a vowel as an aid to vocal production. That is a matter of diction discussed in the preceding chapter. When it is rolled after the *r* it tends to free the back of the tongue when it is stiff or tense, a real hindrance in opening the throat. With two fingers between the teeth, sing various descending scales using the vowel *ah* followed by a rolled *r*. This is not easy, but it pays dividends in securing freedom of the back of the tongue. Then endeavor to sing the other vowels in the same manner without the fingers.

Vocalise 8

C scale. Progress up and down by half steps

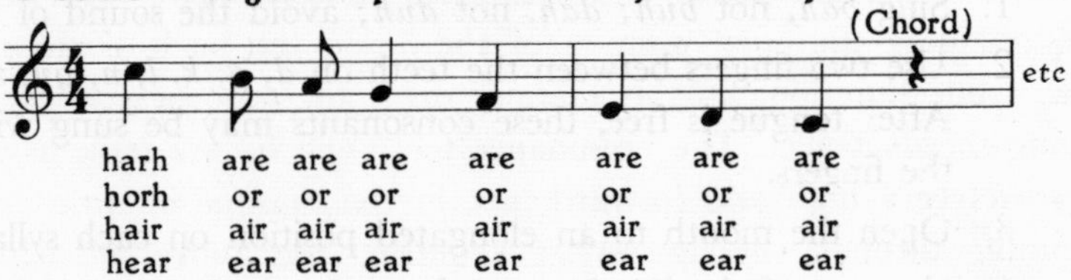

The consonant *w* is a useful one to use as a prefix to vowel study simply because it encourages the active use of the lips. It not only frees the lips but through its use they gradually assume a contour away from the teeth without being deliberately pursed. The author uses in combination the *hw* as a prefix, and the rolled *r* after a vowel: hwar.

Vocalise 9

C scale. Progress up and down by half steps

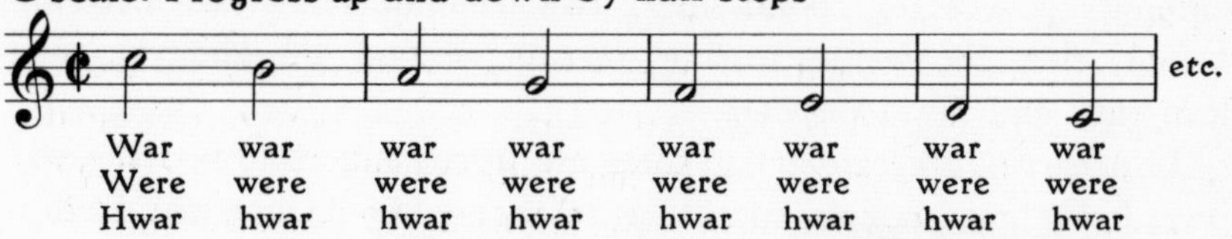

Aside from the above uses, however, consonants are a negative element in vocal production, not a positive asset. They are not to interfere with resonance, breath action and vowel formation. A choral conductor may select troublesome words from the context of the music and practice these words on the pitches of a descending scale. If difficulty is encountered the singers should sing the words without the consonants, that is, just the vowel sounds. Finally, consonants should be added without interfering with or distorting the vowel formations.

Very often it is the initial consonant that interferes with the resonance and alters the vowel sound. Going through the alphabet, as described in the following vocalise, is valuable practice in freeing the articulators so that they do not distort the tone.

Vocalise 10

C Scale, descending:

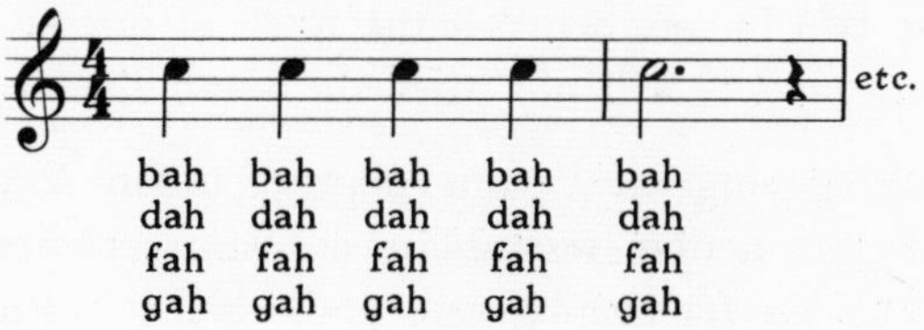

Procedure:

1. Sing *bah,* not *buh; dah,* not *duh;* avoid the sound of *uh.*
2. Use two fingers between the teeth on *d, g, k, l, n, qu,* and *t.* After tongue is free, these consonants may be sung without the fingers.
3. Open the mouth to an elongated position on each syllable.
4. Contour of the lips is away from the teeth.
5. Sing no faster than the speed at which a consistent vowel can be retained. Gradually increase tempo.

Flexibility

A flexible voice is usually a free voice. A free voice is invariably a a lovely voice. Work on flexibility, for it aids in the production of tone, besides being particularly necessary for the singing of certain compositions. For the choral singer two techniques are extremely important: first, the facility to sing *staccato;* second, the ability to sing clean runs and florid passages.

In mastering *staccato* action there are three cautions to be followed: vowel forms must remain consistent, resonance should not vary from a sustained tone, and the breath muscles must be kept firm. These conditions are obtained if the singer draws the tone in and over when singing a *staccato* tone in the same manner as singing a sustained tone. Practice the following vocalise on a descending scale. It will also give the sensation of the tone production used in *staccato* diction discussed in the preceding chapter.

Vocalise 11

C Major Scale, descending

Rather fast

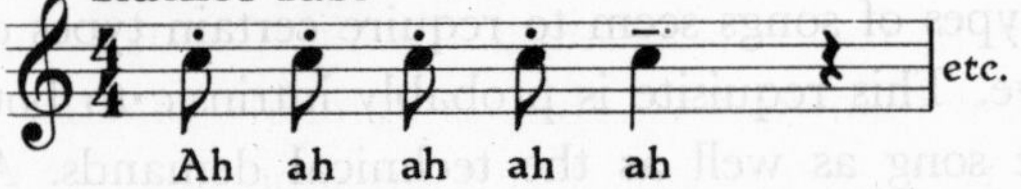

Procedure:

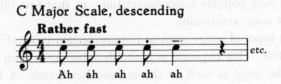

1. Use two fingers between the teeth at first so that diaphragmatic action will not alter the established resonance.

The ability to sing clear runs depends upon a combination of *staccato* and *legato* action, resembling a *semi-staccato* quality. This is the correct technique for singing runs and when it is learned the insertion of an *h* between notes will not be necessary for the chorus to sing clear runs. The degree of detachment depends upon the level of dynamics. For loud passages the run is quite detached; for soft passages the run is less detached, but it must remain clean, with a slight percussive quality on each tone. Develop this skill in the following manner.

Vocalise 12

Progress up by half steps

Rather fast

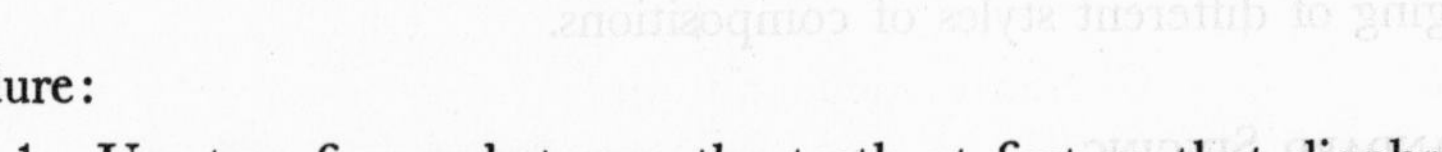

Procedure:

1. Use both parts of this vocalise to E for low voices and G for high voices.
2. Sing part *a staccato* as indicated.
3. Sing part *b* with *staccato* action, but connect the notes as indicated.

TYPES OF TONE

It has been necessary to discuss vocal production as a science based upon acoustical and physiological principles. However, singing is an art and therefore tone must respond to mood and style. Tone must vary with mood and style or else the singing of a chorus will sound the same for all types of compositions. Undoubtedly this is the reason that few opera singers can sing popular songs successfully, or that few folk singers can sing an art song artistically.

Certain types of songs seem to require certain types of tone to make them effective. This requisite is probably intrinsic to both the interpretation of the song as well as the technical demands. A look at these types of tone may be enlightening in our search for the most effective singing of different styles of compositions.

Standard Singing

There is really no term to designate the type of singing which we have presented throughout this book. Standard singing is a term loosely used to indicate the singing of music of a classic nature in contrast to popular and folk music. We have presented the principles of tone production necessary for the expressive singing of this type of music. It is sometimes referred to as a legitimate tone. We are at a loss to know what an illegitimate tone might sound like. "Legitimate" in this sense simply means the type of tone which meets the expressive and technical demands of this style of music.

In Chapter V we pointed out that this type of tone should be colored to express the mood of the composition. Some pieces require a light, lyric tone; other numbers call for a full, dramatic tone. The basic tone must be colored for onomatopoetic effects. As previously pointed out, a majestic chorus by Handel will require a different color of tone than a madrigal by Morley. These contrasts of tone color for different styles of music are all executed within the framework of the vocal technique herein described. The chorus that achieves such coloring of tone without losing its normal beauty has the basis for artistic performance.

Folk Singing

Today the radio variety of folk singer often sings with a tone that is slightly pinched and nasal. So prevalent is this practice that this style of music is often identified with this type of tone. The tone is usually very individual and sometimes quite appealing. Also, there is a nonchalant quality about the tone.

Many composers and arrangers are arranging folk music for concert performances by choral groups. It is not necessary to emulate the tone of the average folk singer in singing these arrangements. Most of them should be sung with a tone correctly produced in accordance with the standards of fine voices. The tone of the opera singer, as popularly conceived is certainly not apropos. Neither is the tone of the so-called "over-trained" singers. To retain the folk character the tone must seem effortless and more natural, if we may use that word.

Occasionally, it seems appropriate to introduce a little humor in the arrangements of American folk songs to mimic for a phrase or two the nasal twang associated with these songs. This tonal device for contrast might be used for an entire, short number but it becomes wearing to an audience very quickly. In the following arrangement the author often uses this folksy effect, as indicated in the excerpt.

Example 79

Sourwood Mountain

American folk song

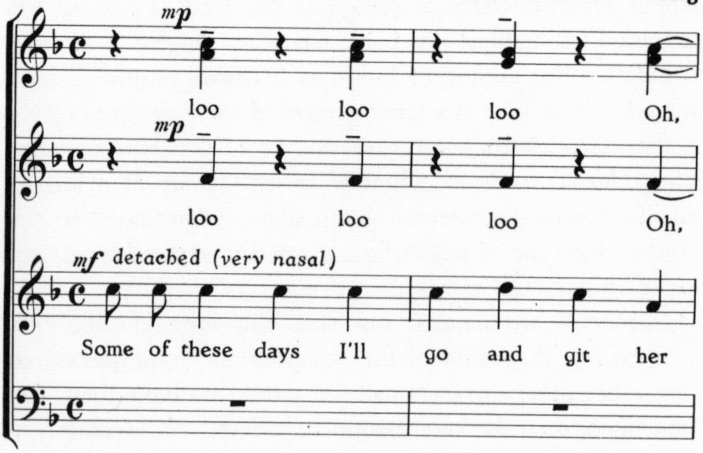

Barber-Shop Singing

At the national contests of the SPEBSQSA (see Chapter I) the author has listened to the quartet finalists, where each one had a different type of tone. One quartet might sing with a nasal quality, another with a strident quality, another with a more "legitimate" tone. In this style of singing the indispensable factor is blend and balance. The type of tone seems secondary. The opera singer is out of place. Voices with tremolos and wobbles are anathema. The most successful quartets seem to be those with a concentrated focus of tone where each member of the quartet produces the voice exactly the same. One quartet which enjoys an international reputation, however, sings with a lovely, lyric quality, but the blend is perfect.

The barber-shop male glee clubs being sponsored by SPEBSQSA which are mushrooming all over the country seem to use a more standard quality of tone. As a result they are not as individual as the quartets except in appearance. Singing with a more legitimate tone enables these glee clubs to expand their repertory, and does not limit them to the barber-shop arrangements of old popular songs which is the preferred diet for these groups.

Popular Singing

Some popular singers have very acceptable voices, but many sing with a tone that is decidedly throaty and consistently a little flat in pitch. Also, the popular singer uses a minimum of vibrato. It seems to be the approved type of tone for this style of singing. Certainly the trained voice with a tremolo or wobble is out of character singing these songs. Popular ensembles usually sing with a tone that approximates that of the soloist.

Many choruses are singing arrangements of popular songs on their programs. For the most part, these are the better type of songs from the Broadway shows. There is no reason for emulating the voice of the popular singer in performing these arrangements. A legitimate tone is most appropriate.

Some choirs are endeavoring to cater to popular musical tastes by imitating radio and television groups. If the conductor trains his group to sing with the prevalent popular tone in singing arrangements of the current popular songs, he is taking a chance on jeopardizing the performance of more permanent repertory. Few groups can sing both types of music equally well. Deliberately developing a popular tone with the group is not wise procedure unless the repertory is to be limited to this type of music.

COMMENTARY

It is very difficult to describe the principles of voice production with sufficient clarity to be useful to the reader. Probably no other technique in any field is surrounded with such an aura of mystery and confusion. Beware of false choral prophets with heretical tonal ideas. By their musical fruits ye shall know them. Voice cannot be taught in a step-by-step sequence, but there can be organization in developing a choral tone. Let us review the sequence of this organization.

Make your vocal goal a fusion of tonal and physical imagery.

Naturalness is the result of correct vocal production.

Extended range in pitch and dynamics, flexibility, intonation, and durability are the tests of a free tone.

Correct posture begets correct tone production.

Devote your immediate attention to the establishing of full and ringing resonance.

Practice the principles of breathing as they relate to establishing resonance.

Produce all vowels in a form consistent with a singing resonance.

Articulate consonants without interfering with vowel formation.

Develop flexibility of the voice to give it added beauty.

Vary the normal tone of the chorus only for some special vocal effect.

Without tone there is no mood; without mood there is no emotion; without emotion there is no music.

Chapter VIII
Special Vocal Problems

The preceding chapter was devoted to the general principles of vocal production. If voices are developed along the lines of the method prescribed, special problems will be reduced to a minimum. Regardless of the efficacy of a general method used with choral groups, there will certainly arise vocal difficulties that puzzle the conductors. In this chapter we hope to anticipate these sundry problems which will confront him in connection with the voices of the singers in these groups. These problems are presented neither in order of importance nor of frequency, but most of them will appear during the career of a choral conductor.

USES OF HUMMING

In the preceding chapter the use of the humming consonants *m, n,* and *ng* as agents for developing resonance was discussed. The belief that humming develops resonance was shown to be a fallacy. The futility of using the humming consonants as prefixes to vocalises for this purpose was explained. A kind of resonance will result from continuous practice of this nature but it is the wrong kind, usually pinched, nasal, and throaty. The correct method of humming was also described in Chapter VI. Review this presentation.

Correct humming does have some constructive uses, however. Fast, light humming vocalises are valuable to give singers a sense of the vocal adjustment necessary to do flexible work. The same type of exercise is valuable for giving men a sense of singing high pitches. Adhering to the law of acoustics, humming should never be used in the development of the high notes of treble voices. (This is discussed at the end of this section.) All of this type of humming should be soft and light and in a "head-voice" quality. Such humming gives a correct sense of a vocal embouchure, that is, an adjustment of the vocal chords. (The vocal embouchure is similar to the lip embouchure of a brass player.) This same vocal adjustment should be sensed when singing flexible passages or soft phrases. We repeat that humming is not used to develop resonance but it may be used to obtain a sense of vocal adjustment for flexible and soft work.

Humming passages written by an arranger or a composer are invariably soft. If he wishes a neutral sound that is loud he will indicate an open vowel sound. As it is very difficult to produce the voice correctly when humming loudly, it is best avoided. Therefore, if a section in a composition is soft and *legato,* humming the section very quietly will give the singers a feeling of the mood. Insist that they sing the words with the same vocal adjustment, not resonance, in order that the mood may be retained. This is a very quick device to tone down a choir for a *pianissimo* passage.

Humming is valuable for practicing parts and for obtaining a blend of harmony. Soft humming enables singers to hear each other more clearly. There is greater uniformity of quality when choristers hum than when singing vowels; therefore, the blend of harmony is more discernible. Also, the resonance of humming is quite pointed and pitches are more distinct.

Arrangers should never write humming for treble voices above top-line F. However, conductors will encounter humming passages written for higher notes because many arrangers do not understand the vocal difficulty involved. The vocal difficulty lies in the acoustical fact that the resonance cavities, functioning like an organ-pipe, cannot adjust to the higher pitches when treble voices hum with their lips closed. Treble voices have three ways in which they may hum high notes: (1) open the lips and hum through the teeth in the manner prescribed in the preceding chapter; (2) hum on a *v* sound with the upper teeth overlapping on the lower lip; (3) open the mouth and hum on an *ng* sound. Any one of the methods permits the throat as a resonator to adjust to the higher pitches.

UNSTEADY VOICES

The tone of a choral group should have life, which means that it should have *vibrato. Vibrato* is the slight variation of resonance that results from the on and offness of nerve pulsation enabling the vocal muscles to function. The variation affects vowel quality, dynamics and pitch. Beauty of tone really depends upon the nature of the *vibrato.*

Tremolo, or wobble in the voice, is the result of the wavering of some muscle or an unsteady deviation in the resonating column. This causes a corresponding wavering in the tone. If it is a small muscle, the wavering will be fast and the effect is called a *tremolo*. If the muscle is a larger one the wavering will be slower, and is referred to as a wobble. Wavering of the tongue causes a *tremolo*. A slight shaking of the head will cause a *tremolo* or a wobble, depending upon the extent and speed of shake. Undue shaking of the breathing or body muscles due to tension will result in a wobble. All of these waverings are the result of muscular tension and result in unsteady and unblending voices.

Young voices seldom have *tremolos* and wobbles. These vocal heresies are an affliction of poor technical training. Often it is the result of endeavoring to develop too quickly a young voice into a mature sound. If the balance between resonance and breath is lost, then tension arises with the unsteady vocal complications.

Voices with marked *tremolos* and wobbles are almost a curse in a choral group. In the first place singers so afflicted are usually insecure in pitch, or we should say, it is difficult to ascertain which pitch they are singing. Secondly, these voices, as a rule, do not blend. The basic quality of a voice may be good, but it will usually stand out if it has a *tremolo* or wobble. Moreover, such voices usually have difficulty in singing flexible passages with facility and clear articulation.

The elimination of *tremolos* and wobbles that have become fixed habits is very difficult, and may necessitate extreme measures. The victims must develop the sensation of more breath against the tone. As a precautionary measure to avoid the unwelcome appearance of any unsteadiness in the voices the author works with the entire chorus. Women's voices are more susceptible than men's to this vocal specter. The general procedure is as follows:

1. Request the choir to whistle a sustained tone on third-space C. Singing is similar to whistling through the vocal chords.
2. Expel the breath on a sustained inaudible *ha*.
3. Sing the same pitch on *hoo* with the same breath action, using two fingers (see p. 164) to insure correct vowel form.
4. Imitate the sound of a hoot owl or a steamboat whistle. (This gives imagery of straight tone.)
5. Continue this exercise on each note of the descending scale.
6. Transfer this technique to the long notes in the compositions being studied.
7. Practice this technique on chords at the end of phrases and sections. These are the notes where the singers are running out of breath and unsteadiness is likely to appear.
8. Retain this technique in all sustained singing.

The author has had striking success in eliminating *tremolos* and wobbles with this technique, as well as securing a steadier tone within an entire choral group. It requires patience, but it will pay dividends in tone and blend.

VOCAL REGISTERS

An understanding of the registers of the voice is of paramount importance if a choral conductor is to develop efficient procedures of singing techniques. No other single aspect of vocal production is so misunderstood or enjoys such variance of opinion. Writers and teachers in the past have differed widely on the matter of registration. Some hold staunchly to the premise that there is but one register throughout the voice, while others point out that there are as many as ten or twelve. The most popular number is three registers: head, middle (or mouth), and chest.

This latter conception of registers is based upon the sensations of resonance. The latest scientific findings indicate that there are two registers in every type of voice and that they are based upon muscular action, with a resultant difference in resonance between the two registers. These two registers are usually referred to as the lower and upper (or *falsetto*) registers.

Briefly, the muscular adjustment for the lower register functions for low and loud tones; the adjustment for the upper register functions for high and soft tones. The soprano part is written primarily in the upper register. Consequently full, rich tones in a soprano voice must be developed. If a soprano voice avoids the use of the lower register in singing low tones this part of the voice will become breathy and anemic. The alto part lies in both registers. That is the reason for the so-called break in the alto voice usually around the *D* above middle *C*. The registers must be coordinated to avoid this break. The tenor part also lies in both registers. Therefore, the tenor must resort to singing *falsetto* on all high notes or he is confronted with the problem of developing the muscles to adjust to singing high, loud tones. The bass part lies primarily in the low register. This is the reason so many basses find it difficult to sing high, soft tones. These must be developed.

The above discussion is quite technical but perhaps we can explain further with some practical suggestions. The upper register is associated with the head voice and light, lyric resonance, the lower with the chest voice and strong, virile resonance. If the vocal procedures in Chapter VII are mastered, few problems will arise over vocal registration. Correct vowel formation, proper resonance and firm breathing muscles are insurance against vocal difficulties attributed to registration. All voices should be trained throughout both registers.

Soprano

The soprano is normally a light, lyric voice. If developed too quickly into a heavy, dramatic voice the muscles of the upper register become over-weighted and as a result *tremolos* and wobbles usually appear. Therefore, in a choral group retain for most singing the normal light, lyric quality in the soprano section. In developing low tones carry the resonance of the top voice into the low registration. When uncontrolled, the heavier quality of the low register is unattractive in soprano voices.

Alto

The "alto break" is partly a result of the vocal line lying just in between the two registers. If alto choristers attempt to carry the low register too high, as do many female jazz singers, the voice will become rough and raucous. In a chorus, the solution is to carry the alto quality of the top voice into the low voice. Do not permit the chest tone to "grab" too suddenly. Then the alto section will gradually gain a rich quality and a blending of color.

Tenor

The tenor part lies in the upper region of the low register. However, when it is used continuously, the muscles become tired and the tone becomes tight and strident. Continual forcing of these muscles causes flatting. Tenors, especially young tenors, should be encouraged to use the *falsetto* voice on high tones in a chorus. This is the normal, natural thing to do. It eliminates forcing. Balance the other parts with the tenor section. The author often instructs the tenor section to "take it easy" during rehearsals. As the tenor voices are developed they may sing the high tones with more virility. It is for this reason that tenors are said to be made, not born. In fact, there are many tenors in high school choirs today that sing baritone because they have not had the instruction to enable them to learn to sing high notes with ease. This omnipresent problem is just over the horizon in our discussion.

Bass

The bass part usually lies in the low and middle part of the lower register of the voice. Because of the *tessitura* of the part, bass voices have a tendency to become closed and heavy. Open them up! Develop high tones with a lyric quality. Utilize the *falsetto* register in developing a conception of high notes the same as with the tenors. Basses tend to cut off all top resonance from their voice. Develop the feeling of archness and overness in the resonance, as described in the preceding chapter.

SINGING ON PITCH

In Chapter IV we pointed out several immediate and general measures which may be used to alleviate, but not eliminate, the vocal sin, poor intonation. It is reviewed in Chapter V in the section on accompanied and unaccompanied singing. It is referred to intermittently in other chapters. In this chapter we will present it in light of the effect tone production has upon it. There are three factors which cause most of the off-pitch and out-of-tune singing: (1) listless physical habits, (2) poor musicianship, and (3) faulty tone.

Listless Physical Habits

Naturally, we are referring to physical habits as applied to singing, although they undoubtedly reflect an attitude in all aspects of life. Physical habits in singing are related to correct posture. As we indicated in the preceding chapter, posture can be erect without being alert. Raising the windows will not cure off-pitch singing in itself but if the fresh air makes the singers more alert, then it may have a positive effect.

Alertness, like enthusiasm, is contagious. If the conductor is alert it may arouse the choristers from their lethargy. Alertness is not a synonym for drive. It is a mental attitude, not a demonstration of physical energy to the point of exhaustion. An alert mind will generate an alert body.

Alertness is evidenced in facial expressions. When eyes are open and bright, choristers are interested. The faces of choristers should not drip and droop; they should literally be lifted as if in the act of looking surprised. We jokingly remark that every singer should look surprised if a tone comes out. The author also uses this device: "push up your cheeks with the palms of your hands; now push up the sides of your head above the ears; leave your faces up there for the remainder of the rehearsal." Or, "lift your cheek bones into the crow's feet of your eyes!" The physical manifestations of alertness sometimes foster a more permanent attitude of alertness. This attitude and physical habit will help offset flatting in pitch.

Poor Musicianship

Music is primarily an aural art. Choristers must learn to hear if they are to sing on pitch. Singing in tune is not an accident; some attention must be given to it! It is amazing how many singers and choirs cannot even sing a single tone on pitch. That is the first step, by the way. Play single pitches on the piano in different ranges of the voice. Have the choir sing them on different vowels. Point out when they are off pitch. Use vocal procedures described in the preceding chapter which will correct the production, which will correct the tone, which will correct the pitch.

Chord Tuning

The above practice should be transferred to the singing of chords. Chords should be sung somewhat softly, so that the choristers can hear each other. Sustain the chords. Pull this part up and that one down until the chord is in tune and on pitch. The chorus will catch breaths as they need them. Sometimes it is amusing as well as instructive to suggest that certain parts sing a little off pitch (indicate whether sharp or flat) and then gradually correct the pitch until the chord is in tune. The other parts must hold their pitch true. This practice teaches the choristers to listen.

Here are a few chord drills which can be practiced. The conductor may also originate others for his particular choral group.

Vocalise 13

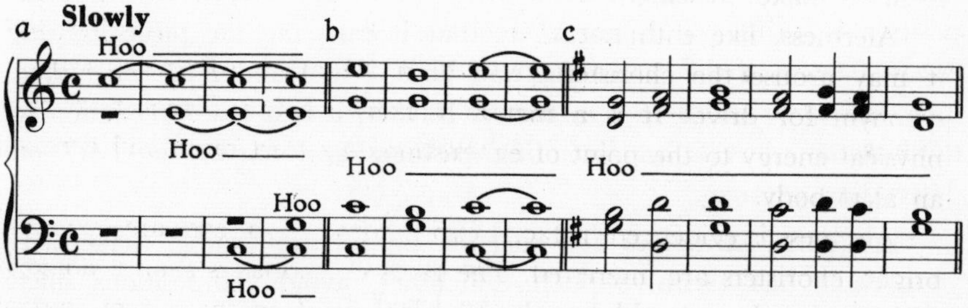

Procedures:

1. Use all vowels. Blend is easier on *ooh,* but do not neglect open vowels.
2. Ascend by half steps with Exercise *a* until the sopranos and basses reach G.
3. Sing Exercises *b* and *c* in the minor mode, as well as other keys.
4. Use various dynamic levels from *p* to *f*.
5. Sing very slowly. Hold each chord until it is in tune. Stagger the breaths.

Apply the above drill to chords in the compositions being rehearsed, especially those chords which are sustained or held. If the chord is *forte,* sing it softly until it is in tune; then the dynamic level may be raised. A chorus that consistently practices with a loud tone will invariably sing out-of-tune! Proceed in the same manner to passages causing difficulty in the music. Hum or vocalize softly on these passages. The goal should be to develop listening habits.

Major or minor. It is interesting to note that choral groups usually sing better in tune in major keys than in minor keys. This observation infers that accustomed hearing affects intonation directly, for choristers are more used to singing and listening to pieces in major keys. By far the larger number of songs in elementary school books and in the choral repertory of school choirs is in major keys.

Therefore, do not limit your vocalises and exercises in chord tuning to major keys. Practice the various ascending and descending minor scales on a neutral syllable, *loo* or *lah.* Also, deliberately select compositions in minor keys for practice, even if these particular numbers are not used on programs. If your group has pitch troubles, avoid a number in a minor key for an exacting performance or a music contest.

Melodic intervals. Some choral groups sing off pitch because they do not hear the sound of a half-step and other melodic intervals. To develop keener discrimination of pitch, practice the singing of major and minor scales. If a choir cannot sing in tune the scale in which a composition is written, it is not likely that it can sing the piece in tune either. Beware of the descending half-steps, 8 to 7 and 4 to 3 in major, 8 to 7, 6 to 5, and 3 to 2 in minor. In fact, it is a wise precaution to think wide intervals on ascending passages and narrow intervals on descending passages.

Chromatic harmonies and melodic figures are trouble makers. If your choir has excessive pitch difficulties, avoid compositions filled with chromatic progressions. There is ample repertory in diatonic harmony until the singers have had a little more experience. It is usually the half step that causes the trouble. Practice the chromatic scale slowly on *lah.* The choristers must hear half steps. Play the troublesome chromatic passages on the piano for the singers to hear; then practice it out of context. Finally, sing the entire phrase or section; if the singers can hear the passage, they will probably sing it in tune.

Wide ascending skips are also a consistent cause of pitch ailments. Tell the choristers to sing on top of the upper note. Instruct them to stretch to the upper note. Tell them to raise their eyes and ears. Caution them to sing the pitch of the consonant on the same pitch as the vowel. (Discussed in Chapter VI.) If the upper note begins with a vowel, introduce a slight aspirate *h.* If the singers hear the interval accurately, then it is only a matter of energizing themselves to reach the upper note.

Faulty Tone

If physical habits are listless and musicianship is poor, the tone will probably be faulty. A good tone, as well as pitch, is dependent upon accurate hearing. Many singers cannot or will not hear themselves mentally. (Perhaps the conductor should not be too harsh in these instances.) As a result, pitch difficulties can be more directly attributed to faulty tone than to any other single factor.

Singing flat. By far the most prevalent habit of singing off pitch is that of flatting. We have presented many immediate devices for correcting it. The basic cause is faulty tone. The first step is to open the resonators so that the tone will be supported by the breath. Heaviness and thickness must be removed from the resonance. The upper throat must be arched, that is, a high palate position, and the sense of the resonance must be high and forward. The sensation of resonance in front of the mouth, in the nose, or under the tongue indicates that the circle of resonance is partially closed and the feel of resonance is not sufficiently "high" and "over." Refer to sections on "Resonance" and "Breathing" in the preceding chapter.

In *forte* singing, "snore" the tone. Line the voices on an *aw* color. Draw the tone "in" and "over." Words are pronounced with elongated movement of jaw and relatively round lips. In loud singing the tendency is to sharp, not flat. The type of tone described should maintain the pitch.

If the resonance is closed, muffled, nasal, or pinched as a result of partially closed resonators, choristers will flat when singing softly. Under such conditions there can be no support with the breath action. Singers have a tendency to energize themselves insufficiently when singing softly, permitting the pharynx to collapse and eliminating open resonance and breath support. When singing softly, show the upper teeth; it helps to take the weight off the voice. "Snarl" the tone. Line the voices on an *ah,* not an *uh,* color. An *uh* color will invariably close the voice and in soft singing it will pull the pitch down. Listen to your choir! If the voices are lined on an *uh* color when singing softly, they will invariably flat. Do not neglect to draw the breath "in" and "over." Elongated movement of the jaw should be reduced to a minimum. Pronounce the words sideways, as if they are coming out of the cheekbones. Choristers should memorize this formula: alert posture + accurate hearing + high-arched tone eliminates flatting of pitch.

Singing sharp. If voices are too open or slightly strident they will usually sharp in high, *forte* passages. Pinched and nasal voices would react in the same way except that they cannot sing loud because of the restricted production. Such voices do not have the balance between resonance and breath. Therefore, when endeavoring to sing loud or high they must force the breath in order to make the tone and this often causes the voices to sharp slightly.

As suggested in the preceding section, line the voices on an *aw* form. Sing with a more elongated position of the jaw. Draw the breath "in" and "over" to counteract forcing of the breath. If choral groups sharp when singing softly, it is invariably a matter of accurate hearing, not tone production. The same basic tonal fault which causes pinched, nasal, closed, or strident voices to sharp when singing loudly will cause them to flat when singing softly. The pharynx is partially closed, the circle of resonance is not completed, and there is no support of the tone.

Singing out-of-tune. If the tone is correct, then singing out-of-tune is a matter of accurate hearing. If there are objectionable *tremolos* and wobbles in voices, it is very difficult to discover which pitch they are singing. If the voices are dark and hollow the pitch has no center and intonation is vague. The pitch can be determined in nasal, pinched, or strident voices, but it is usually off. A tone that has center results from an open-arched throat and proper breath support; this is the one which enables a choral group to sing in tune.

EXTENDING THE PITCH RANGE

There are many voices with a medium pitch range that have an acceptable quality, but few voices seem to be able to maintain a fine tone in the extreme parts of their range. Still, the ability of high voices to sing lyric and dramatic high notes and low voices to sing full, sonorous low notes gives distinctiveness to a choral performance. All voices are trained alike in the middle part of the range. It is in the extremes of the range that one finds variation. This section is devoted to this special problem.

Singing High Notes

There are several negative factors which arise as a result of the inability of choral conductors to develop the high notes of the choristers. First of all, it places limitations on the available worthwhile literature which the choir can sing. Also, the sections with a high *tessitura* suffer because of the singers' lack of ability to cope adequately with the notes in the upper range of the voice. Secondly, to compensate for this technical limitation, arrangers lower the keys of compositions and insert optional notes in the high parts. The lowering of the keys is a partial reason for the prevalence of flatting. It is also sufficient reason for any choral conductor to raise the pitch of any arrangement. Often the piece is merely restored to its original key. Finally, most climaxes are set in the upper *tessitura* of the voices. Part of the thrill of singing is lost if the choristers cannot rise to stirring climaxes. Some of the emotional and aesthetic values of singing are diminished through the inability to sing high notes.

Sing compositions in the keys in which your choral groups sing them best. Do not permit high notes, unless they are excessive, to frighten you away from the performance of a worthy selection. The practice of arranging choral music in lower keys is actually hurting voices. Young people must not get the idea that they cannot sing high. There is no danger of straining voices if they are taught to sing lightly on high tones until their voices are developed.

Treble voices. It is relatively easy to train treble voices (sopranos and altos) to sing high notes. The procedure is to open the throat so that there will be no interference with the action of the large breathing muscles. Acoustically, all vowels gravitate toward an *ah* color as the pitch ascends. Therfore the mouth is opened long and wide on extreme high tones. Vowels need not be deliberately altered to *ah* on high notes, but should be sung in an *ah* vowel form and mouth position while retaining some of their individual color.

Do not use humming or prefixes of humming consonants to develop high notes in treble voices. In singing high notes consistent with the laws of acoustics the resonating column must shorten. This is impossible when the tone is coming out of the nose, as in humming with the lips closed. It is this shortening of the resonating column that gives treble voices the sensation of singing out of the top of their head on high notes. The resonance does not seem to be concentrated high and forward as on lower notes. The resonance seems to fall back, not down, on high notes.

There are many exercises which can be used to develop the high notes of treble voices. The following one is simple. Regardless of the exercise the procedure is as follows: open the resonators, especially the lower throat, gradually alter all tones toward an *ah* color, support the tone with firm breath muscles.

Vocalise 14

Ascend by half-steps to high C

Procedures:

1. Use the deep-set *ooh* vowel at first to secure opening of the lower throat. The use of the aspirate *h* on high notes prevents carrying up too much weight and assures the impact of the breath against the tone. Use two fingers between the teeth to obtain an open mouth position and eliminate the raising of the head or the protruding of the chin. While singing the skip to the high note, push down and out with the right arm, palm down. This prevents lifting or straining with the breath muscles.
2. Use a deep-set *ah* vowel to get the sensation of color on all high notes. If the jaw is especially rigid or the mouth small, use three fingers between teeth. The mouth must be open on high notes! The entire head seems filled with resonance. Again, push down and forward with the right arm. It prevents the body from becoming tense and assures correct breath action.
3. The *ooh* vowel encourages open lower throat and the *ah* vowel produces the correct resonance for high tones. The aspirate *h* assures correct breath action. Attack the high note rather softly, making an immediate *crescendo*. Attacking high notes softly gives a more correct adjustment of the vocal action. Eliminate the fingers and the arm action. Use a mirror to see that the mouth opens long, at least the width of two fingers. Some of the upper teeth should show.

With treble voices the greatest problem is not the singing of high notes, but the singing of high notes and pronunciation of words at the same time. This is not possible unless the circle of resonance is completely open and properly supported by the breath. When this condition is attained, then the movement of the articulators, lips, tongue and jaw, will not interfere or change the resonance. The jaw must be opened on every vowel, regardless of the consonant which tries to prevent it.

Practice the following exercises until freedom of the jaw is secured. Then vocalize on the words set to high notes in the compositions being rehearsed in the same manner. When these places become set in the voice, that is, when the singers have a physical imagery of how they feel, there will be no difficulty in performing them when singing the entire composition.

Vocalise 15

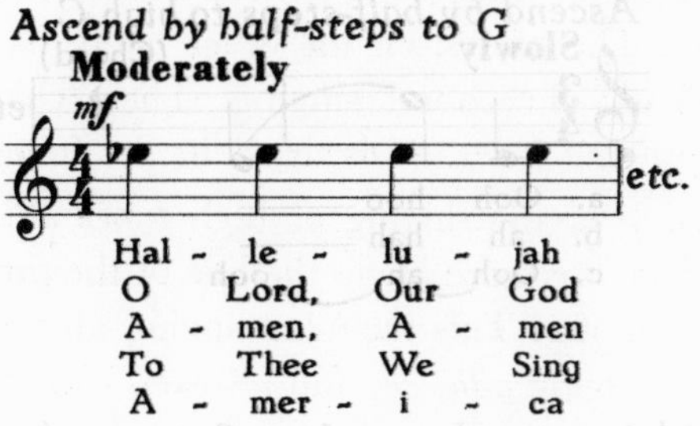
Ascend by half-steps to G
Moderately
mf
etc.
Hal - le - lu - jah
O Lord, Our God
A - men, A - men
To Thee We Sing
A - mer - i - ca

Procedures:

1. Recite the words in rhythm, opening the mouth very long on each syllable. This distorts speech, but it is exactly the physical feeling of pronouncing words on high notes.

2. Sing the words in the vocalise with two fingers between the teeth. It is impossible to pronounce words distinctly with this procedure but it gives the feeling of tonal resonance which must be retained in singing high notes.

3. Now sing the vocalise without the fingers, dropping the jaw on each syllable as in (1), with the same sense of tonal resonance as in (2).

4. Extend the vocalise up to a high B♭ in the same manner.

5. This exercise can be practiced only a few minutes at each rehearsal.

Male voices. The general principles of vocal production apply equally to treble voices and changed male voices except for the singing of high notes. All of the high notes in treble voices lie in the upper register and simply need to be opened up and strengthened. The high notes of a male voice also lie in the upper or *falsetto* register. However, the *falsetto* quality is not acceptable as a virile tone from a male singer. It can be reinforced and strengthened but it always sounds like the voice of a female impersonator. The tenors of the Russian male choirs demonstrate how this tone can be used artistically. This tone is also used extensively by male singers in the Arabic countries in singing their native songs. To develop high, virile, manlike tones, tenors and basses must learn to sing high tones with the lower registration. This requires training and muscular development of the voice.

There is no difference in the training of tenors and basses to sing high tones. However, in choral singing the *tessitura* of the tenor part is high most of the time. Therefore, tenors must be very proficient in singing high tones. The basses, on the other hand, have few high tones which cause difficulty in choral singing. Their chief concern is the singing of resonant low tones. (Discussed in the following section).

As a preparation to the singing of high tones all male voices must be taught to produce the voice along the line of the procedures described in the preceding chapter. This includes singing all vowels with a high-arched resonance; singing *ooh, ee,* and *i* vowels closed; singing all other vowels open and with an elongated position of the mouth, except on very soft tones; and the development of firm breathing muscles resulting from correct posture.

Male voices can sing high notes in three ways: (1) use of the *falsetto* tone, (2) expelling a good, healthy yell and (3) use of the "covered" tone. For the sake of clarification we will deal with each one separately although high notes may have the mixed qualities of all three tones.

The falsetto tone. A high tone in a male voice produced softly will normally be a *falsetto* tone. It is a tone produced with the upper register of the voice. It is a very lyric tone of light texture. Boys consider it to be effeminate in sound, and consequently often resent singing *falsetto.* Nevertheless it is the normal production for changed male voices to use on high tones. It is both easy and natural.

Unless a voice has been strained or forced from wrong use of the low registration practically all voices, both tenors and basses can sing high notes *falsetto* with ease. They need only be instructed to sing very softly on the high notes and the *falsetto* register will function automatically. It will be an anemic and flutelike tone until it is developed, but it will sound, besides usually being on pitch. If male voices are forcing and flatting on high notes, encourage them to sing *falsetto* until they have learned to sing these notes with a stronger tone that is not forced. In tenor parts of an extremely high *tessitura* the tenors should resort almost exclusively to the *falsetto,* or light head voice. In the extreme high range it will sound through any choral group. Top tenors of professional male quartets and male choirs resort to this tone continuously.

The following exercises demonstrate the use of this voice, as well as indicate its use in the development of a more virile tone on high notes. Basses have little use for this *falsetto* voice in choral singing, but practice on these exercises is very beneficial in developing a lyric quality, ease, and freedom on high, soft tones.

Vocalise 16

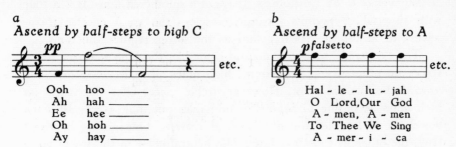

a

Ascend by half-steps to high C

Ooh hoo ______
Ah hah ______
Ee hee ______
Oh hoh ______
Ay hay ______

b

Ascend by half-steps to A

Hal - le - lu - jah
O Lord, Our God
A - men, A - men
To Thee We Sing
A - mer - i - ca

Procedures:

1. Sing the first exercise very softly. (No fingers needed.) Use the aspirate *h* to attack the high tone. Chin should not be raised or protrude. If anyone has a voice that won't "let go" instruct the singer to imitate a steamboat whistle on a high tone. He will immediately get the sense of the *falsetto* register. Carry this exercise to high C in all voices. Very few men will have difficulty in singing this high in the *falsetto* voice.

2. Sing the second exercise in the same *falsetto* quality on selected words. Ascend by half steps to high C. Sing phrases of extreme high *tessitura* in compositions being studied in the same manner. Do not attempt to sing loud in the *falsetto.*

The yell. It may seem strange to discuss the yell in a book on singing. However, the high tones of male voices in some choral groups resemble a yell when sung loudly. A yell is nature's way to make a loud noise in the higher range of a male voice while using the lower register. It is very useful when giving warning of the approach of a lion, or for cheering at football games. Needless to say, it has little function in a choral group.

In making a yell the chin goes up with the pitch, the mouth is spread wide, and the tone is forced out. In the process extrinsic muscles adjust the vocal action permitting the low register to function. It can be demonstrated by using the preceding vocalise with the octave skip on the vowel *ah.* The octave on *F* or *G* are good pitches for such demonstration. Male voices should sing the exercise in this manner a few times to realize physically and tonally the production they should avoid in singing virile high notes.

The "covered" tone. The term "covered" is in quotation marks because so much confusion is associated with it. The "covered" tone used by all well-trained male voices to sing virile high notes does not resemble the dark tone often used by sopranos in the upper middle part of their voices to obtain fullness. It is not a smothered tone. It is a tone with ring which permits intrinsic muscles (the vocal chords, themselves) to adjust the vocal action as the lower register functions.

The "covered" tone is a neutral color like the high notes of treble voices. In other words, on extreme high notes all male voices gravitate toward this neutral color. However, treble voices alter the vowel on high notes according to acoustical principles but male voices alter the vowel on high notes for physiological reasons. One abides by tonal laws, the other by muscular laws. The neutral color in the treble voice is *ah,* in the male voice it is *unh.*

Little scientific study has been made on the production of this tone. It is the stock in trade of all fine male singers, for it enables them to sing high notes with a virile, manlike tone without tension or forcing. In only a few voices do these tones seem to be natural, therefore in most they must be developed. The procedure is to gain a sense of the resonance and then to develop the muscles necessary for the execution of the covered tone. When this quality is developed, tenors and basses have little trouble with high notes. With the absence of strain, and the singing of *oo, ee,* and *i* vowels closed as previously suggested, the prevalent flatting in male voices on high notes will usually disappear.

Vocalise 17

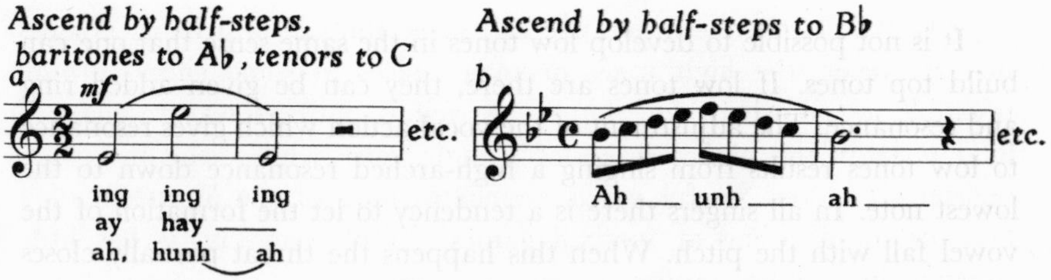

Procedures:

1. Review the first exercise, under *falsetto* tone. It is excellent preparation for developing the "covered" tone.
2. Use two fingers between the teeth on the first exercise to assure a free jaw. The jaw must not be tense.
3. The "covered" tone has nasal resonance. The *ing,* as in sing, will give the correct sensation for this resonance. Use two fingers between the teeth. This will release the voice and free the tongue. Try to retain the virility of the voice. (It may break into *falsetto* on extremely high tones until the vocal muscles are developed).

4. Sing *ay* in the same manner as *ing*, using two fingers between the teeth at first. This vowel is the best and most natural one for developing the "covered" quality. It is simply the *ay* vowel sung with the nasal resonance.
5. Retain the same covered sensation in singing *ah* and other vowels. On the octave skip the vowel seems to shift as follows: *ah-unh-ah*. Be sure to return to an open vowel on the low tone. (Tenors do not cover lower than high G.)
6. Exercise 2 under Vocalise 16 above, demonstrates changing into the covered tone and returning to the open vowel. A five-tone scale is used. When the high note is soft, keep all of the tones open. When the high tone is loud, change into the covered tone and return to the open tone on the descending scale.
7. The "covered" tone must be retained when pronouncing words on high notes at a dynamic level of *mf* and *f*. The skill will come easily after these tones are developed.
8. Carry these exercises up to *F* for basses, *G* for baritones, and *A* or *B♭* for tenors,
9. All male voices should sing open up to fourth line *D*. Basses should cover on *E♭* or *E*; baritones should cover on *E* or *F*; all tenors should sing open up to *F* and cover on *F♯* or *G*.

Developing Low Tones

It is not possible to develop low tones in the same sense that one can build top tones. If low tones are there, they can be given added ring and resonance. The adjustment of the vocal action which gives resonance to low tones results from singing a high-arched resonance down to the lowest note. In all singers there is a tendency to let the formation of the vowel fall with the pitch. When this happens the throat partially closes with a resultant effect on the vocal action. The tone produced is breathy, fuzzy, and with no center; especially on the extreme low tones. These low tones need what is often referred to as a "bite" in the tone.

In developing low tones a five-tone descending scale is sufficient for all voices. Sopranos and altos should sing on an *aw* vowel so that the break between the two registers is reduced to a minimum. Do not permit the "chest" voice to grab suddenly with a raucous quality. The rough, jazz tone has no place in choral singing. Tenors and basses should sing on an *ah* vowel keeping the high, arched resonance. This practice will put ring in the extreme, lowest note. In all voices the mouth is relatively closed in singing low tones.

Vocalise 18

Procedures:

1. Sopranos and altos use the *aw* vowel. Retain a high-arched resonance. Do not permit vowel form to drop in descending. Mouth is open approximately the width of the forefinger. Lips are active and away from the teeth. Face seems lifted as if smiling with the upper lip.
2. Sopranos should sing down to low *A* and altos to low *F*.
3. Tenors and basses should use the *ah* vowel to get more "bite" or center in the tone. When the correct resonance is sensed then the vowel color may be changed to *aw* to secure roundness. In all other aspects follow the instructions given for sopranos and altos in (1).
4. Tenors should vocalize down to low *A,* basses to low *E♭*.
5. Retain the same resonance in practicing the diction exercises. All voices may sing these exercises together.

SPECIAL TREATMENT OF VARIOUS VOICES

We reiterate that the basic training for all voices is the same. However, there are considerations in the treatment of different types of voices which are unique, and are not covered in a general discussion of vocal production. We hope to throw light on some of these problems in this section.

Developing Sopranos

It is in regard to tone that immediate attention should be given to the soprano section. There is usually more variation of tone in this section than in any other during the first rehearsals of a new group. Moreover, this part is so prominent that the chorus will not sound good until there is some homogeneity of tone in the soprano section. The author always gives his attention, first of all, to the sopranos, because it is by improving their tone quality that he can demonstrate the most striking and immediate improvement in the singing of the group.

Soprano voices come in a variety of tones — strident, nasal, pinched, thin, bright, and dark. They also come with and without *tremolos.* To obtain a uniformity of tone practice Vocalise 2 on pg. 163. This should be done at the beginning of each rehearsal for a few minutes. It will release the voice and eliminate all types of throaty tones. Then set the circle of resonance by vocalizing on descending tones, *aw* on loud singing, *ah* on soft singing. Use two fingers inserted between teeth to assure a free jaw. Some exercises can be used to eliminate *tremolos,* as treated at the beginning of this chapter.

On high notes, sopranos simply must open the jaw at least the width of the first two fingers. This is true for both closed and open vowels, which means that the closed vowels will open in quality on high notes. Diction must not interfere with this jaw action. In difficult places of a very high *tessitura,* instruct the sopranos to sing the words with two fingers inserted between the teeth. This device will give them the sensation of the resonance which they must retain on high notes. Then have them recite the words dropping the jaw on each syllable as they speak. They should retain this resonance and jaw action as they sing the words on the high notes. A chorus needs a soprano section with beautiful high tones if it is to produce an acceptable sound.

Developing Altos

There are not many singers with rich contralto voices. Most of the alto sections in school choirs are composed of sopranos who have not learned to sing high notes or who have been placed in this section because they can read notes and carry the alto part. The question is often asked if it does not injure these voices to sing the alto part. The answer is two-fold — not if they use their voices correctly, and not unless undue demands are made on their voices through long and numerous rehearsals. However, since most of the altos in these young choirs are potential sopranos, the conductor should insist that they vocalize just as high as the sopranos on all tonal drill. With this gesture to their vocal welfare he can feel justified in assigning these voices to the alto section.

Because of the range of the part, altos have the intricate problem of smoothing out the "break" between the lower and upper registration. Young voices must not be permitted to sing in the heavy, raucous quality of the popular "blues" singer. It is often called the "chest" voice. In listening to these popular stylists high school girls often endeavor to imitate them by carrying the chest voice far too high. This is injurious to the voice and will not blend in a choral group. On the other hand, alto voices should not sing in a dark, hooty tone in the upper, "head" voice to avoid the individual characteristic of the chest voice. Such production invariably produces disagreeable wobbles so prevalent in mature altos in our church choirs.

To offset these problems the altos must first of all learn to sing in the upper register (from first space *F* up) with an open throat, arched resonance, and firm breathing muscles. Then beginning on the descending *C* scale, vocalize on *aw* and *oh*. Permit the low register to "take hold" where it seems natural, this will be around middle *C* in a descending scale. Do not permit the vowel formation to change, or let the throat or breathing muscles collapse. Then the "shift" will be gradual, and the low voice will gain in richness and color. In choral work, altos should use primarily the color of the head voice, not the heavy, manlike quality of the chest voice.

Developing Tenors

What opera composer was it who exclaimed in desperation, "Tenor is not a voice, it is a disease"? Many a choral conductor must have felt that it is not only a disease, but also contagious.

Most tenor sections have two acute problems; first of all there are not enough tenors to go around. Moreover, many have not learned to sing high notes sufficiently well, so they migrate to the first bass part. The author seldom auditions a baritone section without finding two or three voices that are in reality actually tenor but cannot sing the high *tessitura* of the tenor part. Some individual work with these misplaced tenors enables them to find their true voice and can be used to bolster the tenor section. When this occurs the conductor is more than amply rewarded for his extra time and effort.

Not many tenors are needed to balance the other sections of a choir; they need only be good. The tenor voice must be the most perfectly produced in choral groups because they sing continously in the upper range of the voice. Consequently, during a strenuous rehearsal tenors become tired, and strain and throatiness appear in the voice, accompanied by flatting in pitch. This is a valid reason, aside from those previously pointed out, for rehearsing part of the time in a soft voice. It not only enables the various sections to hear each other better but it also gives the tenors a much needed vocal rest. During such periods they can sing in *falsetto,* or light, head-voice, which is not tiring.

If tenors are weeded out of the baritone section, and all of the available ones trained according to the vocal principles we have presented, there should be a sufficient number of good tenors to carry their part in any mixed choruses. Top tenors for male groups are unquestionably scarce. But like the high-pitched instruments in an orchestra, there does not need to be many of them to balance the lower voices. Choral conductors must be able to make vocal suggestions which will enable tenors to use their naturally high voices with ease and artistry. In the preceding chapter, and in this chapter under the section on "Developing High Notes", the author has described the procedures which he has used with success in developing adequate tenors for various types of choirs. Additional suggestions should not be needed. In his experience with amateur groups he has usually discovered a sufficient number of tenors among the male voices. If not, he sets about developing them.

Using altos on tenor part. Conductors of some amateur choral groups, especially high school choirs, offset the shortage of tenors by using low alto voices on the tenor part. They should sing the part at concert pitch, never an octave higher. There are three problems which arise as a result of this practice. Does it injure girls' voices to sing the tenor part? Is it a musically satisfying procedure to augment the tenor section with altos? Would it be better to sing SAB material where there is such a drastic shortage of tenors?

The question of the advisability of using altos on the tenor part in high school choirs is similar to the prevalent practice of using many soprano voices on the alto part. In answer to the question of the injurious effect on these young voices the response is the same — not if they produce their voices correctly, and not if they are spared too many long and arduous rehearsals. There is one difference; the tenor part is like a very low alto part and altos will often attempt to emulate tenors by singing heavily in the low "chest" voice. This is not good for the voice. Altos should use the voice throughout the complete range. We have emphasized the importance of this for all voices. Therefore, they must not imitate tenors, but should sing like altos even though they are singing the tenor part. Any other procedure is likely to impair the voice and these girls very often have voices worthy of training.

Whether the use of altos on the tenor part is a musical contribution or not is a moot point. Many choral teachers in the high school contend that if they do not use girls on the tenor part, there just won't be any tenor part. Most high school tenors are the young fellows in the ninth and tenth grade whose voices have not settled. They are often unsure musically as well as vocally. If they are placed in the front and center of the choir with a row of "female tenors" directly behind them to give them confidence, a creditable tenor section can be formed. A compromise can also be worked out by using the girls on only the extreme high notes of the tenor part. Then they can switch back and forth between the alto and tenor parts. This can be easily worked out with a little editing. Always remember that the tenors are singing in the upper, brilliant range of their voices, while the girls are singing in their lower, sombre register. The tenor color must come through if the music is to be truly artistic. At best the girls are just a musical and vocal crutch for a weak and crippled tenor section. Use them only as a last resort.

Using SAB and SSAB material. In instances where a shortage of tenors is inevitable is it advisable to use SAB material? There is only one answer, "It all depends upon the material." SAB arrangements that are SATB arrangements with the tenor part omitted should definitely not be used. They are musically incorrect and unsatisfying. If a talented composer or arranger writes a number with the voice combination of SAB definitely in mind, music of worth can be created. There are excellent examples from early Renaissance repertory written for two treble voices and one male voice. It can be done! It is interesting to note that in well written SAB material the parts invariably have a more polyphonic texture. It is intrinsic in the style to endeavor to obtain complete chordal progressions. This combination is especially useful and appropriate for junior high school choruses and excellent arrangers are turning their attention to this combination and producing worthy material. A representative list will be found in the appendix.

As a substitute for the tenor shortage some choral conductors are experimenting with this combination — SSAB. This simply means accepting the inevitable and eliminating male voices on the tenor part. In such arrangements the second soprano is really the alto part, and the alto is the tenor part with modifications. Simple SATB arrangements can be adjusted for this combination. Usually the key has to be raised and the tenor part adapted to the normal range of the alto voice. Even with this precaution the alto part usually lies too low. The music which can be written for this combination is limited. It does not excuse the choral conductor from the task of making an effort to develop bona fide tenors. Some arrangers are endeavoring to bring out acceptable material for the SSAB combination, but it has been received with hesitation and used sparingly.

Developing Basses

In the anxiety over the shortage of tenors, choral conductors have overlooked the tragic shortage of second basses. Yet a good sounding chorus is completely dependent upon an adequate bass section. This is why the best performing choirs have a few more basses than they have sopranos. This balance gives a basic foundation to the overall effect that cannot be matched by any other means.

The middle range of bass voices is developed like any other voice.

They should be lined on an *aw* form to secure roundness and fullness but they should have a high, arched resonance to give the tone center and a lyric quality. Unless basses sing with this resonance, they will flat, and pull the entire choir down with them. With arched resonance they can be the foundation of the choir, and hold the other parts on pitch. Upper tones are developed just as with tenors. Second basses should sing open to sixth space D, "covering" on E♭ or E for *forte* tones. Otherwise these pitches will sound forced and will not blend with the other parts. The vowel formation must not drop with the pitch in singing low tones. The vowel should actually seem to come forward and become "brighter." The mouth is relatively closed and the lips rounded. Without this resonance and mouth position the low tones will be "breathy" and "fuzzy." Basses give a deep organ-like quality to the sound of a choir. Don't neglect them.

The Boy Soprano

There is no justification in training the boy soprano to sing with the hollow, flute-like tone used in some church choirs. For concert performance the boy soprano should be trained like any other soprano. The fine professional boy choirs sing in this manner.

Continuous singing on a dark, hooty tone lined on an *ooh* vowel will tend to cause the lower registration to deteriorate. Then, when the voice changes there will be an irreparable break between the upper and lower registers, or between the singing and the speaking voice. Boys trained in this manner seldom become fine singers in adult life,

Boys should be taught to sing with an open throat, high-arched resonance, and firm abdominal muscles, as presented in this book. Then as the voice changes and lowers they will gradually find their natural range in the alto, tenor or bass parts. When boys are singing correctly they can sing continuously during the change without any injury to the voice. It is questionable practice to have boy sopranos in school choirs sing the tenor part one octave higher for the reason that they do not wish to sit with the girls or because it is effeminate to sing soprano. Let them sit with boys if they wish but insist that they sing the part that fits their voice. These psychological problems must be dealt with individually, for most boys will listen to reason and common sense.

The Changing Voice (Cambiata)

Much confusion has arisen from an effort to classify the changing voice of the boy into definite categories comparable to the adult voice. Such terms as alto-tenor and *cambiata* have been used. As a rule, these terms refer to the limited range often encountered in these voices, a dubious reason for classifying a voice. Boys' voices are so immature, so lacking in individual quality, that it seems more sane to refer to them as high, medium, and low.

A great deal of misunderstanding is evident concerning the changing voice. It is often thought to be a saltatory condition of the voice, that it appears suddenly and disappears rapidly. The fact is, a boy's voice usually begins changing when he is around the age of ten and continues until he is eighteen or even twenty. Often there is a short period when he seems to have little control of the registers of the voice. In the last analysis, this condition is probably due to a long period of improper use of the voice.

The changing voice need not be limited in range if the boy continues to use it properly through the two basic registers of the voice, referred to as the "chest" and "head" voices. Lack of correct use before and during the change causes a separation of the high and low registers of the voice, which results in lack of control. Therefore, every boy must continue to use his voice through both registers during the change.

After the boy has sensed the manliness of the low register of his voice, he psychologically resists using the upper, or *falsetto* register, which sounds effeminate to him. However, it can be pointed out to him that all great men singers, both past and present, make use of this register of the voice. All boys' voices, unchanged, changing, and changed, should vocalize through the "break" so that they will not become limited in range.

The following simple exercise will be helpful in gaining control of the registers of the voice. It is of paramount importance that the throat be opened firmly; therefore, we stongly recommend that two fingers be used between the teeth when singing the exercise, regardless of the vowel. The singing position will be as follows: use left hand, first two fingers between the teeth, middle or third finger on top; chest relatively high, abdomen in, and two feet flat on the floor. Boys are noted for tense jaws; the mouth must be open. (See page 164).

Boys may join in the exercise or drop out at the pitch where it is comfortable for them, depending on the maturity of the voice. However, each boy should attempt to sing through the entire range of his voice. Care must be taken that the chin does not rise with the pitch. Keep it in, and down, without strain. This exercise may seem hilarious to the boys at first but they become accustomed to it.

Vocalise 19

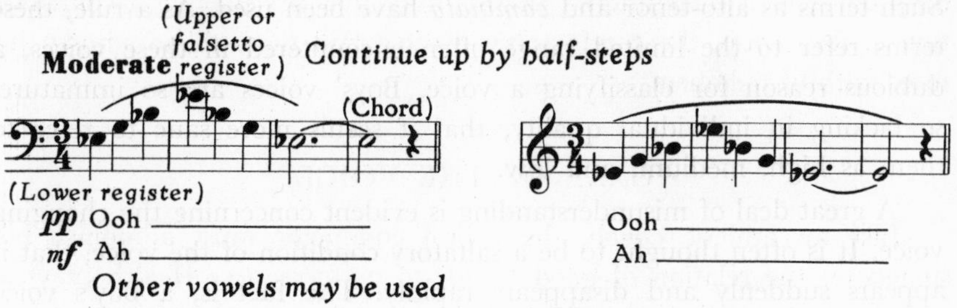

Another current misconception is the idea that it is injurious for a boy to sing while the voice is changing. Have you ever heard a boy of this age yelling on the playground? Remember, there is only one pair of vocal cords and they are used for talking, yelling, and singing. Of course, it is not good for a boy either to sing or to talk at any time, if he is not doing so correctly. Singing during the change, if it is done correctly, will actually be beneficial, and will offset some of the improper use of the voice during play periods.

Naturally, it is impossible in this book to give a treatise on training the adolescent voice. It is no different from training any other voice. The real problem is to continue the use of the high and low registers of the voice throughout the change. Then the boys will not have the limited six note range often assigned to alto-tenors, or cambiatas. The voice will gradually find its normal *tessitura.* The range, when considered with the timbre, will determine the classification of a voice as tenor or bass. In all other phases of vocal production the adolescent boy's voice is trained like any other voice.

The Monotone

There are probably no monotones, but there are undoubtedly people like General Ulysses S. Grant, who is said to have made this statement, "I know only two tunes: one is 'Yankee Doodle', and the other isn't." There are people who find it difficult to carry a voice part in a chorus. We know musicians with keen musical hearing who find it diffcult to carry a voice part because of a faulty voice, personal embarrassment, or lack of any practice.

It certainly is gratifying to note how much improvement these uncertain singers can make with a little patience and individual attention. There is no time during rehearsal for this individual attention but a few minutes before rehearsal, at intermission, or after rehearsal, can do wonders. Sometimes members of the choir who play the piano can work with these delinquents. If they don't improve, they will usually drop out; but if their interest persists until they are making a contribution to the group, the conductor will often find them to be among the most faithful members.

CARE OF THE VOICE

Like an athletic coach, the choral conductor must admonish his singers on the relation of good health to performance. Health plays a major role in good singing. The singer needs to comply with the same "training" rules which apply to an athlete: proper diet, exercise, rest, and other essentials of good health. Invariably when a singer is in "good" voice, he is also in good health. Actually, good health coupled with good singing habits makes the singer less susceptible to colds, headaches, and other minor ailments which directly or indirectly affect the voice.

Colds and Laryngitis

With the prevalence of the common cold, the choral conductor may appear at rehearsal and find fifty per cent of his choristers absent. It is actually becoming a menace to satisfying rehearsals and ultimate artistic choral performance. Although a singer may experience some discomfort in singing with a slight head cold, if his singing habits are correct, it will not be injurious to his voice. If, however, he has a case of laryngitis, the best advice is for him not to sing or speak for the duration of the infection. In laryngitis the vocal mechnism is inflamed with a swelling and reddening of the chords. Singing is difficult and forcing is inevitable. Continual forced singing during such a period of infection may do serious harm to the voice. The only prescription is rest from singing and speaking. During the period of laryngitis, if the chorister is not confined to his bed and continues his other daily activities, he should attend rehearsals, listen to the instructions, and follow his own part. When his voice returns he will be surprised to discover how well he knows the music.

According to medical advice there is no cure for a cold. Aspirin affords some relief, but is not a cure. All doctors prescribe complete rest and a liquid diet. Some cautions can be taken to prevent colds. The first of these is general good health. The author has found vitamin pills, as recommended by the medical profession, a safeguard. Another precaution is sensible dress. Choral teachers in the schools must continually remind their singers to guard against colds by following the simplest precepts of sensible dress. Because of the inclement weather in

New York during the winter season, the author always instructs the male singers in his choir to buy a hat. Girls have to be cautioned not to go out immediately after they have washed their hair. As stated in Chapter II a choral conductor must be more than a musician.

Smoking

Excessive smoking dries the membranes of the throat and irritates the entire vocal mechanism. If continued over a period of time the heat and the nicotine will affect the vocal chords to the degree that the voice will become husky and rough. When the lungs are affected there will be continual clearing of mucous from the throat, which impairs vocal adjustment. The author has been instrumental in persuading many high school youngsters to give up smoking because of the danger to their voices. They were probably just waiting for a sensible excuse. Any young person who is seeking a career as a singer is jeopardizing his chances if he smokes. During intermission with adult groups, if anyone wishes to smoke the author requests that he smoke outside the rehearsal room so that it will not be filled with smoke for the latter part of the rehearsal. Many singers' throats are very sensitive to a smoke-filled room and it causes them decided discomfort when they are singing.

Allergies

Another problem which confronts the choral conductor is the increase in allergies that affect the voices of singers. Many of these allergies affect the tissues of the throat, nose, ear, and surrounding areas which are eventually detrimental to the proper functioning of the voice. Such singers should be advised to seek medical treatment immediately before the vocal apparatus is impaired permanently.

Forcing and Strain

Good, strong, vigorous singing is not injurious to the voice; it is healthy. Much of the soft, anemic, mezza-voce singing is undoubtedly more detrimental to correct production and the general welfare of the vocal action. However, if singers and conductors indulge in long periods of loud singing when the production is throaty, there will inevitably be harmful forcing and strain. If these periods are numerous there may be permanent injury.

Throaty production can be recognized by its nasal, pinched, strident, or breathy quality. After faulty production has been corrected, there should be periods at each rehearsal when the choristers practice at a dynamic level that will enable them to hear all parts and give their voices a rest. Occasional long periods of choral rehearsals for a festival should not be injurious to young voices, but the conductor must beware of the problem of preparing the music for performance without undue taxation of the singers.

Cheering and Cheerleaders

There is nothing more disconcerting for a choral director in the schools than to have a basketball or football game scheduled the day before or the same afternoon as an evening concert. It invariably presages a poor performance. Voices are husky beyond recognition and all sense of nuance and pitch seems to be lost. At the risk of being unpopular, the choral teacher must instill among his singers the precaution of being reserved in their cheering at athletic contests. There is a manner of cheering that is not so injurious to the voice. Tell them to sing the cheers! It is the loud, raucous, unrestrained, and unhibited yelling that must not be condoned in members of choral groups.

Invariably the best singers in high schools and colleges are asked to be cheerleaders. They must be strongly warned by the choral director of the danger of such activity to their voices. There are enough students without singing voices who can serve as cheerleaders. Such activity can permanently impair a voice out of all proportion to its importance.

Vocal Nodes

Nodes are tiny hardened spots that form on the margin of the vocal chords. They result from continued abuse and misuse of the voice. Sometimes only one may form but in most cases there are two which appear opposite each other and prevent proper approximation during the phonation of the vocal chords. They are not limited to singers with a taxing schedule but are also common to public speakers. Cheerleaders invite them. Choral conductors with their strenuous schedules of speaking and demonstration are very susceptible. Healthy voices can withstand heavy demands upon them. Nevertheless, the voice is an intricate mechanism and although tough, there is a limit to what it will undergo.

Very few amateur or school choral groups maintain a schedule of rehearsals which will cause the formation of nodes. If they seem to appear in an individual chorister he should immediately seek medical advice. They are detected through continuous hoarseness and even complete loss of voice. Doctors often prescribe complete vocal rest which causes the nodes to dissolve and disappear. Otherwise it involves a delicate operation and a long period of rest and expert individual vocal training following the operation.

A MATCHING TEST

If you have studied this chapter you should have no difficulty unscrambling these phrases and making them match. The test is to match the phrases in the second column with those in the first column. They represent key statements made in the chapter. Page references are given.

Page		
193	1. Do not use humming or prefixes of humming consonants	a. to faulty tone than to any other single factor.
194	2. Humming is valuable	b. if they are to sing on pitch.
195	3. Young voices seldom have	c. to develop high notes in treble voices.
195	4. Voices with marked tremolos and wobbles	d. almost a curse in a choral group.
197	5. All voices should be trained	e. will normally be a *falsetto* tone.
198	6. These factors cause most of the off-pitch and out-of-tune singing	f. complete rest from singing and speaking.
198	7. If the conductor is alert	g. for practicing parts and obtaining a blend of harmony.
198	8. Choristers must learn to hear	h. in major keys than in minor keys.
200	9. A chorus that consistently practices with a loud tone	i. inevitably have a few more basses than sopranos.
200	10. Choral groups usually sing better in tune	j. the tragic shortage of second basses.
200	11. If your choir has excessive pitch difficulties	k. through both registers during the change.
201	12. Pitch difficulties can be more directly attributed	l. listless physical habits, poor musicianship, and faulty tone.
201	13. Alert posture, plus accurate hearing, plus high-arched tone	m. throughout both registers.
203	14. Sing compositions in the keys	n. eliminates flatting of pitch.
206	15. A high tone in a male voice produced softly	o. it may arouse the choristers from their lethargy.
214	16. In the anxiety over the shortage of tenors choral conductors have overlooked	p. avoid compositions filled with chromatic progressions.
214	17. The best performing choirs	q. will invariably sing out-of-tune.
216	18. Every boy should continue to use his voice	r. plays a major role in good singing.
218	19. Health	s. in which your choral group sings them best.
218	20. During a case of laryngitis the only prescription is	t. tremolos and wobbles.

Chapter IX

Blend and Balance in Choral Singing

Damon and Pythias were inseparable friends in the early days of Sicily. Pythias was condemned to death by Dionysius of Syracuse. Pythias was allowed time to arrange his affairs when Damon pledged his life for his friend's return. Pythias returned and Dionysius, impressed with such loyalty and friendship, pardoned him. Blend and Balance are the Damon and Pythias of choral singing.

ESSENTIAL FACTORS OF BLEND AND BALANCE

Blend and balance might have been included in Chapter III on the basic considerations of interpretation. They could have been included in Chapter IV as basic elements of expression in choral singing. Their importance is mentioned in Chapter V, especially as it relates to the *a cappella* style of singing. However, they are such essential factors in choral singing that an entire chapter is reserved to discuss them. Also, since they are so contingent upon correct vocal production, it was necessary to postpone the presentation of blend and balance until we had presented the chapters on tone and diction.

As good intonation is a prerequisite for any successful choral performance, it is likewise a prerequisite for effective blend and balance. Both of these factors of interpretation must be approached simultaneously. Neglect of blend and balance is one cause of faulty intonation, and conversely, inattention to intonation is a presage of poor blend and balance.

With vocal defects and intonation eliminated as far as possible, and tonal timbres suitable for a varied repertory developed at least partially, the conductor turns his attention to synthesizing the single lines of the chorus into a composite whole. Until the group is transformed into a unified ensemble it is just a body of individual singers singing together. In other words, until there is blend and balance there is no chorus.

RELATIONSHIP OF BLEND AND BALANCE

Blend refers to the uniformity of the quality of tone within and between voice sections; *balance* refers to the equalization of the quantity of tone within and between voice sections. They are inseparable and utterly dependent upon each other. In other words, no blend, no balance; or conversely, no balance, no blend. After a conductor achieves what he believes to be a normal blend, he may observe that a few voices in one section or an entire section are too strong and the blend is gone. He may have attained an acceptable balance between sections and then discover that the quality of a few voices does not blend with the group and the balance is gone. Blend and balance must synchronize.

Both blend and balance are contingent upon homogeneity of tone. Therefore, the approach is to obtain a uniformity of voice quality among the choristers. Some conductors attempt to achieve this quickly by closing or darkening all of the voices to a neutral *ooh* or *oh* quality beyond all recognition of any individual characteristics. In addition to the detrimental effect such a procedure has upon the singing voices of the group, there is so little variety of tone color that all compositions, regardless of style, sound alike. Consequently, the repertory of such groups is generally limited to music that fits this tone.

As we suggested in Chapter VII it is possible to secure blend and balance through a "legitimate" production of the voice, the type of production and tone used by the great singers. Although there is variation in tone among the great singers, there seems to be a common basis for vocal production. Choristers should have individual vocal characteristics like the various timbre in an orchestra but they must subdue these personal qualities sufficiently to secure blend and balance of ensemble. Such a choir tone has personality as an individual voice has personality. Such a choir tone has variety and, at the same time, a unified quality.

The approach to blend and balance is to develop all sections of the choral group, along the tonal lines suggested in Chapter VI. Some conductors attempt to build blend by selecting one individual voice as representative of the quality of each section and endeavor to get the other members of the section to imitate that quality. Some conductors attempt to obtain a blend in each section and then fuse the various sections into one uniform tone. These approaches are not only based upon false psychological principles but also, they absorb too much time from a limited number of choral rehearsals.

Because blend and balance are an integrated unit of choral singing they must be approached with the entire group in an integrated relationship. Since blend and balance should be secured through the fusion of individual timbres they should be approached through a fundamental ensemble tone based upon homogeneity of resonance and uniformity of vowel formation. This group tonal imagery needs refining through continuous attention to various sections and whenever necessary, occasional attention to individual voices. From such procedures should evolve a gradual amalgamation of all the voices and sections into a composite tonal blend and balance.

INTERNAL APPROACH TO BLEND AND BALANCE

The foregoing section gives us some systematic approach to the securing of blend and balance. Developing an adequate and appropriate tone may be called an internal, or intrinsic approach. Although the conductor must be able to "put his finger" on the voice or voices which are impairing the blend and balance of the ensemble, a general method of procedure in attaining them is advisable whenever rehearsal time permits. We suggest these five progressive degrees toward this goal:

1. Develop a conception of blend and balance in the entire ensemble.
2. Consider the blend and balance between the treble sections (soprano-alto) the male sections (tenor-bass) and cross sections.
3. Concentrate on the blend and balance of separate voice sections.
4. Devote attention to individual voices as needed.
5. Attain blend and balance between soloists and the ensemble.

Within the Entire Ensemble

All types of voices with various timbre will appear at the first rehearsal. The qualities will be as individual as the timbre of the violin, the flute, the oboe, the horn, the 'cello, and the trombone. Correspondingly, the voices will be sweet, hooty, reedy, round, resonant or brassy. The orchestral conductor capitalizes upon these individual timbres but the choral conductor must respect their individuality while fusing them into a composite tone.

As previously stated the approach to blend and balance is not that of imitating the tone quality of a particular voice. This would be the same thing as trying to get a flute to sound like a violin. Rather, all voices must obtain a similar tonal imagery through uniform vocal production that is based on sustained speech. This unformity is secured through a homogeneous resonance based on parallel vowel formation.

The larger percentage of voices will be tight and throaty; therefore, they must be freed and released. It is the same as the approach given in Chapter VII. Consequently, as one is developing the voices for technical and interpretive requirements, one is automatically working on blend and balance. The general procedure is to secure a deep, open throat, arched resonance, uniform vowel formation, and finally free articulation of words that does not interfere with or alter the resonance.

Begin in unison with the following exercise which is similar to Vocalise 2. However, it should be sung more softly and the top note held as the group takes time to listen to the blend and balance. This exercise should establish the deep, open throat.

Vocalise 20

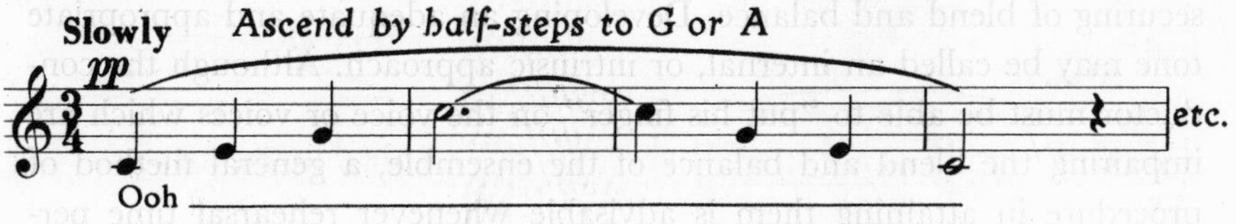

Procedures:

1. Sing softly on an *oo* vowel. Use two fingers between teeth as prescribed. Encourage singers to listen to each other as high note is held.
2. Instruct front row to turn around and face back row. This practice facilitates listening.
3. As soon as a semblance of blend is established, dispense with the aid of the two fingers.

The next procedure is to secure uniform vowel formation with corresponding homogeneous resonance. Herein lies the secret of blend and balance in tone quality. Sustained tones on a descending major or minor scale will suffice. Alternate between modes.

Vocalise 21

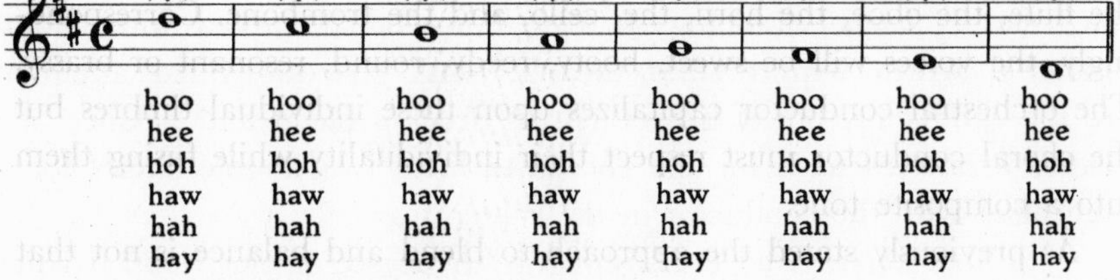

1. Sing various vowels at a *mp* dynamic level. This enables voice sections and individual singers to hear each other.
2. Use two fingers between teeth in the beginning as prescribed on page 164.
3. Experiment with various rows, sections and individual singers facing each other to encourage careful listening.
4. Practice the singing of a swell on each note, being careful to avoid any distortion of blend and balance.

Simultaneously with the securing of blend and balance in unison there should be practice in singing chords with these factors of choral singing in mind. Such exercises are often used for "tuning up", but they have greater meaning when the effort to ensure correct intonation is joined with the purpose of establishing blend and balance. See "Chord Tuning," p. 199.

Vocalise 22

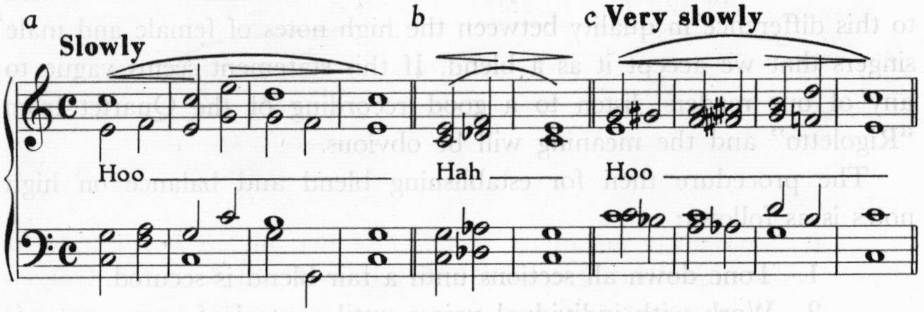

Procedures:

1. Use different vowels.
2. Sing Exercise *a* also in minor. In Exercise *b* ascend by half steps one octave. Sing Exercise *c* in different keys.

From practice on selected exercises the group may move to the singing of hymns and easy choral pieces in unison and in parts with the primary concentration on blend and balance. If the rehearsal room has movable chairs an excellent device is to divide the chorus into double quartets and seat them in several circles. This arrangement is conducive to fostering keener listening. It should not be attempted with choral material which requires that the choristers give undivided attention to the conductor, but it is excellent to develop blend and balance. An easier arrangement is for the chorus to form two double circles for a rehearsal with the conductor in the center.

On high notes. After establishing a fair degree of blend and balance in the middle range of the group, attention will probably be needed on the high notes. Unless voices are used correctly there will undoubtedly be strain and lack of control when singing in the upper range. Individual voices will force and be too prominent; other voices will strain, affecting the blend. The first step is to tone down voices that impair blend and balance. If it is difficult to discover these voices, reduce the dynamic level of the entire group in high passages, even at the temporary sacrifice of emotional climaxes. Then, as high notes are brought into control a stronger dynamic level can be resumed. (Don't drive a car at full speed until it is broken in).

Develop high notes in all voices along the lines suggested in Chapter VIII. On high, soft work the blend will be almost automatic unless there are some nasal, pinched soprano voices. If this blemish appears, line the soprano section on an *oo* form when singing high notes softly. In *forte* singing the loud tones of the treble voices do not actually blend with the "covered" tones of the male voices, because they are singing in different registers. However, our ears have become so accustomed to this difference in quality between the high notes of female and male singers that we accept it as a blend. If this statement seems vague to any of our readers, listen to a good recording of the Quartet from "Rigoletto" and the meaning will be obvious.

The procedure then for establishing blend and balance on high notes is as follows:

1. Tone down all sections until a fair blend is secured.
2. Work with individual voices until control of upper notes is apparent.
3. Increase dynamic level of the entire group according to the interpretive demands of the music, safeguarding blend and balance at all times.

On low notes. When blend and balance have been achieved in the middle and upper range of the voices there should be little difficulty in the lower range. Two problems are evident; balancing the bass voices on low notes in *forte* singing, and blending the alto voices with the other sections when they sing in the lower register, or "chest" voice.

Sometimes composers forget themselves and write extremely low tones for basses in *forte* passages. It is impossible to secure the tonal volume necessary to balance the other sections regardless of the number and maturity of the bass voices. There is only one solution; that is the singing of such extreme low notes one octave higher. Seldom is the effectiveness of the music impaired by this device. In extremely low ranges in soft passages basses, as a rule, have little difficulty in balancing the other voice sections.

Example 80

The Shepherd's Story

Dickinson

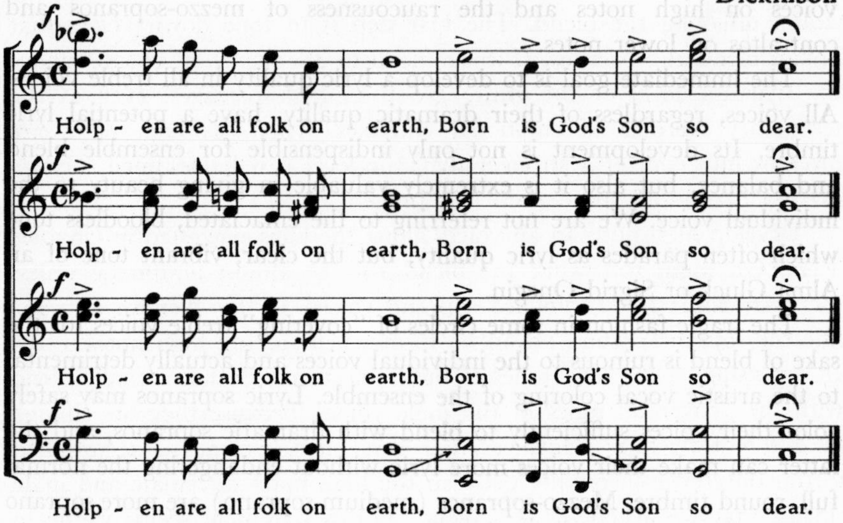
Holp - en are all folk on earth, Born is God's Son so dear.
Holp - en are all folk on earth, Born is God's Son so dear.
Holp - en are all folk on earth, Born is God's Son so dear.
Holp - en are all folk on earth, Born is God's Son so dear.

In the preceding chapter it is pointed out that altos should not be permitted to sing in the raucous tone of the popular "blues" singer. If condoned it will affect the quality of the voice throughout the range and jeopardize blend and balance, regardless of the *tessitura*. The altos must retain the resonance of the upper registration in the low voice as the "chest" voice takes hold. To attain this color, vocalize alto voices down the scale on an *oh* vowel to the extreme lower tones. Retain this resonance and color in articulating words. This is the alto quality that has the color of the *chalemeau*, or lower register of the clarinet; they must not sound like a bassoon on an escapade. This quality gives a fullness and roundness to the alto section that blends and balances with the other sections.

Between Voice Sections

After a fair degree of blend and balance is attained within the entire ensemble, attention may be directed to blend and balance between individual sections. If the procedures in the preceding section have been followed, this practice can probably be reduced to a minimum. A feasible approach is to work first with treble sections, then male sections, and finally various combinations of cross sections.

Treble sections (soprano-alto). Here the problem is to blend lyric and dramatic sopranos, mezzo-sopranos, and contraltos into a homo-generous color which is adaptable to the vocal demands of various styles of compositions. The urgent need is to eliminate stridency in the soprano voices on high notes and the raucousness of mezzo-sopranos and contraltos on lower notes.

The immediate goal is to develop a lyric quality in all treble voices. All voices, regardless of their dramatic quality, have a potential lyric timbre. Its development is not only indispensible for ensemble blend and balance, but also it is extremely valuable in giving beauty to the individual voice. We are not referring to the emaciated, bloodless tone which often parades as lyric quality, but the clear, vibrant tone of an Alma Gluck or Sigrid Onegin.

The tragic fashion in some circles of "covering" treble voices for the sake of blend is ruinous to the individual voices and actually detrimental to the artistic vocal coloring of the ensemble. Lyric sopranos may safely color their voices sufficiently to blend with dramatic sopranos, and the latter can make their voices more lyric without endangering the normal full, round timbre. Mezzo-sopranos (medium-soprano) are more soprano than contralto, but they should be assigned to the alto part. A mezzo-soprano should not be permitted to sing the high soprano part in a chorus even though this may be her personal preference. For these voices to sing continuously in the high *tessitura* of the first soprano part will produce strain. Even the second soprano part will prove taxing. The contralto is a rich, sonorous voice which gives body to the treble sections. To achieve this normal timbre the lower register is not avoided, but the misuse of the "chest" voice to the point of harshness must not be condoned. It is safe procedure to place lyric sopranos on the first soprano part, dramatic sopranos on the second soprano part, mezzo-sopranos on the first alto part, and contraltos on the second alto part.

Every mixed chorus should occasionally sing a number for three-or four-part treble voices where undivided attention can be given to the matter of blend and balance of voices in these sections. Passages in mixed-voice arrangements that are written for treble voices alone can be used for the same purpose. The following type of exercises can be of additional assistance.

Vocalise 23

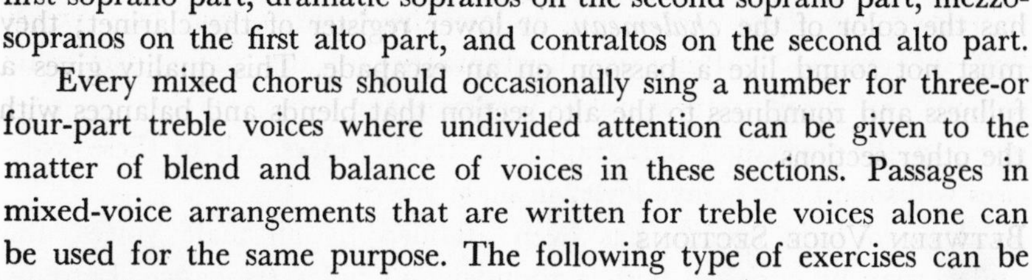

Procedures:

1. Use two fingers between teeth (see p. 164) with the first vocalise until blend and balance are evident.
2. Sing all exercises on different vowels and various dynamic levels.
3. Sing all exercises using *crescendi* and *diminuendi* as indicated.
4. Regardless of the section assignment in the chorus divide the voices into four equal parts for the last vocalise.

Within male sections (tenor-bass). The problem of obtaining blend and balance within the male section is similar to that of the treble sections. The conductor is usually presented with lyric and dramatic tenors (we hope), baritones in abundance, a sprinkling of bass-baritones or *basso cantate,* and an occasional *basso profundo.* This variety of timbre must also be transformed into a uniform color. It is usually the extreme voices, such as the high tenors and low basses, which cause the most difficulty. Tenors have a tendency to be pinched and strident and basses lean toward a heavy, grumbling sound.

The approach, as with the treble sections, is to develop a rich, lyric quality throughout the male sections. Use soft exercises in the *falsetto* to release the tenor voices and to get the baritone and bass voices "off the ground." After some light practice of this nature the male sections can profit immeasurably by doing the same exercises as those given in the preceding paragraphs for treble voices. All of these exercises will sound one octave lower in male voices.

After a lyric quality has been attained by all male voices, the timbre may be enriched with a rounder and fuller resonance. Extreme high notes and low notes should be developed along the lines prescribed in Chapter VII. Occasionally, the conductor should select a suitable number for male voices alone where complete attention can be given to blend and balance. This practice will carry over into the selections for mixed voices.

The following exercises are excellent to develop a conception of a light, lyric quality. They should be supplemented with the vocalises suggested for securing blend and balance within treble sections.

Vocalise 24

Ascend by half-steps to high A *Descend by half-steps to low F*

1. Sing exercises very softly with a falsetto tone.
2. Ascend by half steps for one octave.
3. Carry into the lower registration the same feel of resonance as in the upper registration.

Within cross sections. If the method of vocal production has been followed as suggested in Chapters VII and VIII, and if the procedures for the entire ensemble have been followed as suggested in this chapter, there should be little problem in securing blend and balance between the various combinations of female and male vocal sections. It is primarily a matter of giving the various sections a chance to hear each other together. The exercises described in the above section for treble voices are useful. In singing these exercises sopranos always sing the high note, altos always sing the low note except when singing with the basses, tenors always sing the high note except when singing with the sopranos, and basses always sing the low note.

The various combinations of cross sections are soprano-tenor, soprano-bass, alto-tenor, and alto-bass. These various combinations may sing sections of the music together. Not only will this practice give the singers a better sense of blend, but also it will secure accuracy of their parts. The sections should stand facing each other or form a circle for this practice; this facilitates hearing. In the usual seating arrangement of a chorus, male sections seldom really hear the treble sections. With adequate voice production, the above practice is the most efficient procedure by which to obtain blend between female and male voices.

Separate Voice Sections

After working with the entire ensemble and combinations of vocal sections, added attention will undoubtedly need to be given to separate sections. Correct voice production for all types of voices has been outlined and prescribed in preceding chapters. These procedures need to be continued with the separate voice sections. We re-emphasize that blend and balance result from a uniformity of production, not from the imitation of some individual voice in the section.

Processes must be employed which will enable the singers of each section to hear each other. While working with the entire ensemble on blend and balance the conductor may have each of the separate sections sing the vocalise several times. Each section may rehearse the melodic passages of the music being studied, not alone for notes but primarily to obtain tonal imagery of blend. Singers should be instructed to blend with those choristers sitting on each side of them. If sitting in rows, each row should stand and face each other during this sectional practice; if chairs are movable each section may sit in a circle. These methods foster attentive listening and are priceless in developing a composite tone quality within each section.

Individual Voices

It is likely that sooner or later the conductor will be confronted with the necessity of working with individual singers who seem to have inconsonant voices that are incompliant. There are usually two types, the timid voice with a reedy quality that cuts through the blend, and the "eager beaver", who feels complete responsibility for the performance of his section or even the entire ensemble.

The latter chorister reminds us of the story of the Welsh basso, Mr. Jones, who had a dream. In this dream he was singing in a chorus of 1000 sopranos, 1000 altos and 1000 tenors. He was the only bass. The chorus was singing double forte when the meticulous conductor interrupted the singing with a rap on his stand and this remark, "A little less volume on the bass part, Mr. Jones."

The Mr. and Mrs. Joneses are valuable members of most choruses, especially church choirs. If their assurance and over-zealousness can be tempered slightly they may fulfill their leadership aspirations while making a genuine musical contribution to the ensemble. A private interview with the conductor can reveal to the singer the necessity for curbing his vocal enthusiasm. It should be pointed out that he or she has a voice of fine quality but its power impairs the blend and balance of the ensemble. These singers are immediately apologetic in a disguised, patronizing manner. The conductor should take this opportunity to work with the singer to reveal to him the extent of the dynamic level of the voice to be used with the ensemble. A secret signal can be worked out between the conductor and singer which will warn the singer when his voice is too strong for blend and balance.

With the reedy or strident voice which mars blend, the conductor should tactfully arrange an appointment for remedial instruction. This singer either fails to hear the tone quality used by the other choristers in the section, or fails to realize the physical coordination needed to produce such a tone. Return to the instructions in Chapter VIII. Such a voice needs to be freed and released. A little work will usually give the singer the tonal imagery of the quality necessary to blend with the ensemble. After this barrier has been removed, the physical imagery for coordinated production will follow quickly. If there are several of these singers they may be interviewed together.

In choral groups of more than thirty singers it is often difficult for the conductor to determine the unblending voices, unless he occasionally takes the time to listen to each individual voice. This procedure is usually impossible during rehearsals of limited duration. In some groups it is often embarrassing to the very voices which the conductor is trying to discover and help. The author usually schedules periods before and after rehearsals when he can hear the individuals of each section. The ones who need help may be detained and given remedial vocal measures. Following this procedure only infrequently are these discordant voices unable to fulfill their rightful place within their respective sections. It takes time, but for the conscientious choral conductor it is time well spent.

Soloists and Ensemble

In oratorio societies and church choirs, as well as in incidental solos for the music of other choral groups, there is always the problem of blending and balancing solo voices with the ensemble. There are two approaches; either reduce the dynamic level and tone quality of the soloists to match that of the choristers, or augment the dynamic level and round out the tone quality of the choristers to match that of the soloists. It is evident that the latter method is unquestionably the most tactful, feasible, and musical approach.

In oratorios, cantatas or anthems where the soloists are singing together they cease to be four soloists and are a quartet. All the interpretive considerations which apply to a very small choir are applicable in these situations. When the quartet is singing with the choir it should emulate the work of a double choir, except in this case one choir is composed of four singers while the other one is larger. The larger choir should not overbalance the smaller choir and the quartet should blend with the ensemble of choristers. Interplay between the two is absolutely necessary for an artistic performance.

When a composer or arranger assigns a passage to a soloist he expects it to be prominent. In such musical situations the ensemble is in the position of an accompaniment and should be so treated. The soloist should have some opportunity and liberty for individual expression. This personal quality should be confined to the musical limitations imposed by good taste. The interplay between the conductor and the soloists should circumscribe these artistic boundaries. The conductor is the final source of interpretation but on the other hand he is not singing the solo. The maturity and experience of the soloist will determine the degree of musical authority which the conductor should exert. The soloist has the responsibility of subjecting any artistic idiosyncracies to the expressive considerations dictated by the music itself.

The idea that solo voices cannot blend with a chorus is erroneous. We have held to the premise throughout this book that there should be no difference between the tonal production of fine solo singing and fine choral singing. If the chorus sings with an incongruous or incompatible tone quality, then it will be difficult for legitimate soloists to blend with it. Conversely, if the soloists have a tone production which is not acceptable in accordance with approved standards, they will not blend with a choral group. Such singers, however, should not be asked or employed to sing solos. The author has never had any difficulty in incorporating solo singers into an ensemble. His conception of tone production is similar for both styles of singing.

EXTERNAL APPROACH TO BLEND AND BALANCE

Although the essential factor in securing blend and balance is a composite and homogeneous ensemble tone, other devices of a more external nature may be introduced to abate and absorb conflicting sounds. These involve the number of singers on each part, the shifting of voices on parts, the interchange of parts, a slight alteration of parts, and the unlimited possibilities represented in formations of voice sections. These external approaches are expedient measures when blend and balance cannot be attained through the internal approach, as presented in the preceding section.

Numerical Balance of Parts

Probably the most immediate external factor contributing to blend and balance is the assignment of an equal number of voices on each part. The internal factor of a uniform tone is still the essential criterion, but the equal distribution of voices is the framework within which it can be realized most quickly. The author recalls that one of his best sounding festival groups was an All State High School Chorus of 200 singers with 25 voices on each of the eight parts.

In a mixed choir of 60 singers *where the voices are of nearly equal maturity,* the following distribution would probably be ideal: 16 sopranos, 14 altos, 12 tenors and 18 basses. This number of bass voices gives a fundamentally solid sound to the choir; this number of sopranos is adequate without making the choir sound top heavy; 14 altos are sufficient for an inner part; finally, fewer *good* tenors are needed to balance the other parts since they are generally singing in the higher *tessitura* of the voice. This distribution is primarily designed for *a cappella* singing or for performance with a piano or organ accompaniment. When an instrumental accompaniment such as a band or orchestra is added, more sopranos will probably be needed to balance with the dynamic level of the accompaniment.

The author realizes that such an ideal situation must be a selected choir to be discussed in the next chapter. Seldom do teachers inherit such a choral utopia. They are often lucky if they have enough boys to form a mixed chorus. The vocal distribution at the first rehearsal may simulate the following: 30 sopranos, 20 altos, 4 tenors, and 6 basses. Don't give up the musician-ship! We pass on to other factors which may relieve this choral dilemma.

Shifting of Voices

As mentioned above most amateur choirs are completely unbalanced in the number of singers on each part. Many unselected choruses in high schools may boast of some such distribution as follows: 50% sopranos, 25% altos, 10% tenors and 15% basses. It is difficult by any stretch of the imagination to conceive how a balance can be achieved with such an uneven distribution of voices. Still, it is not completely hopeless. The first step is for the other sections to concentrate on listening to the tenor section. Tell the choristers that if they cannot hear the tenor section, they are singing too loudly.

Any or all of the external approaches will alleviate the situation, but one of the most effective is the judicious shifting of voices on the various parts. In all such groups there are sopranos who can sing alto, altos who can sing tenor, and baritones who can sing tenor when the range is not too high. These singers should be weeded out through audition and personal interview. An appeal can be made to these singers to use their vocal versatility for the performing needs of the choir.

These choristers should be seated in a position where they can shift from one part to another without disrupting the normal arrangement of the various sections. In soft passages that employ a medium range little shifting will be necessary because a few tenors can balance many sopranos and altos in such passages. The device is needed in loud passages, forte climaxes, sections with a high *tessitura,* and in difficult phrases with intricate melodic and rhythmic figures.

Loud passages. In loud passages an uneven distribution of voices is very evident. In such passages instruct the voices doing double duty to shift to the other part as long as necessary. These sopranos may sing alto, low altos may switch to tenor and a few baritones may bolster the tenor section if necessary. This shifting of voices must be worked out in advance by the conductor so that no rehearsal time is wasted in making the changes.

This device can also be used in shifting voices to bring out melodic passages and themes in fugal entrances.

High passages. If the tenors have a very high section which they cannot handle and it does not seem advisable to alter the part, then the only solution is to shift some alto voices to the tenor part on this passage. When this is done some of the sopranos may be needed to sing alto. There might be instances in a very high bass part when the tenors need to shift to this part while the altos carry the tenor part alone. As mentioned above, the personnel of this shifting of parts must be worked out in advance by the conductor.

Difficult passages. At times, tenors will have phrases which are so intricate that they are not able to sing them accurately. In such instances the conductor should have a group of low altos which he can shift immediately, to strengthen this part.

Interchange of Parts

The interchanging of parts is a procedure very similar to the shifting of voices to obtain balance, except that entire sections are assigned to sing some part other than the one usually sung. The use of "female tenors" described in the preceding chapter is an example. This practice must not be a permanent interchange, however. As in the following example, some arrangers are actually writing in a cued part to signify this interchange of the alto part for the tenor part in a high *tessitura.*

Example 81

How Lovely Is Thy Dwelling Place

Brahms

Alteration of Parts

Although the usual reason for altering parts is to avoid extreme high notes in the tenor part, or extreme low notes in the alto and bass parts, this practice is also a device for improving balance in musical figures which contain notes in the extreme ranges of these parts. It should not be condoned except in an emergency as a last resort. A conductor should make every effort to develop his groups so that they can perform the parts as written. These alterations should be limited to the changing of a few notes in a musical figure from one part to another. It is a mark of efficiency on the part of a conductor if he or an assistant writes in these alterations before the reading of the number by the choir. The following example is typical.

Example 82

Here Yet Awhile, from "St. Matthew Passion"

Bach

mf
loosed by Thee, Shall be-come a welcome por-tal
loosed by Thee, Shall be-come a wel-come por-tal
loosed by Thee, Shall be-come a wel-come por-tal
loosed by Thee, Shall be-come a wel-come por-tal

SEATING AND STANDING FORMATIONS

Although there are many factors which enter into the choice of seating and standing formations of a chorus, the consideration of blend and balance is undoubtedly the most important. Some formations are selected for appearance, some to improve intonation, and some to give support to weak sections, but the dominating reason should be blend and balance. The following diagrams are designed for mixed choruses, but the same principles apply to other choral groups. Diagrams for these groups will be presented under each type in the next chapter.

Rehearsal and Performance

Whatever may be the preferred formation of voice parts, every effort possible should be made to retain this arrangement in both rehearsal and performance. It will save time and confusion later if singers are assigned to regular seats at rehearsals, in the same arrangement by row and number as they will stand for a performance. Appearance, strength and quality of voice, and height must all be taken into consideration in making these seating assignments.

Such formations may occasionally be changed at rehearsals when a conductor wishes to give added attention to a section. He may bring the boys down in front to work more closely with them. As already suggested in this chapter, sections may be seated in four circles or the entire chorus in a double circle to work especially on blend and balance. Such changes add a little novelty to the routine of rehearsals. The conductor should also be continually alert for desirable changes in seating of individual singers, when it will improve the ensemble. As a rule, the stronger and better voices should be distributed throughout a section. They should not be permitted to congregate in the front row but they should be persuaded that their voices are more valuable in the rear of the section.

Diagram 14 or 15 of the block arrangement of voice sections as presented under "Traditional Formations" is the usual seating for chorus rehearsals. It is by far the most efficient for learning the music quickly. Choruses which use one of the "Newer Arrangements" or "Novel Arrangements" for performance may sit in a block arrangement while learning new music, then switch to the concert arrangement during the final rehearsals before a performance.

At public performances there is no reason why a chorus cannot shift formations between groups or even between numbers. In polyphonic music, especially of the Baroque era, where fugal entries and contrapuntal lines need to be clear and distinct, the traditional formations or block arrangements of voice parts are best. In homophonic music whose effectiveness depends upon a complete fusion of parts, one of the newer formations which mix the voices of the various sections is superior. Therefore if a choir has a varied repertory it should have various suitable formations to reap the ultimate in artistic choral singing. Unquestionably when a chorus sings with an orchestra or band accompaniment one of the traditional formations with a block arrangement of voices is the "safest", as well as the most effective.

Traditional Formations

Traditional seating arrangements of amateur choirs have probably evolved from those simulated by church choirs. Blend and balance are difficult with these traditional block arrangements; individual parts are too obvious and the sopranos are usually too prominent. Study the following diagrams before reading the explanation. It is evident that many choral conductors give very little thought to the artistic validity of such arrangements. Seemingly, they take the attitude that what was good one hundred years ago in choral singing is still good today. They are probably right, partially so at least. However, the finest choral work today is being done by conductors who are willing and sufficiently daring to experiment with varied formations of voice parts which are adaptable and appropriate for the choral groups under their direction.

Diagram 14

Tenor	Bass
Soprano	Alto

Most four-part singing groups use this formation. It probably originated from the idea that the men were taller and should be in the rear while the high voices should be on one side of the platform and the low voices on the other. Before the use of choir risers there was some logic to the first reason. With the universal use of risers it is no longer valid. There is really no musical basis for the second reason except possibly that composers of church anthems very often write passages as a duet between sopranos and tenors or altos and basses. Seldom does one find duets for soprano and bass in anthems. Also, since there are more sopranos than any other part and fewer tenors, this formation affords a balanced appearance on the stage. Sopranos are invariably too prominent, musically and physically with this arrangement.

Diagram 15

Bass	Tenor
Soprano	Alto

This formation preserves the placing of the men in the rear because they are taller than the ladies. In switching the tenors and basses the outer voices are on one side of the platform while the inner voices are on the other. Since these parts are closely allied at times in polyphonic writing it is claimed that performance of this style of music is improved by making the interplay of contrapuntal lines more striking. Also, the idea is advanced that pitch is improved with this arrangement because the fundamental tone of the basses will prevent the sopranos' wavering from the key. This claim is vindicated only if the basses sing on pitch themselves. The appearance of balance on the platform is thrown slightly askew because the larger sections are on the same side. For the same reasons as in the preceding formation, blend and balance are difficult.

Diagram 16

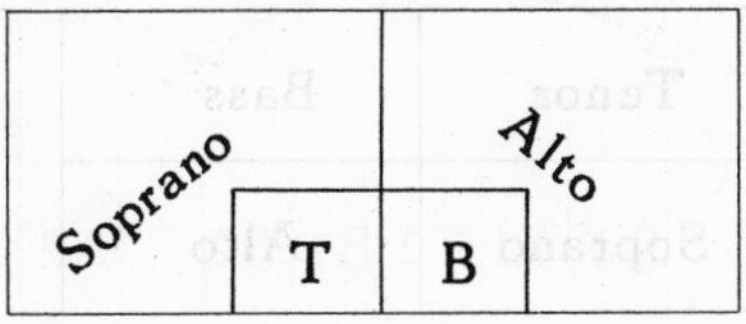

The dearth of boys in school choirs caused the choral teachers to break with tradition and formulate the above formation. It was the only solution to secure some semblance of balance when the girls often outnumbered the boys four to one. It is the prevalent one used in unselected mixed choirs today and it works fairly well. Since this arrangement places the taller boys in front the use of choir risers or platforms is necessary.

Diagram 17

T 1	T 2	B 1	B 2
S 1	S 2	A 1	A 2

This formation is the usual one for choirs which sing eight-part music. It is the same as Diagram 14 except that the parts are divided. It provides a balanced appearance on the platform, but it has the same inherent weakness for obtaining blend and balance. The sopranos generally overbalance the other parts and in this block arrangement a fused tone is difficult to obtain.

Diagram 18

B 1	B 2	T 1	T 2
S 1	S 2	A 1	A 2

This formation is also used in choirs which sing eight-part music. It is a variation of Diagram 15. The same positive and negative features apply to both. Blend and balance are difficult unless there is practically the same number of singers on each part.

Diagram 19

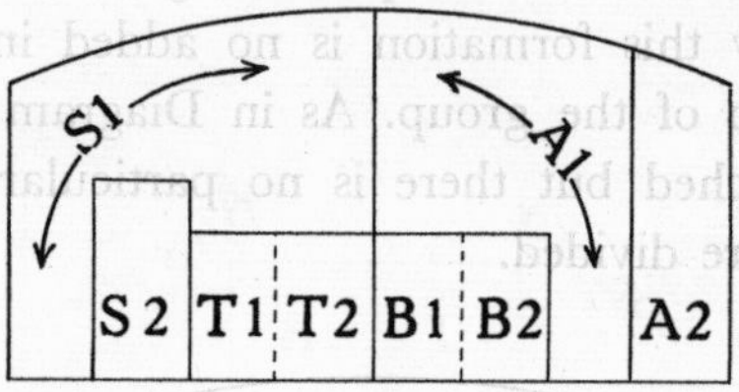

Choruses with a shortage of male voices but which are still able to perform eight-part music often use this seating formation. The author has often used it with large festival choruses. It is the same as Diagram 16 with each part divided. It is an expedient arrangement to improve balance. The use of some type of choir risers is indispensable.

NEWER FORMATIONS

Choral conductors are beginning to discover the difficulty of securing blend and balance through block formations of voice parts. Consequently they are experimenting with the mixing of the various sections. In the past they have undoubtedly been fearful that the singers could not carry their respective parts unless they were grouped together. This anxiety is probably the reason why most choral conductors still use the traditional formations. Nevertheless, we are discovering that the average chorister has more musical independence than we surmised if we give him the challenge of carrying his own part without contingent forces. All of the newer formations are based upon the established observation that blend and balance are obtained more readily when voice parts are mixed. To the novice conductor unfamiliar with this procedure, the fusion of parts is almost unbelievable.

Diagram 20

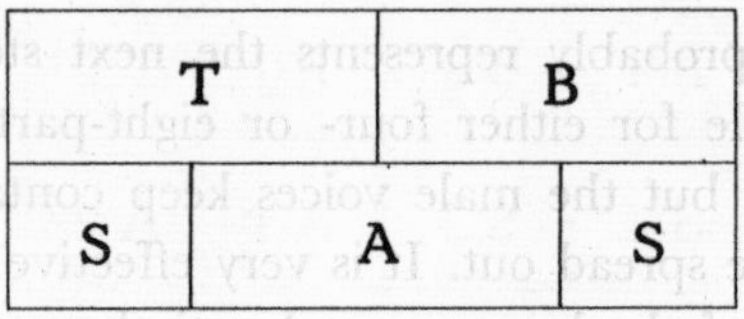

Most mixed choruses are dominated numerically by sopranos. It is a musical blessing that they usually carry the melody. The first step in mixing voices is to divide the soprano section. The above formation illustrates this arrangement. If the conductor will listen from the rear of an auditorium to the blend and balance with this formation in contrast to Diagram 14 he will be amazed and delighted with the improvement resulting from this simple change. Since the sopranos are carrying the melody this formation is no added imposition upon the general musicianship of the group. As in Diagram 15 the tenors and basses may be switched but there is no particular advantage to this since the sopranos are divided.

Diagram 21

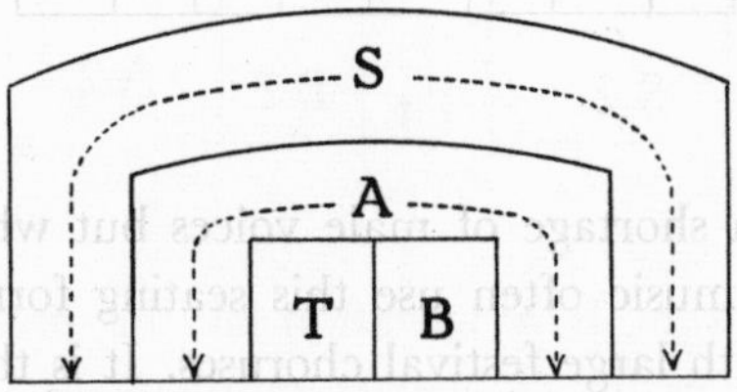

This formation is similar to the preceding Diagram 20 but it is designed for choirs with a marked shortage of male voices as shown in Diagram 16. It has all of the advantages of both formations, namely, by dividing the sopranos the melody comes from more than one spot on the stage and by bringing the male voices to the front a better balance is achieved. It is an excellent voice arrangement for the average high school choir or any amateur group where there is a shortage of tenors and basses.

Diagram 22

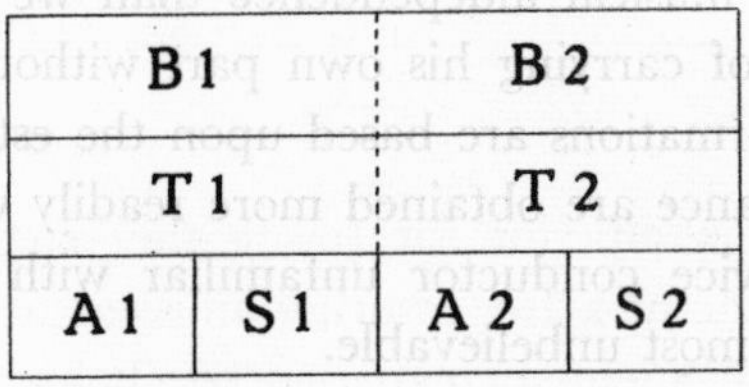

This formation probably represents the next step in mixing voice sections. It is suitable for either four- or eight-part music. The treble sections are divided, but the male voices keep contact with their part, even though they are spread out. It is very effective to have the fundamental voice sound of the basses spread entirely across the back of the choir. Since the tenors are in front of the basses there is usually a better balance between the two sections. The division of the treble parts is not only conducive to a better blend, but also it fuses these parts sufficiently to engender a more even balance with the male parts, even though the tenors and basses are outnumbered. It is obvious that this formation is excellent for double choir work. The author recently performed the double motet of Bach, *Sing Ye To The Lord* with this formation.

Diagram 23

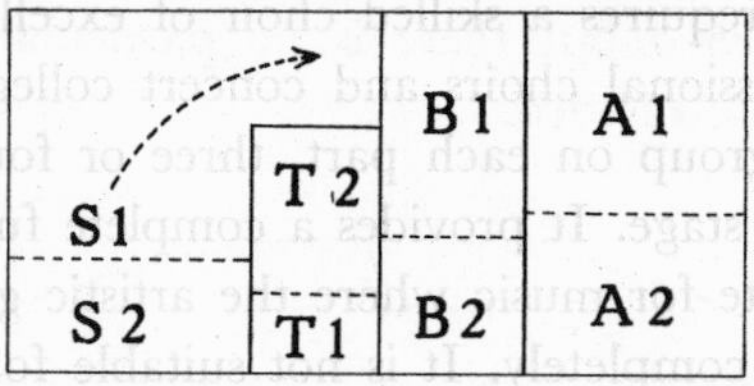

The above diagram is a variation of the preceding Diagram 16 except that it provides for eight-part numbers. It is a very convenient way of seating a large festival group since the assignment of chairs is a simpler process. Also, because as a rule the second sopranos, the first tenors, the second basses, and the second altos are smaller numerically than their counterparts, a better balance usually results. Try it when your voice distribution follows that pattern.

Diagram 24

B 1	T 1	B 2	T 2
A 1	S 1	A 2	S 2

This formation is superior for fusing the parts and still retaining the necessary compactness for assuring musical accuracy. The author often uses this arrangement for experienced choirs and festival choruses which have an almost equal distribution of voices and are adequately prepared musically. The blend and balance which can be achieved with this formation is par excellence. It is equally suitable for homophonic and polyphonic music as well as double choir singing. Also, there is a smaller choir (S1, A2, T1, B2) within a larger choir which may be used alone on soft passages and a double quartet in the center which may be used for antiphonal effects.

Diagram 25

B 1	S 1	T 2	A 1
A 2	B 2	S 2	T 1
A 1	T 2	B 1	S 1
T 1	B 2	S 1	A 2

This formation requires a skilled choir of excellent musicians. It is often used by professional choirs and concert college choirs. It simply distributes a small group on each part, three or four singers, over the various parts of the stage. It provides a complete fusion of voices. It is especially appropriate for music where the artistic goal is to blend and balance all sections completely. It is not suitable for music which contains contrapuntal lines that need to be clear-cut for the most effective performance. It is the formation which the author uses for radio broadcasts and recording.

Diagram 26

A	T	B	S	A	T	B	S
T	B	S	A	T	B	S	A
B	S	A	T	B	S	A	T
S	A	T	B	S	A	T	B

This formation represents the ultimate in the distribution of voices. It almost looks like a bingo board. The choir is composed of quartets that are mixed. It requires an experienced and well-trained choir. If all other factors are under control, this arrangement should produce superior blend and balance. It was quite a fad for a period, but one sees and hears it less often at present. Perhaps this is a reflection on the musicianship of our choristers. It is undoubtedly this factor which causes conductors to avoid this formation. It is obvious that this formation requires a nearly equal number on each part. This requirement alone eliminates it as a possibility for most conductors. It does have one valuable concomitant however. Since the choir is divided into quartets, the singers can be encouraged or required to practice the music in quartets or double quartets as preparation for a full rehearsal. It is also an impetus for developing a small ensemble program. (See Chapter X.)

Novel Formations

Conservative conductors may look askance at the newer choral formations presented in the preceding section. If so, they will undoubtedly speak out with vehemence against any suggestion of the novel formations presented in this section. They will exclaim that our job is not to entertain, but to interpret the finest in choral music for interested listeners. In this opinion the author concurs completely.

However, even our artistic world is changing. With the advent of television and the wandering cameras, an audience, even a cultured one, often expects more than a concert. On television the shifting camera enlivens even a string quartet concert for many people. True lovers of chamber music may refute this comment. Professional choral groups are continuously shifting their voice formations. Choral conductors of amateur groups should not completely close their minds, their eyes and their ears to the possibilities of new and novel formations.

It is not necessary to emulate the elaborate formations of the football band. The dominating aim should always be artistic singing, not entertainment. For that matter there are many levels of entertainment. It does not have to be cheap and puerile. Beautiful singing can be entertaining as well as cultural and educational.

Most of the novel formations are better suited for smaller choirs ranging from sixteen to thirty-two voices. Beyond that number they become cumbersome and lose their *raison d'être.*

Diagram 27

B	G	B	G	B	G
G	B	G	B	G	B
B	G	B	G	B	G
G	B	G	B	G	B

The above diagram is usually referred to as a boy-girl formation. The voice parts should be distributed, as well as the sexes. It is an excellent arrangement for rhythm numbers, folk songs and music of the theater. It is often used for a program of light numbers, as in a musical revue.

Diagram 28

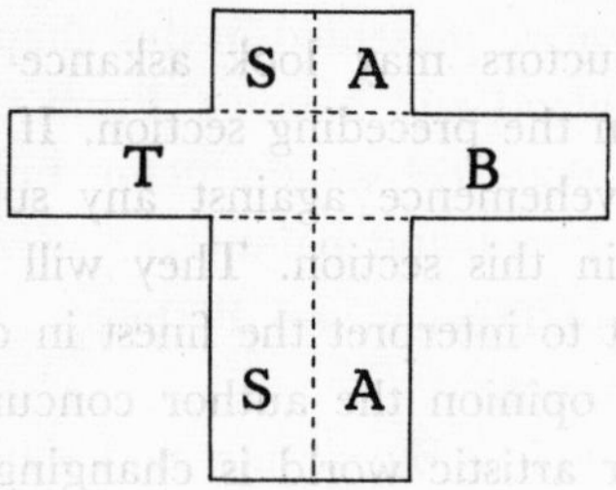

A beautifully robed choir formed in the shape of the cross supported with artistic lighting effects can establish a mood with certain sacred numbers not possible by the use of traditional concert formations. Such formations have no place in the performance of oratorios, masses, or the bulk of our heritage of great sacred choral music. It is more appropriate for music with a distinct mood or dramatic character. The voice parts may be distributed in various ways.

Diagram 29

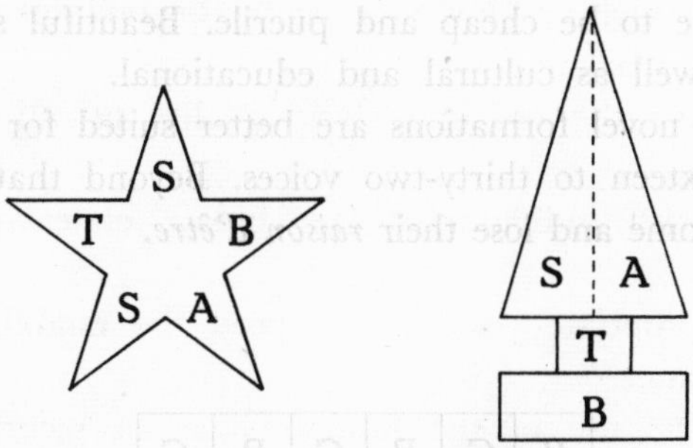

At Christmas time the choir may form a star to sing the sacred part of the program and then change the formation to a Christmas tree to sing the secular part of the program. Such formations seem to be particularly enjoyable in programs presented by choral groups of young people. Voices may be distributed in different patterns. Risers or platforms are a must.

Other possibilities. Through the use of different costuming letter formations are possible in singing patriotic and alma mater songs. Casual grouping of a small choir around the piano is relaxing and informal for light numbers. The enterprising conductor and his choristers can invent many other ideas for choir formations. As a parting caution may we urge the conductor not to become so involved in formations that he loses sight of the goal of singing beautiful music artistically.

REVIEW

There are many devices presented in this chapter which a conductor can use in developing blend and balance. From the following list check the procedures which you feel a conductor might use to contribute to the development of blend and balance.

1. Tell the story of Damon and Pythias.
2. Improve intonation.
3. Neutralize all voices by closing and darkening tone color.
4. Obtain a homogeneous quality through uniform vowel sounds.
5. Stress the individual vocal characteristics of the singers.
6. Develop, first of all, a conception of blend and balance in the entire ensemble.
7. Imitate the tone quality of a particular voice.
8. Give no attention to blend when practicing the notes of voice parts.
9. Foster keener listening between voice sections.
10. Tone down all sections until a semblance of blend and balance is secured.
11. Work on high and low notes as the beginning step in obtaining blend and balance.
12. Encourage the use of a lyric quality by all singers in the ensemble.
13. Work with individual voices before endeavoring to blend sections.
14. Use appropriate vocalises to speed the establishing of blend and balance.
15. Avoid the use of the falsetto voice in securing blend and balance in male voices.
16. Make no attempt to blend soloists with choristers.
17. Shift voices from one part to another to bring out melodic passages and fugal entries.
18. Never alter parts to secure blend and balance.
19. Interchanging parts may be used with integrity to obtain balance of parts.
20. Use the same seating and standing formations at rehearsals and performances.

Chapter X

Types and Organization of Choral Groups

Along with the primary purpose for choral groups discussed in Chapter I, other factors of organization need to be considered. The organization of a choral group must have an impetus which usually comes from a sponsoring institution, an enterprising conductor, or a group of enthusiastic choristers. Each of these participants may have a set of objectives aside from the primary purpose.

The Sponsoring Institution

There are many sponsoring institutions for choral groups: schools, colleges, churches, civic clubs, community organizations, recreation commissions, and industries. Schools consider such groups as a part of the educational program, public relations, a booster to school morale, and recreational and social activities. In addition to these objectives colleges consider choral groups a part of the music training program. Churches sponsor a choir program primarily for religious services. Civic clubs and community organizations wish to improve the cultural status of their towns and cities. Recreation commissions desire to expand their program. Industries feel impelled to provide activities for their employees to foster loyalty and general well being.

The sponsoring institution has five responsibilities: (1) to furnish an adequate rehearsal hall with a piano kept in tune, chairs for the choristers (not too comfortable), choir risers or platforms and a conductor's stand and podium, (2) to set aside funds for the purchase of music needed by the chorus, (3) to employ a conductor who has the personality and musicianship to realize the primary purpose (see Chapter II), and (4) to engage an accompanist who will support the conductor and can serve as assistant conductor, and (5) to provide an auditorium and equipment for public performances. In addition, most sponsoring organizations also provide some means for the dressing or robing of the choir.

Regardless of other objectives, the sponsoring institution must not belittle the primary purpose of the artistic singing of beautiful music if it expects to maintain a continuing organization. The fulfillment of this purpose should be turned over to the conductor without interference. Any adverse criticism publicly will simply jeopardize his work and position with the choristers. The purpose succeeds or fails through his ability and efforts.

The Conductor

There is no reason why a conductor should not instigate and organize a chorus through his own efforts. His reasons may be manifold. He may be doing a job which includes other services; he may wish to make more money; he may wish to enhance his social and musical prestige in the community; he may sincerely wish to share his experience in singing beautiful choral music with others. All of these reasons are valid but unless the last one is paramount he will lose interest in his work and in the personnel of the group. When this happens, the chorus will be short-lived, or, it will struggle along in ignominy.

At this point the reader should reread the first part of Chapter II. He should have a clearer perspective of the personal and musical responsibilities of the conductor. They are really demanding and challenging. If the conductor is so impressed with his musical ability and knowledge that he is impervious to the human values in this job, he will blunder. On the other hand, if he fails to place standards of perfection on both himself and his singers, the resultant personal and musical dissatisfaction will cause loss of interest. The artistic singing of beautiful music is the only solution.

The Choristers

A group of choristers is often the impetus for the organization of a choral group. These interested persons usually have only one reason for coming together — their liking of singing and their enjoyment of singing with other people. When this purpose is achieved their goal is fulfilled. Other subsidiary personal desires must remain subservient to the main purpose. Every choral group needs leaders, but if their leadership expresses itself in social ambition or a wavering from the central goal, it cannot be tolerated. These attitudes lead to disaster.

Election of Officers*

Every choral group functions differently. In some the conductor fulfills all duties, musical, mechanical and janitorial. In others he appoints one or two assistants to help him with details which will

* A complete discussion of the organization of choirs will be found in "Building a Church Choir," Wilson, H. R. and Lyall, J. L., Schmitt, Hall & McCreary Co., Minneapolis, 1957. Chapter V.

assure a smooth-running rehearsal. A few choral groups elect a full quota of officers.

When officers are elected they should have definite functions in the smooth running of the choral group. The argument, often advanced, that the election of officers is democratic, seems to us to be a false one. Democratic procedure is not a matter of electing officers; it is a manner of living from day to day. Unless officers have real functions that serve the electors, their election may actually be undemocratic. If the conductor or choral teacher is dictatorial in temperament the election of officers will not change his conduct. It is the cooperation within the group, and the recognition which individuals receive in the act of making music that gives choral groups their value as democratic organizations.

We do not mean to give the impression that we are against the election of officers for choral groups. If they are made to serve a purpose in certain situations, the practice is a valid one. In many college, church, and community choruses, these officers serve a real function and warrant their existence.

What officers can be of genuine service in the efficient functioning of a chorus? We have mentioned them indirectly above, but it may be well to list them again. These officers are almost indispensible in the help they can give the conductor in producing a smooth-running singing organization. A conductor's musical responsibilities are jeopardized when he is laden with administrative detail. On the other hand, he must not be aloof from the organizational factors conducive to successful rehearsals and performances. These positions are not just honorary, they are a necessity.

(1) Business Manager

This office should be filled by an energetic person who has executive ability. The business manager may be appointed or elected after the conductor has carefully outlined his duties to the organization. The choristers will feel more responsibility toward a qualified person whom they have elected. He will cooperate closely with the conductor in all business details associated with the organization. He will handle all publicity, ticket sales, and financial problems. He will cooperate with the conductor in all arrangements for transportation. He will have the power to appoint committees to assist him. In choral groups sponsored by industries, civic clubs and recreation commissions, the business manager is often appointed by the governing body of the institution.

(2) Librarian

This office should be filled by a person who is responsible and enjoys this type of work. The librarian may be elected but it is usually better for the conductor to appoint someone who is interested. If he or she is elected the conductor must impress upon the choristers the important responsibilities of the office prior to the voting. The librarian will have charge of cataloguing, filing, repairing, passing out, checking out, and collecting all music.

(3) Wardrobe Custodian

This position is often taken as a joke, but believe us, it is not. It is only necessary in choral groups which perform in uniform dress supplied by the organization. It is generally wise to appoint some interested young lady in this rather thankless job. She is responsible for the checking in and out of robes for a concert, or season, depending upon the policy of the organization. She must attend to the cleaning and repairing of robes or uniforms. She should have two or three robes or uniforms on hand at each performance for the forgetful choristers.

(4) Assistant Conductor

This office should be filled by a person who has leadership qualities and superior musical ability. In choral groups sponsored by outside organizations he is often employed for his services. In such situations the accompanist may serve as the assistant conductor to function as a substitute during any emergency or indisposition of the conductor. In school choral groups he may be elected by the students after they have had the opportunity to observe several of their own number conduct the organization. The assistant conductor should attend every rehearsal and have charge of arranging the set-up of chairs and risers for rehearsals and performances. He should have rotating assistants for this chore. He should be able to take charge of the rehearsal in the absence of the regular conductor.

(5) Accompanist

This very important officer is usually employed by the sponsoring organization or appointed by the conductor from among persons best qualified. The judgment of the conductor should be the determining factor in the appointment of the accompanist. There must be no personal or musical friction between the working rapport of these two. They must have a sincere mutual respect for each other. A proficient accompanist may serve in the capacity of assistant conductor. In schools the choral teacher usually selects the accompanist from among qualified students. For additional suggestions concerning the responsibilities of the accompanist see Chapter V.

The Choir Constitution

All phases of the organizational policies of a choral group should contribute to the primary purpose of the artistic singing of beautiful choral music. A choir constitution can clarify the purpose and policies of the choir, describe the responsibilities of its members and save valuable time in needless arguments over little problems which arise.

A choir constitution should be brief and explicit. To function effectively, it should be sufficiently flexible to yield to needed changes. If it becomes busy work, it should cease to exist as superfluous to the organization. The experience of formulating a constitution is excellent educational experience for young people. In all organizational activities, however, the true goal of the chorus must not be lost, nor must anything be permitted to interfere with this goal.

A short, simple constitution usually embodies the following properties:*

1. Preamble — Statement of the purpose
2. Leadership — Method of securing or relinquishing services of a conductor
3. Membership — Qualifications and eligibility of members
4. Officers — Election of roster of officers
5. Committees — Provision for standing committees
6. By-Laws — Description of rehearsal schedules, rules, penalties and dues

The author has led different choral groups that have been successful both with and without constitutions. Most choristers resent any kind of regulation but, on the other hand, there needs to be some indication of willingness to accept responsibility if the chorus is to be perpetuated. If a constitution is formulated and seems to contribute to a smooth-running organization, then it has its place. If it becomes an agent for friction it should be abolished. Ultimately the success of a chorus does not depend upon officers or a constitution; rather, it survives and

* A complete description and example of a choir constitution can be found in "Building a Church Choir," Op. Cit.

flourishes to the direct ratio that the conductor is able to make rehearsals and performances an enjoyable and inspirational experience for the choristers.

Budget

It is true that the best things in life are free but many good things in life cost money. One of these things is a successful choral group. It is most depressing to see a chorus struggling along, ill-housed, with a piano out-of-tune, with one piece of music between three or four choristers, etc. When beautiful singing emerges from such adverse conditions, it is certainly a tribute to the conductor and the singers. The author recalls the remark of a young lady who had a fine group at a festival. She had taught the music to the choristers by rote from one piece of music which she had purchased herself. That is determination and devotion above and beyond the call of duty.

There must be a business-like attitude toward a budget. There seems to be a general notion that musicians are not reliable or business-like. Perhaps this has been all too true in some phases of the music profession. In the world of today the conductor must acquaint himself with the financial routine of such items as budgets, requisitions, and accounts. If he can prove himself to be an efficient business person rather than one who keeps haphazard accounts or is dilatory with budgets, he will find his path toward achieving his musical purpose a much smoother one.

If a conductor is not familiar with the financial routine of the sponsoring institution he should sit down with the administrator and have it explained to him. After he understands the routine, he must be diligent in observing it. The conductor who knows his business will keep himself informed of available materials and sources of supply. He will have his name placed on the mailing list of a number of publishers. In examining new books and music, he should adhere to the ethical practice of sending for music on approval, rather than requesting complimentary copies. He should see to it that, if not purchased, the material is returned in saleable condition. He will anticipate his needs at least a year in advance in order that he can accurately make out his budget the preceding spring. He will properly fill out requisitions and order blanks, and take pains to present valid reasons for his requests. He will keep his personal accounts separate from school accounts in order that there may be no misunderstanding or confusion about payments.

Conductors should respect and refrain from infringing upon the copyright law. Publishers are most cooperative with conductors and choral teachers, but they have a right to the protection of their copyrighted works. It is unlawful to print on the blackboard, typewrite, or mimeograph music or other materials from a published book without permission from the publisher. Unless it is public domain (56 years old) arrangements cannot be made of copyrighted music without the permission of the publisher. Every conductor should acquaint himself with the copyright law and observe it.

Unless the artistic purpose of a choral group is realized its existence seems rather futile. To be successful these things are paramount: pleasant rehearsal quarters, a piano in good condition, a minimum of one copy of music for two singers, and a proficient conductor and accompanist. These necessities may be supplied by the sponsoring institution, individual patrons, or dues and assessments of the choristers. The conductor and accompanist must be adequately paid and the other requirements fulfilled or the obstacles for survival are insurmountable. In an initial venture all of these basic needs for success may not be forthcoming but if the conductor and choristers can persevere and demonstrate musical results, Orpheus seems to bend a listening ear, and patronage and support appear.

SELECTIVE OR NON-SELECTIVE

This entire book is based on the premise that the purpose of choral groups is the artistic singing of beautiful music. This premise would seem to imply that choruses should be selective to attain this purpose. This inference is not necessarily true.

First of all, when a choral group is organized it is usually only those persons interested in singing who seek membership. This very interest generally signifies some musical ability. Secondly, if challenging music is selected for repertory the less interested ones will gradually drop out. This same type of singer often withdraws anyway after the novelty of the activity has worn off. Occasionally a misfit will persist in membership. His handicap may be an unblending voice quality or the inability to sing a tune in tune or carry a voice part. The conductor must use tact and discretion in an interview with such a chorister as to the advisability of continuing in the chorus. As a rule the chorister will ask to resign if he senses that he is detrimental to the welfare of the chorus. It is also possible that with a little instruction he can correct his limitations and become an acceptable member.

It is certainly much easier to take a group of selected singers and develop them into a fine chorus than it is with a group of nonselected singers. It is a genuine tribute to a conductor if he can produce quality out of quantity. Developing an artistic group from unselected singers is a real challenge. Also the conductor's mission of bringing fine music to more people is fulfilled to a greater degree when he works with an unselected group.

By the above observations we do not mean to imply that there should be no selective groups. Some choruses have such a strenuous schedule of performance that selectivity is almost a pre-requisite for membership. Also, every choral conductor needs the stimulus of working with a group endowed with technical facility and musical sensitivity. It is a balm that will lighten the remainder of his labors.

Testing of Voices

Non-selective group. In a general chorus, voices are not tested for selection but for classification. At the first rehearsal, the author usually requests the singers to take their seats in the section where they are accustomed to sing. It is advisable to divide a chorus into eight parts at the outset. If there is a shortage of altos, urge some of the second sopranos to switch to this part. Then urge a corresponding number of the over-abundance of first sopranos to change to second soprano. In the male voices it may be necessary to urge a few of the baritones to sing bass in order to assure balance. Tenors, if any, will be self-sufficient.

After a general seating formation is obtained, ask for a show of hands of those people who are doubtful about which part they should sing. Ask these people to remain after the rehearsal for an audition to classify their voices. If there are too many to audition conveniently after one rehearsal, several periods may be necessary. It is better not to take valuable rehearsal time for this assignment of voices to sections but it may be necessary in some school situations because of schedule conflicts.

After this immediate aid to doubtful singers is given, the conductor should try to reserve time after each rehearsal until he has heard all of the voices in the chorus. If the chorus is too large to make this feasible, he should make himself available to any chorister who would like to have him test his voice. This personal attention is appreciated and gives added assurance to many singers. It gives the conductor a much better understanding of the vocal potential of his group and enables him to select music that is more appropriate for it.

Do not give a test in sight-singing to unselected singers. It will only be embarrassing to the student and discouraging to the conductor. Sufficient reading power can be developed through the rehearsing of music. (See Chapter XI). True, many compositions will be learned by rote and by ear with the help of the piano. But why not? Isn't music for the ear? With this method a skilled conductor can gradually improve the general musicianship of a group of choristers until they become quite proficient in learning new music.

Use some simple test such as the following to get acquainted with the singers and to classify the voices. *Remember, a voice is classified by the quality as well as the range.* This principle should always be followed. Take care because some altos sing as high as sopranos, some tenors sing as low as baritones and some basses sing as high as baritones. Misplacement of voices causes added difficulty with pitch and blend and balance.

1. Play unrelated notes skipping up and down, to determine the student's ability to match tones.
2. Use a simple arpeggio vocalise on the vowel *ah* to determine the upper range of the voice. Use a descending five-tone scale to determine extreme low range. (Use two fingers between teeth to assure normal voice production).

3. Sing some easy song to determine the quality of the voice and the ability of the student to sing a tune. ("America" is suitable. The author uses "Drink To Me Only With Thine Eyes.")

A simple test of this type is always interesting to the student and establishes a personal rapport with the conductor. The conductor makes the following discoveries about the chorus:

1. The outstanding voices and the voices that are especially weak and need individual attention.
2. Voices of limited, or extensive range.
3. Potential leaders and soloists in various sections.
4. Boys' voices that are still changing and need careful watching.
5. Classification of voices which he may divide into eight parts: first and second sopranos, first and second altos, first and second tenors, and first and second basses.

Selective group. It should be considered an honor to belong to a selective choral group and the members should be willing to meet specific, although not necessarily rigid, qualifications. Applicants should be sincere in their purpose and should give evidence of an ability to:

1. Sing an easy song rhythmically and expressively, with a pleasing quality of voice.
2. Vocalize over an extended range of approximately an octave and a fifth. (Use arpeggios with two fingers between teeth.)
3. Carry a voice part independently. (Play a hymn while singer carries his part.)
4. Read music of moderate difficulty, employing diatonic progressions. (Easy hymns will suffice. Use Bach Chorales for advanced groups. Audition singers in quartets.)

These requirements are far too difficult for the elementary and junior high chool choirs discussed in the next section. They are also very exacting for high school students. Adjustments can be made in view of the quality of performance expected and in light of other musical opportunities in the curriculum. At this point we would like to suggest that if it is necessary to choose between character and an exceptional voice for a selected group, choose character. A more serious type of chorister is needed for selective choral work, one with integrity and a sense of responsibility. No prima donnas or pseudo-Caruso's please! Also, it should be added that artistic singing is emotional, but mentally controllable, and one cannot overstress the necessity of the right mental attitude for a successful selective choral group. Mental stability is far more important than vocal ability.

Pitch Range of Voices

In the previous section we stressed the fact that voices should be classified by the quality as well as the range. However, very often the voices of choristers are not developed and it is difficult to utilize the quality with any degree of assurance in classifying the voice. In these instances the conductor must resort primarily to the range of the voice for the assignment of a part. Also, even though a singer may have an extended range, the *tessitura* of a high part may be too taxing for him and he should be assigned to a lower part. Likewise, it is just as harmful to assign a normally high voice to a part where the *tessitura* lies low. For this reason it is often necessary to continue to reclassify voices as they develop.

Range does give an important clue to the classification of voices. It gives a conductor an understanding of what to expect from a voice until further development of quality. Therefore, we are giving the normal ranges of singers for different types of choral groups at various age levels. The white notes represent comfortable ranges and the black notes represent extreme ranges.

Elementary School Choir

SA Choir

Junior High School Choirs

SATB Choir

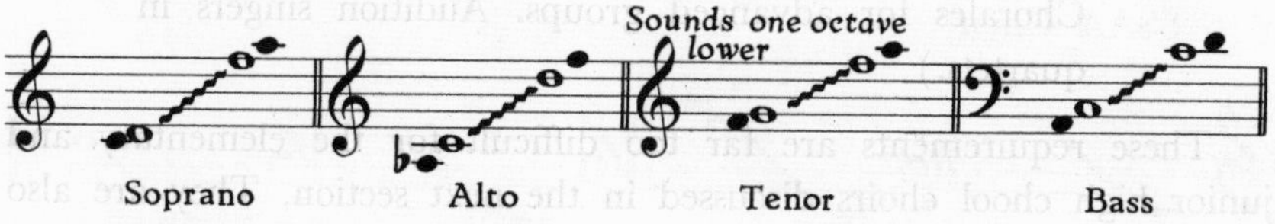

SAB Choir

SSA Choir

High School Choirs

SATB Choir

SSA Choir

TTBB Choir

Adult Choirs

SATB Choir

SSAA Choir

TTBB Choir

Ranges for a double mixed choir are the same as those for SSAA and TTBB choirs.

TYPES OF CHORAL GROUPS

We have endeavored to cover the major considerations in the organizing of all types of choral groups. However, some of these groups have specific and unique problems which need to be considered individually.

Elementary School Choir

The major share of the music taught in the elementary school is, and should be in the classroom. However, we feel that there is a place for a selected elementary school choir. Such an activity should be available for the more talented children, above and beyond the music presented in the general classroom. Moreover, music teachers, after years of preparation in music, need the satisfaction and inspiration of working with interested and more talented pupils. It gives them a musical lift, and more zest for all of their work.

A choir of youngsters from the elementary school can be a delight both to behold and to hear. As a rule, the membership should be limited to the fourth, fifth and sixth grades. There can be a simple tryout for admission or the members can be selected by the teacher from her knowledge of their singing in the classroom. Ability to sing a tune with a moderately wide range should be the only requirement. Tone quality and part-singing can be taught in the choir.

The better policy in the classroom is to divide the class equally in singing two-part music. Then the singers switch parts on different songs. In the sixth grade, and occasionally in the fifth, some pupils show a preference and an adaptability for carrying the alto part. In the selected choir each singer should be assigned to a permanent part. The alto part is usually sung by the older children and the younger children are generally assigned to the soprano part.

The singers should be divided into four parts at the outset even though two-part singing is all that is anticipated. Such division readily permits the shifting and interchanging of parts as well as conserving rehearsal time for the occasional division of parts. The following diagrams represent the possibilities for voice formations.

Diagram 30

S	A

a.

The traditional seating and standing formation. It is a good plan at rehearsals to learn the music but it is not conducive to the proper blend and balance because voice parts are segregated.

S	A	S

b.

Superior to the traditional arrangement for blend and balance. It divides the melody so that the melody is heard from different parts of the stage. Also, since altos are usually the older children and taller it provides a nice stage appearance.

A 1	S 1	A 2	S 2

c.

Best arrangement for blend and balance. Through the division of both parts the voices are fused together. Parts can be easily shifted to strengthen a weak section. Choir needs to have considerable security in ability to carry parts.

The elementary school choir should number anywhere from twenty to a hundred singers. Sixty is a good compromise to secure the ultimate of musical clarity and contrast in dynamics. The minimum of organization is necessary. The teacher may select a few responsible pupils to assist her with details. The accompanist must be competent and experienced. Another teacher, a talented mother, or a qualified high school student are all possibilities. If the teacher is especially proficient at the piano and the group is not too large, the teacher may serve as both conductor and accompanist.

The elementary school choir can be a service to both the school and participants. It can represent the school in many different types of functions. It can be used to establish better community relations. It is invaluable to the pupils as an effective part of their musical training. It provides the teacher with an outlet for continuing her association with artistic musical endeavor. It provides an opportunity for the children to develop an enduring attitude of appreciation for beautiful music.

The boys' choir. In answer to the problem of interesting boys in music, some singing teachers in the elementary school organize a boys' choir. When such a group is organized it usually replaces any other type of selected elementary school choir. The boys selected for the choir should be made to feel that it is an honor which carries with it the responsibilities of industry and discipline.

It is organized in the same manner as the elementary school mixed choir. The formation of voices and arrangement of parts are similar. Through the cooperation of the mothers of the boys, uniform dress can be devised. The author prefers some apparel other than robes for these "young men" and, as a rule, so do they. Repertory for these boys is similar to the music for the selected, mixed elementary school choir, except that a cowboy or novelty tune can be included on a program.

Boys' voices should be trained with the same procedures we have prescribed for any soprano or alto. They should not be permitted to yell just because they are boys nor, on the other hand, should they be permitted to sing in a dark, hooty, unnatural color. When boys with unchanged voices sing with a lovely, clear tone the only word to describe the quality is "heavenly."

A boys' choir can be a delight to the teacher, the school, and the community. These boys often serve as leaders in the classroom toward fostering general musical improvement through the school.

JUNIOR HIGH SCHOOL CHOIR

Musical activity in the junior high school should be similar to that in the elementary school. The major emphasis of music instruction should be found in the class for general music. Talent begins to lift its head at this age and it should have more chance to flourish in opportunities other than those offered by the classroom music. We are discussing junior high schools consisting of grades seven through nine. However, the comments are applicable to junior high schools embodying only the seventh and eighth grades.

The selected choir should be a mixed choir consisting of young people genuinely interested in singing fine music together. The only vocal requirement necessary is the ability to sing a melody of fairly wide range, on pitch. The teacher may select the membership from his acquaintance with the ability of the singers in the general music classes.

Acrid controversy usually arises as to whether these choirs should sing SAB or SATB material. The individual situation must determine the repertory. An SATB choir is more musically satisfying, but if there is a shortage of boys' voices it had better be an SAB choir.

The general superiority of SATB music is widely recognized, but it should also be remembered that some of the finest early choral music was composed in three parts. Junior high schools should not sing SAB arrangements which are SATB compositions with the tenor part omitted. But when a composer or arranger demonstrates an understanding of the SAB combination and writes accordingly, artistic musical results can be achieved. A representative list of such numbers will be found in the final chapter.

A homogeneous choral tone for junior high school groups should be developed in the same manner as the voices of any other choir. The principles of voice production are the same. The so-called changing or adolescent boys' voices should not be treated as freaks in need of special or eccentric vocal methods. Review the discussion of these voice procedures in Chapters VIII and IX.

Voice formations for the SATB choirs were discussed in the preceding chapters. Formations for SAB choirs present practically the same problems. A few of them may be valuable for the directors especially interested in junior high school choirs.

Diagram 31

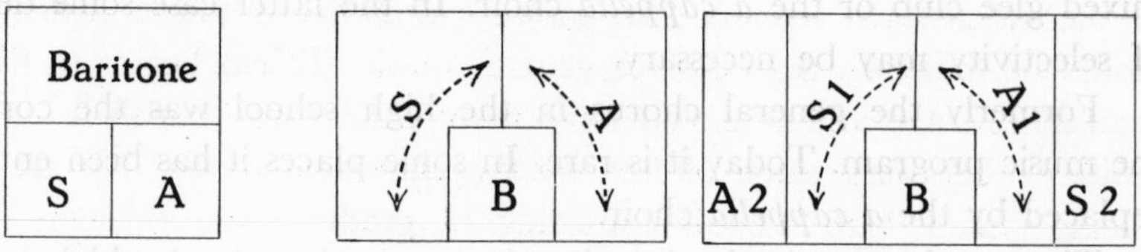

a. This is the traditional vocal formation for SAB choirs, with nearly an even number of singers on each part. It is an excellent arrangement to learn parts but since parts are segregated it is not conducive to blend and balance in performance.

b. This formation is the traditional one for SAB choirs where there is a shortage of boys. It has the same virtues and faults as diagram *a*.

c. This formation employs the traditional features of diagrams *a* and *b*. It also provides a division of the treble voices and, by mixing parts, a much better blend and balance is possible.

Senior High School Chorus

The singing activities of the senior high school offer a golden opportunity for bringing to fruition that sensitivity to the beautiful in music which we feel is most urgently desired in all students of this age group. Is it not, then, a misfortune that many students fail to continue their interest in singing after junior high school? Can this be due to the failure of the high school to offer adequate opportunities? The boys' voices are beginning to settle into tenor and bass classifications. A few genuine contralto voices are in evidence. Soprano voices are fuller and more mature. A large and varied field of choral literature is available. Music that represents the genius of the great masters is ready to lead these young people to even greater heights of aesthetic enjoyment. For these reasons opportunities for singing *must* be presented in the senior high school in order to make these boys and girls aware of the joy of singing with their more developed voices.

One opportunity is through a "general chorus," which is just exactly what the name implies — a chorus for everybody. Every student who indicates a vigorous, or even a feeble desire to sing should be encouraged to become a member. There are some high schools that make provision for every student to sing in one big chorus once a week. The chorus will vary in size, according to the enrollment in the high school. In a large school the chorus may enroll several hundred students; there may be a beginning and an advanced chorus, or there may be a chorus for each grade. In a small high school the general chorus may become the mixed glee club or the *a cappella* choir. In the latter case some degree of selectivity may be necessary.

Formerly the general chorus in the high school was the core of the music program. Today it is rare. In some places it has been entirely replaced by the *a cappella* choir.

The trend toward selective choral organizations in the high school is probably due to the fact that the general chorus has confined its efforts to community singing and the repertory has never passed the "Over the Bounding Main" stage. This is a reflection upon the musical ability of the choral teachers rather than upon that of the students.

Do not underestimate the ability of high school students. These young people like a real challenge. They like to feel that they are accomplishing something, that they are "going places." The singing of music that is too easy and trivial becomes a chore. It is not necessary to resort to the banality of much of the popular music of today if the conductor can make the singing of great music a thrilling experience. Most of the majestic choruses from *Messiah* are within the vocal and technical capabilities of these young people. Other masterworks which are suitable will be found in the final chapter.

A cappella choir. There are students in the high school who are eager to participate in choral ensembles which challenge their individual musical ability and enable them to devote more time to singing the wealth of choral literature than is possible in the general chorus. While it is the first job of the high school to provide singing experiences for the entire student body, it should also provide special musical opportunities for talented students. A great deal of the material available to the small selective groups calls for exacting performance. The enthusiasm with which gifted high school students accept and master this challenge is often one of the greatest delights of the choral teacher.

In Chapter V we compared accompanied and unaccompanied singing and extolled the virtues of the latter. *A cappella* singing is especially suitable for selected groups. It is through this style of singing that the subtle aesthetic and spiritual values of artistic singing are truly attained.

Permanent values exist only when there are intrinsic qualities of merit. Unaccompanied singing, first of all, approaches a pure means of vocal expression. It enhances the meaning of an idea expressed musically. It is personal, intimate, and sincere. It is less trammeled by externals. *A cappella* singing requires careful and complete use of the voice, because it alone must carry the burden of expression. The singing is not borne along by an accompaniment. The singer feels the responsibility of expressing the musical idea. He is stimulated by this direct and personal approach to the song. He is freer to express himself sincerely and beautifully.

Secondly, unaccompanied singing facilitates more careful listening. The true musical experience must be approached through listening. There are many opportunities for listening to music. Too many people can *hear,* but they never *listen.* Listening is the completion of the musical experience which is approached through hearing. It is in this approach that the unaccompanied choir justifies itself and gives richer rewards than those offered by choral units that sing only accompanied music. When there are no external distractions, the singer is freer to listen to what is going on tonally, harmonically, and dynamically. Heavily accompanied choral singing may even impair a young singer's sensitivity to accuracy of pitch, quality of tone, unified articulation, and delicate shadings of dynamics and nuance. Truly, if the young singer is to receive a genuine musical experience through beautiful vocal expression, the psychological procedure is to introduce him early to unaccompanied singing. This approach should be used before the student reaches the senior high school and unaccompanied singing should continue to be an important part of his musical experiences.

A third value which is significant in *a cappella* choirs lies in the type of material available. A large percentage of unaccompanied music is from the literature of the church. The great contribution of sixteenth and early seventeenth century composers such as Palestrina, Orlando di Lassus, Byrd, Morley, and others, was the perfection of small vocal forms. The motet and madrigal are the highest musical expressions of these composers. By more modest means they express a musical idea as complete as the fugue, the cantata, the opera, and the symphonic forms of the eighteenth and nineteenth centuries. There is a wide difference in the scope of the musical idea, but the earlier forms are the equal of the later forms in quality.

Therefore, the *a cappella* choir has a wealth of beautiful music especially suited to its needs. Nor is it necessary to search the archives of modal music for *a cappella* literature. An increasing demand for unaccompanied choral music has produced striking and effective arrangements of a wide variety of folk songs, as well as the best musical efforts from some of our contemporary composers.

For these foregoing values may the *a cappella* choir continue to flourish in our high schools. Tone production, blend and balance, and voice formations for these groups have been discussed in previous chapters. The first part of this chapter gives assistance in the selection of members for this ideal type of choral group. Also, organizational procedures have been given. We add a blessing to the conductor and choristers of these groups in their pursuit of artistic singing.

General College Chorus

For consideration of the general college chorus little needs to be added to the discussion given in the preceding section of the senior high school chorus. It provides a cultural activity that leaps the confines of departmental lines. It is an experience that can weld a widely heterogeneous student body into a common artistic goal. It may establish closer community ties by inviting members from the surrounding environs. A college chorus can make an extremely valuable contribution to the aesthetic life of the campus. In looking around the average American college campus, the latter need is obvious.

A college chorus should sing the great masterpieces of choral literature. If a tradition is established for singing the best repertory, the students attracted to the chorus will be those with the most interest and superior ability. With this method of screening, all applicants should be admitted to membership. If a misfit happens to find his way into the chorus he can be handled on an individual basis. Many fine college choruses have been organized and maintained on this informal and democratic basis.

The oratorio is the standard musical diet for most college choruses. Many of the master composers have devoted their most serious efforts to the oratorio as a means of musical expression. Many of them are within the vocal resources of the college.

A satisfying performance of most oratorios is dependent upon adequate soloists. Amateur soloists, as a rule, are disappointing. It is not a question of denying local soloists experience, but it is rather a matter of giving everyone concerned the finest spiritual and artistic experience in singing and listening to great music. The experience must not suffer from the lack of satisfactory soloists. Naturally, if there is a promising student or satisfactory vocal soloist in the locality, he should be given a chance. The importing of special soloists for the oratorio is traditional procedure. Long and tedious rehearsals are not required of the chorus for the sake of the soloists as in the case of an opera production. Chorus and soloists can rehearse separately. As a result, through the singing of expert soloists the performance is often as keen a musical experience for the chorus as for the audience.

The college chorus should join with the college orchestra for many performances. However, great pains must be taken to see that the orchestra is as well prepared as the chorus. It is a most disappointing experience for the chorus to work diligently all semester on a major work, and then to have the performance impaired by an inadequately trained orchestra. It is far better to use the combination of a piano and organ as the accompaniment for the performance. All things considered, it is advisable for the choral conductor to direct the final performance. The chorus usually responds more enthusiastically to the conductor with whom it has been rehearsing.

If an oratorio is used during the year, it should be supplemented by easier choral material with emphasis on *a cappella* numbers. In these compositions the conductor can center attention upon singing as a tonal art. Care of the voice should be stressed and the love of sustained, legato singing developed. These young people need music which seems to present the emotional qualities of immediate interest as well as music which will nurture mature emotional development.

College Concert Choir

Much of the finest choral singing in our country is being performed by college concert choirs. The vocal and musical maturity plus unbounded enthusiasm of the students enables these groups to rise to any choral challenge. The college concert choir is often the outstanding performing group on the campus. It is the pride of both schools and community. It often represents the school on concert tours and at music conferences.

To be a member of the concert choir should be a mark of distinction. The membership should consist of college students who not only have the musical ability, but also realize their responsibility to the school in their deportment at rehearsals, in concerts, and on choir trips. Singers should be auditioned as described for selective groups at the beginning of this chapter. A core of officers should be appointed and elected to aid the conductor in rehearsal mechanics and the management of performing activities. The choristers, in cooperation with the officers and conductor, should formulate a constitution or at least a body of rules for continuing membership.

The entire gamut of fine choral literature is open to these groups. Under wise and efficient leadership the sesamé to artistic choral experience is attainable. The major share of the singing should probably be *a cappella* but the repertory should not be limited to unaccompanied music. There are many suitable compositions in this style. Also, especially challenging are many works which utilize a small combination of instruments as an accompaniment. The Bach cantatas are a rich repertory for this type of performance. The choral conductor is singularly blessed who has the opportunity to develop a fine college concert choir.

Church Choir

The problems involved in developing a successful church choir are manifold. We refer one more time to a recently published book for which we served as co-author. The unique functions of church choirs can be investigated in this book.* All of the aspects of artistic choral singing as presented in our present discussion are applicable to the singing in the choir loft.

As we stated in Chapter I, the primary purpose of a church choir is to create an atmosphere conducive to spiritual worship. To be spiritual, music must be beautiful; sincerity is not enough. In a worship service there is no excuse for banal music of a secular variety sung in a haphazard or nightclub manner.

Choir rehearsals must be regular and meaningful. Music must be appealing and spiritual in quality. The problem of changing and improving the musical taste of a congregation is a deliberate, discerning process. However, people invariably respond to beautiful music sung artistically. The choir director must not use the Sunday service as a college class in music appreciation. His continual search should be for understandable music that is in good taste.

In organizing a church choir, steps toward a constitution and a roster of officers should be taken as soon as feasible. The size of membership will be partially determined by the size of the choir loft or chancel. When applications exceed the available space a move may be made to make the choir more selective by raising the standards of performance. Such a policy is completely in accord with the primary purpose of church choirs.

Seating arrangements of voice sections for church choirs are the same as those for any mixed choir, except in churches where there is a divided chancel. The following diagrams present a few of the many possibilities.

Diagram 32

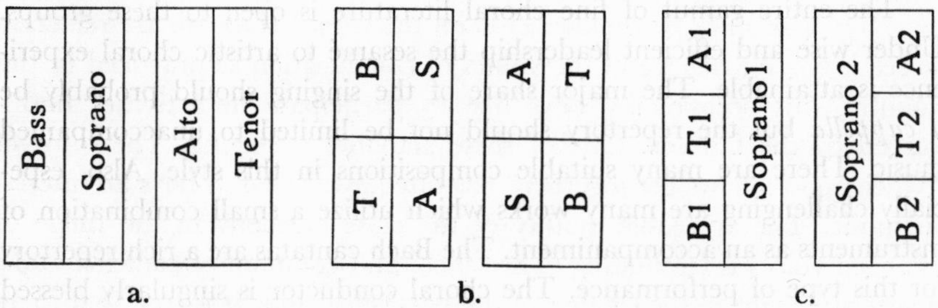

*Op. cit.

a.	b.	c.
The traditional formation for a divided chancel choir. When there is an overabundance of sopranos they may occupy one side with the other parts facing them. Blend and balance are difficult in this arrangement.	A newer formation for divided chancels. By dividing the parts equally, a much better blend and balance can be obtained. Choir must be quite experienced for this arrangement.	An excellent formation for antiphonal singing or double-choir work. It is conducive to excellent blend and balance. The weaker sections should be shifted to the outside.

Community Chorus

There was a time in the musical history of our country when nearly every hamlet had a community chorus. It had a social as well as a musical purpose. With the inroads made on creative activity in our present life the spread of community choruses is gradually diminishing.

One comforting trend is for the community chorus to combine with the college chorus. In communities which are fortunate enough to have a college, the general chorus still functions. This arrangement usually assures the chorus of the dynamic leadership needed for its continuance and success.

With the gradual disintegration of a community chorus, many conductors have endeavored to yield to individual demands for easier and lighter music of a popular variety. This procedure is disastrous. The talented singers who usually carry these groups lose interest and drop out. Soon the conductor is left with a small group of singers who are unable to sing any type of music adequately. It has been the author's experience that the conductor should hold to his standards, reveal the beauty of great music to his choristers, and work with enthusiasm and conviction for his ideals. Only this emphasis on the permanent values of singing will encourage the singers to be steadfast.

Male Glee Clubs

Boys' glee clubs. Is the glee club on the wane? If so, we are reluctant to see it go. We believe in the values of co-education as practiced in this country, but occasionally boys like to participate in activities undisturbed by the fair sex. One of these activities is singing. The spirit of "when good fellows get together" has often awakened in boys an interest in music. The agreeable quality of the close harmony in the range of changed voices is fascinating. The school and community audiences take a special delight in the singing of the boys' glee club. It is true that there is a shortage of first tenors, not only in high school but everywhere. Make a specialty of developing them. (Procedures can be found in Chapter IX.) Only a few are needed to balance the other voice parts of the glee club.

The term "glee" originally meant an unaccompanied song for three or more voices. It was not confined to boisterous songs of merriment. Many two- and three-part arrangements of worth are being published to meet the needs of these high school groups. The rehearsals can be made a social occasion, as well as a time for work. One of the answers to interesting high school boys in singing is to have a glee club.

Men's glee clubs. In some countries in Europe, notably Wales and Germany, there is a long tradition of outstanding male glee clubs. This tradition emigrated to this country and blossomed during the period of the great expansion. Today few men's clubs exist except those sponsored by some organization or institution, notably, industries, service clubs, professional organizations and the colleges, especially those for men only. Barber-shop glee clubs sponsored by the SPEBSQSA are the vogue today.

The latter glee clubs are a wonderful outlet for men who like to sing, but they are limited in repertory. Many conductors, realizing this limitation, are reaching out for more variety and more classic literature. This movement may be the wellspring for a resurgence of the male glee club in America.

Many colleges have proved that the male glee club can be as artistic an organization as a concert choir. The singing of a fine male glee club is thrilling. The repertory of every mixed choir should have several numbers for male voices alone. The parts for a standard male glee club are called tenor I, tenor II, bass I (or baritone) and bass II; those of a barber-shop glee club are designated as tenor, lead, baritone, and bass. Since the voices are of uniform timbre and in the lower range of the pitch scale, it is not necessary to mix them. Here are the usual voice formations for each type of glee club.

Diagram 33

Standard Male Glee Club

T 2	T 1	B 2	B 1

Barber Shop Glee Club

Tenor	Lead	Bari-tone	Bass

Girls' Glee Club

There is an abundance of material for girls' glee clubs, much of it questionable. Don't forget that high school girls on the whole are more mature than the boys. Study carefully the beautiful songs of Brahms for ladies' voices. Three-part songs seem to be the most suitable for high school. In senior high schools, however, many four-part songs are possible. Do not purposely avoid them. They are richer in harmonic texture and more satisfying in unaccompanied singing. Many girls may sing the second alto part if they do not sing with forced chest quality. Mature ladies' glee clubs should emphasize four-part music in their repertory. Every mixed choir should have in its repertory several numbers for treble voices alone. The celestial quality of these lyric voices offers variety, and often provides the highlight of a musical program.

As with the male glee clubs, because treble voices have a similar timbre it is not as necessary to mix the voice parts to secure blend and balance, except in groups where there is an over-abundance of first sopranos. In these groups it is advisable to divide the first sopranos as in diagram *b* below.

Diagram 34

a. Girls' Glee Club

S2	S1	A

b. Girls' Glee Club (Divided Soprano 1)

S1	S2	A	S1

c. Ladies' Glee Club

S2	S1	A2	A1

Small Vocal Ensembles

In high schools and colleges there should be singing experiences for students of all degrees of musical ability. The general chorus invites all students to participate in expression through song. The choir and the glee clubs are more selective. Small vocal ensembles, such as madrigal groups, boys' quartets and double quartets, girls' trios and double trios, provide opportunities for students of superior talent. Small ensembles in our music education program are one guarantee for the development of leaders for the future.

Small singing groups have values other than giving the student with superior musical ability an opportunity for more extensive study. First of all, these groups contain the core of a program that will develop a musical America. What is happening to all the young students who play in our large high school and college orchestras and sing in our large choruses? After graduation do they put their music on the shelf and confine their vocalizing to bathroom warbling? Too often they do, even when opportunities for participating in musical organizations are provided by the community. Experience in small singing ensembles in the high school stimulates the desire to keep this form of expression alive after graduation.

It is much easier to organize small groups in the community than large choruses which involve considerable expense and superior leadership. Formation of singing groups can be stimulated by presenting a plan to the general chorus, the choir, and the glee clubs. This plan should include a description of various ensembles such as the madrigal group, mixed quartet, girls' trio and sextet, boys' quartet and octet.

Regular rehearsals should be planned to be held weekly, bi-weekly, or even once a month in various homes by members who are in the habit of meeting together socially. Each group should have a student leader who sings with the group. The leader may be the accompanist. Occasionally time should be taken from chorus and choir rehearsals for these groups to present numbers that they have been practising. Large numbers of such small informal groups carried into adult life will nurture a singing America.

The small ensembles which are selected to represent the school can be very effective in contributing to the musical life of the community. These groups are usually composed of the most talented singers in the school. They should do artistic work. Moreover, because of their size there are no difficult problems of organization. This fact is very important in filling singing engagements. Rehearsals are easily arranged. Transportation is no problem. The singing of these groups is most appropriate for club meetings and informal gatherings. A small meeting place is not only adequate but actually advantageous. If they sing well, they will be in continuous demand. However, this demand can be overdone. Some policy should be worked out as to the number of appearances that a small ensemble should make each month.

The type of singer selected for the small ensembles representing the school should be reliable and responsible. Although the teacher will probably be well acquainted with the superior students, a try-out is not only fair, but is also tactful. This try-out should include all suggestions offered for selecting members of the *a cappella* choir, but the test should be even more exacting. It should include reading and singing part-songs. A natural blend of voices is very necessary for these small singing ensembles, and the director should hear the voices together before making a final selection. Great care should be taken to select students who will work together. Often students will form such groups on their own initiative and come to the teacher for help.

In these groups the students will naturally have a greater voice in the selection of music that they are to sing. If a good job has been done in building a repertory of fine music in the chorus and choir, there need be no fear for the music that they will select for themselves. Undoubtedly, the teacher will need to guide them continually in developing criteria for the selection of music. At times it may be necessary for him to point out the inadvisability of including a certain number in their permanent repertory. The teacher remains the guiding spirit in the picture, but he should give the students as much freedom in the selection of music as their discriminating power warrants. They must be made to realize that they are building a permanent library for the school. Each group should be permitted to check out music from the choral library of the school.

Any group smaller than twelve voices should not be conducted; they should be so carefully rehearsed that they can sing independent of direction. For this reason, singing in these small ensembles is often a more satisfying individual musical experience than singing in a large chorus or choir. Students develop independence, leadership, responsibility, and cooperation that is more active and personal than that resulting from participation in larger groups. By all means let us as music educators direct some of our attention and energy to these small singing ensembles.

PROJECTS

1. Draw up a plan for the organizing of a community choral group. Take into consideration sponsorship, leadership and membership.
2. Outline a corps of officers which you feel would be needed for a mixed choral group, discuss the manner in which they attain office, appointed or elected, and describe the nature and duties of each office.
3. Draw up a typical constitution for a mixed choral group.
4. Make out an annual budget for some choral group with which you are familiar. Defend all of the various items of the budget.
5. Audition twelve members of your class or individual friends and classify them for membership in a mixed choir.
6. Visit one rehearsal of every type of choral group described in this chapter. Write up your reactions. Read Chapter XI as preparation for your visit.

Chapter XI

The Choral Rehearsal

The ultimate success of a choral conductor stands or falls upon his attitude toward and his procedures in rehearsals. The rehearsal must be an exciting adventure for both singers and conductor. If it becomes a laborious chore, little will be accomplished and the rehearsal might as well be cancelled for the good of everyone concerned. The value of a rehearsal should be measured by the pleasure and sense of achievement it gives the singers. The motivation of an impending performance should be secondary.

The rehearsal itself should achieve all of the values of choral singing as presented in Chapter I. The performance may supply a supplementary motivation, but it should not be necessary for the fruition of choral values. The persistent and consistent goal of the rehearsal must be as high a level of artistic singing as possible within the capability of the group. This goal does not preclude the recreational, social, cultural, spiritual, and aesthetic considerations from rehearsal attitudes and procedures. In fact, the primary goal will be more readily achieved when the rehearsal is conducted in an atmosphere which capitalizes upon what may be referred to as extra-musical values. These qualities of the rehearsal, rather than being detrimental, are actually beneficial to the primary purpose.

REHEARSAL OBJECTIVES

The psychologists tell us that to be successful any cooperative human endeavor must be pleasurable, possess a sense of "belongingness," and provide a perception of personal and group achievement. Choral rehearsals must be conducted in such a manner as to capitalize on these qualities. The choral conductor may well ask himself simple questions such as these: Do the choristers enjoy the rehearsals? Do I enjoy them? Do all of the choristers seem to be a vital part of the group or do some of them seem to be left out? Is the rehearsal a cooperative venture and adventure between the conductor and the group and among choristers?

Do the choristers learn something? Am I learning something? Successful rehearsals are dependent upon the objectives engendered from positive responses to such self-searching questions.

Musical Development

The essence of the choral rehearsal must be musical growth. This growth includes appreciative discrimination, familiarity with repertory, vocal development, and improvement in singing skills. All of these factors indicate a growth in general musicianship which is the logical central organizing objective of any group rehearsal.

Some conductors may feel that choristers are not interested in their improvement in musicianship, that exploring the ramifications of musical development will tend to slight personal and social values, that with the pressures of public appearances there is simply no time at rehearsals to concern themselves with anything but learning the music. The author's experience with students and choristers has been almost the opposite attitude. Unless choristers feel that they are improving both individually and as a group, they will lose interest. Unless sufficient emphasis is given to musical development, personal and social values will be diminished. And unless general musicianship is developed, rehearsals become repetitive, tedious, and a sense of achievement is minimized.

Choristers must have the feeling that they are learning something to remain interested. Choristers sometimes refer to the fun which they have had at a rehearsal, but they more often refer to how much they have learned at a rehearsal. Choristers sometimes refer to how much they like the conductor or what a good fellow he is, but they more often refer to how much he has to offer them in learning to sing.

Rehearsals must not be approached with the attitude of only making them pleasurable, democratic, and pseudo-inspirational at the sacrifice of musical values. Rather, they should be approached with the determination of emphasizing musical development in the group, thus making the rehearsals enjoyable, democratic, and genuinely inspirational.

Enjoyable Experience

Rehearsals must be enjoyable because it is in such an atmosphere that the goal of a choral group is achieved and singing values are realized. We must remember that no one will learn what he will not accept; anyone will lose interest in an activity that does not give him some form of pleasure. Severity of manner in itself does not instill a desire to learn. Amiability with a purpose usually gains better results. A friendly attitude need not sanction a slackening of artistic standards. It is the gradual working toward musical perfection that makes rehearsals enjoyable.

An enjoyable experience is fun, but it is also more than fun. An enjoyable experience gives pleasure, but it is also more than pleasure. In each rehearsal let everyone have at least one satisfying musical experience. What is meant by a musical experience in a chorus? Simply this: it is the joy of singing with abandon some beautiful piece of music. It is the sheer joy of singing that causes faces and eyes to light up and awaken the imagination. Each rehearsal period must provide these experiences. Imagination is stirred through an understanding of the text and the message of the music. "With abandon" implies the opposite of self-consciousness. It means giving one's self unreservedly to the music. It is apparent in the vital *pianissimo* as well as in the restrained *fortissimo*. It is through such experiences as these that a genuine appreciation of beautiful singing in a choral body will develop. From this growth both the conductor and choristers will derive their greatest source of genuine pleasure.

Democratic Environment

Some people revel in authority because of the feeling of aggrandizement that it provides for them, and for the power over their fellowmen which it affords. It is found among many politicians and administrators and, unfortunately, it is even evident in some choral conductors. Some conductors adopt a superior attitude because of the wealth of musical knowledge which they enjoy in contrast to the poor, ignorant chorister. They represent the musical aristocracy among the unmusical peasantry. Some conductors seem to feel that a dominating and demanding personality and attitude is absolutely necessary to get results. Very often this attitude in rehearsals is only a defense to conceal their own personal and musical limitations.

This idea of democracy in rehearsals is not to be taken lightly. The callous use of unreasonable tactics of force have no more place in a choral rehearsal than they do in government. Democracy implies kinship with other people more or less fortunate than onself; it implies a consideration of the welfare of others as well as one's own welfare. Ask yourself if, in exasperation, you have chosen someone in the chorus on whom to inflict your sarcastic chastisement. If so, was it meted out deservedly, or was it to detract attention from your own limitations? Have you used authoritative measures because you were not sure of yourself? The best conductors get artistic results faster and better through democratic means. They are sufficiently sure of themselves to be considerate of the other fellow.

Democratic behavior observes and accords to every individual certain "unalienable" rights and certain inescapable corollary responsibilities. Every chorister has the right to expect democratic treatment from the conductor, but he in turn has definite responsibilities which preclude his taking advantage of such consideration. The conductor exercises his leadership by the consent of the choristers, out of respect to his greater musical knowledge. He appeals to their reason to subject individuality for the success of a cooperative enterprise.

Someone has said that a democracy exists first for the privilege of doing the thing for which one is most aptly suited, and secondly, for recognition in doing it. By recognizing publicly worthwhile achievement of whatever nature, students not only acquire this democratic spirit of recognizing merit, but they are stimulated to greater achievement. A word of praise to a vocal section here and a word of commendation to a soloist there will excite the entire group to greater endeavor.

It is often stated that the cooperative performance in music is a demonstration of the democratic spirit. In such a performance the individual must contribute not only some skill, however elementary, but also must be able to participate with others toward achieving a common end. These musical organizations are often called "laboratories" for developing the desirable traits toward cooperative spirit and democratic understanding.

As a final observation let us point out that music as an art is undemocratic, because it is relentless in its demands for expressive performance before it will reveal its beauties. However, since its beauties are revealed through the bodies, the feelings, and the minds of human beings, just like human beings its spirit flourishes best in a democratic environment.

Aesthetic Satisfaction

It is difficult to "put one's finger" on the subtle meaning of aesthetic satisfaction. In a chorus, however, it is reflected in the bodily attitudes, the facial expressions, and the musical responsiveness of the singers. When it is experienced by the whole group it pervades the entire room or auditorium. In simple terms aesthetic satisfaction implies a glow of general well-being in response to something beautiful. It further implies the sensitivity to react to something beautiful. It also infers the presence of something beautiful to which to react and respond.

Aesthetic satisfaction results from responsiveness to an artistic creation in some media. Choristers must produce their own aesthetic satisfaction through artistic singing. The music is not beautiful until they make it beautiful. Appreciation, discrimination and refinement of taste are the concomitants aesthetic experiences. That is why artistic singing must be the goal of every choral group and why each rehearsal must be conducted in such a manner that aesthetic satisfaction will be realized. It may be only the lovely color of a single unison tone, the richness of an individual chord in a composition, the turn of a phrase, the surge of a climax, or the poetical quality of the text. When these experiences occur, linger on them, for they are the musical life-blood of a chorus.

The responsiveness of the choristers to music is largely determined by the responsiveness of the conductor to music. The lead comes from him. Unless he is musical "to his finger tips", the rehearsal is likely to be drab and barren of aesthetic value. Yelling, ranting, and stomping the feet are not a substitute for artistry. On the other hand, lackadaisical procedures and compromise of high standards of performance are not the answer. Music will impart its message only to those who are willing to give of themselves unstintingly in exploring its secrets and beauties.

REHEARSAL PLANS

The responsibility for the success of rehearsals rests upon the conductor. Careful preparation not only makes for efficient rehearsals, but it is also conducive to more enjoyable rehearsals. Nothing is more distracting to a choral group than for the conductor to "breeze in the last minute" as if his attendance were an afterthought, completely disorganized as to what to do, and undecided as to what music to practice. The conductor should always give the impression at rehearsal of having important things to do. That means arriving early and leaving late. It means not wasting time and "dilly dallying" during rehearsals. Vary the pace of the rehearsal, yes, but convey the feeling that the artistic performance of music is a worthwhile endeavor and must be approached with keen anticipation and serious intent.

Rehearsal Schedules

Careful consideration of rehearsal schedules contributes immeasurably to successful rehearsals. The rehearsal should be held at a time when people feel like working. Morning hours are usually good. Immediately after lunch is not the best time, although this warning has nothing to do with the idea that one should not sing on a full stomach. It is simply that singing requires energy and alertness, and people, as a rule, do not feel very energetic or alert immediately after lunch. The middle of the afternoon is not bad, unless it is immediately after school, in which case there are too many distracting influences. Just before dinner in the evening, when body energy is at a low ebb, seems to be one of the poorest times of the day. Evening is a good time for rehearsals, unless the day is so strenuous for the participants that they do not respond to the relaxation that a good dinner and change of outlook afford. Community choruses, industrial choral groups and church choirs seem to function best with evening rehearsals. It is wise for church choirs to have a short rehearsal to "run over" the anthem before the Sunday morning service.

A rehearsal should be only as long as it can be made interesting. At the close there should always be the feeling that there is more to be accomplished. A lively one-hour rehearsal will accomplish more than a two-hour rehearsal that drags. A two-hour rehearsal should provide for a short intermission of at least ten minutes. Rehearsals less than forty-five minutes long usually bring disappointing results. Thirty-minute rehearsals are too short and too rushed.

A wise conductor will begin on time and end on time. Once the habit of starting late is established it becomes progressively worse. He should start on time even if there are only a few members present. The late comers will soon get the idea that he means business. A few pointed remarks on responsibility and cooperation may be apropos occasionally, but do not give a weekly sermon on tardiness. Repeated threats lose their effectiveness. If the chorus has within its constitution a set of rules relating to such matters, the conductor should see that the members abide by them. Also, stop on time. Little is accomplished by running over a few minutes The singers may have made other engagements after the rehearsal. It might be well for all choruses to have a finishing bell such as the class bell in the high schools. When rehearsals run over the scheduled time, choristers usually become inattentive and fidgety. The author's pet remark to restless singers is "Don't worry about the time. I am a union man, and I will stop on time even if it is in the middle of an eighth note."

Rehearsal Facilities

As mentioned in the preceding chapter, an adequate rehearsal room and equipment must not be underestimated in their effect upon a choral rehearsal. In some situations conductors may feel that they are lucky if they have any room at all in which to practice. Also, we know conductors who practice in rooms where no piano is available and the singers must stand. That is determination! If a fine performing group can be developed under handicaps, the impression the chorus makes usually stimulates the sponsoring institution to provide more suitable quarters and equipment. To do the best work a choral group should be furnished with the following facilities: (1) a suitable room,

(2) a conducting podium and stool, (3) appropriate chairs, and (4) a piano in good condition.

Rehearsal room. Size, lighting, ventilation, and acoustical properties are the chief factors to consider for a choral rehearsal room. The room should be sufficiently large to give the chorus some approximation of its sound in an auditorium. When choral groups practice in an extremely small room they are lost when asked to perform in an auditorium. In schools the auditorium stage is a good place to practice except for the demands by various study groups for the use of the auditorium during a school day.

Needless to say, the rehearsal room should be well lighted and well ventilated. Singers have enough difficulty reading music in good light without imposing upon them the handicap of poor lighting. Singing requires a constant change of air. Someone should be assigned to keep the room well ventilated at a temperature which will stimulate activity. Take heed, however; singers are sensitive to drafts. Plenty of fresh air helps to offset drooping spirits and sagging pitch.

Careful consideration should be given to the acoustical properties of the rehearsal room. It should be neither too live nor too dead. If it is too live, the singing of the group will sound muddled and lack clarity, choristers will have difficulty hearing each other, and the conductor gets a wrong conception of the quality of the performance. If it is too dead, the singing will sound lifeless and rehearsals will be disappointing. What is needed is a room sufficiently live acoustically to give resonance to the singing without impairing clarity of pitch, parts, and diction. An oblong room with the singers seated at one end is usually more satisfactory than a square room where the singers are facing a nearby wall. Anyone desiring information concerning rehearsal rooms and equipment can secure valuable information from the Music Educators National Conference (MENC), NEA Building, 1201 16th St., N. W., Washington 6, D. C.

Conducting podium and stool. A conductor should not be too high above a chorus. Tilting the chin or craning the neck to see the conductor causes incorrect posture for singing. Unless it is a very large group, it is better for the conductor to be near the singers, and practically on the same level. Then if the singers hold their music in the proper position, they can see the conductor with ease. A podium about a foot in height is the best answer rather than a high platform. Then the conductor is freer to leave the podium to assist voice parts and listen attentively to individual voices or sections.

As far as we are concerned a conducting stool is a must. There was a time when we felt that a conducting stool was a sign of physical decrepitude. With the advance of years and with experimentation the author has found that he is just as efficient conducting rehearsals while seated upon a stool as when standing. The conservation of one's energy is immeasurable. Festival rehearsals which sometimes endure for five or six hours are "rough." A conducting stool need not diminish a conductor's enthusiasm and energy, in fact he can maintain a better pace for a longer period of time when using a stool. Get a good one, one with a leather seat and back!

Rehearsal chairs. Choral chairs should be designed to beget correct singing posture. They should be straight-backed so that it is easy to sit in an erect position on the edges of the chairs. Auditorium seats of the lounging variety simply double the work of the conductor. Since many rehearsal rooms are used for multiple purposes conductors are forced to resort to folding chairs. If so, try to secure the one with the straightest back. Regardless of the chairs, insist that while singing, choristers sit with two feet flat on the floor and with their backs away from the seats. At the present time, permanent choral chairs as well as choral folding chairs which are conducive to correct singing posture are being manufactured. Write to the MENC.

Rehearsal piano. Our modern piano, tuned to the well-tempered scale, is said to be out of tune with the "pure" scale, even when it is in tune. Be that as it may, it is absurd to endure a piano that is out of tune with its out-of-tuneness. There is nothing as discouraging to the author as to direct a choral rehearsal when the piano is flat in pitch, out of tune, and uneven in scale, with some notes not sounding.

We are devotees of unaccompanied singing, but the judicious use of the piano at rehearsals expedites immeasurably the learning of the music. Good piano tuners are on the decline, both in availability and capability. We are convinced that every choral conductor should take a course in the repair and tuning of the piano. A good upright piano will suffice for rehearsals if a grand piano is not feasible. Let us not continue to arrange and prepare for all other aspects of successful rehearsals and then have them ruined by a "wretched" piano.

Rehearsal Attendance

The problem of attendance is a part of rehearsal planning. The best medicine to assure regular attendance is to hold rehearsals in which objectives are realized. If rehearsals are enjoyable, educational, democratic, and inspirational, a chorister will overcome almost any adversity to attend. Convenient rehearsal schedules and pleasant rehearsal facilities also engender regularity of attendance.

Another factor which bears upon rehearsal attendance is the human trait of being needed. Let every chorister be aware of the fact that attendance is checked at each rehearsal. This practice will give him the assurance that his presence is needed. If a choir constitution exists and contains a set of rules for attendance, they should be strictly adhered to. Rules that are not observed are detrimental rather than beneficial.

REHEARSAL PREPARATION

Successful choral rehearsals are not "hit or miss" affairs. They are the result of careful planning and thorough preparation. The gifts of verbal and musical improvisation are valuable, but they should not be completely depended upon by the conductor in directing rehearsals. The goals for which we plan and prepare are usually realized.

Musical Preparation

Conducting a chorus is more than simply rehearsing and performing. It involves homework. The conductor must not only take the prime responsibility for selecting the music, but also he must familiarize himself with it so as to be able to present it efficiently and effectively to the chorus. Any conductor who takes recourse in learning the music *with* the choir is inviting disaster. Very few conductors are sufficiently talented and experienced to appear before a chorus unfamiliar with the music and still direct a superior rehearsal. In fact, it is the talented and experienced conductors who inevitably make it a point to prepare themselves musically for every rehearsal.

Until he has gained musical assurance through experience, every novice choral conductor should set up some routine such as the following to prepare himself musically before every rehearsal.

1. Read through the accompaniment of each selection on the piano.
2. Read through the voice parts on the piano if they vary from the accompaniment.
3. Practice with conducting movements the setting of the tempo of each selection to be rehearsed.
4. Practice conducting movements in intricate rhythmical passages.
5. Practice singing the difficult sections of each voice part for demonstration purposes.
6. Read the text aloud, with special attention to meaning and diction. The conductor should be able to clarify the poetical meaning of the text and pronounce each word correctly. He should be sure of the meaning and phonetics of foreign texts.

7. Arrange for an assistant, or music secretary to make corrections or minor changes in all copies of the music. This practice is the only efficient one for this troublesome detail. Corrections and changes made by choristers are invariably unsatisfactory.
8. See that the accompanist has all music in advance of rehearsal for study and practice.

The accompanist has a similar responsibility to the conductor. So many choral rehearsals are impaired by incapable or indifferent accompanists. The qualifications of an accompanist were described in Chapter V. At present we are concerned with his preparation for rehearsals. Few accompanists read music with sufficient facility to warrant neglect of the study of the music previous to a rehearsal. He must be able to play it competently so as to give his undivided attention to the conductor. His preparation for rehearsals should include the following:

1. Practice the accompaniment of each selection until it is "under his fingers."
2. Play through the parts in open score (unless the music is in complicated contrapuntal style) until he can play them with facility.
3. Study individual contrapuntal parts to be able to play them for sectional practice.
4. Anticipate the need for simple transpositions such as flats to sharps and sharps to flats in unaccompanied numbers.

Social Preparation

A friendly atmosphere in the room is one of those intangible elements which contributes vitally to successful rehearsals. The following are a few means for establishing a congenial spirit for work during the rehearsal!

1. A social committee should be present to greet and welcome all new members.
2. The conductor should make himself available to the members before and after rehearsal. He should endeavor to arrive ten minutes before rehearsal and remain ten minutes afterwards. These informal chats with the conductor are greatly appreciated by the members, and stimulate them to put forth added effort.
3. The conductor should make a few introductory remarks of greeting and a short description of rehearsal plans. Anything approaching a lecture is out of place. Save it.
4. The conductor should introduce new members to the chorus during a rehearsal break.

5. The reciting of a little personal incident during the rehearsal is a natural device for the conductor to use in order to encourage social rapport with the group.

Rehearsal Room Preparation

An efficient rehearsal depends largely upon the physical preparation of the rehearsal room. Much time can be wasted on details, such as arranging the chairs and distributing individual copies of music. A corps of officers is needed to take the responsibility of checking the room and the music for rehearsal.

1. If chairs are movable they should be arranged in advance of the rehearsal time according to the instructions of the conductor.
2. Heating and ventilation should be checked so that the best working conditions for singing exist.
3. Singers should be assigned seat numbers to avoid confusion at the beginning of the rehearsal.
4. Singers should be given a music number and the corresponding envelope or book containing all of the music to be rehearsed as they take their seats. After the rehearsal singers may turn in music or check it out for study. This practice is a greatly needed time-saver.

REHEARSAL PROCEDURES

Rehearsal plans may be carefully laid and rehearsal preparation given adequate attention, but if the conductor lacks the personal attributes and choral techniques necessary to carry out the objectives of a successful rehearsal, plans and preparation come to naught. It would be convenient if we could produce a set pattern of rehearsal procedures, which could be followed in all situations and under all conditions. However, a fixed method is not only impossible, but also inadvisable.

Moreover, no conductor should permit himself to adopt a set pattern of rehearsal procedures. Avoid such a routine as vocalizing, reading new music, working on familiar numbers, closing with a favorite selection. Also, abstain from the practice of budgeting time such as ten minutes on "warming up" on exercises, ten minutes on sight-singing, twenty minutes learning new compositions, fifteen minutes perfecting old numbers, five minutes reviewing some selection preferred by the chorus. This practice is deadening to interest.

A rehearsal should be an anticipated event for the choristers. Vary the rehearsal! Sometimes start with a brilliant number familiar to all.

Exercises for vocal development should apply directly to the task at hand — the artistic singing of choral music. Spend the most time on the music which needs it most. Pace the rehearsal to maintain interest and renew weary bodies and spirits.

In his experience, the author has observed many types of rehearsals. Perhaps a description and comment upon these representative rehearsals may be most helpful to the reader in checking on his own effectivenss of procedure and in assisting him to formulate his choral practices. Following the presentation of these typical rehearsals various aspects of rehearsal procedures will be discussed separately. These rehearsals will be designated by letter. Naturally, there are many variations within the different types. While writing the descriptions of these rehearsals the author was impressed with their resemblance to train rides which he has taken. He has facetiously added characteristic sub-titles.

TYPES OF REHEARSALS

Rehearsal A (Whistle-stopper). One type of rehearsal we have observed consists of reading through one piece of music after another with little or no comment. Verbal directions for dynamics and tempos for the entire piece are given to an inattentive chorus. Occasionally, the director points out wrong notes which are being sung by one of the sections. Rarely does he admonish the singers to pronounce the words more distinctly. Never is any suggestion made for the improvement of tone quality! Notes are "drummed out" in difficult passages for the various sections. After the music is read through again in a desultory fashion it is put away for the day only to be brought out at the next rehearsal and exposed to the same treatment.

Comment: This description is not exaggerated, for we have seen many such rehearsals. It might be referred to as a time-killing rehearsal in which neither the leader nor the students hold any objectives. There may be a public performance in the distant future, but it is too far off to excite any enthusiasm for immediate application of energies. Conductors who indulge in such procedures are either indifferent or they just do not know what to do or what a rehearsal is all about.

In this kind of rehearsal, choristers are bound to learn something; a smattering of information here and a technical detail there. However, no worthwhile or permanent learning can take place because the activity has no direction. Moreover, there may be negative attitudes instigated, such as deceiving the conductor, feigning effort, and devising tricks of misbehavior.

There may be many factors involved which cause conductors to hold these random rehearsals but the deficient results suggest the lack of any definite purpose. Surely there is little pleasure, musical growth is practically nil, any democratic values are accidental, and aesthetic satisfaction is completely missing. It would almost seem better to dispense with such choral rehearsals and devote the time to more meaningful activities.

Rehearsal B (The Pleasure Excursion). Then we have observed rehearsals, especially in schools, where a good time seems to be the primary purpose. "It is kids this, and kids that. We must do a good job at the parent-teachers association next week." To be popular with the choristers seems to be the chief aim of the conductor. His approach is to use their vernacular and try to be one of them. Confusion and restlessness usually prevail but a spirit of friendliness often pervades the rehearsal. Any musical results are attained through persuasion.

The customary procedure is to "warm up" on vocal exercises for a few minutes. Seldom is tone mentioned during the remainder of the rehearsal. New music is struggled through, parts are rehearsed separately, and the music is put together again. The director coaxes the singers to give attention to various facets of interpretation, such as tempos, dynamics, and diction. Clarity of pronunciation is usually slighted, because it calls for too much meticulous work. Nearly all elements of expression are presented by suggestion rather than demonstration. Intonation evolves from faith. Music is selected which the "kids" are sure to like. Little assiduous study of the artistic performance of worthwhile music is evident.

Comment: There is no question that many of the choristers enjoy rehearsals of this type. They like the spirit of cameraderie. The conductor is a "great guy." Rehearsals are a social and entertaining affair. The music is secondary. The singers are willing to work on it to please the conductor. Such rehearsals become a "mutual admiration society." These choral groups seldom have an exacting schedule of public performances. Possibly they fulfill the requirements expected of them. Democratic activity is present, but without direction. Aesthetic satisfaction is present to some degree, or at least there is a general physical and emotional feeling of well-being.

Rehearsal objectives are partially realized accidentally, but they remain nebulous. They need organization and focus. Permanent values and continuous musical growth are questionable. Rehearsals deteriorate into a social setting. The artistic performance of fine music ceases to be the primary purpose and motivating force of rehearsals.

Rehearsal C. (The Shuttle). Then we have observed rehearsals almost the direct opposite of the two preceding. All motivation and effort is geared to one or two performances each year, or the exacting requirements of a contest-festival in the spring. At each rehearsal concentration is limited to the study of one or two numbers. Perhaps one entire rehearsal is devoted to some technical detail. Sectional rehearsals are a regular part of the schedule. Singing an occasional wrong note is considered heresy. Technical perfection is the immediate and ultimate goal.

The conductor is usually business-like and gets right down to the task at hand. The music is the important thing here, the singers are secondary. He has no intention of being embarrassed in public performance with an unprepared group of singers. In school groups, anything below a rating of *I* in the spring festival is an insult to his musical skill. If this should happen the roof of his musical ego would collapse.

The inevitable "warm up" vocalises are present, including some tune-up exercises. A run-through of the music is next, then down to the important task. Parts are analyzed and practiced thoroughly, and wrong notes and poor intonation are eliminated before an effort is made to put the parts together. The conductor continually harps on clean diction without, however, offering concrete procedures to correct the faults. Suggestions for improved tone are scientific and exact. (They often sound as if they were read from a book). Factors of interpretation such as rhythmic figures, dynamics, accent, and phrasing are approached in the same studious manner. Nothing is left to chance, "even to the raising of an eyebrow."

Comment: The objectives of this type of rehearsal are the opposite to those of rehearsals *A* and *B*. They are narrow and extreme. The single purpose is there, but it needs to be achieved in the perspective of the larger musical, personal, and social values. Technical perfection is confused with artistry although artistic singing is dependent upon technical proficiency in all phases of music, tempo, tone, pitch, diction, dynamics, phrasing, nuance, and accuracy of notes. However, there must be that added element of understanding and responsiveness to musical and literary content.

There is little zest in this type of rehearsing. The pleasure comes from the motivation of pleasing an audience, taking a trip to the festival, and winning a high rating. There is musical growth, but it is fragmentary and lacking in continuity or wholeness. Democratic environment is sacrificed in order to achieve a limited, unremitting goal. The musical ends justify the dogmatic means. Such meager musical fare and impoverished rehearsal opportunities seldom provide genuine aesthetic satisfaction. We are not condoning slip-shod performance but pleading for more all-inclusive musical experiences in the rehearsal. A choral rehearsal should be self-sufficient in obtaining the broad objectives of artistic choral singing; procedures should not be dictated or determined by an impending public performance.

Rehearsal D (Twentieth-Century Limited). The choral rehearsal should be a challenge. We repeat that the rehearsal is the true test of the conductor; the public performance is a by-product. There should be a balanced approach to the realization of all the objectives of the rehearsal. In fact, their complete fruition is the result of the interdependence and interrelationships of the musical, personal, and social values. Broad and permanent musical values fail to flourish in a rehearsal devoid of extra-musical values. The chorister is a many-sided person and his whole being must be taken into consideration in any learning situation. Therefore, musical values cannot be stressed at the complete disregard of extra-musical values, hoping that they will come about incidentally. However, neither is the reverse true; that is, musical values will not flourish if only the extra-musical values are emphasized.

Moreover, musical growth which is worthy of the name consists of more than technical facility or one phase of musical development. It embraces understanding, comprehension, and insight. Interpretation is not a composite of various technical elements added together but an expressive imagery to which all of the elements of music, physical, emotional and mental, contribute. Consequently, all of the technical aspects of a rehearsal such as tone production, dynamics, diction, blend and balance, and musical accuracy should not be treated in the abstract but related immediately to the interpretation of the music being studied.

A large repertory, the subject matter of music, is worthy, but it is not necessarily the highest accomplishment of rehearsals. Repertory should be a tool to a deeper understanding and artistic response to music. In realizing the objectives of choral rehearsals a large repertory performed in a desultory fashion can be as ineffective as the highly technical performance of limited repertory which lacks musical understanding. The goal is to use as varied a repertory as possible which can be developed to an artistic level of performance in light of rehearsal time and the capabilities of the group.

The above remarks serve as a preface to the description of rehearsal procedures recommended by the author. The perplexing problem is the approach in learning the music. Our contention has been that better results are possible through the realization of the major objectives of rehearsals, namely: enjoyment, musical development, democratic setting, and aesthetic satisfaction. With these objectives functioning, the best procedures in learning the music are the ones which obtain the most musical results in the shortest possible time. Here is where the true ability of the conductor is revealed. Personality, conducting techniques, or one's own performing ability will not offset the lack of results, in this case a musical, finished product.

As described in the discussion of the preceding rehearsals the usual procedure taken by most choral groups in learning music is what might be called the *note approach.* Let us review it. A new composition is introduced. Sometimes an attempt is made to read a section of it in parts with the piano. Then each voice part goes over this section alone several times. The section is again sung in parts to see the improvement. Each section is reviewed in this manner until there seems to be some mastery of notes and rhythm. Then diction and phrasing are given attention. Suggestions for tone are sometimes introduced along the way. Finally, the interpretation is imposed upon all of these elements, with a gradual correction and refinement of notes and rhythm.

There are three things wrong, if not downright wicked, in exposing singers to such a mechanistic procedure. First of all, it is tedious and boring; secondly, it does not get fast results; finally, it does not get musical results.

Nothing is more tiring than "beating out notes," one part at a time. Practically none of the emotional or poetical qualities of the music survive this procedure. Rehearsals become hard, laborious work; singers lose interest and become indifferent; and, in younger groups, discipline problems arise.

Now let us look at another way of learning new music. We are going to be bold enough to call it the *musical approach*. In this approach, one essays to give an introduction to the entire piece of music. This may be done in several ways. If the singers have a certain amount of reading power, they should endeavor to sing through the entire piece in parts with the piano or with the aid of other instruments. In case the music is too difficult for this approach then it may be played completely through by the accompanist while the group follows the score. (Be sure the accompanist is warned in advance.) This same approach may be taken for an easy number where it is desirable for the accompanist to demonstrate mood and phrasing at the outset. If a fine recording is available the number may be introduced by playing it for the group. A recording should not be used unless the interpretation is one of which the conductor approves. The first conception of the choristers is difficult to erase. The author has found this approach extremely valuable when especially fast results are needed. Recordings may also be used after a group has learned a composition to compare interpretations.

After the entire number is introduced to the group, sections of it can be worked out. This is the point at which we recommend a radical departure from the usual note-to-note method. An approach must be taken through which all of the elements that make up the heart of the music are reached simultaneously — mood, words, rhythm, dynamics, phrasing, and even correct notes. It can be done with practice and experience.

The answer is for the group to speak the words in the musical rhythm with correct diction (both as to style and tone), proper dynamics, nuance, and phrasing. This can be done in one process if the teacher will demonstrate these things. Each phrase may be repeated several times in this manner and even broken down into smaller sections to show the inflection and nuance of the words, especially at the end of phrases. (Always look to the words for the secret of phrasing choral music.) Then try to do the same thing in singing the parts. If the singers do not get the notes let the accompanist play the parts. Then have the group try again to sing the parts. Work out phrase after phrase in this manner, endeavoring to take as large a section of the music as possible at a time, until the entire piece is covered. After the rough edges are knocked off in this way, more attention can be given to details of interval, tone, and special effects. By the time the notes are learned the interpretation is realized. Musical expressiveness and musical accuracy are arrived at simultaneously. The general procedure for this method of learning music is as follows:

1. Read the words in correct tempo and rhythm giving attention to style, tone and diction.
2. Sing the parts in the same manner.
3. Correct parts — contrapuntal sections may have to be practiced separately.
4. Reread words in difficult passages with correct style and diction.
5. Sing the parts of these sections in same manner.
6. Sing the entire composition with proper interpretation.
7. Review and refine until satisfactory.

Comment. The author has found several advantages in this procedure. First of all, the singers are aware of the mood and interpretation of the music from the beginning. Secondly, they actually learn the music more readily, that is, strange as it may seem, the notes and parts come faster. Finally, the singers, over a period of time, gain more reading power in this manner than when a mechanical approach to reading is taken. Therefore, each time a new piece of music is tackled the process becomes easier, and the finished product is attained more quickly, with greater artistic effect. This procedure is simply putting into practice what we know about the most efficient psychological procedures in an effective learning process, as well as realizing all of the objectives that should be inherent in every rehearsal. Try it!

As an added note we should give warning that this method is not as feasible in slow, contrapuntal music of the early Renaissance period. In this music each part is an independent voice line. Groups singing this music should have some reading facility. Otherwise, each individual voice line will need to be practiced and then fused together. Contrapuntal music with strong rhythmic characteristics should be learned in the method described above.

Discipline

If the difficulties were only vocal and musical, the life of the choral conductor in the public schools would be a comparatively peaceful existence. But he is dealing with young individuals, full of red blood and energy, who through his leadership are led to a greater understanding of music and a deeper love for its beauty. The path has many turns and obstructions. Many times this enthusiastic energy, for which we are truly thankful, causes dissension in the ranks when misdirected, and our old bugbear discipline arises.

The development of the spirit of cooperation is the problem of the individual conductor, and depends largely upon his teaching ability, leadership, enthusiasm, knowledge of his subject, and tact. The secret of solving most disciplinary problems is to be found in the creating of interest by keeping the singers busy. Insist on an attentive posture when singing. Utilize their hands and bodies in exercises for vocal development. Do not spend needless time with one part while another part has nothing to do but get into mischief. If a singing part needs individual attention, be sure to employ the entire chorus at brief interims. If corrective measures are necessary, do not threaten and then do nothing about it. In securing discipline avoid using an individual as a "bitter example" before the entire group. See him after rehearsal. This does not, however, rule out an admonishing word to individuals during a rehearsal. Impress on the group the fact that order and cooperation are imperative for the smooth and efficient running of the rehearsal. A sense of humor helps!

Inertia

A more dangerous enemy than discipline, encased in the word "inertia", is waiting to frustrate the hopes and goals of the choral conductor. Inertia is in evidence in every department of choral work.* It is evident in the irregular manner of going on and off the platform at a concert, the listless rising and sitting of the chorus, the attack and release of notes, and the lack of responsiveness to the beat of the conductor. These defects can be corrected, but they will persist unless the conductor is blessed with unlimited patience and unrelenting perseverance.

In such instances as those mentioned above, inertia can be detected and tactfully corrected; but there is one place where it is a more deadly weapon because it is not obvious, and its presence is not suspected by the singers. This place is in the articulation of words. All singers seem to succumb to this evil unless it is forcibly thrown off. In Chapter VI, p. 123, three steps were presented for overcoming inertia in diction.

Following the Beat

One aspect of inertia which needs added attention at this point is responsiveness of the singers to the conductor's beat. However, it is usually more than inertia so we are treating it separately. Very often it is due to the lack of decisiveness of the conductor's beat. On the other hand, it may be the stilted pattern of the beat which precludes the flexibility of phrase line. What we are trying to say is that some conductors are lucky that the singers do not follow their beat. However, since efficient conducting is one of the most important requisites of successful rehearsing, we must assume that there are other factors which contribute to this lack of attention to the beat.

Inexperience of the choristers is often the basic reason for unresponsiveness to the conducting beat. They are simply not used to following it. In such situations, the conductor should explain what his conducting movements portray. The author does this with all new groups. Then he explains the necessity of holding the music up, so that the minimum of eye movement is needed to see it, while at the same time, watching the conductor. Following these suggestions a few devices may be introduced.

1. Practice a series of attacks and releases at different dynamic levels on a single chord. Hold the chord for different periods of length so that complete attention is needed for sharp cut-offs. Make no verbal instructions as to loudness or softness but be sure the dynamic level corresponds to the conducting indication.

***Choral Technique and Interpretation,* H. Coward, Novello and Company, London, p. 73.

2. Sing some short number with which the singers are familiar. Warn them that you do not intend to take the accustomed beat. Regardless of the markings, vary the tempo and dynamics throughout the singing of the piece. Indicate both gradual and sudden changes of tempo and dynamics. If this will not awaken the group, nothing will. Most choristers enjoy this game of "following the conductor", and it imprints upon their minds the absolute necessity of attention and responsiveness to the beat, if the singing is to be uniform and expressive.

Developing Voices

Chapters VII and VIII were devoted to the techniques of tone production and special vocal problems. Now we are concerned with the procedures to be used in rehearsals for developing voices. Probably a few points in outline form will be the most concise manner of presenting these procedures.

1. Abstract "warming up" exercises at the beginning of every rehearsal are ineffective. The voice is sufficiently exercised through the daily habits of normal speech.
2. Vocalises may be used at the beginning of the rehearsal if they are directed toward some specific aspect of tone production, or if they lead naturally into the study of some musical selection.
3. To develop a tone line, hymns or simple songs may be sung in unison on a neutral vowel such as *ooh* or *ah*. These may be used at the beginning or middle of a rehearsal.
4. Exercises which relate to some vocal problem encountered in the music being practiced should be improvised during the rehearsal.
5. All work on diction should be synchronized with tone study throughout the rehearsal.

Developing Music Reading

As one music educator has said, "The best way of learning to read music is to read it." If a rather large repertory is learned by the chorus, employing the procedures described in Rehearsal D above, a fair degree of reading power can be developed by the singers. The "stumbling block" with most singers is rhythm. If rhythmic assurance can be secured through the reading of words in rhythm, trouble is seldom encountered within the idiom of the voice parts. Learning each voice part by rote will not improve music reading. A procedure which emphasizes the rhythmic sweep of the music is the approach to take in enabling a chorus to grasp the intricacies of musicianship, thus gradually facilitating reading. Repertory can be augmented by methods directed toward sight-singing.

1. At each rehearsal spend a little time with a sight-singing book adaptable to group instruction.*
2. Read through a number of hymns or easy community songs in parts, using the piano as an accompaniment. Call attention to time signatures, key signatures, starting chord, unusual rhythmic figures, wide intervals, and chromatics. Choristers should become aware of these things.
3. Repeat the process in #2, dispensing with the piano.
4. Read the words in rhythm of easy harmonic choral numbers. Correct difficult rhythms. Sing the parts with the piano. Sing the parts without the piano.

Introducing New Music

Also in the description of Rehearsal D, approved procedures were presented for learning new music. These might be overlooked; therefore, an outline of do's and don't's in introducing new music may be helpful in this controversial aspect of choral rehearsals.

DO'S

1. After a few appropriate remarks about mood and style, endeavor to read the entire composition with the assistance of the piano. A skilled accompanist will be able to play the piano part and at the same time cue the weaker voice parts. Use the correct tempos throughout the piece.
2. If the chorus has any reading facility, it should attempt to read easy unaccompanied numbers without assistance from the piano. The accompanist should remain alert to support the voice parts in troublesome spots.
3. In difficult or extremely fast compositions, read the words with correct rhythm. Practice the parts of difficult passages, then sing the entire number following the suggestions in #1 above.
4. In short mood numbers the author often has the accompanist play through the entire composition before having the chorus sing it. This procedure provides a more musical first-reading. The accompanist will appreciate an opportunity to practice the number in advance of the rehearsal.
5. Introduce a new number by playing an excellent recording of it. Two precautions should accompany this procedure, however; the interpretation should be standard, and the mechanical aspects of the recording should be superior. The first precaution is necessary because a chorus will inevitably follow the interpretation as a model and the second is advisable because of the futility of

* We suggest "Sing A Song At Sight," Wilson, H. R., Schmitt, Hall & McCreary Company, Minneapolis.

listening to poor reproductions. This approach should be limited to compositions that have been recorded by superior choral groups. A list of them may be found in the Appendix.

DON'T'S

1. Do not give a musicological lecture on the composer and the background of the music. A few remarks may be appropriate but they should be made to set the mood for the first reading of the music.
2. Do not give a theoretical lecture on the analysis of the form, the harmonic content, the number of fugal entrances, and the style. A few remarks about the style which will contribute to an expressive first reading are helpful, however.
3. Do not go through the entire composition pointing out dynamics, expression marks, and changes of tempo. This is a waste of time. The singers will probably not pay attention and are not likely to understand. If there are difficult spots or certain effects are desired, practice them for a few minutes before singing the piece. A conductor's conducting technique should reveal at the first reading the manner in which a composition should be sung.
4. Do not practice each part by rote before endeavoring to read the parts. This approach is detrimental to musical development, besides being antithetic to sound phychological procedures of learning.

Reviewing Old Music

The repertory of choral groups should include both new and old music, that is, numbers to which they are introduced by the conductor and numbers with which they are already acquainted. Someone has said that popular music is familiar music. Sometimes choristers will not respond to a piece of music upon its first presentation to them, regardless of the tactics. If the singers are indifferent to it after a rehearsal or two of concentrated effort, the shrewd conductor will put it away for a time and bring it out again when the chorus has grown with training and experience.

Familiar music should be treated with the same intent with which new music is introduced. Neither the conductor nor the chorus should consider it a time-saver or something to fill a program. A higher degree of perfection should be striven for than that experienced in the previous performance of the number. The chorus should have improved in music ability, tone quality, and diction habits. In truth, it is a new chorus tackling old music. Therefore, the new performance should be something creative rather than repetitive drill. Each review of a number should be an additional effort toward perfection. Perhaps it will retain a permanent place in the repertory.

Sectional Rehearsals

In principle, sectional rehearsals for "pounding out notes" should not be necessary. They should be scheduled only as a last resort. They carry to the extreme the unsound mechanistic routine of learning separate parts, putting the parts together, and fabricating an interpretation upon the element of musical accuracy. We repeat that these procedures do not conform with approved psychological laws of learning. An adequate technical performance may be accomplished with this process, but seldom is a meaningful, artistic performance fulfilled.

At choral festivals where speed is paramount, sectional rehearsals of various voice parts are usually scheduled. In this situation where time is at a premium and where the energies of the guest conductor must be conserved, there may be some validity for sectional rehearsals. However, whenever the author is serving as guest conductor for festivals he insists that each composition be rehearsed by him with the entire chorus before being practiced in sections. This procedure assures him that the singers have some conception of the tempo, mood and style of the piece before beginning to work on detail. When singers seem both physically and vocally tired he has often cancelled sectional rehearsals with no apparent loss in technical and musical results. He has also discovered that when choruses "prepare the notes", it is sometimes more difficult to "whip them into shape" for performance than if he introduces the music to them.

Closing the Rehearsal

Every rehearsal should end on a thrilling note with the choristers anticipating the next rehearsal as they leave the room or hall. The ending may be on a loud, climactic mood or it may be on a soft, meditative mood. The rehearsal should not just stop; it should culminate. Choristers that practice assiduously for an hour or more on a single work or several compositions deserve this consideration. The author usually has the chorus stand and sing as artistically as possible one of the numbers on which they have been working. Then the singers can feel and hear the musical results of their labors.

CONDUCTOR'S REHEARSAL

1. In your own words, relate the values of the objectives of the choral rehearsal discussed in this chapter.

2. Make rehearsal plans for the following types of choral groups: elementary school choir, junior high school chorus, high school a cappella choir, church choir, college concert choir, and community chorus. Include schedules, facilities and problems of attendance.
3. Select one composition for each type of chorus under #2, and practice the musical preparation necessary to present it at a rehearsal.
4. Visit six choral rehearsals of different types of choral groups and appraise the rehearsals in light of the types presented in this chapter.
5. Without referring to the text, enumerate the number of devices you can remember for securing discipline, overcoming inertia, following the conductor's beat, developing music reading, and introducing new music.

Chapter XII

Building Choral Programs

The success of a choral program depends upon the quality of the music performed. It must be beautiful music. Our first concern therefore, must be with the choice of the music. As obvious as this factor may seem, many programs seem to be planned with little consideration for it.

TASTE IN MUSIC

It seems to be impossible to discuss the selection of music for choral programs without becoming involved in the matter of taste. Appreciation of fine music is invariably bound up with impressive performance. When fine music is beautifully performed it never fails to elicit a favorable response from all types of listeners. It is when great music is performed in an indifferent and unimpressive manner that audiences are likely to turn to music of a more entertaining and temporary variety.

We have seen many choral enterprises begin with great zest and hope. At the first sign of flagging of interest on the part of any of the members, the music committee and conductor begin to compromise with music standards. The first step is to interpolate lighter music and cater to the popular taste. Subsequently, the best singers usually withdraw. Secondly, in order to activate membership social hours after rehearsals are introduced and free tickets to all concerts are issued. The latter inevitably go begging. Morale rapidly deteriorates and another musical endeavor, which began with high expectations, ends in disillusionment.

In a discussion of taste in choral performance there are three human factors to consider: the conductor, the singers, and the listeners. Each one has a point of view to contribute.

The Conductor

Most choral conductors have had excellent training in music and are desirous of sharing their experiences with a group of singers. As a rule, in their college education they were introduced to and developed an appreciation for fine choral music. In the beginning they usually select music of high calibre for their choruses. Unless they can draw an impressive and artistic performance from choral groups their goal becomes increasingly difficult. If, with experience, they can actualize the objectives of the rehearsal presented in the preceding chapter, their aim will be assured.

Some choral conductors have a tendency to sell both singers and listeners short. They contend that their singers and audiences are not ready for the best in music. This viewpoint leads to the practice of "starting where they are" and attempting to lead them gradually up the Mt. Olympus of musical taste. This procedure works for the path of easy to difficult music, but not from the bad to the good. To gain an appreciation of fine music, singers and audiences should not only be introduced to it directly, but they should also be saturated with it. The public reaction to superior radio programs and recordings in the past twenty years is evidence of the validity of this belief.

A few choral conductors take the opposite tack. They have strong, opinionated ideas of what constitutes good music. They usually have a decided preference such as the following: no music written since 1700 is worth doing; Bach alone is first, last, and always; 1900 was the beginning of music. Too often their attitude is that anyone is a musical ignoramous who does not agree with their likes and dislikes. The music they select for the chorus may be very good music but a heavy dose of any particular style inevitably generates rebellion. The conductor does not impose his taste on singers and listeners; he leads them to an understanding and appreciation of all types of fine music. This is his duty and privilege.

The Singers

If the beauties of fine music are revealed to choristers, they invariably prefer the good and enduring to the cheap and temporary. All singers, as well as high school students, invite a challenge to their vocal and musical powers. Compositions that are completely beyond their technical ability cause discouragement, and even resentment. On the other hand, the singing of music that presents no challenge becomes a bore as well as a chore.

Singers need a balanced diet of easy and challenging music. Conductors and singers should not become confused between taste and difficulty. Just because it is easy is no sign that it is bad, and just because it is difficult is no sign that it is good. Easy music may be good and difficult music may be bad. Taste is developed through exposure, association, and understanding of all technical levels of fine music. The only way to push the tawdriness out of one's life is to fill it with fine things.

It is always interesting to the author to see the reaction of young people at a choral festival toward the music on the program. At the beginning of the rehearsals it is usually the Broadway hit or the rhythm folk song to which they respond most readily. But later in the rehearsals there is a gradual shift of response and preference to the better music on the program. At the end of the festival they usually choose as their favorite the number with the deepest and most inspiring musical expression. We must confess that we make every effort both in time and energy to reveal the spiritual qualities of the best numbers to them. Nor do we withhold telling them our preference of the numbers on the program. Some conductors comment that we are influencing the students' judgment. Our response is that we sincerely hope so.

The Listeners

Appreciation is knowing and feeling the worth of something. There are several ways to listen to music, such as the sensuous, associative, and intellectual, but appreciation of a piece of music will depend upon the degree of responsiveness to it. An American may go to a French play and grasp the gist but completely miss the jest. The same American may listen to a piece of modern music and grasp the general mood but completely miss the true meaning. Continued association with the language of music will enable him to grasp both the mood and meaning of new and old music.

Conductors are prone to write off too quickly the musical responsiveness of audiences. The musical public is often considered ignorant or boorish. The best is too good for them. This attitude has been proven false time and time again, yet it persists. American audiences are accustomed to the best and they will respond to the best in music when it is presented in the best manner.

SELECTION OF MUSIC

A conductor may build a program from entirely new repertory or he may turn to music that is in the library of the organization. If it is a program of miscellaneous numbers it is sane and safe procedure (sane for the budget and safe with the chorus) to mix the new with the old. Choristers continually need new music to hold interest, but they relish equally well a return engagement with old musical friends. Regardless of whether it is new or old repertory, there are four factors which the conductor must consider in selecting music for a program. These are the quality of the music, the quality of the text, the suitability for the chorus, and the type of audience.

The Music

The music should be worthy. Rehearsals are time-consuming and demanding of much human effort. Only worthwhile music merits this degree of attention. But the evaluation of good and bad music is sometimes baffling. The safest criteria are its lasting qualities. In this respect beauty is like truth. Veritable values are the permanent ones. The best music seems to have eternal life.

Therefore, to develop discrimination it would seem wise to steep oneself in the classics. Most of these compositions have passed the test of time. Some of the early music unearthed by scholars may well have remained in their resting places, in light of their usefulness for performance. The compositions of representative composers of earlier periods (as listed in Chapter V) should serve as a beginning guide. As this music becomes familiar through association, appreciation and discrimination of all music is enhanced. This does not necessarily imply a fondness for all music, in fact, the reverse is usually true.

Sometimes judgment on music is based on its association. Most music which has survived the ravages of time has evolved from the more beautiful and spiritual experiences of man. Consequently, the predominance of good choral music is sacred.

Sincerity is the mark of worthy music. Sometimes one wonders about the sincerity of certain contemporary compositions. Is the composer being different just for the sake of novelty? Honest experimentation must be encouraged. Innovation must not be denied. History has shown that what is new today may be old tomorrow, and even what is bad today may be good tomorrow. However, one cannot be shocked into appreciation; this is a slow, meditative development. Effect for the sake of effect is not true art. Sincerity comes from honest conviction.

Worthy music has the stamp of originality. Study the compositions of the early and classic composers. Although they bear resemblances, each composer's music has its own elements of originality. The music of these periods which does not contain the distinction of individuality has passed on into oblivion. In examining new publications, a conductor should ask himself whether the music has a touch of originality or if it is merely a rehash of former musical cliches or styles which have been better expressed by another composer or arranger. Worthy composers and arrangers are not imitators; they are searching for new musical expression.

Workmanship is a primary essential of worthy music. Regardless of how simple, it must demonstrate the craftsmanship of the composer. This simply means complete control of melodic, harmonic, and contrapuntal devices as well as the other techniques of composition. Accent of words and music should coincide, voice parts should be interesting, and the accompaniment, if any, should be a contribution to the musical expression. It is in the writing of accompaniments that many composers and arrangers reveal their limitations as craftsmen. The least one can expect is that the music be grammatically correct. Some publications of choral music today suggest musical illiteracy. The true composer or arranger is an artisan as well as an artist.

To recapitulate, the conductor should ask himself these five questions in selecting music for a choral program: does it have permanent qualities; is it associated with worthwhile human experience; is it sincere; does it have originality; and does it demonstrate capable workmanship? These are the earmarks of worthy music.

The Text

Choral music has one unique advantage over instrumental music (although many musicians call it a limitation) namely: its association with literature. Therefore, a very important consideration, second only to music in building a choral program, is the text. The texts should have genuine literary value. As we stated in an earlier chapter, fine texts usually beget fine music. There are no particular objections to novel or humorous songs, but even these texts should be set in a manner sufficiently musical so that they are a pleasure to rehearse.

Worthy texts contain the same qualities as worthy music discussed in the preceding section; permanency, worthwhile associations, sincerity, originality, and workmanship. We have covered considerable space in this book emphasizing the need for unity of text and music. Expressive words are as important as expressive music.

It is interesting to note how fine words seem to strengthen a melody and trivial words have a tendency to weaken or cheapen it. As an English drinking song, *Anacreon in Heaven,* the melody for *The Star-Spangled Banner,* seemed doomed to extinction, but as a dignified national anthem it has been raised to distinction. The popular songs based on the beautiful melodies of Tschaikowsky and Schubert are short-lived, but the original melodies continue to give musical satisfaction. If music is supposed to enhance the mood and meaning of a text the words must be worth this attention and devotion.

The Chorus

In selecting music, the choral conductor must know the limitations of his chorus but he must not underestimate the capabilities and appreciative powers of the singers. His job is to lead them persuasively to ever "bigger and better" efforts. This means an improvement in quality, difficulty and quantity of music.

He remains adamant in his preference for fine music, but he continues to present this position with understanding and tact. Very often the author will say to a young group of choristers, "Of all the numbers we are rehearsing, this one is my favorite. Sing it for me at the concert." To hear them "come through" is to realize that a forward step toward better music has been made. A classic may be introduced with this remark, "This composition is in the permanent repertory of all outstanding choruses. It will undoubtedly have the same appeal for us after we have learned it." Or a modern composition may be presented with the comment. "This one is really different. I am not sure that I understand it myself. Let us work on it a few rehearsals to see if we can discover what the composer has to say." If it is worthy music the chorus will eventually respond favorably toward it.

Music must be within the capabilities of a choral group, but still remain a challenge. Recently, at a festival, the author heard a rendition of an eight-part number from the Russian liturgy with only three basses and one tenor in the choir. He is still trying to discover how the conductor expected to divide one tenor. This is a ludicrous example, but many conductors in their effort to emulate professional or more experienced groups select music far beyond the limitations of their chorus. Division of voice parts, pitch range of parts, dynamic demands, intricate rhythmical patterns, chromatic melodic lines, dissonance of harmonies, and finally, maturity of expression, all are factors to be considered in selecting music for an individual choral group.

Aside from these considerations the author has one other rule; the music should be worth the rehearsal time necessary for performance. The objection to using present-day popular music on programs should not be based on the fact that it is popular, but rather on the fact that it is usually not worth the amount of rehearsal time necessary for its preparation. If arrangements of popular songs can be performed effectively with a minimum amount of rehearsal time, then they have their place.

Some of the masterpieces of choral literature are worthy of a full year's rehearsal by a choir for an initial performance as well as warranting a return to it many times for complete musical fulfillment. We have heard music at state-competition festivals which a choir has spent the entire year preparing, music that was not worth more attention than the time of approximately two or three rehearsal periods. (We are not referring necessarily to the popular song, which seldom appears on these programs anyway). It is a sound criterion for a director in selecting a choral number to ask himself, "Is this piece of music worth the time necessary for my choir to make it ready for performance?"

This latter observation leads to the quantity of music selected for a chorus to prepare for a specific program. The chorus should not attempt to sing more music than it can do well. The author has heard too many programs where one or two numbers were performed adequately, while the remainder of the program, evidently due to lack of rehearsal time, was sung badly. When this happens, the entire program leaves a bad impression. Reading through a quantity of music is commendable but the numbers to be presented for public performance should be limited to those which the chorus can do well. It is more advisable to supplement the choral performance with solos, instrumental numbers, small ensembles, or even community singing.

The Audience

A final factor to be considered in choosing music for a program is the audience. Music is what it is because it expresses an infinite number of moods. In other words, there is music for every place and occasion. A thoughtful director will not present the same numbers for a church vesper service as for a civic club dinner. However, this does not mean that it is necessary to sing cheap music or sing "down to the audience." Any audience resents being sung "down to" as many artists have discovered in their concert tours. Our job is to lift an audience "up to" something.

Nevertheless, deliberately trying to educate an audience to appreciate fine music through usual academic procedures is a rather futile business. However, if a conductor simply concentrates on an impressive and expressive performance of beautiful music, his audience will gradually respond and gain enjoyment and appreciation of fine music. The achievement of this goal is indeed a rewarding and glorious privilege.

FACTORS IN PROGRAM BUILDING

A program should be composed not only of works of art but it should be a work of art itself. "Throwing together a few numbers without rhyme or reason" does not constitute a program. Like a painting, it must contain unity in variety and variety in unity, represented by symmetry, form, rhythm, and contrast.

A Unified Program

A program should have unity; that is, a deliberate attempt should be made to select numbers for a reason and with some relationship to each other. The unity is often secured by dividing the numbers into groups, such as: Sacred Music, Folk Music, Modern Music. Sometimes they are simply indicated as groups I, II, III, and IV. The general practice is to begin with sacred music and end with secular music of a lighter vein. Or, the program often begins with early music and ends with contemporary music. Too often this latter type of program has a deadening effect, with the audience merely enduring the first half of the program while waiting for the second half, generally of a more lively quality.

It is important that at the very beginning a feeling of *rapport* be established between the performers and the audience. Hence it is wise to select opening music which will assure the complete attention and enthusiasm of the audience. The following is one good basic plan for a mixed choir. Even this very general plan can become stereotyped and needs much variation. Substitutions which better fit individual situations may be used instead of the music listed.

1. Choral Prelude
   A song of praise of music, the Creator, or some universal theme
2. Folk Songs
   Lively folk dance tune
   Quiet number (treble voices)
   Spiritual (male voices)
   Vigorous folk song
3. Sacred Songs
   Early contrapuntal work
   Quiet unaccompanied number (male or treble voices)
   Liturgical music (Russian, Jewish, etc.)
   Hymn of praise
4. Contemporary Songs
   Contrapuntal style, not too dissonant
   Homophonic style, rhythmic variety
   Ballad style (treble or male voices)
   Popular, novelty or modern style
5. Choral Postlude
   A patriotic number or one with majestic quality on a noble theme

Another plan to gain unification of a program is to use music which reflects the different moods suggested by a special occasion. For example, a short choral program for a Thanksgiving service can represent the various qualities of the spirit of thankfulness, highlighted by numbers expressing reverence, gratitude, supplication, and praise. A narrator reading selections from the Bible, or suitable poetry, will help to set the mood for the choral numbers.*

THANKSGIVING SERVICE

1. Instrumental Prelude
2. Call to Worship
   *The Lord's Prayer — Wilson (CM)
   Come, Ye Thankful People, Come (Audience) — Elvey
3. The Spirit of Reverence
   Thanksgiving Reading
   Let Thy Holy Presence — Tschnekoff (SB)
4. The Spirit of Gratitude
   Thanksgiving Reading
   Gratitude — Thomas (GS)
5. The Spirit of Supplication
   Thanksgiving Reading
   Misereri Mei — Lotti (GR)
6. The Spirit of Praise
   Thanksgiving Reading
   *Psalm 150 — Franck (GS)
   Now Thank We All Our God (Audience) — Luther

Still another plan for unifying a program is to select some literary idea or quotation around which groups of numbers may be organized. A short Christmas assembly program can be planned around the text, "Glory to God in the highest and on earth peace, good will toward men."

CHRISTMAS ASSEMBLY PROGRAM

1. Prelude (Brilliant chorus expressing the general theme of the program)
   *Fanfare for Christmas Day — Shaw (GS)
2. Glory to God in the Highest
   Hark! the Herald Angels Sing (audience) — Mendelssohn

*All compositions and arrangements are for SATB unless otherwise indicated. However, conductors will find that many of the numbers are available also for different combinations of voices. Only abbreviations are given for the publishers. See index for key. An asterisk preceding a composition indicates that it is available in recording. See list in index.

*Love Came Down at Christmas	Wilson (MM)
*Alleluia	Thompson (ECS)
Glory to God in the Highest	Pergolesi (GS)
(or) Hodie, Christus Natus Est	Willan (CF)
3. Peace on Earth	
It Came Upon the Midnight Clear (audience)	
*Dona Nobis Pacem (TBB)	Old German Canon (SHMc)
A Christmas Chant	Wilson (CM)
4. Good Will Toward Men	
*Glory to God (from "The Messiah")	Handel (GS)
*For Unto Us a Child is Born (from "The Messiah")	Handel (GS)
Joy to the World (audience)	Handel

Other Christmas programs can be planned around a centralized theme, such as "The Animals of the Christmas Story." A narrator may read the appropriate text from the Bible, or suitable poetry, perhaps the words of the song to be sung. Here is an example especially suitable for young people.

THE ANIMALS OF THE CHRISTMAS STORY

1. Choir: Silent Night (concert version)	Gruber (SHMc)
(or) In the Stillness of the Night	Wilson (JS)
2. Narrator: "The Lamb" by William Blake	
3. Choir: Little Lamb, Who Made Thee	Wilson (BH)
(or) Carol of the Sheep Bells	Kountz (GM)
4. Narrator: Sixteenth Century (Yorkshire) words from "The Storke" by Clokey (JF)	
5. Choir: The Storke	Paul (SB)
6. Narrator: Words from the Czechoslovakian carol by Krone (CF)	
7. Choir: The Birds and the Christ Child	Krone (CF)
(or) Carol of the Birds	Cain (SHMc)
8. Narrator: "The Barn" by Elizabeth Coatsworth	
9. Choir: The Friendly Beasts	Richards (HWG)
(or) The Friendly Beasts (audience)	Old French Carol
10. Narrator: And so, for nearly two thousand years has been told the story in different ways of the humble birth of the Christ Child, the vision of the shepherds in the field and the journey of the Magi from the Orient.	
11. Choir: The Shepherd's Story	Dickinson (HWG)
(or) Noel	Wilson (SHMc)

*See foot-note on page 307.

Many other ideas can be developed around centralized themes which will give more unity to Christmas programs as well as added literary and musical meaning.

Lights of Christmas. As in the preceding programs, a narrator may be used. This idea makes use of the various types of light associated with the Christmas story and builds up to the climactic thought of the Christ as the Light of the World. The program should include music containing in its text reference to: the heavenly light seen by the shepherds, the star of the East, and candles and torches. For a final number any one of the following is appropriate:

Swedish Yule Carol	Gaul (GM)
Christ Is the World's True Light	Stanton (OUP)
Break Forth, O Beauteous Heavenly Light	Bach (several editions)

Note: The author has often combined this program with the Jewish celebration of Hannukah or "The Feast of Lights." The Hannukah story and music should precede the Christmas story and music.

Christmas Everywhere. This idea is based on the poem "Everywhere, Everywhere, Christmas Tonight" by Phillip Brooks. The development of this theme is obvious. Build the program around the carols of all countries.

Characters of the Christmas Story. Use songs of Mary, Joseph, the shepherds, the innkeeper, the Wise Men and Jesus, the Prince of Peace.

Christmas Scenes. The traditional scenes depicted by tableaux and accompanied by the singing of appropriate carols or concert songs.

Christmas Cards. Season's greetings in songs of various places and peoples; Christmas Card tableaux on the stage.

Christmas Candlelight Service. Choose songs which fall into three groups, calling them *The Advent, The Nativity* and *The Rejoicing;* or the groups may be called *Heaven's Message, The Christ Child,* and *Earth's Welcome.*

The same plan of using a centralized theme or unifying idea may be used for general choral programs not celebrating a special occasion such as Christmas or Easter. A program may be based on the words of an individual song, as follows:

SING YOUR SONGS

1. Choral Prelude

O Sing Your Songs	Cain (HF)

2. Songs of Nature

Now Is the Month of Maying	Morley (GS)
Midsummer Song	Delius (BH)
Autumn	Gretchaninoff (GS)
*Winter	Wilson (MM)

3. Songs of God
   *Cantate Domino — Pitoni (BM)
   *Call to Remembrance — Farrant (BM)
   *Glory to God — Bach (GR)
4. Songs of Love
   Love Song — Brahms (GR)
   *At Parting (TTBB or SATB) — Wilson (TP)
   My Spirit Sang All Day — Finzi (GS)
5. Choral Postlude
   Remember Our Songs — Rhea (CP)

One teacher worked out a very interesting and varied program for young people in the elementary school based upon the words of the composition, "A Tribute to Song" (BM). It is equally applicable for junior high schools.

LET THERE BE SONG

1. A Tribute to Song (SA or SAB) — Wilson (BM)
2. Narrator: "The Great Creator moved through space,
   His magic wand touched every place,
   He gave a song to the robin's throat . . ."
3. Robin, Robin, Sing Me a Song (vocal solo) — Spross (GS)
4. Narrator: "And to the brook a rippling note . . ."
5. Song of the Brook (piano solo) — Lack (GS)
6. Narrator: "A song to the wind . . ."
7. Windy Night (SA) — Malin (KJ)
8. Narrator: "A song to the sea . . ."
9. Song of the Sea (SA) — Strong (SHMc)
10. Narrator: A song that sings in the heart of me . . ."
11. Holla le, Holla lo (SA) — Czechoslovakian (BM)
12. Narrator: "Let There Be Song!"
13. Reprise: "A Tribute to Song" — Wilson (BM)

Other ideas which have been used by the author include the following:

MUSIC OF THE FAITHS

1. Choral Prelude: One God for All — Savino (CM)
2. Protestant Music: Motet by Bach or representative anthems.
3. Catholic Liturgy: Short mass or individual numbers from the

*See foot-note on page 307.

early contrapuntal school (Palestrina, di Lassus, Arcadelt, etc.)

4. Jewish Liturgy: Selections from a typical Friday evening service or a representative group of individual numbers. A fine closing number for this group is Psalm 150 — Lewandowski (SHMc).

5. Choral Postlude: Majestic number with brotherhood theme.

MUSIC OF OUR NEIGHBORS

1. Choral Prelude: Marches of Peace — Mueller (CF)

2. Music of Canada: Folk music and contemporary compositions. (The liturgical motets of Willan (CF) are excellent).

3. Music of Mexico and Latin America: Folk music and contemporary compositions. (Some unusually interesting numbers have been written by Chavez, Villa-Lobos, Mignone, and Varese.)

4. Choral Postlude: Era of Peace — Williams (BM)

The following program simply makes use of alliteration. It represents three aspects of life in which music is used.

MUSIC IN WORK, WORSHIP, WAR

1. Choral Prelude
   O Softly Singing Lute — Borowski (JF)

2. Music in Work
   The Erie Canal (Early American folk song) — Scott (SP)
   Night Herding Song (Cowboy song) — Wilson (SHMc)
   The Peasant and his Oxen (Jugoslav folk song) — Aschenbrenner (CF)

3. Music in Worship
   Kyrie in D Minor (or an easier Bach number) — Bach (GS)
   Cherubim Song — Glinka (BH)
   *Jacob's Ladder (spiritual) — Wilson (GR)
   Praise — Rowley (OUP)

4. Music in War
   The Swazi Warrior (Zulu marching song) — Wood (CF)
   Yankee Doodle (traditional) — Reynolds (CM)
   Meadowlands (Cossack marching song) — Wilhousky (CF)

5. Choral Epilogue
   Glory (chorus and orchestra) — Rimsky-Korsakov (MPH)

Patriotic programs may be organized around such ideas as the following example:

*See foot-note on page 307.

ALL-AMERICAN CHORAL CONCERT

1. Choral Prelude: Star-Spangled Banner
   (audience and chorus)
2. Early American: Three Fuguing Tunes — Billings (MM)
3. Folk Songs: spiritual, folk ballad, cowboy song,
   mountain dance tune
4. Contemporary Choral Music: representative numbers
5. Choral Postlude: America, the Beautiful
   (concert version) — Ward (SHMc)

This one may be used for a general patriotic program or one which commemorates the birthday or memory of Abraham Lincoln.

MUSIC OF, BY, AND FOR . . .

1. Choral Prologue
   Salutation — Gaines (JF)
2. Reading of the Gettysburg Address
3. Music of the People
   Skip to My Lou (American folk song) — Wilson (SHMc)
   Oft in the Stilly Night (SSA) — Stevenson (CF)
   (Said to be Lincoln's favorite song)
   When Johnny Comes Marching Home (concert version)
   Lambert (CF)
4. Music by the People (audience participation)
   America, the Beautiful (use descant with choir)
   Ward (SHMc)
   Medley of Gay-ninety songs (audience alone)
   Appropriate popular songs of the day (choir sings with audience)
   America — Bloch (BS)
   (Choir sings it first; then repeats with audience.
   Obtain permission to print words on program).
5. Music for the People
   Holiday Song — Schuman (GS)
   All Music — Wilson (GS)
   Stomp Your Foot (from "Tender Land") — Copland (BH)
6. Choral Epilogue
   A Song of Democracy (chorus with orchestra)
   Hanson (CF)

Here are some other ideas for consideration:

1. Music of One Composer. (Program should include some instrumental music for contrast).
2. Music of Two Composers. (Mozart-Brahms, Bach-Britten, Schubert-Stravinsky are good combinations).

3. Style in Music
   a. Early contrapuntal (16th and 17th century)
   b. Classic period (18th century)
   c. Romantic period (19th century)
   d. Contemporary compositions (20th century)
4. Poets in Song (emphasis on the text)
   a. Choral Prelude
      The Poet's Monument — Gretchaninoff (GS)
   b. The Bard from England
      Settings of poems by Shakespeare
   c. Poets of Foreign Lands
      Settings of French, German, Italian and Spanish texts sung in the original languages
   d. Poets from Home
      Choral settings of the works of American poets
5. Song and the Dance
   All types of choral dance music. Some of it may be used as an accompaniment for choreography
6. Music of the Masters
   a. Choral Prelude: A Thing of Beauty (words by Keats) — Wilson (CF)
      (Used only for the purpose of setting the mood)
   b. Music of Palestrina, Vittoria, di Lassus, Gibbons, Byrd, Morley or Purcell
   c. Music of Bach, Handel, Schubert or Brahms
   d. Music of Vaughan Williams, Holst, Britten, Kodaly, W. Schuman, R. Thompson, Copland and others
   e. Choral Postlude: Hallelujah Chorus (from "Mount of Olives") — Beethoven (CF)

In light of our first statement that music is the thing, it may seem like wasted energy to give so much time and thought to planning programs with some literary unity. However, the director will find this work most rewarding in the enthusiastic response of the singers in rehearsing such a program, and in the added interest on the part of the listeners.

A Varied Program

In the effort to obtain unity in a program one must not forget the necessity for securing variety within a unified whole. If the reader will acquaint himself with the preceding programs he will discover not only literary unity but musical variety as well. Variety means more than a cursory selection of numbers having no relationship to each other. Variety must be planned. Its achievement involves care in the selection of numbers contrasted as to key, time, tempo, length, mood, style, period, and composer. A workable plan is to decide upon a centralized theme to give the program unity and then to search for numbers which will give the necessary variety within groups. If the theme is not conducive to a wide variety of music materials, do not use it. It is better to eliminate the idea of a literary theme if it interferes in the building of a well balanced music program. If a theme occurs to you that is worth developing, publishers are more than willing to assist you in the search for suitable material.

One way of securing variety in a choral program is to include some instrumental music, either piano or small ensemble. If this is not possible, try at least to include a vocal solo or a small choral ensemble on a program. Solos and small ensembles are usually introduced between groups of choral numbers. These incidental numbers need not necessarily fit the main theme of the program but may be completely different and individual. They offer a musical relief from a parade of choral numbers for an entire evening.

Occasionally a conductor secures variety by having the different types of choral organizations under his direction perform in a single concert. These concerts are usually sponsored by schools where several conductors serve. In building this kind of program care must be taken that time is not wasted in marching the groups on and off the stage. The author has seen festival programs of this nature that resemble track meets more than choral concerts. If the stage is large enough arrangements can be made so that several groups are on the platform at one time. Also the space in front of the stage may be used to seat the younger groups. Numbers which combine all the groups are a genuine contribution to these programs. These concerts are often greatly enjoyed by the community.

Following are two programs of this nature. One is for Christmas and the other is for a spring concert.

ANNUAL CHRISTMAS CONCERT

1. Choral Prelude — Combined groups, SATB with junior choir

Let Carols Ring	Wilson (B3)

2. Elementary or Jr. H.S. Treble Choir

A Christmas Song	Diers (BM)
By the Manger	Franck (GS)
A Merry Christmas	English carol (BM)

3. High School Boys' Glee Club or Double Quartet

Masters in This Hall (TBB)	English carol (BH)
Lo, How A Rose E'er Blooming	Praetorius (CM)
A-Rockin' All Night	Spiritual (TP)

4. High School Girls' Glee Club
   - Ave Maria — Arcadelt (BM)
   - Lullaby of Jesus — Polish carol (B3)
   - Rise Up, Shepherd, an' Foller — Spiritual (BH)
5. High School Choir
   - Carol of the Bells — Leontovich-Wilhousky (CF)
   - Three Kings — Willan (CF)
   - Yuletide Is Here — Davis (Gal)
6. Choral Postlude — Combined Groups
   - A Merry Christmas (incorporates familiar carols) — Savino (CM)

ANNUAL SPRING FESTIVAL

1. Choral Prologue — Combined Groups
   - Gloria in Excelsis — Mozart (TP)
2. Junior High School Choir
   - Bells of St. Michael's Tower — Knyvett (BM)
   - O Lord Our God — Schvedov (BM)
   - Res' My Shoes — Wilson (BM)
3. High School Girls' Glee Club
   - At Eventide It Shall Be Light (from "The Holy City") — Gaul (TP)
   - May Day Carol — Taylor (JF)
   - Devotion — Strauss (EV)
4. High School Choir
   - Tenebrae Factae Sunt — Ingegneri (BH)
   - He's Got the Whole World In His Hands — Spiritual (SHMc)
   - Sourwood Mountain — American folk song (SHMc)
   - Let Not Your Song End — Cain (HF)
5. Choral Epilogue — Combined number utilizing all groups
   - Alleluia — Hummel (GR)

Directors should remember that there is nothing more deadening for a group of singers than to repeat the same numbers year after year. Concert programs by high school and college choirs often repeat fifty percent of the last year's program. Sometimes a song is repeated in order to improve upon a previous performance. That is a different matter. But beware of repetition just because the composition happens to be in the library and half of the choir is familiar with it.

It is unfair to ask singers who already know a song to go through the tedious rehearsals necessary for other singers to learn it. Why? Because this is not the way people grow in musicianship or gain an ever-widening appreciation of choral literature. Also, the resultant *ennui* should never occur in a choral rehearsal. Moreover, the same thing can be said of the director, who should never be satisfied with performing the same choral numbers year after year, but should be constantly developing his musicianship and growing in his knowledge of the wealth of fine choral literature. A basic collection of standard choral music of various styles is a good thing to have in the library of a school because it offers a wide variety of carefully selected music from which to build programs.

Combined Numbers

In some music departments the instrumental conductor and the choral conductor are not on musical terms with each other. The best way to come to a musical understanding is for them to work together. The most immediate way of working together is to plan numbers which combine choral and instrumental groups at the various school concerts. Take turns conducting.

In schools and colleges where both departments are functioning effectively, the singing in combined numbers is an inspiration and a growing musical experience. Some of the great composers wrote their finest choral music with orchestral accompaniment. Many of these are being transcribed for concert band. Contemporary composers and arrangers are adding to the combined repertory. On one or two concerts each year the choral director should take the initiative to program one or two combined numbers. As an accompaniment for voices an orchestra serves better than a band, but in the absence of the former do not despair of using the latter. These combined numbers usually open and close the concert.

Extended Works

Two patterns of choral programs seem to be prevalent: one consists of a single work for the entire concert, while the other consists of groups of miscellaneous numbers as indicated in the examples in this chapter. College choruses and community choruses seem to prefer to perform a lengthy cantata or oratorio for their programs. School groups and college concert choirs favor the miscellaneous program. Most church choirs and professional choirs plan both types.

There is a rich repertory of single works for adult groups. There is nothing more inspiring than rehearsing and singing a great master choral work. Moreover, a performance of a cantata, an oratorio, or opera in concert form, has public appeal. We strongly urge such groups not to limit their music repertory to single works. They might give an occasional program of miscellaneous numbers or combine the two types by singing a work of approximately thirty minutes in length for the first half of the program and miscellaneous numbers for the last half of the program. The relief from the heavy diet of single works is enjoyed by both the chorus and audience.

Although the repertory of extended works for school groups and *a cappella* choirs is limited, there are a number of worthwhile things which have been published. We strongly urge all conductors of these groups to search for more extended and rewarding compositions. We will list several in the Appendix and give the timing. A choral composer usually does his best work when his creative effort is devoted to an extended work. Avoidance of rehearsing and performing these works means failing to come in contact with many composers' most serious efforts. Except for especially young groups, every conductor should attempt to perform at least one work of ten minutes in length or more at each concert. When this is done concerts are more impressive and enjoyable to singers and listeners alike. The work becomes the highlight of the program.

Dramatics and Dancing

For years choral conductors have experimented with the use of dramatics and dancing with choral music. With the advent of television which has capitalized upon the visual aspects of music performance there has been added impetus in this direction. In the author's experience, the addition of these arts to choral numbers detracts from the singing. However, if the combination seems to be something unique in itself, such as an opera, there is no reason why they should not be included on choral concert programs. They give variety and serve as a break in a long string of miscellaneous numbers.

The most obvious manner of using dramatic effects is through *lighting,* for example, subdued lights for soft numbers and love songs, and bright lights for patriotic songs. This practice can become very "corny." The audience gives more attention to the lights than to the music. We can imagine effective use of lights for pageants, tableaux, to spotlight solos, and for specific Hannukah, Christmas, and Easter programs. Otherwise, our advice would be to tell the stage electrician to stay away from the light switchboard.

Tableaux are especially appropriate for religious observances where choral music is used. We have even seen an effective performance of Part III of *The Christmas Oratorio,* by Bach, synchronized with proper tableaux. Recently the author was introduced to a cantata by Joseph Roff, *The Christmas Story,* where a color film strip of Christmas masterpieces of painting was synchronized with the singing. Any presentation of this kind however, distracts the attention given to the singing, and consequently the chorus has a tendency to be careless in the quality of performance. Therefore, they should be used only on very special programs.

Dramatic skits with choral accompaniment are being included as a novelty on programs. They are usually bonafide folksongs sung as a dialogue. The arranger capitalizes upon the dramatic element and writes a choral part to accompany it. The characters, usually two, sing and dramatize the action in costume in front of the chorus. The result is a miniature opera. These novelties certainly consist of better music than many of the compositions labelled as humorous novelties or encore numbers. Perhaps it is a more authentic manner of presenting these folk songs with dialogue than the more prevalent concert arrangements. The author has succumbed to this trend, and has arranged six American folk songs as "Choral Skits." (See Appendix).

The final extraneous activity to consider which can be included with choral singing is choreography. But here we are dealing with an art that is normally associated with music. Is there any reason why dancing should not be performed with choral music as well as with instrumental music? Is the fact that choral music contains words a barrier? Choreography should only be combined with choral music where the meaning of the words is obvious.

The author has seen very effective choreography performed with beautiful singing of Thompson's *Alleluia.* Also, he has seen a story dramatized in modern dance, impressively performed with the concert choral arangement of the spiritual *Go Down, Moses.* Typical dance songs arranged for choral groups may employ dancing in performance and augment the aural art with the visual. In this manner, the author has presented striking choral and dance performances of, *Song of Old Spain,* Granados-Savino; *Skip To My Lou,* American folk song; and *I Got Rhythm,* Gershwin.

In these latter examples, the dance was the outgrowth of the music. Dances may be either those traditionally performed with the music or they may be stylized, employing dance forms. In the former examples in the above paragraph, the choreography was an entity in itself. The music served only to suggest the dance movements, and consequently, had a tendency to become subordinate. Combining these two arts in this manner requires sensitivity and ingenuity or the results are ineffective for either art. On the other hand, it seems natural to combine dance music, either instrumental or choral, with the dance. Conductors in schools can well explore with the dance teacher the possibilities of joining together in projects which combine choral music with the dance on school music programs.

Length of Programs

There is one factor which all conductors must keep in mind; that is the fatigue of the listeners. The singers become tired but they are active. The listeners become tired, and through inactivity are lulled to inattention, or even sleep. As one exasperated conductor put it, "If I can keep my audiences awake, I feel that I have fulfilled my artistic responsibilities."

The general concert should be a diversified program, and in school concerts more than one music organization should be utilized. However, it is not necessary for every organization to perform at every concert. Save this type of program for the spring festival. As a rule it is better to feature one organization at each concert and support this group with one other large group, small ensembles, or solos. This plan avoids too many delays in the shifting of groups of performers and paraphernalia, and eliminates programs of undue length. One hour of music, including the necessary pauses between numbers, with added allowance for changing the stage, is usually ample time for a school concert. Professional concerts or the singing of oratorios by college and community groups with naturally be longer. Plan the time of your program and stick to it!

PLAN A PROGRAM

The following diagram is a pattern which may be followed for a conductor to assure himself that he has fulfilled the elements of good program building. This is an example of a miscellaneous program, (see p. 306) the type with which most conductors are concerned. Using this example as a model, plan two programs, one for a special occasion, such as Christmas, and the other for a general concert.

MISCELLANEOUS PROGRAM FOR CONCERT CHOIR

NAME	COMPOSER OR ARRANGER	KEY	METER	TEMPO	APPROXIMATE TIME	DIFFICULTY 1 TO 5	PERIOD	STYLE A=accompanied U=unaccompanied	MOOD
Prelude									
To Music	Schubert	E major	4/4	Mod. fast	2:10	1	Romantic	Harmonic-A	Exuberant
Folk									
Elijah Rock	Hairston	G minor	C	Mod. fast	2:00	2	Spiritual	Rhythmic-U	Intense
Balm in Gilead	Dawson	A major	4/4	Slow	2:45	2	Spiritual	Melodic-U	Peaceful
In Silent Night	Brahms	E♭ major	3/2	Mod. slow	2:30	2	German	Harmonic-U	Flowing
Ho-La-Li	Luvass	F major	2/4	Fast	1:45	2	Bavarian	Staccato-U	Gay
Early									
Dancing & Springing	Hassler	C major	3/4	Fast	1:45	3	17th Century	Contra-puntal-U	Light
The Silver Swan	Gibbons	G♭ major	C	Slow	1:50	3			Meditative
Sweet Love Doth Now Invite (TTBB)	Dowland	A major	4/4	Moderate	2:45	3			Amorous
He Is Good and Handsome	Passereau	C minor	C	Fast	2:30	4			Delicate

NAME	COMPOSER OR ARRANGER	KEY	METER	TEMPO	APPROXIMATE TIME	DIFFICULTY 1 TO 5	PERIOD	STYLE A=accompanied U=unaccompanied	MOOD
Sacred									
Heavenly Light	Kopolov-Wilhousky	D minor	Free	Slow	2:15	3	19th Cent.	Harmonic-U	Reverent
Te Deum (SSA with soprano solo)	Wilson	D major	3/4	Moderate	5:50	5	Contemporary	4 continuous sections-A	Majestic
Emitte Spiritum tuum	Schuetky	B♭ major	C	Mod. slow	3:15	4	19th Century German	8-part harmony-U	Sustained to Majestic
Contemporary									
Three Shakespearean Songs									
1. Full Fathom Five	V. Williams	F major	4/4	Slow	3:10	5	Contemporary	Harmonic-U	Pictorial
2. The Cloud-Capp'd Towers		Transient minor	4/4	Very slow	2:50	5		Harmonic-U	Sombre
3. Over Hill, Over Dale		E minor	6/8	Fast	1:30	3		Contrapuntal-U	Happy
Postlude									
Jubilant Song	Dello Joio	C major	Shifting meter	Fast, slow, fast	3:40	5	Contemporary	Rhythmical and contrapuntal-A	Ecstatic

Chapter XIII

The Choral Performance

The time has come! All of the long hours of rehearsal are about to bear fruit. Excitement prevails. Nerves are on edge. How will the concert go? Will we have a large audience?

Perhaps we should examine the public performance to see if it is worth all of the anxiety. The author makes a point of not worrying about concerts. If the group is well rehearsed there is nothing to be concerned about. There may be a slip or two but they are seldom noticed and even if they are, they detract little from the performance. The work is done; the concert is something to be enjoyed by both performers and audience.

ATTITUDES TOWARD PUBLIC PERFORMANCE

Much of the anxiety over public performance is due to one's attitude toward it. Naturally there are mixed emotions in the attitude of the conductor and choristers toward a concert but they may be separated into three general attitudes which we will label, theatrical, academic or pseudo-academic, and communal.

Theatrical

Some choral groups approach a concert as if they were putting on a show. Their primary aim is to impress the audience (or critics) with theatrics. Singing is just a means. Many times these groups sing well, but there are so many extraneous factors in the performance that it suffers in artistry. The conductor uses the concert to build personal and professional prestige in the community.

Very often these groups resort mostly to novelties and neglect programming fine music. They emphasize bizarre choral effects; they attempt to imitate professionalism. The conductor builds the reputation of being a "terrific showman." He should be concerned more with his reputation as an artist. In fact, most fine artists are fine showmen, but their showmanship is a concomitant of their superior performances. Compliments to such groups are often directed to all aspects of the performance except the singing. A conductor should be able to determine the artistic quality of his work by the nature of the compliments which he receives. If they are pointed toward the moving quality of the singing, then he can be reassured.

There is a dramatic quality about the appearance of a well-trained chorus which presupposes a theatrical atmosphere at a concert. We would not exclude this quality from public performance. We are only pleading that ostentatious theatrics not be the aim or the dominating factor in the giving of a concert. When theatrics are practiced the artistry of the singing is neglected. The conductor and chorus fail to fulfill their reason for being.

Academic or Pseudo-Academic

A few conductors approach a concert bent on educating the audience. They treat the situation as if it were a class in music appreciation. Their aim is to instruct. Elaborate program notes are printed on the program or presented verbally. The performance reflects this attitude; it is stiff and formal. An intellectual atmosphere pervades the hall. Acknowledgment of applause is either discarded or indifferent. The chorus appears solemn with little change of expression.

There are attributes to this point of view. The program usually shows careful planning and is impeccable in taste. Within the capabilities of the group the numbers are generally sung with technical perfection. A sense of dignity becoming to artistic endeavor is present. But it lacks a human quality; it lacks *rapport* with the audience. The musical chasm between singers and listeners is not bridged.

It is true that some choral concerts convey this academic impression when it is just a lack of security on the part of the choristers and the conductor. Public performance is a completely new experience and they are suffering from stage fright. Repetition of the experience will overcome this condition. Sometimes the cause is insecurity of the music. Only careful preparation will offset this dilemma. The only known cures for uneasiness and stage fright are adequate experience and complete musical security. At these concerts there is always a feeling of, "Let's get this thing over with as quickly as possible."

Whether the attitude is academic or pseudo-academic, the performance is usually stilted. The former may have the quality of intensity but lacks the heightened emotion so necessary for artistic singing and audience response. The latter often has a quality of indifference, resulting from a feeling of personal and musical inadequacy, and the performance is phlegmatic. If the listeners are parents and friends, they will endure it.

Communal

There are good and bad aspects in the attitudes discussed above. Perhaps we can preserve the good and eliminate the bad in a communal approach. By communal, we mean a community spirit. It implies sharing oneself and one's talents with others. The conductor and chorus have been working hard preparing and experiencing the performance of beautiful music with each other. They give a public performance to share these enjoyable musical experiences with both friends and strangers. This spirit of sharing is the attitude which should determine the atmosphere of the concert hall.

This attitude possesses the best attributes of the theatrical and academic attitudes. If the singers wish genuinely to share their music, they will rehearse with the diligence necessary to have something worthwhile sharing. This preparation will include not only a technical performance within their capabilities, but also an emotional quality which they have experienced to make the music live. The dramatic aspects are present without theatrics. Program notes and verbal remarks are brief and designed to set the mood of the piece. The acknowledgment of applause is gracious and reflects sincere appreciation. The concert becomes not a show, not a music lesson but an enjoyable evening of making music together. It is this type of public performance which often causes a conductor to exclaim, "The singers outdid themselves."

VALUES OF PUBLIC PERFORMANCE

The author has often dreamed of choruses which felt no obligation to give concerts. With these imaginary groups the pleasure of rehearsing fine music together would be sufficient to realize the objectives and values of such organizations. He has even experimented with giving concerts of oratorios where the chorus sat in the auditorium as part of the audience. Only the orchestra and visiting soloists were on the stage. It was a fine musical experience for the choristers, but in every case it was evident that it would have been a more enjoyable occasion if they had been on the stage with the soloists. Listeners also seem to prefer a traditional type of concert. From these experiments the author is convinced that choral groups to be successful socially, culturally and musically need to give concerts.

Motivation

Singers in choral groups should be introduced to a wide variety of compositions. Lest acquaintance with all these compositions be superficial and a careless attitude on the part of the students prevail, a few numbers should be practiced with such attention to detail that they can be performed as perfectly as the ability of the group permits. This caliber of performance calls for long, sustained practice on individual compositions. Choristers grow restless during such rehearsals unless there is a concert in the offing. Only then will they understand the conductor's careful attention to detail and insistence upon perfection. During such preparations, the choristers are more willing to strive for exact rhythm, phrase nuance, uniform tone quality, dynamic shadings, and clear diction.

After the performance many choristers will return to careless habits and attitudes toward musical study. However, some of them will be made aware of the patience and care necessary in artistic effort. All of them will retain at least some of the things that they learned in the preparation for the concert. A number of these preparations will develop a desirable attitude toward careful artistic effort, and students will become dissatisfied with a slovenly performance for any audience. In this way public performance engenders a deeper appreciation of artistic singing.

Social Values

The sociological significance of music in our culture is realized through public performance. The expression of individuals or groups to other individuals or groups through the medium of tone conveys the message of the music. There must be a performer, even though through mechanical means, and an audience, even though it is the performer himself, or there is no music. In other words, *music must be performed to exist.* There is usually a friendly audience for most choral performances and music serves as means of bringing the performers and the audience into closer relationships. In this way the public performance fosters an affinity between the chorus, the sponsoring institution and the community.

In the second place, most of the performing at school and college functions is done by various groups of students. Preparation for these performances requires the wholehearted cooperation of all the participants. Although individual artistic effort is encouraged and rewarded, the perfect musical ensemble is the result of collective effort. Education toward a democratic spirit brings forth fruit in the choral ensemble as it prepares for public performance.

Integration

In schools and colleges the public performance tends to unify the various divisions of the music department as well as to enlist the cooperation of the entire school. In presenting their joint concerts to the general public the choral and instrumental instructors must resolve their differences and combine all forces for a successful performance. This attitude is reflected in the work of the students who discover for themselves the effectiveness of the different media for making music. A public concert includes solo and group performances by both singers and instrumentalists. The composition classes can also make contributions. Discriminative listening can be encouraged through the performance itself, through the rehearsing of the music, and through the use of the same material in general music classes. The entire school can be enlisted to aid in the publicity. In this way the public performances give direction and purpose to the musical activities which consequently not only foster a deeper appreciation, but also make music a more meaningful part of life.

Publicity

It is not possible to discuss the public performance of choral groups merely in terms of the preceding educational values. The practical values of advertising the sponsoring institution or the conductor and raising money are so often the prime objectives that they must be given some consideration.

It is perfectly legitimate and commendable to acquaint the public with the work of the chorus. On the other hand, advertising the chorus can become a harmful practice if the choristers are exploited solely for the personal aggrandizement of the conductor, or if such demands for public performance are made on their time and energy that practically all cultural and aesthetic values are impaired.

Choral performances which demonstrate the vital part that music can play in the artistic and cultural life of a school or community should be sufficiently publicized to attract an audience of sympathetic and discriminative listeners. By producing results and bringing evidence of these results to the public eye and to the attention of the administrators of the sponsoring institution, the conductor is able to secure money for better materials and equipment for the chorus. In this way public performances contribute to a more artistic singing organization.

PLANNING THE PERFORMANCE

An artistic concert does not just happen; like the rehearsal, it must be planned in order to be successful. In fact its success is probably in direct proportion to the degree of careful planning. There are many details to preparation, but the major factors are the preparation of the music, rooms and equipment, appearance of the group, financing and advertising.

Preparation of the Music

This entire book has been devoted to the ways and means of preparing music for performance. The rehearsals may have been enjoyable and musically satisfying but it is at the concert that the conductor and chorus reap the rewards of hard work. It must be as nearly perfect as they can make it or there will be a sense of futility after the concert. Preparation of the music is the most important factor for the fulfillment of their goals.

Memorization. Should the singers memorize the music? There is no question that they will perform the music better if memorized thoroughly. If the music is only partially memorized it is wiser and safer to use music. When groups have memorized the music they can be more attentive to the interpretative indications of the conductor. Also, they present a more unified and attractive appearance. For a higher standard of performance memorization is advisable.

If rehearsal procedures are followed as suggested in Chapter XI memorization is not such a formidable task. By the time the music is ready for performance most of the choristers will have memorized it. A little review for the entire chorus with attention to difficult places and it is ready for the concert. Learning music through sectional and individual part rehearsing is not conducive to fast memorization; in fact, it presents a barrier. When a group grasps the emotional mood and unity of the entire composition from the beginning, memorization comes easily and naturally.

Memorization of music applies only to a program of miscellaneous numbers. Concerts of extended numbers or single works need not be memorized. It is far better to spend the time in building musicianship and reading through other material. It is best not to make a fetish of memorization, even though it can contribute to a more artistic performance.

Our contention has always been that if a chorus memorizes the music the conductor should conduct from memory. Memorization of the music improves the artistry of the performance. One thing is certain, if the conductor has no music he will keep his "nose out of the score." A conductor usually pleads lack of time as his refusal to memorize any music. To tell the truth, it is easier to memorize the conducting of a piece of music than it is to memorize the words and music of any of the parts, except possibly the melody. Naturally, if the conductor is not sure of himself he should use music. The responsibility of the concert rests on his arms and shoulders. The real criterion of the performance depends upon the way in which he can obtain the most artistic singing from the group.

Warm-up rehearsal. If at all possible the conductor should arrange to be with the chorus for a few minutes before going on the platform. (However, it is too late to make corrections in the music or suggest changes in interpretation.) He can utilize this time to vocalize the group and run through a number which needs to be set. If there is time, the author runs through the first number and then practices entrances by singing the first phrase of each number in the program. This practice eliminates any doubt of the procedures and establishes complete understanding as to pitches between the conductor and accompanist. He expresses a few appreciative and encouraging remarks and the concert is ready to begin.

Rooms and Equipment

Unless he has very reliable assistants, the conductor, himself, had better check all mechanical details of the concert. To avoid mistakes it is well to have an itemized list of things to do. We would suggest this order: the auditorium, the platform, the additional rooms.

The auditorium: lights, ventilation, programs, ushers, marking off reserved sections.

The platform: lights, flowers, position of choir risers, position of piano (it should have been tuned in advance), conductor's podium, conductor's stand, final check of all music, both selections and pages, before placing it on stand (do not trust this final detail to anyone else), test public address system, if used, and placement of all microphones.

Additional rooms: dressing room for conductor and soloists; dressing rooms for chorus, one for men and one for women, warm-up rehearsal room (use same room for lining up sections to march on stage), distribution of music to chorus.

Appearance of Group

A choral group actually seems to sing better when dressed in robes or some type of uniform. The visual unity seems to give tonal unity. When a chorus is called upon often to sing for the public, it is much more impressive when robed. The type of robe or uniform will depend somewhat upon the repertory of the group, but robes or some uniform dress are definitely a part of the equipment for organized singing activities.

The expense of robes is prohibitive for large choruses. These groups present a lovely appearance, however, if the ladies wear black skirts with white blouses (no jewelry please) and the men wear dark suits with dark four-in-hand ties. Evening dress is always appropriate for very special evening occasions. The author has attended several high school and college choir concerts where the first half of the program in a rather serious vein was sung in robes while the lighter, latter half of the program was sung with the girls in pastel-shade evening dresses and the boys in tuxedos.

Robes certainly do save a conductor many headaches. They cover a multitude of sins of apparel. Robes will transform a motley group of teen-agers into a uniform group of singers. The impressiveness of their appearance inspires a more expressive performance.

Financing and Advertising

In planning a choral concert the problem of financing always arises. The author has always believed that local concerts should be open to the public as part of the social and cultural activities of that community. If this policy were followed it would be the responsibility of the sponsoring institution, school, college, church, industry, or recreational association to finance the concert. On occasions, this may be impossible due to the fee for the auditorium, advertising, and programs. Two other ways to finance a concert are free-will offerings or tickets sold in advance. The price of the tickets should be commensurate with the anticipated expenses of the concert and not be geared to making a profit. If the concert is being presented to raise money for some cause such as robes, choir risers, music, or charity, it should be announced in the advertising and on the programs.

An advertising program should be planned whether or not there is a charge for the concert. At intervals there should be announcements in the local papers with a final release of the program. Church bulletins and school papers should carry notices. Conspicuous bulletin boards and front windows of important stores should contain brochures and posters. Announcements should be made at public gatherings. A telephone committee should be organized to spread word concerning the concert. An active ticket committee should be appointed. The entire membership of the choir should be drafted for publicity purposes. When a conductor and chorus have something of worth to share there should be a representative audience at the concert with whom to share it.

THE PERFORMANCE

Finally, we have come to the actual concert itself. We have covered the general aspects of the attitudes toward a concert, the values in giving a concert, and the factors in planning for the concert. Now let us look at those little details which may arise during the concert that either mar or embellish the performance.

The Role of the Conductor

The conductor may think that he is the most important personage at the concert, but he is mistaken; it is the audience. Without the audience the occasion would be just another choral rehearsal. Therefore, his function is not to impress the audience, but it behooves him to win the audience. His attitude should not be one of condescension, but of appreciation.

His true attitude may be reflected in his mannerisms, his entering and leaving the stage, his recognition of applause, his acknowledgment of soloists and accompanists, and his incidental remarks to the audience. His entrances and exits should be dignified but free from self-consciousness, not too fast and not too slow. His bowing should reflect the mood of the piece which has just been sung; slower and more serious for sacred numbers and faster and more enthusiastic for light, secular numbers. His acknowledgments to other performers should be more than a nod; he should give them an opportunity to stand and share the applause. Stage deportment of this kind should be practiced and criticism enlisted from qualified persons. This is not a phase of the conductor's art to cast aside lightly.

The conductor must communicate complete musical security to the chorus. Incompetence is difficult to camouflage. He must be genuinely secure in the job to which he is assigned. When he faces the chorus his bodily attitude and face should reflect the mood of the piece which the chorus is going to sing. The singers tend to respond and return this mood. From this point on he must be completely absorbed in the music; nothing must distract him, his concentration must not waver, even for an instant. Of course, if some young lady in the chorus faints, the music should be stopped and someone should attend her. Human beings come before music. Recently we heard a conductor proudly claim that the chorus "kept right on singing" even though a chorister had fainted. Occasional minor incidents in an audience, however, should not interrupt the concert.

Humility, coupled with personal and musical confidence, best describes the necessary attributes for a conductor at the concert. He should think of himself as a channel through which the message of the music is borne. If the message is comprehended by the listeners he will receive many compliments. In answer to these he should give credit to the chorus. Probably the most appropriate comments are, "Thank you." or, "I am pleased that you enjoyed it," or an occasional, "I was proud of the chorus." Compliments are given in friendliness and graciousness. The conductor should not take them too seriously, but search his own heart and head as to whether the chorus came up to expectations.

Decorum of the Chorus

Regardless of the conduct in rehearsals a group of young people usually behaves in an exemplary fashion at a concert. It is the physical and musical inertia spoken of earlier, against which the conductor and chorus must be ever alert. The marching on and off the stage should be practiced and a system devised consistent with the best platform etiquette. Entrances and exits should be executed without confusion, and in a positive manner. Each singer should be assigned a number, by row and position, in advance. This eliminates misunderstanding and disorder in finding places. Techniques for standing and rising should be practiced. A device of the author is to request each singer to imagine that a string is attached to his nose. The conductor holds the strings. He pulls all of these strings for the chorus to rise and pushes for the chorus to sit.

Perhaps a word should be said about gum and young choral groups. The author has attended some concerts of school groups when he could not tell whether the choruses were singing or just chewing gum. It is a sad commentary on American life but young people must be told to get rid of their gum. They forget that their jaws are wagging.

In the correction of all of these details the chorus must never lose sight of their real goal, the artistic singing of the music which they have rehearsed. The attitude of the chorus toward the audience must parallel that of the conductor. They should not try to impress the audience, but should try to win the audience through their conduct and through their singing. It has been the experience of the author that if singers of all ages realize their mission and responsibility they rise to the occasion.

Presenting Music to the Audience

As a rule, music is sufficient unto itself. Little need be said about it. Any written and verbal statements should be designed primarily to set the mood of the composition. Long musicological discourses and detailed theoretical analyses are inappropriate for most amateur performances. Whatever is written or said should contribute directly to the enjoyment of the music.

A note about the composer and style of the composition is sufficient. If the poetry is short and its meaning too subtle to grasp as the chorus sings, the words may be printed on the program. If the music is so contrapuntal that it is difficult to understand, the words may also be printed. As we have stated before, we do not see the necessity of printing long, familiar texts. Following them often distracts the attention of the listeners.

At informal concerts the author has felt that the audience enjoys the music more if he makes a verbal comment about each number. This, also, should be limited to setting the mood of the music. It may be just a note about the composer and the style of the music. If the mood of the music is completely dependent upon understanding the meaning of the text, and if the nature of the writing makes it difficult to grasp the words the chorus is singing, the author has found it very effective to read the poem prior to the performance. An example is, "The Silver Swan" by Gibbons where the beauty of the words is so completely interwoven with the mood and meaning of the poem.

> The silver swan, who, living, had no note,
> When death approached, unlocked her silent throat!
> Leaning her breast against the reedy shore,
> Thus sang her first and last, and sang no more.
> Farewell, all joys, O death, come close mine eyes;
> More geese than swans now live, more fools than wise.

Securing the Pitch

There must be no mistakes in the giving of the pitch. The author has witnessed musical tragedies from lack of attention to this detail. Complete understanding must exist between the conductor and whoever is giving the pitch. Then it needs to be rehearsed with as much care as the music.

If a pitch-pipe is being used to give the pitch, the singers will need considerable practice on each number to obtain their respective pitches. They will need to take their pitches from a keynote and retain them silently until the conductor's cue to begin. For the first number some conductors attempt to have the voice sections obtain their pitches off stage and retain them while marching on stage. This is a stunt and is a risky business. There can be too many unexpected delays before beginning the concert to take this chance.

If a piano is used the pitch should be the first chord, given in the mood of the piece; soft pitches for soft attacks, firmer chords for louder attacks. If the chorus is insecure in taking its pitch in this manner, the pianist may play the first musical figure or phrase. Humming of the chord by the chorus should not be necessary. There are two criteria for giving pitch; it should set the mood for the composition and should be given in a manner which provides complete musical security for the choral group performing the music. See Chapter IV for additional discussion of how to secure the pitch.

Radio, Television and Recording Performances

Broadcasting. The school or community concert audience is quite different from the radio or television audience. The former usually has a personal interest in the performers which colors judgment. The radio audience listens primarily to be entertained; the personal interest is lacking. Also, the enjoyment by a member of the school or community concert audience is not confined to what he hears alone. He is affected by the physical appearance of the group.

The radio listener does not have this visual aid (it is even limited on television) and judges a performance by what he hears, comparing it to the work of professionals. Finally, the school audience is sympathetic, and, if the performer and conductor are enthusiastic, the listeners are often impervious to poor intonation, uneven attacks, and inadequate interpretation. On the other hand, the microphone is merciless. It is an ultra-sensitive ear which records what it hears accurately and objectively. Poor intonation, thin and colorless tone quality, "muddy" and unrhythmical performance seem actually to be intensified. Undoubtedly, there should be a script which informs the listener that the broadcast or telecast will be done by an amateur group, but this should not be used as an apology for a poor performance. Amateur choral broadcasts and telecasts must be of a very high standard if they are to be accepted by the public.

Preparation. Several of the problems unique to broadcasting can be eliminated if they are considered during the period of preparation. If the rehearsal room is treated acoustically and reverberation is eliminated, sounds will resemble more closely those heard in a radio studio. Secondly, the conductor must learn to listen as objectively as possible. Since the microphone is only one ear instead of two, more accurate judgment may be made if he will shut his eyes and listen to the rehearsal occasionally with one ear stopped tightly. Another device to eliminate visual aid in hearing is to turn the back to the performing group and cup the hands behind the ears. If conductors do this they will hear more accurately the effects as they will sound over the air.

A third consideration in preparing for a successful radio or television appearance is deliberately emphasizing those performance factors which are vital to good broadcasting. The most marked of these is pitch discrepancy. The good teacher will ever be alert for poor intonation, but must be doubly so for broadcasts. Likewise, extra care must be devoted to precision in attacks and releases of tone, for they contribute to rhythmical clarity which is so essential in radio performance. Also, *crescendos* and *diminuendos* should not be too sudden, and dynamic extremes should be limited. If the volume of tone exceeds a certain point, it will be necessary for the radio engineer to turn the volume control down to a void "microphone rush," and vise-versa; if it becomes too soft, he will have to turn the control up, otherwise the music may not be heard at all. When the engineer is forced to do this, the performance is uneven and rough. To obtain a smooth performance the dynamics must be retained within limits so that the engineer can "let it ride". In other words, there should be no interference with the dynamics through the manipulation of volume controls. The newer and improved microphones of today provide for a sufficiently wide range of dynamics to assure artistic interpretation.

On the air. For the broadcast or telecast itself, the music teacher must assume responsibilities and, in turn, be willing to trust the radio engineer and producer with certain details. The conductor must turn in his program allowing ample time for the copyright clearance of all numbers to be broadcast. This information includes the name of the composition, composer, arranger, and publisher. If a number is being performed from manuscript, a written statement granting permission for broadcasting must be secured from the composer. If it is an arrangement, proof must be provided that the words and melody are in the public domain (56 years old). This information is very important to the broadcasters because they must be extremely careful not to break copyright laws. Their copyright staffs are eternally vigilant lest broadcasting companies be legally forced to pay millions in damages for infringement of rights. Much delay and misunderstanding can be avoided if the teacher will cooperate with the broadcasters in this matter.

The musical numbers of the program must be carefully timed by the conductor, saving an adequate amount of time for the announcements. The conductor should provide sufficient background information from which the broadcaster can write suitable continuity. This is one more reason for submitting programs early, for no continuity can be written until the program has been received at the station and approved. In addition to continuity writers, radio stations employ engineers who take care of the technical phases of the broadcast and production managers who supervise the presentation of performances before the microphone, adjust the balance of voices with instruments, work with the engineer in the placement of the microphone, and, in general, do everything in their power to assure a smooth performance. Ordinarily radio engineers and directors are competent, and they can be relied upon to put the program on the air to its best advantage, but they cannot be expected to make it better than it is. The conductor's safest procedure is to adhere carefully to the instructions of the director.

One of the most intricate problems in broadcasting large music groups is the placement of the microphones. This is really a function of the radio engineer and program director; the conductor must, naturally, accept their suggestions. When one microphone is used for the chorus it should be placed at a distance and height where it will receive the composite tone most favorably without admitting room reverberation. As a rule, a large choir will sound better if the conductor is guided by the following suggestions: 1.) do not have the piano directly between the singers and the microphone; 2.) large choral groups should sing full voice but as suggested previously, they should be careful of dynamic extremes; 3.) small groups of singers will blend and balance better if they stand in a mixed-up formation as suggested in Chapter X; Diagram 4.) small groups will sound better if they cut their dynamic level about fifty percent. Over a microphone these procedures are conducive to more uniform performance.

These remarks are only suggestions and the advisable procedure is for the conductor to have his chorus in the studio one hour before broadcasting time to solve any problems with the engineer and director, and to assure the most favorable reception.

Diagram 35

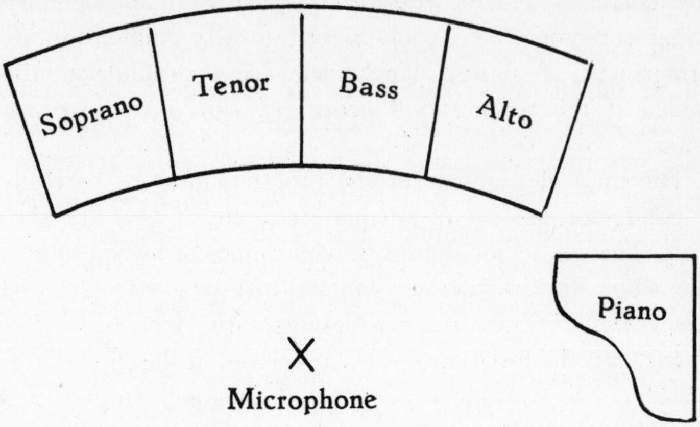

The Festival Performance

We have no magic formula for conductors which will enable them to obtain automatically superior ratings for their groups at festivals. If the rating is paramount, then take only the best singers; if the rating is secondary, then take the "whole gang." If two numbers are sung, select contrasting numbers, including a slow, smooth one. Sing only the best music on these occasions. As a judge for many festivals, the author finds that the two most distressing faults which mar singing performances are intonation and lack of blend and balance. These two factors are so apparent that the judge is forced to give them weighty consideration in his evaluation. Many other technical details are more likely to be regarded with less severity. The only sure formula for obtaining superior ratings is to sing good music within the capabilities of the group in the most artistic manner possible.

If any reader of this volume is requested to serve as guest conductor for combined festivals, the first and foremost factor to consider is the program. Only the best is good enough for such occasions. These young people are usually the more talented students from the schools and are capable of giving a superior performance of challenging music. The conductor should be very familiar with at least fifty percent of the program. In other words, he should have performed at least that many numbers on previous concerts. Only with this past experience with the music will he be able to introduce and utilize procedures for learning the music with the speed and assurance necessary for preparing a finished program in the limited rehearsal time available. Most of the conducting, tonal and rehearsal procedures presented in this book have evolved from the author's experience as a conductor of music festivals.

POST MORTEM

The performance is over. How did it go? Shall we forget it, or shall we talk it over? Aside from the sharing of the musical work of a choral group with an interested audience, the author feels that the public performance has one other valid purpose; it serves as a learning experience. Evaluation is a part of learning, so an appraisal of the concert should be a valuable part of the experience.

At the next rehearsal after the performance, the author usually makes a few appreciative and praiseworthy remarks to the chorus and then asks for general remarks and reactions from the members. This open discussion may be carried on as long as there are appropriate contributions. After this period the conductor may give his general criticism of the performance and then he may discuss the singing of individual numbers, pointing out the elements which made one number go extremely well, followed by the factors which marred the performance of another. If he desires he may practice certain points at this time and review specific selections. Then with some succinct remarks as to the technical and expressive elements which should be emphasized to make the singing more artistic, he introduces a new work and the chorus is embarked upon another musical adventure.

Appendix

RECORDINGS

We have mentioned the use of recordings in introducing new music and expediting the learning of music. Any conductor wishing to make a collection of useful choral recordings will refer to the catalogues of standard companies which he can secure on request. In Chapter XII we have listed certain compositions which are available in recording. These are listed below. Some of them were performed by the Concert Choir of Teachers College, Columbia University, directed by the author. These will serve as a demonstration of many numbers usually found in the repertory of high school, college, church and community choruses. The other recordings listed are those with which we are familiar and which we believe will be helpful in study by the conductor and chorus.

Beloved Choruses from THE MESSIAH (Handel) Westminster WN 18099
London Philharmonic Choir, London Symphony Orchestra —
Herman Scherchen, Conductor.

Ceremony of Carols, A (Britten) — London LL 1396
Copenhagen Boys Choir
11 original Christmas numbers for SA choir with optional harp accompaniment.

Choral Musicianship Series, Bk. I, Silver Burdett Company
Fourteen selections for demonstrating SA arrangements.

Choral Selections, Accompanied, PAR Recordings CS 7000, Box 209, Madison Square Station, New York, N. Y.
Concert Choir, Teachers College, Columbia University
H. R. Wilson, Conductor
One World — O'Hara, Ave Verum Corpus — Mozart, America My Own — Cain, May Day Carol — Taylor, Glory to God — Bach, Hallelujah Amen — Handel, In the Stillness of the Night — Wilson, Psalm 150 — Lewandowski.

Choral Selections, Unaccompanied, PAR Recordings CS 7001 (address above)
Concert Choir, Teachers College, Columbia University
H. R. Wilson, Conductor
Break Forth, O Beauteous Heavenly Light — Bach, Ave Maria — Arcadelt, Cherubim Song No. 7 — Bortniansky, Tenebrae Factae Sunt — Ingegneri, A Joyful Christmas Song — Gevaert, Lo, How a Rose E'er Blooming — Praetorius, Jacob's Ladder — Wilson, Alleluia — Thompson.

Christmas Hymns and Carols, Victor LM - 2139
Robert Shaw, Conductor

A new recording of Christmas carols, beautifully sung a cappella. Excellent for demonstration of style and diction.

Christmas Songs and Anthems, PAR Recordings (address above)
Concert Choir, Teachers College, Columbia University
H. R. Wilson, Conductor
Fanfare for Christmas — Shaw, The Shepherd's Story — Dickinson, The Three Kings — Willan, Magnum Mysterium — Vittoria, Winter — Wilson, other familiar choral numbers.

Concert of Sacred Music, Col. ML - 5048 and 5203 (12″)
Mormon Tabernacle Choir of Salt Lake City
J. Spencer Cornwall, Conductor
Miscellaneous anthems from standard repertory.

Creation (Haydn) Decca Dex-138
Soloists, Choir of St. Hedwig's Cathedral

Early Renaissance Music, Unaccompanied, PAR Recordings CS 7002 (address above)
Concert Choir, Teachers College, Columbia University
H. R. Wilson, Conductor
Sacred: Adoremus Te — Corsi, Cantate Domino — Pitoni, Agnus Dei — Hassler, Resonet in Laudibus — Handl, Call to Remembrance — Farrant, Let All Ye Sons and Daughters Sing — Leisring
Secular: Dancing and Springing — Hassler, Mother, I Will Have a Husband — Vauter, The Silver Swan — Gibbons, He Is Good and Handsome — Passereau, Sweet Love Doth Now Invite — Dowland, Which is the Properest Day to Sing — Arne
Note: Decca has a complete series of recordings of early music beautifully performed by the Brussels Pro Musica Antiqua.

Folk Songs of the New World — Capital P-8324
Roger Wagner Chorale
Excellent recording of folk songs often found on concert programs.

For Everything There Is a Season (Rosza) — Music Library Recordings MLR 7071
Concert Choir, Teachers College, Columbia University
H. R. Wilson, Conductor
Side 2: A Thing of Beauty and The Finger of God — Wilson
Sixty-Seventh Psalm and Harvest Chorale — Ives

Great Sacred Choruses — RCA Victor LM 1117
Robert Shaw Chorale
Hallelujah — Handel, Heavens are Telling — Haydn, Ave Verum — Mozart, Hallelujah — Beethoven, He Watching Over Israel — Mendelssohn, Thou Must Leave Thy Lowly Dwelling — Berlioz, Sanctus — Gounod, God So Loved the World — Stainer

Magnificat in D Major (Bach) Decca 9557 (12″)
Soloists, Chorus, and Ainsbach Bach Festival Orchestra

Miscellaneous Selections, ABC-Paramount ABC-195 (12″)
Concert Choir, Teachers College, Columbia University
H. R. Wilson, Conductor
Compositions and Arrangements of Dr. Wilson

Side 1: The Lord's Prayer, Remember Now Thy Creator, Lullaby of Jesus, Long Ago in Bethlehem, Te Deum Laudamus, The Twenty-Third Psalm
Side 2: Off the Road, Coffee Grows on a White Oak Tree, Paw Paw Patch, At Parting, A Rockin' All Night, A Phantom of Delight, Peace Must Come Like a Troubadour

Requiem (Fauré), Capital P-8241 (12")
Roger Wagner Chorale, Concert Arts Orchestra
Roger Wagner, Conductor

Requiem (Mozart), Victor LM 1712 (12")
Robert Shaw Chorale
Robert Shaw, Conductor

Sacred Music Around the Church Year, Concert Hall - CHS-1100 (12")
Trapp Family
Psallite — Praetorius, Resonet et Laudibus — Handl, O Bone Jesu — Palestrina, and other miscellaneous numbers

Sweet and Low, Victor LM-1800
Robert Shaw Chorale
Side 1: Four Schubert Songs for Male Voices
Side 2: Miscellaneous

Three Motets (Bach), ARC Decca 3040
1. Singet dem Herrn, 2. Der Geist hilft, 3. Füschtedich nicht

Three Motets (Bach), ARC Decca 3041
Jesu Meine Freude, 2. Komm, Jesu, Komm, 3. Lobet den Herrn all Heiden

Treasury of Easter Songs, LM 1201
Robert Shaw Chorale
Hymns and carols beautifully sung a cappella.

CHORAL COLLECTIONS

There seems to be considerable controversy over the use of collections by choral groups. If it is a careful selection and edited in a scholarly manner, a collection is certainly a saving on the budget. Unless a majority of the numbers are usable by an organization, the collection should certainly not be purchased. The author often employs a basic collection for a choral group and supplements it with individual numbers. There are excellent collections for younger groups. These groups, however, deserve separate compositions also as part of their repertory. Older groups, unless they are singing a single work, seem to prefer single octavo numbers. We are including collections for different voice combinations which we have found useful in many situations.

1. *Collections of Series*

A Cappella Singer, The, Ed. by H. Clough-Leighter, E. C. Schirmer
Three books of superior material primarily from the 17th and 18th century.
Mixed voices — 30 numbers
Women's voices — 30 numbers
Male voices — 25 numbers

Auditorium Series, Schmitt-Hall & McCreary Co.
Inexpensive booklets for all types of voice combinations. Write to publisher for catalogue.

Choral Musicianship Series, Arr. and Ed. by Wilson, Silver Burdett Co.
Easy selections, 12 to 14 numbers both sacred and secular in each book for various voice combinations. Suggestions and procedures for developing and musicianship and learning the music. Book I — SA, Book II — SSA, Book III — Boys' Voices, Book IV — SAB, Book V — SATB. Book I, SA has been recorded. See list of recordings.

Choral Program Series, Arr. and Ed. by Wilson, Silver Burdett Co.
Easy numbers, both sacred and secular, for various voice combinations.
Book I — SA, Book II — SSA, Book III — Male Voices, Book IV — SAB, Book V — SATB (easy), Book VI — SATB (more difficult).

Sing a Folk Song, Arr. by Churchill, Plymouth Music Co.
Thirty easy folk songs — 19 for mixed voices, 4 for male voices, 5 for treble voices.

Tribute to Song, A, Boosey and Hawkes
Two books with a variety of material especially suitable for school choral groups.
Mixed voices — SAB — 17 miscellaneous sacred and secular numbers.
Treble voices — SSA — 14 miscellaneous sacred and secular numbers.

2. *SATB Collections*

Five Master Choruses, Schmitt-Hall & McCreary Co.
Glory to God in the Highest — Pergolesi, Lacrymosa (Day of Weeping) — Mozart, Crucifixus (Crucified) — Bach, Requiem Aeternam (Peace and Rest Eternal) — Verdi, Hallelujah Amen — Handel. All five anthems are standard repertory. Excellent buy.

Select A Cappella Choruses, Ed. by Noble Cain, Schmitt, Hall & McCreary Co.
Fourteen carefully selected numbers. Very reasonable.
(See 1. above)

3. *SAB Collections*

Collection of Sacred Choruses, Harold Flammer, Inc.
Eleven selections including arrangements of some old favorites. Moderately difficult.

SAB Choral Book, The, Ed. by Thomas, Concordia Publishing House.
Excellent collection for an inexperienced group.

SAB Chorister, The, Arr. by Heller, Schmitt, Hall & McCreary Co.
Easy arrangements of music of high caliber — 23 selections.

Sing Praise, Arr. by Lenel, Concordia Publishing House.
Two volumes of excellent sacred music for SAB.
(See 1. above)

4. *Treble Voice Collections, SA and SSA*

Green Hill Three-Part Sacred Choruses, The — Davis, E. C. Schirmer.
Unusually fine arrangements of anthems chosen from the best religious music of many churches, countries, and centuries. 38 anthems in all.

Let There be Song — Siegmeister and Ehret, Bourne Music Co.
Twelve varied numbers for treble voices.

Rejoice and Sing — Ehret, Belwin, Inc.

Excellent sacred collection for unison or two part.

Schirmer's Two-Part Choruses for Junior Choir, G. Schirmer, Inc.

A standard collection of sacred music.

Singing Bee, A, Gearhart, Shawnee Press.

Forty-nine easy songs for SA group. Good fun.

Unto Thee We Sing, Arr. by Heller, Schmitt, Hall & McCreary Co.

Twenty-eight superior arrangements for SA of carefully selected sacred music. (See 1. above)

5. *Male Voice Collections*

Harvard University Glee Club Collections for Male voices.

Superior material. Write to E. C. Schirmer & Co. for information.

Selected Songs for Men, Arr. by Christensen and Wycisk, Augsburg Publishing House.

Arrangements of hymns and well known selections. 68 in all. 57 are sacred. (See 1. above)

6. *Christmas Music Collections*

Christmas — its Carols, Customs and Legends, Arr. by Heller, Schmitt-Hall & McCreary Co.

Over 75 familiar and unfamiliar carols, plus authentic information extremely valuable in building programs.

Christmas Cheer, Arr. by Wilson, Consolidated Music Co.

Five sections: familiar carols, other favorite carols, novelty Christmas songs, spirituals, special music.

7. *Sight Reading Material*

Sing a Song at Sight, Wilson, Schmitt-Hall & McCreary Co.

A practical and rapid method of developing music reading, individually or in groups.

EXTENDED WORKS

All choral groups, even the younger ones, should consider doing more extended and challenging works than those usually represented by individual octavo numbers. We are not listing the standard oratorios and cantatas, except those which are in the capabilities of most amateur groups. We are calling attention to some numbers, which, although not of the dimensions of larger works, are certainly worth considering to add impressiveness to public concerts. For these numbers we have given the approximate length of time. After a chorus has exhausted this list they are ready for the great masterpieces.

1. *Sacred*

Ceremony of Carols, A — Britten, Boosey & Hawkes.

Eleven attractive numbers for SA with optional harp accompaniment. About 20 minutes.

Christmas Oratorio — Saint-Saens, G. Schirmer, Inc.

For mixed chorus and solos. Choral parts are very easy but solos are difficult. About 45 minutes in length.

Crucifixion — Stainer, G. Schirmer, Inc.
The standard oratorio in many churches for the Lenten season. Not difficult. About 45 minutes in length.

For Everything There Is a Season — Rosza, Broude Brothers.
A dramatic motet in modern vein based on text from Ecclesiastes. Divided parts. Difficult. About 15 minutes.

For Unto Us a Child Is Born — Bach, Galaxy Music Corp.
For mixed voices and contralto, tenor and bass solos. About twenty minutes in length. Not difficult.

Gallia — Gounod, G. Schirmer, Inc.
A lovely motet of about 20 minutes in length. Soprano soloist needed. Easy and effective.

Gloria — Vivaldi, G. Ricordi & Co., Inc.
An easy but effective setting of the Gloria section of the mass. Latin or English. Mixed chorus with soloists. About 30 minutes in length.

Glory Around His Head, The — Meyerowitz, Broude Brothers.
Text by Langston Hughes. A cantata in contemporary vein of the Resurrection. Mixed voices with one medium-voice soloist. Medium difficulty and different.

Hear My Prayer — Mendelssohn, G. Schirmer, Inc.
A short cantata within the musical ability of most choirs. About 12 minutes in length. Good soprano soloist needed.

Holy City, The — Gaul, G. Schirmer, Inc.
A universal favorite which is within the means of most church choirs. Four good soloists needed. About 45 minutes in length.

Hymn of Praise — Mendelssohn, G. Schirmer, Inc.
An effective cantata of about 45 minutes. Four soloists needed. Medium difficulty.

Jeanette-Isabella — Elsmith, Summy-Birchard Co.
A song-play for children around the old French carol. About 20 minutes in presentation. As many as 40 or 50 children can be used.

Jesu, Priceless Treasure — Bach, G. Schirmer, Inc.
A motet of approximately 25 minutes in length. No soloists. Composed for SSATB. Difficult.

Lord Is a Sun and Shield, The — Bach, H. W. Gray.
An easy cantata for general purposes; soprano, alto and baritone solos. Approximately 15 minutes.

Magnificat — Bach, G. Schirmer, Inc.
An exciting work. About 30 minutes in length. Four soloists needed. Difficult.

Messiah (Christmas Section), The — Handel, G. Schirmer, Inc.
Listed here to call attention to the availability of just the Christmas section. Closes with the "Hallelujah Chorus" of Part II. A challenge for all church choirs.

Now Thank We All Our God — Bach, G. Schirmer, Inc.
Also excellent edition published by H. W. Gray Co. Moderately difficult. About 20 minutes in length.

Rejoice, Beloved Christians — Buxtehude-Dickinson, H. W. Gray Co.
A short cantata that is very easy. Soprano, alto and bass solos. Especially suitable for Advent.

Requiem — Fauré, H. T. FitzSimons Co.
Mixed chorus with soprano and baritone solos. A beautiful work and not difficult. About 45 minutes in length.

Requiem — Mozart, G. Schirmer, Inc.
Latin edition. Excellent edition in English — H. W. Gray Co. A masterwork suitable for the average choir that desires a challenge. Medium difficult. Four soloists needed.

Rex Gloria — Gaines, Summy-Birchard Co.
A Christmas recessional. Mixed voices, solo quartet, ad lib., solo violin and narrator. About ten minutes in length. Very effective.

Te Deum Laudamus — Wilson, Mills Music Co.
A hymn of praise for treble voices with soprano solo; optional violin and 'cello parts, 4 contrasting sections. Approximately 6 minutes. See list of recordings.

Thanksgiving for Victory — Vaughan Williams, Oxford University Press.
Mixed voices, soprano solo, and speaker. About 15 minutes in length. Very effective.

This Is Christmas — Burt, Shawnee Press.
An easy choral pageant of attractive new music. Approximately 15 minutes.

Thou Very God and David's Son — Bach, G. Schirmer, Inc.
Difficult work of about 12 minutes in length.

Three Fuguing Tunes — Billings, Mercury Music Corp.
1. Creation; 2. When Jesus Wept; 3. Be Glad Then America.
Early American, about 9 minutes in length. Not difficult.

Three Motets, Op. 29 #2 — Brahms, G. Schirmer, Inc.
1. Create In Me, O God, a Pure Heart; 2. O Cast Me Not Away;
3. Grant Unto Us the Joy of Thy Salvation.

Upon This Rock — Wilson, G. Schirmer, Inc.
An oratorio of about 50 minutes in length. Based upon the life of St. Peter. Unaccompanied small choir used for recitatives. Four soloists needed. Orchestration available. Medium difficulty.

When the Christ Child Came — Clokey, Summy-Birchard Co.
Easy cantata for solo voices with mixed choruses. Orchestration available. A great favorite.

2. *Secular*

Five Songs, Op. 104 — Brahms, G. Ricordi & Co.
A series of five beautiful songs which make a superior group. Rather difficult, approximately 12 minutes. 1. Night Watch, No. 1; 2. Night Watch, No. 2; 3. Lost Happiness; 4. Lost Youth; 5. In Autumn.

Peasant Cantata — Bach, Peterson Publications.
One of the two secular cantatas which Bach composed. Approximately 30 minutes in length.

Songs of Conquest — McDonald, Elkan-Vogel Co.
Cycle for mixed voices. Rather difficult and 12 minutes in length. 1. The Breadth and Extent of Man's Empire; 2. A Complaint Against Bitterness of Solitude; 3. A Declaration for Increase of Understanding Among Peoples of the World; 4. The Exaltation of Man in his Migrations and In Surmounting Natural Barriers.

Songs of Nature — Dvorak, Broude Brothers.

Five lovely songs for a delightful group. Not difficult — approximately 10 minutes. 1. Melodies Steal Into My Heart; 2. Vesper Bells Ring; 3. Golden Sunlight; 4. Slender Young Birch; 5. This Day.

Testament of Freedom — Thompson, E. C. Schirmer.

Four settings for TTBB from the writings of Thomas Jefferson. Orchestration available. Not too difficult. Approximately 15 minutes. 1. The God Who Gave Us Hope; 2. We Have Counted the Cost; 3. We Fight Not for Glory; 4. I Shall Not Die Without Hope.

'Twas the Night Before Christmas — Darby, Shawnee Press.

Easy and light setting of Clement Moore's famous poem. May be dramatized. SATB or SSA.

MISCELLANEOUS COMPOSITIONS*

There is a wealth of octavo material to fit the needs of any choral group. However, "Can you suggest some suitable or new materials?" seems to be the never-ending cry of choral conductors wherever we go. Festival lists and catalogues put out by publishers are usually long or confusing and the novice has difficulty in selecting numbers from these with confidence. The author is familiar with all of the numbers given in the following lists. They lean toward the classics and contemporary music which he feels are generally neglected by choral groups. He also favors original compositions instead of arrangements. The lists are designed primarily for inexperienced conductors since the experienced conductor is usually familiar with sufficient material for his needs. Never should any conductor, however, relinquish his ardent search for better material for his groups because the music he selects is his guidepost to success. The author has taken the liberty of listing his publications which seem to have aroused the most favorable reception by conductors and choral groups. He will send an additional list to any reader who requests it. A new list of modern contemporary choral music for all voices may be secured from the Music Educators National Conference (MENC).

No price is given for individual copies because prices are constantly changing. The average price for each octavo is 20¢, however, although there are variations depending upon the length of the number.

The difficulty of each number is indicated by a rating scale from 1 to 5: 1 = very easy; 2 = easy; 3 = moderate; 4 = moderately difficult; 5 = difficult. (The 4 and 5 ratings usually imply a number with division of parts.)

*All numbers preceded by an asterisk will be found in the list of recordings.

Materials are classified as follows:

a. Voice combinations: mixed, treble, male.

b. Types of material: sacred, secular, folk (including spirituals).

c. Christmas (all voice combinations).

d. Combined numbers (all voice combinations).

Title	Composer or Arranger	Key to Publisher	Diffi-culty	A* U* O*	Description
1. *Sacred — Mixed Voices*					
Achieved Is the Glorious Work	Haydn	GS	3	A	A glorious anthem
*Adoramus Te	Corsi	BM	4	U	Flowing
Adoramus Te	Perti	GR	3	U	17th century
Advent Motet (2nd Movt.)	Schreck	KJ	4	U	Entrance scene
*Agnus Dei	Hassler	BM	2	U	Prayerful
Agnus Dei	Pergolesi	MM	3	A	Beautiful setting
Agnus Dei	Wilson	JS	4	U	Antiphonal — 8 part
All Breathing Life	Bach	GS	5	A	From motet "Sing Ye to the Lord"
All In An April Evening	Roberton	GS	2	O	Quiet and peaceful
Alleluia	Hummel	GR	3	A	Festival Chorus
*Alleluia	Thompson	ECS	4	U	Required repertory
Almighty and Everlasting God	Gibbons	SB	4	U	Standard anthem
Almighty God Who Hast Me Brought	Ford	BM	1	A	Dignified
And the Glory of the Lord	Handel	GS	3	A	From the *Messiah*
Ave Maria	Stravinsky	BM	3	U	Unusual setting
Ave Maria	Villa-Lobos	CM	3	O	Classic in style
Ave Verum	Mozart	GS	2	A	Deep spiritual quality
Ballad of the Trees and Master	Wilson	BH	4	O	Unusual setting of this beautiful text
Behold I Stand at the Door	Bach	HWG	3	U	Chorale
Bless the Lord, O My Soul	Ippolitov-Ivanov	HWG	3	U	Easy and effective
Blessed Are the Meek	Wilson	CF	1	A	Beatitude, medium voice solo

* Throughout this section A = accompanied; U = unaccompanied; O = optional.

Title	Composer or Arranger	Key to Publisher	Diffi-culty	A* U* O*	Description
Brazilian Psalm	Berger	GS	5	A	"Alleluia" may be ordered separately
*Call to Remembrance	Farrant	BM	2	U	Meditative
Cantate Domino	Hassler	BM	3	O	"Sing to the Lord"
*Cantate Domino (Sing to the Lord)	Pitoni	BM	2	U	With praise. English words
Cherubim Song No 7	Bortniansky	SHMc	3	U	Always good, a cappella
Cherubim Song	Glinka	BH	3	U	Contrasting sections
Children's Blessing	Wasner	GS	2	U	With devotion
Chorus of Angels	Schubert	GS	2	O	Harmonic
Create in Me, O God, a Clean Heart	Wilson	MM	4	O	Much contrast, a cappella
Creation, The	Richter	HF	4	U	Climactic
Creation, The	Scott	TP	4	U	Concert piece with narrator
Crucifixus	Bach	PM	3	A	B Minor Mass, English words
David's Lamentation	Billings	CF	2	U	Slow and sustained
*Dona Nobis Pacem	Arr. Wilson	SHMc	1	U	Old German canon — SSA, SAB or SATB. Appropriate for Christmas
Emitte Spiritum Tuum	Schuetky	SB	4	U	"Send Forth Thy Spirit"
Fanfare for Easter	Wilson	BM	4	O	Good opener
Festival Song of Praise	Mendelssohn	BM	4	A	Stirring festival chorus
Finger of God, The	Wilson	GR	4	A	Poem from "Abt Vogler" by Robert Browning
Give Us Faith for Today	Wilson	GS	1	A	Easy and tuneful
Gloria in Excelsis	Mozart	GS	2	A	Standard repertory. English words

* Throughout this section A = accompanied; U = unaccompanied; O = optional.

Title	Composer or Arranger	Key to Publisher	Diffi-culty	A* U* O*	Description
Gloria Patri	Palestrina	GS	2	U	Antiphonal
Glory Now to Thee Be Given	Bach	CM	2	A	Majestic chorale
*Glory to God	Bach	GR	4	A	Stirring, good opener
God of Our Fathers	Mueller	CF	2	O	Festival chorus
*God So Loved the World	Stainer	GS	2	U	From "The Crucifixion"
Go Not Far From Me, O God	Zingarelli	JS	2	O	Contrasting sections
Great Is the Lord	Handel	MPH	3	A	Majestic
Hallelujah Amen	Handel	GS	3	O	From "Judas Maccabeus"
Heavenly Light	Kopyloff-Wilhousky	CF	2	U	Sustained in free rhythm
*Heavens Are Telling, The	Haydn	GS	4	A	From "The Creation"
Here Yet Awhile	Bach	BH	4	A	From " St. Matthew Passion"
*He Watching Over All the World	Mendelssohn	SP	3	A	From "Elijah"
Hospodi Pomilui	Lvovsky	MPH	3	U	Russian chant
How Lovely Is Thy Dwelling Place	Brahms	GR	4	A	From "German Requiem"
How Lovely Thy Place	Kubik	HWG	3	O	Psalm 84
Hosanna to the Son of David	Gibbons	GS	5	U	A superior challenge
I Beheld Her, Beautiful As a Dove	Willan	CF	3	U	Beautiful phrasing
If With All Your Hearts	Wilson	GR	3	U	Antiphonal effects
I Thought On the Lamb of God	Wilson	Volk	2	U	"All In an April Evening"
Jesus and the Traders	Kodaly	BH	5	U	Dramatic
Kyrie Eleison	Bach	GS	5	A	From "B Minor Mass'
Laudate Dominum in Tympanis	Palestrina-Klein	JF	5	U	Festival chorus for 3 choirs
Legend	Tschaikowsky	HWG	3	O	Story of Crucifixion

* Throughout this section A = accompanied; U = unaccompanied; O = optional.

Title	*Composer or Arranger*	*Key to Publisher*	*Diffi-culty*	*A* U* O**	*Description*
Let All the World in Every Corner Sing	Roberton	GS	1	O	Stirring
*Let All Ye Sons and Daughters Sing	Leisring	BM	3	U	Double chorus, SSA and SATB
Let Thy Holy Presence	Tschesnekoff-Ehret	PA	2	U	Effective arrangement
Let Thy Holy Presence	Tschesnekoff	SB	4	U	8 part, original
Lord, Make Me An Instrument of Thy Peace	Wilson	B3	5	U	St. Francis' Prayer
Lord, Now Lettest Thou Thy Servant Depart in Peace	Wilson	B3	3	O	Nunc Dimittis
Lost In the Night	Christensen	Aug	3	A	Most effective
Now Shall the Grace	Bach	HWG	5	U	Short motet for double choir
Now Thank We All Our God	Arr. Mueller	GS	4	O	Brilliant arrangement
O Come, O Come Emmanuel	Arr. Niles	CF	1	U	SSAB, also suitable for Christmas
O Come Ye Servants of the Lord	Tye	BM	1	A	Easy anthem
O Sacred Head Now Wounded	Bach	JS	1	O	From "St. Matthew Passion"
O Saviour of the World	Goss	SHMc	2	O	Standard repertory
O Saviour Rend the Skies	Brahms	Ox	5	U	Theme and variations
O Sing Unto the Lord a New Song	Mead	HF	3	A	Forceful
Praise	Rowley	Ox	3	A	Brilliant
Praise Ye the Lord of Hosts	Saint-Saens	BH	1	O	From "Christmas Oratorio"
Psalm 150	Franck	GS	4	A	Wonderful setting
*Psalm 150	Lewandowski	SHMc	3	O	Hymn of Praise
Rejoice In the Lord	Wilson	B3	2	A	Brilliant
Remember Now thy Creator	Wilson	B3	2	U	Modal in style

*** Throughout this section A = accompanied; U = unaccompanied; O = optional.**

Title	Composer or Arranger	Key to Publisher	Diffi-culty	A* U* O*	Description
Rise Up, My Love, My Fair One	Willan	Ox	3	U	General or Easter
Salvation Is Created	Tschesnekoff	JF	3	U	Original, beautiful, divided parts
Salvation Is Created	Tschesnekoff-Ehret	BM	1	U	Useful arrangement
Sanctus	Bach	GS	5	A	From "B Minor Mass"
Sanctus and Hosanna	Mozart	BH	3	A	Two contrasting sections
Sanctus and Hosanna	Schubert	BH	4	A	From "Mass in G"
Save Us, O Lord	Matthews	HTF	1	O	Surging
Sing and Rejoice	James	HTF	4	O	Majestic, divided parts
Sing We Now With One Accord	Praetorius	GS	1	O	Forceful
*Sixty-Seventh Psalm	Ives	MM	5	O	Modern harmonies
Song of Praise, A	Mozart	CM	2	U	Ave Verum, English words only
Souls of the Righteous	Noble	SHMc	3	O	Standard repertory
Te Deum	Holst	Gal	4	A	Stately
*Tenebrae Factae Sunt	Ingegneri	BH	4	U	English words
Thanks Be to God	Lowell	BM	3	A	Strong melody
Thanks Be to God	Mendelssohn	SHMc	5	A	From "Elijah"
There Shall a Star Come Out of Jacob	Mendelssohn	SHMc	4	A	Famous standard anthem
Thy Kingdom Come	Berger	GS	5	O	Modern harmonies
To Thee We Sing	Archangelsky-Tellep	SHMc	3	U	Smoothly and sustained
Turn Back O Man	Holst	GAL	3	A	Sturdy anthem, accomp.
*Twenty-Third Psalm	Wilson	BM	4	U	Pastoral setting
We Praise Thee	Gretchaninoff	RH	2	U	Solemn
With a Voice of Singing	Shaw	GS	2	A	Jubilant

* Throughout this section A = accompanied; U = unaccompanied; O = optional.

Title	*Composer or Arranger*	*Key to Publisher*	*Diffi-culty*	*A* U* O**	*Description*
Ye Watchers and Ye Holy Ones	Arr. Zanzig	ECS	3	A	Old German melody, accomp.
2. *Secular — Mixed Voices*					
All Music	Wilson	GS	3	U	Poem by Whitman
America My Own	Cain	HF	1	A	Melodious—all types of arrangements
April Is In Her Lovely Face	Morley	GR	2	U	Lovely madrigal
Ballad of Brotherhood	Wagner	EV	4	O	Contrasting moods
Ballad of Green Broom	Britten	BH	3	U	Animated
Beautiful Dreamer	Foster	SF	3	U	Serenely
Begin the Beguine	Porter	MPH	3	A	Excellent arrangement of popular song
Bluebird, The	Stamford	Gal	3	U	Larghetto
Cantical of Freedom	Copland	BH	5	A	Choral finale
Come Let Your Hearts Be Singing	Gestoldi	BM	3	U	Early German
Come to the Fair	Martin	BH	3	A	All types of arrangements
Concert Epilogue	Cooper	GS	3	A	Choral postlude
Cuanto le gusta	Ruiz	Sou	2	A	Mexican rhythm song
Cuckoo Song	Lemlin	GS	3	U	16th century
*Dancing and Springing	Hassler	BM	3	U	SSATB, gay madrigal
El Cumbanchero	Hernandez	Sou	2	A	Mexican street dance
Eres Tu	Sandoval	Sou	3	A	"Are you," soprano solo with chorus
Farmer's Wife Lost Her Cat	Mozart	EBM	3	O	Delightful

* Throughout this section A = accompanied; U = unaccompanied; O = optional.

Title	*Composer or Arranger*	*Key to Publisher*	*Diffi-culty*	*A* U* O**	*Description*
Fire, Fire My Heart	Morley	GS	5	U	Five-part madrigal
Fireflies	Arranged	ECS	1	U	Excellent novelty
Fog	Sommervell	BM	3	O	Words by Sandburg
Go Down Death	Scott	TP	4	U	Rhythmical and intense
Go Lovely Rose	Wilson	Mills	4	U	Romantic
Happy and Gay	Peuerl	BM	2	U	Early German
*He is Good and Handsome	Passereau	BM	4	U	Early French
*Holiday Song	Schuman	GS	3	A	Unusual
I Got Rhythm	Gershwin	MPH	3	A	Popular song
In These Delightful Pleasant Groves	Purcell	GS	3	U	Delightful
Kye Song of the Saint Bride	Clokey	SB	1	U	Delightful
Lamento Gitano	Grever	Sou	3	A	A gypsy lament
Las Agachadas	Copland	BH	5	U	Spanish dance
Let My Soul Rise in Song	Rhea	SB	3	O	Surging
Let Our Great Song Arise	Wilson	GS	4	O	Stirring prelude
Linden Tree, The	Schubert	CM	2	A	Nostalgic
Little Song of Life, A	Kanitz	SHMc	2	U	Quiet and simple
Little White Hen, A	Scandello	BM	3	U	Different
Love Song	Brahms	GR	3	O	Study for phrasing
Love Songs	Brahms	ECS	3	A	Two-piano accompaniment. Waltz tempos
Vol. I — 4 songs					
Vol. II — 6 songs					
Madame Jeanette	Murray	Ox	2	U	Required repertory

* Throughout this section A = accompanied; U = unaccompanied; O = optional.

Title	*Composer or Arranger*	*Key to Publisher*	*Diffi-culty*	*A* U* O**	*Description*
Morning	Speaks	GS	2	A	Contrasting moods
Music of Life	Cain	GS	4	O	Overpowering
My Spirit Sang All Day	Finzi	GS	3	O	Joyous
Nightingale, The	Tschaikowsky	SB	3	U	Easy part writing
O Brother Man	Wilson	Mills	5	U	Whittier's poem — 8 parts
O Lord Don't Leave Me Now	Wilson	WM	4	A	In the style of a spiritual
O Mistress Mine	Murray	CF	3	U	Tranquil
O Sing Your Song	Cain	HF	4	O	Brilliant
*Off the Road	Wilson	JS	3	O	Thoughtful poem
One World	O'Hara	BM	3	A	Popular closing number
Onward Ye People	Sibelius	Gal	3	A	Festival number
Out of the Silence	Jenkins	GS	3	A	Sweeping
Paper Reed by the Brooks, The	Thompson	ECS	3	U	Quiet and serene
*Peace Must Come Like a Troubadour	Wilson	B3	3	A	Excellent closer also SSA
*Phantom of Delight, A	Wilson	GR	4	U	Words by Wordsworth
Polly Wolly Doodle	Kubik	Sou	4	A	Paraphrase on old song
Radiant Stars	Cui	ECS	3	U	Nocturne
Railroad Reverie	Sacco	GS	5	A	Sound effects
Remember	Piket	AMP	4	U	Christina Rosetti's poem—modern
Riding Along a Valley	Wilson	CM	3	O	Slow and dreamily
Russian Picnic	Enders	GS	3	A	Good fun
She Walks In Beauty	Wilson	BH	4	O	Flowing and free
*Silver Swan	Gibbons	BM	3	U	SSATB, magnificent

* Throughout this section A = accompanied; U = unaccompanied; O = optional.

Title	Composer or Arranger	Key to Publisher	Diffi-culty	A* U* O*	Description
Six Chansons	Hindemith	AMP	4	U	Contemporary. Excellent as a group
1. The Doe					
2. A Swan					
3. Since All is Passing					
4. Spring Time					
5. In Winter					
6. Orchard					
Sleigh, The	Kountz	GS	3	A	Exciting
Some Folks	Foster	SF	3	A	Light and rhythmical
Stomp Your Feet	Copland	BH	4	A	Two-piano accompaniment
Sunrise	Taneyef	HF	4	U	Builds to dramatic climax
Sweet Day So Cool	Roberton	GS	3	U	It is sweet
*Thing of Beauty, A	Wilson	CF	4	U	Poem by John Keats
Three Chorales from Tagore	Creston	GS	5	U	Contrasting moods
To An Ancient Picture	Wolf	GR	3	U	Soprano solo with humming chorus
To Her Shall I Be Faithful	Schoenberg	EBM	5	U	Based on German folk song
To Music	Schubert	SHMc	2	A	Excellent opener
Tune Thy Music To Thy Heart	Rowley	GS	4	U	Lovely
You'll Never Walk Alone	Rodgers	SP	3	A	Fine popular song
Younger Generation, The	Copland	GS	3	A	Humorous
Waiting	Bacon	Sou	4	A	Tranquilly
Weep O Mine Eyes	Bennett	BM	3	A	In flowing style
When Gran'ma Danced the Polka	Frey	B3	2	A	Novelty

* Throughout this section A = accompanied; U = unaccompanied; O = optional.

Title	Composer or Arranger	Key to Publisher	Diffi-culty	A* U* O*	Description
When I am Frae My Dearie	Barnes	SB	3	U	Poem by Robert Burns
When To Her Lute Corinna Sings	Harris	MM	3	U	Allegretto grazioso
*Which Is the Properest Day	Arne	BM	2	U	Lively
3. *Folk Songs — Mixed Voices*					
Amen	Hairston	BM	3	U	Lovely spiritual
An Evening's Pastoral	Shaw	GS	1	U	Peaceful
At Sundown	Hofland	KJ	3	U	Lento con molto espressivo
Balm In Gilead	Dawson	Tusk	2	U	Reverent spiritual
Cindy	Wilson	SHMc	3	O	American dance tune
*Coffee Grows on a White Oak Tree	Wilson	SHMc	3	A	American, a little different
Cotton Needs Pickin'	Reynolds	CM	2	O	Southern folk tune
Deep River	Reynolds	CM	2	O	Beautiful spiritual
Erie Canal	Scott	SP	3	A	American work song
Ezekiel Saw de Wheel	Dawson	Tusk	4	U	Stunning spiritual
Ezekiel Saw de Wheel	Wilson	SHMc	1	A	Simple, but effective
Finding A Husband	Bartok	GS	5	U	Hungarian Folk song
Hold On	Houston	BM	4	U	Very rhythmical
In Dat Great Gettin' Up Mornin'	Cook	WM	4	A	Stirring spiritual
*In Stilly Night	Brahms	CM	2	U	Slow in free rhythm
*Jacob's Ladder	Wilson	GR	3	O	Arr. for any voice combination
Kathryn's Wedding Day	Luvaas	SB	3	O	Czechoslovakian
Listen to the Lambs	Dett	GS	4	U	Freely transcribed from a spiritual

* Throughout this section A = accompanied; U = unaccompanied; O = optional.

Title	Composer or Arranger	Key to Publisher	Diffi-culty	A* U* O*	Description
Little Bird	Kubik	Sou	5	A	American sketch
*May Day Carol	Taylor	JF	2	A	English — all types of arrangements
Mountains	Luvaas	SB	1	U	Slow and sustained
My Lord What A Mornin'	Burleigh	GR	4	U	Slow and reverent
Old Boat Zion, The	Shure	JF	4	U	White spiritual
Ride the Chariot	Smith	KJ	3	U	Strong rhythm
Scandalize My Name	Reynolds	CM	3	O	Syncopated
Schlof Bobbeli	Siegmeister	TB	2	U	Pennsylvania Dutch lullaby
Set Down Servant	Shaw	SP	3	U	Rhythm spiritual
Skip To My Lou	Wilson	SHMc	3	O	Play party song — also SSAA
Song of the Halutzin	Gaul	MPH	4	O	Palestinian folk song
Soon-ah Will Be Done	Dawson	Tusk	3	U	Dramatic spiritual
Sourwood Mountain	Wilson	SHMc	3	U	Southern mountain tune
Were You There	Burleigh	GR	4	U	Spiritual
Yandee Doodle	Reynolds	CM	3	A	Traditional American
Yonder, Yonder	Gaines	TP	3	U	Plaintive Russian folk song
4. *Sacred — SAB*					
Ave Verum Corpus	des Pres	GS	3	U	16th century
Cast Thy Burden	Mendelssohn	BH	2	A	Chorale from "Elijah"
It Shall Be Light	Gaul	BM	3	U	From "The Holy City"
O God of Life	Franck	BM	3	A	"Panis Angelicus"

* Throughout this section A = accompanied; U = unaccompanied; O = optional.

Title	Composer or Arranger	Key to Publisher	Diffi-culty	A* U* O*	Description
O Lord Our God	Schvedov	BM	3	O	Reverent
Our Lord Is a Rock	Davis	SB	3	O	With energy
Praise Ye the Lord	Saint-Saens	BH	2	A	Majestic
5. *Secular — SAB*					
America, My Homeland	Dykema	BH	2	U	With trumpet solo
As Torrents In Summer	Elgar	BH	3	O	Long a favorite in SATB
Bells of St. Michael's Tower, The	Knyvett	BH	3	O	Sound effects
Come Sing This Round With Me	Martini	BM	3	O	Canonic
Cranberry Corner, USA	Klein	BH	3	A	Rhythmic
Deaf Old Woman, The	Davis	Gal	2	A	Dialogue
Kentucky Babe	Geibel	BH	2	A	American lullaby
Res' My Shoes	Wilson	BM	3	A	Bounce tune
Night Has a Thousand Eyes, The	Wilson	BH	1	A	Lovely poem
Sail, Sail Thy Best, Ship of Democracy	Hanson	CF	1	A	Unison chorus
Shepherd's Song	Elliot	RH	2	A	Pastorale
To Music	Schubert	SHMc	3	A	Beautiful song
6. *Folk Songs — SAB*					
Blue Tail Fly, The	Ehret	BH	2	A	Minstrel song
Jesus Walked This Lonesome Valley	Ehret	BH	3	A	White spiritual
Let Us Break Bread Together	Ehret	BH	2	A	Reverent spiritual

*** Throughout this section A = accompanied; U = unaccompanied; O = optional.**

Title	Composer or Arranger	Key to Publisher	Diffi-culty	A* U* O*	Description
Cindy	Wilson	SHMc	3	A	American dance tune
Holla-li Holla-lo	Wilson	BM	3	O	Bavarian folk song
Little David Play on Yo' Harp	Wilson	SHMc	3	O	Rhythmic spiritual
May Day Carol	Wilson	BH	3	A	English folk song
Rock-A-My-Soul	Wilson	BH	3	A	Rhythmic Spiritual
Salangadou	Wilson	BH	3	A	Creole folk song
Soldier Won't You Marry Me	Wilson	BH	2	A	Dialogue song
Were You There	Wilson	BM	2	U	Beautiful spiritual
7. *Sacred — Treble Voices (SSA unless indicated otherwise)*					
Agnus Dei	Bizet	GS	4	A	Soprano solo with chorus and optional string accompaniment
At Eventide It Shall Be Light	Gaul	TP	3	U	From "The Holy City"
Ave Maria	Arcadelt	BM	3	O	Free rhythm
Eternal Life	Dungan	GS	3	A	St. Francis' prayer
Gentle Jesus, Meek and Mild	Wilson	BM	1	A	SA — also Christmas
God's Dawn Brings Day	Lowell	EV	3	A	Useful for general occasions
I Lift Mine Eyes	Pfautsch	SB	3	A	SA — stately and serene
Laudate Dominum	Mozart	ECS	3	A	SSAA — hymn of praise
Lift Thine Eyes	Mendelssohn	GS	2	U	From "Elijah"
Love Divine All Love Excelling	Stainer	GR	3	A	SA — Challenging
Non Nobis Domine	Quilter	BH	3	A	Stirring
Omnipotence	Schubert	GS	4	A	Forceful

* Throughout this section A = accompanied; U = unaccompanied; O = optional.

Title	Composer or Arranger	Key to Publisher	Diffi-culty	A* U* O*	Description
Praise Ye the Lord	Saint-Saens	BH	1	A	Majestic
Psalm 150	Lewandowski	SHMc	3	A	Allegro maestoso
Te Deum Laudamus	Wilson	Mills	5	A	SSA with soprano solo
Thirteenth Psalm, The	Brahms	Gal	5	A	Challenging
Tota Pulchra Es Maria	Wilson	EV	3	U	"Thou Art Beautiful, O Mary"
Vere Languores Nostros	Lotti	BM	2	U	"He Bears Our Burdens"
8. *Secular — Treble Voices*					
Alice in Wonderland	Fine	MPH	4	A	Modern style
The Knave's Letter					
The White Knight's Song					
Beautiful Soup					
As Costureiras	Villa-Lobos	GS	5	U	SSAA — "Sewing Girls"
Bought Locks	Mennin	CF	3	A	Clever
Cease Your Bitter Weeping	Kodaly	BH	5	U	Solemn — divided parts
Ching-A-Ring-Chaw	Copland	BH	3	A	Minstrel Song
Come Let Us Start a Joyful Song	Hassler	BM	4	O	Good opener
Come You Maidens	Tschaikowsky	BH	3	A	Dance from "Eugene Onegin"
Death of Trenar, The	Brahms	HWG	4	A	Dramatic-accompaniment includ-es two horns
Devotion	Strauss	EV	3	A	Magnificent song
Dream Lullaby	Savino	BM	1	A	Lovely melody
Dream Song	Stringham	MPH	4	A	Exquisite

* Throughout this section A = accompanied; U = unaccompanied; O = optional.

Title	Composer or Arranger	Key to Publisher	Difficulty	A* U* O*	Description
Enchanting Song	Bartok	BM	3	U	Giocoso
Fly Singing Bird	Elgar	HWG	4	A	Optional 2-violin obbligato
From the Land of the Sky-Blue Water	Cadman	EM	2	A	Famous song based on Indian theme
Holiday Song	Schuman	GS	3	A	Unusual
How Merrily We Live	Este	ECS	3	U	17th century
Infant Joy	Wilson	MM	3	A	Poem by William Blake
Lazy Afternoon	Siegmeister	EBM	2	A	From "Ozark Set" — harp or piano
Loon, The	Strom	SHMc	3	A	Modern harmonies — flutes or violin obbligato
Lullaby	Byrd	BM	3	U	17th century
Mocking of Youth	Bartok	BM	3	U	Humorous
Mother Goose Suite	Horton	Wit	3	U	Six short numbers
'Mother I Will Have a Husband	Vautor	BM	4	U	Contrapuntal
Musetta's Waltz Song	Puccini	BH	3	A	From "La Boheme"
Music	Klemm	SF	1	A	Very popular
Music that Brings Sweet Sleep	Hesch	BM	1	A	Poem by Tennyson
My Mother Bids Me Bind My Hair	Haydn	SHMc	3	A	Exquisite
Nightingale, The	Weelkes	ECS	3	U	17th century
Now I Lay Me Down to Sleep	Thompson	ECS	3	U	Canonic
O Lovely Night	Ronald	BH	4	A	Beautiful song
Our Lullaby	Savino	Mills	2	A	Lovely melody
Peace Comes to Me	Murray	BH	3	A	Modern harmonies

* Throughout this section A = accompanied; U = unaccompanied; O = optional.

Title	Composer or Arranger	Key to Publisher	Diffi-culty	A* U* O*	Description
Songs My Mother Taught Me	Dvorak	CM	1	A	SA — famous song
Spring	Bartok	BH	4	U	Fast and light
Spring	Pfautsch	MPH	4	U	SSA — gay
Symphony of Flowers, A	Savino	CM	3	A	Tuneful
These Things Shall Be	Barney	BM	2	A	SA — Stirring
Think on Me	Scott	Gal	2	U	Quiet love song
Though Philomela Lost Her Love	Morley	Gal	2	U	16th century
To Music	Schubert	SHMc	2	A	Fine opener
Tribute To Song, A	Wilson	BM	1	A	SA — good opener
Waters Ripple and Flow	Taylor	JF	3	A	Czechoslovakian — also SATB
Were My Songs with Wings Provided	Hahn	Mills	2	A	Dreamily
When At Dawn	Schuman	BH	2	A	Delightful song
Who Would	Hunt	BM	2	A	SA — orchestra song
Wooing of a Girl, The	Bartok	BH	3	U	Descriptive
9. *Folk Songs — Treble Voices*					
Can You Count the Stars	Roff	SP	1	A	German folk song
Early One Morning	Davis	Gal	2	A	Lovely
Listen Young Maidens	Dalarac	SP	2	A	French begerette
My Friend John	Peloquin	MPH	4	A	French folk song
Tell Me, Mama	Wecherlin	BH	3	A	French begerette
Twenty Eighteen	Taylor	JF	3	A	Old English

*** Throughout this section A = accompanied; U = unaccompanied; O = optional.**

Title	Composer or Arranger	Key to Publisher	Diffi-culty	A* U* O*	Description
Bird's Courting Song	Wilson	BH	3	A	New England
Black is the Color		BH	3	A	American Ballad
Cindy		SHMc	3	O	SSAA dance song
Climb Up Ye Chillun		BH	3	A	Shoutin' spiritual
Crawdad Song		SHMc	2	A	Lazy rhythm
Git On Board Little Children		BM	2	A	SA — favorite with elementary choirs
He's Gone Away		BH	3	A	American Ballad
He's Got the Whole Wide World		SHMc	3	O	Beautiful spiritual — also SATB
Mary and Martha		EV	2	A	SA or SSA — spiritual
O Mary Don't You Weep		B3	3	A	Rhythmic spiritual
Paw Paw Patch		B3	3	A	Play-party song — also SATB
Skip to My Lou		SHMc	3	O	SSAA — play party song — also SATB
10. *Sacred — Male Voices (TTBB unless indicated otherwise)*					
Ave Maria	Arcadelt	BM	3	U	Free in style
Blessing, Glory and Wisdom	Bach	KJ	4	A	Majestic
Crucifixus	Lotti	ECS	4	U	Worthwhile
Give Us Faith for Today	Wilson	GS	1	A	Reverently
God Ever Glorious	Lvoff	BH	1	O	Majestically
Lead Me Gently Home	Berwald	GS	1	O	Long a favorite
Last Words of David, The	Thompson	ECS	4	A	Forceful

* Throughout this section A = accompanied; U = unaccompanied; O = optional.

Title	Composer or Arranger	Key to Publisher	Diffi-culty	A* U* O*	Description
Praise Ye the Lord	Saint-Saens	BH	2	A	Majestically
Richard de Cartre's Prayer	Terry	Gal	3	U	Modal in character
With a Voice of Singing	Shaw	GS	3	A	With spirit
Ye Watchers and Ye Holy Ones	Davidson	ECS	3	A	17th century German melody
11. *Secular — Male Voices*					
Above the Clouds	Savino	CM	2	A	Soaring
Angler's Song, The	Lowes	BH	2	A	TBB — firmly
*At Parting	Wilson	TP	2	U	Barbershop harmonies
Brothers, Sing On	Grieg	JF	3	O	Vigorous
Come Away, Come Away, Death	Key	Sou	4	U	TBB — Shakespeare's words
Come Where My Love Lies Dreaming	Foster	SF	3	O	Serenely
Dance My Comrades	Bennett	HF	2	A	Popular in high school
Dedication	Franz	HF	2	U	With sincerity
Go Lovely Rose	Thiman	Gal	3	U	Beautiful harmonies
Here is Thy Footstool	Creston	GS	3	U	With simplicity
I Bought Me a Cat	Copland	BH	3	A	Children's song
In My Arms	Loesser	SP	2	A	Popular song
Let Not Your Song End	Cain	HF	4	A	With life
Lullaby	Brahms	GS	2	O	Gently
On the Trail	Grofe	B3	3	A	From "Grand Canyon Suite"
Passing By	Purcell	SB	2	U	Simple and charming

* Throughout this section A = accompanied; U = unaccompanied; O = optional.

Title	*Composer or Arranger*	*Key to Publisher*	*Diffi-culty*	*A* U* O**	*Description*
Shadow March	Protheroe	BM	2	O	Standard repertory
Stomp Your Foot	Copland	BH	4	A	Square dance — two-piano accompaniment
Stout-Hearted Men	Romberg	MPH	1	A	Very popular
*Sweet Love Doth Now Invite	Dowland	BM	3	U	Especially suitable for male voices
Tarantella	Thompson	ECS	4	A	Superb, excellent accompanist needed
Thou Hast Made Me Endless	Creston	GS	5	O	Majestic
Upon the Mountain	Davis	GS	3	U	Very fast
Vale of Tuoni	Sibelius	RDR	3	U	Very slow
We Be Three Poor Mariners / We Be Soldiers Three	Ravenscroft	BM	2	U	Vigorously
When Good Men Sing	Plank	SB	2	U	Spirited
With a Hey and a High and a Ho Ho Ho	Mizzy	BM	2	A	Cute popular song
12. *Folk Songs — Male Voices*					
*A-Rockin' All Night	Wilson	TP	1	O	Lullaby
Climbin' Up the Mountain	Smith	KJ	2	U	Jubilantly
Erie Canal, The	Wilson	SHMc	1	A	TBB — American work song
Good-bye Ol' Paint	Wilson	SHMc	1	A	TBB — cowboy song
Joshua Fit de Battle Ob Jericho	Cookson	RH	2	A	TB easy and effective
Rock-a My Soul	Regier	SB	3	U	Rhythmical
Wade in de Water	Hall	GS	3	O	Steady with rhythm

* Throughout this section A = accompanied; U = unaccompanied; O = optional.

Title	*Composer or Arranger*	*Key to Publisher*	*Diffi-culty*	*A* U* O**	*Description*
		CHRISTMAS			
	(All voices — SATB unless otherwise indicated)				
*A-Rockin' All Night	Wilson	TP	1	O	Spiritual, SATB, SSA, TTBB
As I Out Rode This Endres Night	Stevens	Sou	4	U	TBB, Allegretto
Behold the Star	Dawson	Tusk	4	O	Rhythm chorus with tenor solo
Behold That Star	Ehret	BH	2	A	SAB — rhythmical
Birthday of a King, The	Neidlinger	BH	1	A	SAB — well-known song
*Break Forth, O Beauteous Heavenly Light	Bach	SHMc	1	O	Chorale
Bring a Torch Jeanette Isabella	Dickinson	HWG	3	U	Also TTBB — French carol
Carol, A	Bacon	Gal	4	A	SSA — Old English
Carol of the Bells	Arr. Wilhousky	CF	2	U	Russian — SATB, SAB, SSA, TTBB
Carol of the Birds	Cain	SHMc	3	O	Traditional French carol
Ceremony of Carols, A Wolcom Yule There Is no Rose Balulalow As Dew in Aprille This Little Babe Deo Gracias	Britten	BH	3-4	A	Six good numbers with contrast; also for SA with five additional numbers. See "Extended Numbers."
Christmas Carol, A	Broecht	BH	1	A	Simple — mostly unison
Christmas Dance of the Shepherds	Kodaly	BH	3	U	SA — dance rhythm

* Throughout this section A = accompanied; U = unaccompanied; O = optional.

Title	Composer or Arranger	Key to Publisher	Diffi-culty	A* U* O*	Description
Christmas Song	Diers	BM	2	A	SA — canonic
Fanfare for Christmas	Shaw	GS	2	A	An excellent opener
Five Narrative Carols	Pfautsch	SB	3	U	SSA voices with optional flute obbligato
Four Miniature Polish Carols	Arr. Kozinski	EV	1	U	Delightful
Fum, Fum, Fum	Catalonian Carol	BM	2	A	SA ,SAB — Jolly march
Go Tell It on the Mountain	Cooke	CM	3	O	Jubilant
Gloria! Gloria!	Caldwell	SHMc	3	A	A rewarding anthem
Glory to God in the Highest	Hammerschmidt	MPH	4	A	Double SSA chorus
Glory to God in the Highest	Pergolesi	GS	3	A	Standard repertory — accomp.
God Rest You Merry, Gentlemen	Arr. Pfohl	CF	2	O	Excellent arrangement
Greensleeves	Lefebre	Gal	1	U	SSA — Christmas words
Hark Now, O Shepherds	Arr. Luvaas	SB	3	O	Bohemian carol
Hodie Christus Natus Est	Willan	Ox	4	U	Superior
How Far Is It to Bethlehem	Shaw	HWG	3	O	Quiet mood
Hushing Carol	Kountz	GS	2	U	Unusual
Infant King, The	Pohlmann	SHB	2	A	SAB — rather fast
In the Stillness of the Night	Wilson	JS	1	O	Tuneful—SATB, SAB, SA, SSA
I Stand Beside the Manger Stall	Bach	GS	2	O	Chorale
I Wonder as I Wander	Arr. Niles	GS	3	U	Beautiful—soprano solo-Also SSA
Jacques, Come Here	Donovan	Gal	3	O	French — allegro giocoso
Jesus, Jesus Rest Your Head	Arr. Niles	GS	2	U	Armenian — SATB, SSA
*Joyous Christmas Song	Gavaert	GS	3	U	A favorite Christmas song
Long Ago in Bethlehem	Wilson	Mills	3	U	Modal flavor — divided parts

* Throughout this section A = accompanied; U = unaccompanied; O = optional.

Title	*Composer or Arranger*	*Key to Publisher*	*Diffi-culty*	*A* U* O**	*Description*
*Love Came Down at Christmas	Wilson	MM	3	A	A new setting
Lullaby of Jesus	Wilson	B3	2	A	SSA — Polish carol
Lullaby of Mary	Wilson	B3	2	A	SA—Joseph Dearest, Joseph Mine
Lullaby on Christmas Eve	Christiansen	Aug	1	O	Lovely — soprano solo
Masters in This Hall	Ehret	BH	2	A	SAB — Joyful
Masters in This Hall	Arr. Whitford	SHMc	2	O	Colorful atmosphere
Merry Christmas, A	Warrell	Ox	4	U	Spirited — also SAB arr. published by BM
Moon Shines Bright, The	Wilson	BM	3	A	SAB — also general
Noel	McLemore	GS	3	U	SSA — excellent
Now is the Carolling Season	Priesing	SP	3	U	Gay and seasonal
*O Magnum Mysterium	Vittoria	BM	4	U	A wonderful mystery — English words
On Christmas Night	Arr. Ehret	Volk	2	A	Sussex carol—SATB, SAB, SSA
Patapan	Arr. Wilson	SB	3	O	Burgundian carol — SATB,SSA, TBB
*Resonet in Laudibus	Handl	BM	3	U	From early period — English words
Rise Up, Shepherd an' Foller	Wilson	BH	2	O	SSA — moderately fast
Shepherd's Christmas Song	Dickinson-Reiman	HWG	2	A	Folk song in lovely setting
Shepherds Keep Their Flocks, The	Bach-Ehret	JS	1	O	Quiet chorale
Shepherds, Shake Off Your Drowsy Sleep	Ehret	MM	1	A	SSA — French carol

*** Throughout this section A = accompanied; U = unaccompanied; O = optional.**

Title	Composer or Arranger	Key to Publisher	Difficulty	A* U* O*	Description
*Shepherd's Story, The	Dickinson	HWG	4	U	A universal favorite — soprano, tenor, baritone solos
Silent Night	Gruber-Wilson	SHMc	2	O	Concert version with descant — also SA
Sir Christemas	Benjamin	BH	5	U	With baritone solo
Sledge Bells, The	Roberton	GS	3	U	Fast and light
Sleep of the Child Jesus	Gavaert	GR	1	U	TTBB — delicate
Sleep of the Infant Jesus	Arr. Christy	SHMc	2	O	Flemish carol
Susan Belle	Abbey	MM	3	O	Secular carol
Swedish Yule Carol	Gaul	Gal	3	A	Brilliant
*Thou Must Leave Thy Lowly Dwelling	Berlioz	BH	3	A	From "The Childhood of Christ"
Three Carols Tyrley Tyrlow Balulalow The Sycamore Tree	Warlock	Ox	3	U	English — unusual. Difficult accompaniments
To Bethlehem Singing	Wilson	BH	3	U	Puerto Rican carol
To Us Is Born Immanuel	Praetorius-Buszin	SHMc	2	U	Joyous and dignified
Two Kings	Clokey	JF	3	A	Brass accompaniment
Virgin Unspotted, A	Billings-Dickinson	MM	2	U	Early American
Wassail Song	V. Williams	Gal	4	U	Old English
Welcome Yule	Kraehenbuehl	AMP	4	U	SSA or TTBB—Christmas madrigal
Wonder of the Darksome Night	Priesing	SP	4	O	Lovely

* Throughout this section A = accompanied; U = unaccompanied; O = optional.

Title	Composer or Arranger	Key to Publisher	Difficulty		Description
		COMBINED NUMBERS — ALL VOICES*			
America, the Beautiful	Ward	SHMc	3	E	Concert version
Battle Hymn of the Republic	Howe	SP	3	E	Stirring
Ching-da-ra-sa	Fry	B3	2	B	Novelty
Danny Downbeat	Wilson	JS	4		Drum solo with chorus
Festival Song of Praise	Mendelssohn	BM	3	O	Prayer and hymn of praise
Glory	Rimsky-Korsakov	MPH	4	O	Famous Russian melody
Hundredth Psalm, The	Williams	Gal	4	O	Majestic
Jesu, Joy of Man's Desiring	Bach	SB	2		Strings — choral prelude
Land I Love, The	Savino	CM	1	E	Easy to put together
Last Words of David, The	Thompson	ECS	4	O	Majestic
Let Us Walk In the Light	O'Hara	GR	3	B	Dignified
Melodic Caravan, A	McHugh & Fields	B3	3	B	Potpourri of popular songs
New World, A	Savino	BM	3	O	SSA or SATB
One World	O'Hara	BM	3	E	Climactic
Pledge of Allegiance	Wilson	JS	1	B	May be sung in unison or SATB
Preludes to Eternity	Liszt-Reibold	SP	3	O	Based on "Les Preludes"
Song of My Land	Wilson	EPM	3	B	Patriotic poem by Karl Bratton
Spookie-Boogie Hop	Wilson	JS	3		Percussion sound effects, novelty
Te Deum Laudamus	Wilson	Mills	5		Strings—SSA with soprano solo
To American Youth	Wilson	JS	2	B	Stirring words by Bratton
To Music	Schubert	SHMc	3		Strings—beautiful song
Vincent Youman's Selections	Youman	B3	3	B	Medley
Wizard of Oz Selection	Arlen	B3	3	B	Tunes from the show

*In this section the accompaniment is designated as follows: O = orchestra; B = band; E = either.

Name	Key
Associated Music Publishers, Inc. 1 W. 47th St. New York 36, N. Y.	AMP
Augsburg Publishing House 426 S. 5th St. Minneapolis 15, Minn.	Aug
Belwin, Inc. 250 Maple Ave. Rockville Center, N. Y.	Bel
Big Three Music Corp. 799 — 7th Ave. New York 19, N. Y.	B3
Boosey & Hawkes, Inc. P.O. Box 418 Lynbrook, N. Y.	BH
Boston Music Co. 116 Boylston St. Boston 16, Mass.	GS
Bourne, Inc. 136 W. 52nd St. New York 19, N. Y.	BM
Broude Bros. 56 W. 45th St. New York 36, N. Y.	BB
Concordia Publishing House 3558 So. Jefferson Ave. St. Louis, Mo.	Con
Consolidated Music Co. 240 W. 55th St. New York 20, N. Y.	CM
Elkan-Vogel Co., Inc. 1716 Sansom St. Philadelphia 3, Pa.	EV
Carl Fischer, Inc. 56-62 Cooper Sq. New York 3, N. Y.	CF
J. Fischer & Bro. Harristown Rd. Glen Rock, N. J.	JF
H. T. FitzSimons Co. 615 No. La Salle St. Chicago 10, Ill.	HTF
Harold Flammer, Inc. 215 W. 19th St. New York 11, N. Y.	HF
Galaxy Music Corp. 2121 Broadway New York 23, N. Y.	Gal
The H. W. Gray Co., Inc. 159 E. 48th St. New York 17, N. Y.	HWG
Neil A. Kjos Music Co. 525 Busse Highway Park Ridge, Ill.	Kj
Edward B. Marks Music Corp. 136 W. 52nd St. New York 19, N. Y.	EBM
Mercury Music Corp. 47 W. 63rd St. New York 23, N. Y.	MM
Mills Music, Inc. 1619 Broadway New York 19, N. Y.	Mills
Music Press Tuskegee Institute Tuskegee, Alabama	Tusk
Music Publishers Holding Corp. 488 Madison Avenue New York 22, N. Y.	MPH
Oxford University Press 1600 Pollitt Drive Fair Lawn, N. J.	Ox
Plymouth Music Co. 2908 The Americas Building Rockefeller Center New York 20, N. Y.	PM
Theodore Presser Co. Bryn Mawr, Pa.	TP
Pro Art Publications 469 Union Ave. Westbury, N. Y.	PAP
G. Ricordi & Co., Inc. 16 W. 61st St. New York 11, N. Y.	GR
R. D. Row Music Co. 353 Newbury St. Boston 15, Mass.	RDR
E. C. Schirmer Music Co. 221 Columbus Ave. Boston 16, Mass.	ECS
G. Schirmer, Inc. 3 E. 43rd St. New York 17, N. Y.	GS
Schmitt-Hall & McCreary Co. 527 Park Ave. Minneapolis 15, Minn.	SHMc
Shawnee Press, Inc. Delaware Water Gap, Pa.	SP
Silver Burdett Co. Morristown, N. J.	Sil
Southern Music Co. 1619 Broadway New York 19, N. Y.	Sou
Jack Spratt, Music Publisher 77 W. Broad St. Stamford, Conn.	JS
Summy-Birchard Co. 1834 Ridge Ave. Evanston, Ill.	SB
Volkwein Bros. 632 Liberty Ave. Pittsburgh 22, Pa.	VB
The B. F. Wood Music Co., Inc. 24 Brookline Ave. Boston 15, Mass.	BFW
Words & Music 1270 — 6th Ave. New York 20, N. Y.	WM

INDEX